Big Is Beautiful

Big Is Beautiful

Debunking the Myth of Small Business

Robert D. Atkinson and Michael Lind

The MIT Press
Cambridge, Massachusetts
London, England

This book was set in ITC Stone Sans Std and ITC Stone Serif Std by Toppan Best-set Premedia Limited. Printed and bound in the United States of America.

Library of Congress Cataloging-in-Publication Data is available.

ISBN: 978-0-262-03770-9

10 9 8 7 6 5 4 3 2 1

Contents

Preface

Small business is the basis of American prosperity. Small businesses are overwhelmingly responsible for job creation and innovation. In addition, small businesses are more productive than big companies. As they power the American economy, small business owners are the basis of democracy in America, whose health depends on the existence of a large and growing number of self-employed citizens. Yet Washington, controlled by big business and engaged in "crony capitalism," systemically discriminates against small businesses.

Every word in the previous paragraph is false or misleading. Small businesses create many jobs but they also destroy many jobs because most small businesses fail. Virtually all big firms are more productive than small ones—that is why they got big and that is why they pay their workers more. Only one particular kind of small firm contributes to technological innovation, the technology-based startup, and its success depends on scaling up, either on its own or in affiliation with large corporations, which are themselves extremely innovative because they can marshal the resources needed to invest in innovation.

Nor is it true that democracy and liberty in the United States depend on maximizing the number of Americans who are self-employed. In the United States as in other nations, economic development is marked by the replacement of self-employed farmers and peddlers and artisans by a majority of citizens who work for medium-sized to large firms. Civil rights and voting rights and freedom of expression are far safer in today's American economy with its many big corporations than they were in the agrarian America of the past, when a small-proprietor majority coexisted with slavery, segregation, and the denial of rights to women and sexual minorities.

All of this is demonstrably true—and we have written this book to demonstrate it. Why, then, is small business the most sacred of sacred cows in the United States, and other nations as well?

The cult of small business in America can be attributed to two schools of thought—producer republicanism and market fundamentalism. Producer republicanism, which holds that a republic must rest on a majority of self-employed small farmers and small business owners, is a relic of the Jeffersonian agrarian republicanism of the preindustrial era. Producer republicanism has been anachronistic for more than a century, although it enjoys periodic short-lived revivals and is enjoying one at present among progressives.

The small business cult is also reinforced by market fundamentalism. Market fundamentalism assumes that all markets are naturally competitive markets atomized among many small firms, in which competition, in the absence of government favoritism or business cheating, would soon whittle down any firm that temporarily got bigger than the rest. This is a good description of firms in technologically stagnant, labor-intensive sectors of the economy, such as local shoe repair companies. But it ignores the centrality in modern advanced economies of such sectors as manufacturing, transportation and infrastructure, and high-tech retail, which are characterized by economies of scope and scale. In these industries, the supposed "laws" that students learn in Econ 101 do not apply: monopoly can be efficient and rivalry among a few big oligopolistic firms can drive innovation.

These are the themes we develop in *Big Is Beautiful*. Following a discussion of the small-is-beautiful rhetoric in chapter 1, in chapters 2 through 7 we detail the advantages of scale that have led businesses in America to become big and continue to get even bigger.

In the second half of the book, chapters 8 through 13, we turn to the politics and policy of business. Political corruption is a genuine problem, but public policy is warped as much or more by small business pressure groups as by large firms. We argue that from the nineteenth century to the twenty-first, American antitrust or competition policy has been warped by a harmful bias against big firms as such. While using antitrust legislation to assault many firms guilty only of the crime of success, the US government, motivated by a confused mix of populist and free market ideology, has showered favors on small firms, the greatest beneficiaries of so-called crony capitalism.

We conclude by calling for size neutrality in government policies toward business—including in taxation, financing and subsidies, procurement, and regulation—combined with a focus on new high-growth business, not small business, that is, on dynamic startups that can transform the economy, not on small businesses whose owners do not engage in innovation and do not seek growth.

Our motive in writing *Big Is Beautiful* is not hostility toward small firms, some of which have vital functions to play in a dynamic economy that includes firms of all sizes as well as nonprofit research institutions and growth-promoting government agencies. Our intervention in this debate is motivated by our conviction that boosting America's economy-wide productivity makes all other public policies easier to achieve. The best way to boost productivity is to remove obstacles to the replacement of small-scale, labor-intensive, technologically stagnant mom-and-pop firms with dynamic, capital-intensive, technology-based businesses, which tend to be fewer and bigger. The current "small is beautiful" belief, held by both sides of the political aisle, represents a major barrier to that necessary and beneficial reallocation. But doing so will require debunking the small-is-beautiful myth while at the same time working to restore the reputation of large firms as engines of progress and prosperity.

The eighteenth-century writer Jonathan Swift said that "whoever could make two ears of corn, or two blades of grass, to grow upon a spot of ground where only one grew before, would deserve better of mankind, and do more essential service to his country, than the whole race of politicians put together." We should not let nostalgia for the village life and small-scale economies of an idealized past blind us to the benefits of the kinds of businesses that are most likely to make two ears of corn or blades of grass grow where only one grew before.

Acknowledgments

We thank the Smith Richardson Foundation for the financial support that made the research and writing of this book possible. In addition, we would like to express our appreciation for the helpful comments of the three anonymous reviewers in the Smith Richardson review process and the three anonymous reviewers in the MIT review process.

Rob Atkinson thanks John Wu and Kaya Singleton for research and editorial assistance and his wife, Anne-Marie, daughter, Claire, and son, David, who patiently supported his writing efforts during family time.

I   History and Present Trends

1 Belittled: How Small Became Beautiful

Small is beautiful. And big is bad. That is the consensus shared by Americans across the political spectrum, from the anticapitalist left to the libertarian right.

Support for small business is one thing all modern American presidents agree on. For Gerald Ford and Jimmy Carter, "Small business to each of us represents the very heart of economic opportunity in America and a linchpin of our social and economic cohesion."[1] For Ronald Reagan, "The good health and strength of America's small businesses are a vital key in the health and strength of our economy ... indeed, small business is America."[2] George H. W. Bush had a plan "for what we can do for small business."[3] Bill Clinton agreed, asserting that "virtually all of the new jobs come from small business."[4] For George W. Bush, "It makes sense to have the small businesses at the cornerstone of a pro-growth economic policy."[5] President Obama declared that "small businesses are the backbone of our economy and the cornerstones of America's promise."[6] And for Donald J. Trump, "The American dream is back. We're going to create an environment for small business like we haven't had in many, many decades!"[7]

Politicians spend much of their time ritualistically praising small business. Between 2010 and 2012, the phrase "small businesses" showed up in the *Congressional Record* more than 10,000 times.[8] The pollster Frank Luntz told National Public Radio, "I've tested 'small-business owner,' 'job creator,' 'innovator,' 'entrepreneur' and nothing tests better than 'small-business owner' because it represents all of those."[9]

The embrace of small business is bipartisan. The 2016 Republican Party platform proclaimed:

A central reason why the 20th century came to be called the American Century was the ability of individuals to invent and create in a land of free markets. Back then they were called risk-takers, dreamers, and small business owners. Today they are the entrepreneurs, independent contractors, and small business men and women of our new economy.[10]

Not to be outdone, the 2016 Democratic Party platform stated, "Democrats also realize the critical importance of small businesses as engines of opportunity for women, people of color, tribes, and people in rural America, and will work to nurture entrepreneurship."[11]

As one book on small business notes, "Politicians love to love small business. The rhetoric is familiar: Small-business owners dare to dream, buck tradition, support their churches, defend freedom and possess faith, intellect, and daring. For politicians, praising small business is like kissing babies—and about as meaningful for those involved."[12] This celebration of small business is not confined to America. Political leaders around the world sing the praises of small business. For example, the prime minister of Australia, Malcolm Turnbull, has said that small business is "the backbone of our nation's economy."[13]

If small is beautiful, big is ugly. Indeed, if you want to demonize something today, simply put the word "big" in front of it. In a Democratic presidential debate in 2007, John Edwards denounced "big tobacco, big pharmaceutical companies, big insurance companies, big broadcasters and big oil companies."[14] "Big Pharma Is America's New Mafia," the *Daily Beast* headline screams, leading some to wonder, what exactly is "Small Pharma"?[15] An apothecary grinding powders in a shop? Also, we suspect that the critics of "Big Oil" have other goals in mind than defending the interests of small oil-and-gas companies.

But it seems that any industry can now be afflicted with what Louis Brandeis called "the curse of bigness." Wal-Mart is "Big Box."[16] Then there is the sinister "Big Beer." The *Los Angeles Times* tells us: "Venture offers craft breweries an alternative to 'selling out to Big Beer.'"[17] Democratic senator Ed Markey decries "Big Broadband."[18] "Big Tech," a collection of large Internet firms like Google, Facebook, and Microsoft, has, according to liberal scholar Robert Reich, become "way too powerful."[19]

The writer and activist Michael Pollan dismisses the benefits of low prices from "Big Food":

The power of the food movement is the force of its ideas and the appeal of its aspirations—to build community, to reconnect us with nature and to nourish both our health and the health of the land. By comparison, what ideas does Big Food have? One, basically: If you leave us alone and pay no attention to how we do it, we can produce vast amounts of acceptable food incredibly cheaply.[20]

"This Is Why You Crave Beef: Inside Secrets of Big Meat's Billion-Dollar Ad and Lobbying Campaigns" is a headline from *Salon*.[21] Another magazine, *Vice*, denounces the "Big Chicken industry" (the companies are big, not the chickens).[22]

Even nonprofit institutions can have the adjective "big" thrown at them by their critics. Large environmental organizations are described and denounced as "Big Green" both by conservatives and some progressives.[23] "Big Science is broken," declares *The Week*.[24] *LA Progressive* magazine even demonizes "Big Religion."[25]

If big business is bad, its alliance with big government is even worse. The conservative journalist Jonah Goldberg warns: "The bigger the business, the more reliable the partner for government."[26] In 2012, Republican governor of Louisiana Bobby Jindal told Politico, "We've got to make sure that we are not the party of big business, big banks, big Wall Street bailouts, big corporate loopholes, big anything."[27]

Only about one in ten Americans are self-employed, a number that has been falling for more than a century, and only a fraction of that number employ other people. In other words, most Americans are wage earners who work for others, including the more than half the population that works for medium-sized and large corporations, government agencies, or nonprofits. And yet our political discourse stigmatizes the large and successful organizations that employ much of the American workforce and instead idealizes the self-employed small business owner. It is hardly surprising that a Gallup poll in 2005 showed that, given the choice, 57 percent of Americans would prefer starting their own business to working for others, compared to 40 percent who would prefer to be employed by others.[28] This is the case even though, as we discuss in chapter 4, the earnings and benefits of the self-employed and those working for small business lag those of workers who are employed by large corporations.

Why is the gap between the reality and the reputation of big business so large? And why, as we detail in chapter 12, do governments fall over themselves to bestow favors on small businesses? One reason is politics. Former

House Speaker Tip O'Neil once said that all politics is local, and when it comes to local politics, small business outweighs big business because there are many more small firms than large firms in any congressional district. One student of small business writes: "As one lobbyist put it, 'Even though they're small, they're big in their local communities.'"[29] If you are a member of Congress advocating a more level playing field between big and small, you can be sure that when you go back to your district you will be hearing from local car dealers, accountants, real estate agents, restaurant owners, and all the other types of small business: "Why are you opposed to the hard-working small business owner?" Responding with the abstract argument that higher productivity is likely to result if the government does not pick winners based on size would only provoke the following retort from your opponent in the next election: "Congressman X wants big business to come in and destroy your jobs."

A second reason for the mystique of small business is ideology. In chapter 2 we show that there is a long tradition in the United States of seeing small business as aligned with the core values and traditions of the republic. A nation founded by overthrowing an oppressive king was not about to substitute one kind of undemocratic monarchical rule for a rule by big business.

This historical American tradition notwithstanding, big businesses enjoyed at least somewhat favorable views from World War II to the 1970s. As a new economy emerged after World War II, so too did a new organizational system. This became the era of the large organization—big corporations, big government, and big labor—all of which were governed by a new ethos of management. Activities that in the prior factory era were associated largely with individual proprietors or small firms now became the province of large national corporations. In the 1960s, John Kenneth Galbraith captured the change:

Seventy years ago the corporation was confined to those industries—railroading, steam boating, steel making, petroleum recovery and refining, some mining—where, it seemed production had to be on a large scale. Now it also sells groceries, mills grain, publishes newspapers and provides public entertainment, all activities that were once the province of the individual proprietor or the insignificant firm.[30]

The rise of corporate America after World War I also meant a change in the way Americans looked at businesses. Bigness was seen as the ultimate achievement, while small firms were seen as ones that failed to become big. As Galbraith argued, "Being in an earlier stage of development it [the entrepreneurial firm] did less planning. ... It had less need for trained personnel that the state provided. Its technology being more primitive, it had less to gain from public underwriting of research and markets."[31] Small firms were looked down on as a second-class group characterized by lower wages, lower management quality, and higher insecurity. Again, Galbraith: "The entrepreneur as many see him, is a selfish type motivated by greed, and he is furthermore, unhappy."[32] This was the era of the manager, not the entrepreneur.

As large corporations came to dominate the economic landscape after the first part of the twentieth century, the control and management of business enterprises also changed in a fundamental way. In the factory economy, corporations were largely instruments of their entrepreneurial owners. Such men as Carnegie, Harriman, Ford, Eastman, DuPont, and, of course, Rockefeller were known as corporate titans. Yet as corporations grew and became ever more complex, with a vastly increased need for management and administration, they became controlled by a class of professional managers. Scholars argued that control was now separate from ownership. Adolph Berle of Columbia University, a leading member of Franklin Roosevelt's "Brains Trust," went so far as to conclude that the large corporation gave no rights to the owners of the enterprise, so it was up to a class of enlightened managers to guide the corporation. It wasn't just New Dealers who held this view; Republican senator Robert Taft, known as Mr. Conservative for his rock-ribbed midwestern conservatism, stated, "The social consciousness of great corporations is promoted by the glare of publicity in which they must operate, and by a management attitude now approaching that of trusteeship, not only for the stockholders, but for employees, customers, and the general public."[33]

As business professor Marina Whitman has noted, during the heyday of the corporate economy, between 1950 and 1973, America's large corporations became private institutions endowed with a public purpose.[34] They provided stable jobs, supported the arts, encouraged employees to become involved in their communities, and assumed leadership positions in civic organizations. There was a widely shared sense that the corporation was committed to the local community, that the corporation's goals, the worker's, and the community's were in sync. Because managers had almost unlimited discretion, with less pressure from financial markets and global competition than today, they could afford to view their role this way. As Michael Useem has observed, "Managerial capitalism tolerated a host of company objectives besides shareholder value."[35] The newfound legitimacy of postwar business was reflected in public opinion surveys. One poll from 1950 found that 60 percent of Americans had a favorable opinion of big business, with 86 percent of the public having a favorable view of General Electric and over 70 percent having a favorable view of General Motors.[36] In 1952 the eminent scholar of business Peter F. Drucker observed:

> We believe today, both inside and outside the business world, that the business enterprise, especially the large business enterprise, exists for the sake of the contribution that it makes to the welfare of society as a whole. Our economic-policy discussions are all about what this responsibility involves and how best it can be discharged. There is, in fact, no disagreement, except on the lunatic fringes of the Right and on the Left, that business enterprise is responsible for the optimum utilization of that part of society's always-limited productive resources that are under the control of the enterprise.[37]

But by 1975 polling by Gallup found that only 35 percent of respondents had a great deal of confidence in large companies, compared with 57 percent who said they had a great deal of confidence in small companies.[38] By 1984 a survey of journalists found that 80 percent rated the credibility of small business owners as good or excellent, but only 53 percent gave the same rating to corporate CEOs.[39] The write-up stated: "When asked whether small businesses should have less government regulation than larger businesses, 56 percent of a sample of adults agreed they should; unsurprisingly, so did a large majority of small business owners and managers. Likewise, the public believes that large corporations don't need any more help from government."[40]

Attitudes toward big business have become even worse in the last decade. In 2009, 59 percent of Americans surveyed believed that big business made too much profit, up from 52 percent in 1994.[41] Likewise, when asked if too much power was in the hands of big corporations, 70 percent said yes, up from 59 percent in 1994. Even 59 percent of Republican voters agreed. When asked whose ideas they trusted to create jobs, in 2011 79 percent of Americans trusted small business owners' ideas and only 45 percent trusted the ideas of CEOs of big corporations.[42]

In 2016, 86 percent of millennials thought small business had a positive effect on the way things were going in the country, while only 38 percent of them had the same view of large corporations. Baby boomers had an even lower opinion of large corporations, with just 27 percent of them having a positive view of them.[43] In 2016, Gallup found that while 68 percent of people had confidence in small business, only 18 percent felt that way about large business.[44]

Why are large firms so suspect today? One factor is the proliferation of high-profile corporate scandals, including Enron's accounting scandal, the Tyco executive stock fraud, Goldman Sachs's manipulation of derivative markets prior to the housing crisis of 2008, Barclays bank's manipulation of international LIBOR rates, Volkswagen's "dieselgate" and lying about auto emissions, Turing Pharmaceuticals' jacking up prices on an HIV drug 500 percent, and most recently Wells Fargo pressuring employees to manipulate customers into adding accounts. But in light of the 1.7 million C corporations (businesses whose income is taxed separately from their owners' income) in the United States, it would be a surprise if there were no scandals.[45] Larger firms are easier to single out for blame. Even though the mortgage collapse that led to the global recession of 2008–2009 was caused largely by fraudulent small, independent mortgage originators, the blame fell on large banks that manipulated the packaging of the loans.[46]

Big businesses also suffer from the fact that they are much more visible than small ones. When a large firm lays off 3 percent of its workers, it makes the national news. When a small firm goes out of business, it is barely noticed. When a small firm does something immoral, unethical, or dangerous, few people hear about it and even fewer remember it. As Richard Pierce writes, "Does anyone remember the name of the small firm that shipped partially full containers of oxygen generators fraudulently labeled empty on the Value Jet plane that crashed in the Everglades?"[47]

Another source of the animus against big business is that many of the industries that contemporary progressives do not like—including oil and gas, tobacco, agribusiness, and pharmaceuticals—are characterized by large firms because of scale economies of production and innovation. Even if these industries were characterized by small firms, many on the left would still rail against them.

Even more important is that globalization has corroded the reputation of big business through undermining the assumption of an alignment of interests between companies and the nation. In 1953, Charles "Engine Charlie" Wilson, then the president of General Motors, was asked during his confirmation hearing to become the US secretary of defense in the Eisenhower administration whether he would be able to make a decision adverse to the interests of GM. Wilson famously answered that he could— but also that he could not conceive of such a situation "because for years I thought what was good for the country was good for General Motors and vice versa." We have little doubt that Wilson, and most US CEOs of the time, believed this, as it was mostly true. However, as the US economy globalized and US corporations became, in the words of former IBM CEO Sam Palmisano, "globally integrated enterprises," such a statement would be seen as anachronistic by many Americans today.[48]

Note that Wilson did not say what was good for General Motors was good for Michigan, where GM is headquartered. By that time GM had already located some of its production in lower-wage southern states. GM had moved beyond its roots as a "Michigan company" to become an "American company." Hence, in a logic that would later play out again in the move toward globalization, what was good for GM in the 1950s was evidently not always good for its home state. And if GM had no complete loyalty to Michigan, neither did Michigan car buyers, who were indifferent to what state their car was made in.

US consumers and US corporations had moved from regional to national in their orientation. But even national firms went out of their way to demonstrate loyalty, or at least claim it, to the communities they produced in. In a local newspaper ad in the Syracuse, New York, paper titled "Shake, Syracuse," GM proclaimed: "So count on us, in our production of goods and services, to share in the prosperity you are so ably helping us attain with the people who live and work here as our neighbors."[49] They did the same in Muncie, Indiana, where the company ad read, "Our main concern is with the hope that folks here are also glad to have us as their neighbors."[50]

Today the situation is in one way no different. Instead of US companies "off-stating," they are offshoring. Instead of multistate, national companies, we have multinational, global companies. And instead of buying nationally, most American consumers buy globally, demonstrating almost no loyalty to buying American-made goods. Price and quality are king; origin and production location at best are afterthoughts. But having a warm or even a neutral feeling toward large multinational corporations is much tougher when they must satisfy the demands of global stakeholders, not just national. Being loyal to communities in a particular nation is very different from being a globally integrated corporation loyal to no place.

Even more damaging to the reputation of big business than globalization, perhaps, has been the rise of the shareholder value movement, which tolerates no other corporate purpose than producing short-term profits. Until the late 1970s, there was a general view held by corporations that their mission was not just to increase stock price but also to serve other constituencies, including the firms' workers, the communities in which the companies were located, and the nation. And before the 1980s, most US corporations made investment decisions on the basis of expectations of long-term returns.

But beginning in the 1908s, changes in the institutional system of US investing and management, under the rubric of the "shareholder value movement," changed all that. How investment funds were structured and their managers were rewarded meant that funds moved money around in search of the quickest return, regardless of where long-term value might be found. How managers were compensated—increasingly with stock options that were not always related to actual managerial performance—reflected this new view that a manager's job was to maximize value for the shareholders. And because managers themselves became key short-term stockholders (through the significant growth of stock options), they made even more effort to enhance the welfare of short-term stockholders, including by boosting dividends and through stock buybacks.

Now stock price was all that mattered, and the best way to get that price up was to engage in frenetic bidding wars to get the best CEO and top-level management team, which meant a massive increase in executive compensation. The rise of the shareholder value movement and its later evolution into corporate short-termism, or what some call quarterly capitalism, meant that CEOs were rewarded for downsizing firms, limiting investment in capital stock (in order to maximize return on net assets), and paying attention solely to the bottom line.

This focus on short-term returns was not rational in the sense of maximizing returns for society, or even for companies (if returns are defined as maximizing the net present value of all future profits). And it certainly was not rational in terms of maintaining good will on the part of citizens toward corporate America. The shareholder value revolution not only led to growing inequality and less job security for workers, it also hurt economic performance. Indeed, as companies began paying out more in dividends and engaging in stock buybacks as a way to boost stock prices for short-term investors, relatively less was available for investing in activities that would boost long-term innovation and productivity.

Giving intellectual legitimacy to this new short-termist orientation was the increasing dominance of neoclassical economics after the late 1970s. Neoclassical economics defined a well-functioning economy as one in which everyone pursued his or her self-interest in price-mediated markets and the principal role of government was to get out of the way.

With the rise of the shareholder value movement came a shift in the political role and orientation of the corporate community. Prior to the mid-1980s many CEOs, such as GM's Charlie Wilson, GE's Reginald Jones, Hewlett-Packard's John Young, DuPont's Irving Shapiro, and Loral's Bernard Schwartz, saw their role not just as CEO but as corporate statesman. But around that time the role of "business statesman" began to fade. Executives came under increasing pressure to focus ruthlessly on boosting profits and share prices. Those who didn't risked losing their jobs or seeing their companies swallowed up in hostile takeovers. This is not to say that some of today's CEOs don't try to play some broader role, but overall, US corporate leaders have abdicated their roles as statesmen for roles as CEOs alone. In his book, *The Fracturing of the Corporate Elite*, Mark Mizruchi observes:

[After] World War II, American business leaders hewed to an ethic of civic responsibility and enlightened self-interest. ... In the 1970s, however, faced with inflation, foreign competition, and growing public criticism, corporate leaders became increasingly confrontational with labor and government. As they succeeded in taming their opponents, business leaders paradoxically undermined their ability to act collectively.[51]

A survey by the corporate organization Committee for Economic Development supported this observation, finding that the three biggest barriers to business leaders taking a more active role in public issues were "concern about criticism others have experienced; shareholder pressure for short-term results; and belief that a CEO should focus on his/her company."[52] For the CEOs, it became a collective action problem. Why step up and fight for big business and the US economy generally when it only meant taking valuable time away from your company? As a thought experiment, try to name a current CEO who is seen as a leader for good policy for the American economy.

Finally, as both major US political parties have become more politically polarized, each for different reasons has developed an antipathy toward large business and support for small. In the 1950s and 1960s, one reason Republicans were willing to support small business policies, including by creating the Small Business Administration, was to deflect criticism that Republicans were "the party of big business."[53] Now, under the influence of the libertarian right, much of the GOP indulges in outright vilification of large business. Indeed, when the Republican Speaker of the House can publish an op-ed in the bible of big business, *Forbes* magazine, titled "Down with Big Business," it reflects a particular brand of free market, classical liberalism that hews more to Adam Smith's view of the world of small firms competing against each other, at odds with reality in the industrial and postindustrial world of large firms.[54] Speaker Ryan equated big business with a "pernicious threat to free enterprise." Big business not only generates "crony capitalism" but also leads to government nationalization of the economy. He wrote, "Big businesses' frenzied political dealings are not driven by party or ideology, but rather by zero-sum thinking in which their gain must come from a competitor's loss. Erecting barriers to competition is a key to maintaining advantage and market share." This is the same reason why the conservative magazine the *American Interest* proclaims, "Small business should be priority number one."[55]

Left-wing populists have made common cause with right-wing libertarians in their disdain for large business, co-opting the language of the market fundamentalist right to paint their antipathy to large business in the guise of support of markets. In a speech decrying big business and praising small, Senator Elizabeth Warren (D-MA) made her position clear: "I love markets! Strong, healthy markets are the key to a strong, healthy America."[56]

Conservatives and libertarians emphasize free markets and deregulation as liberating forces to break up the procrustean bed in which crony capitalists and big government bureaucrats sleep together. For its part, the localist left wants to use the hammer of antitrust policies to break up concentrations of economic power. Meanwhile, in the political center, a combination of investments in "human capital" and support for "entrepreneurs" was supposed to concoct the magic small business creation elixir for America's advanced industrial economy. In short, the libertarian right, the neoliberal center, and the liberal left tend to agree in their idealization of small business.

The decline in the reputation of big business has also been part of a broader cultural shift. Today's widespread megalophobia (fear of large things) can be dated back to the 1970s. Around the time that the British economist E. F. Schumacher's book *Small Is Beautiful* became an international bestseller in 1973, American culture underwent a transformation of values.[57] New Deal liberalism, which took pride in big hydropower dams, multilane highways, and powerful rockets, was dethroned by the left-wing counterculture, which opposed dams, loathed automobiles, and preferred the exploration of inner space. On the right, conservatives and libertarians extolled the virtues of unfettered free markets and criticized not only excessive government regulation but also complacent, sclerotic corporations seeking to pervert Adam Smith–style capitalism into crony capitalism. The new right was inspired by Ayn Rand to go Galt; the new left was inspired by Tolkien to go hobbit.

Can a consensus that is so broadly based be wrong? Yes—if it is based on lazily repeated clichés and inherited myths rather than on fact and analysis. What is called the "antimonopoly tradition" informs most of the criticism of big business in the United States and many other countries. The antimonopoly tradition has two somewhat incompatible strands. One is "producer republicanism"—the belief that a democratic republic can exist only in a society in which most citizens are self-employed family farmers or small business owners. The other strand is "market fundamentalism"—the belief that in all markets, absent private conspiracy or public intervention, competition would maintain a majority of small firms by quickly cutting down to size any large firms that happened temporarily to appear and gain significant market shares.

Our argument is that the antimonopoly tradition is intellectually flawed and the policy prescriptions inspired by it are worthless or in many cases dangerous. Both producer republicanism and market fundamentalism are intellectual relics of preindustrial agrarian society. Producer republicanism is irrelevant because the self-employed are a small minority in advanced industrial societies. At the same time, the neoclassical economics on which market fundamentalism is based, while useful in describing the interactions of small firms in truly competitive sectors, is worse than useless in understanding the dynamics of markets characterized by imperfect competition and dominated by innovative oligopolies in industries with increasing returns to scale, such as aerospace, information and communications technology, life sciences, agriculture, and energy. Trying to use the antimonopoly tradition to understand a modern economy based on high-tech, capital-intensive enterprises with transnational supply chains and networks is like trying to find your way through twenty-first-century Manhattan using a map from the eighteenth century, when few structures were more than one or two stories tall and much of the island was still farmland.

Our purpose in writing this book is to debunk the small-is-beautiful consensus. But we do not intend to replace it with an equally simple-minded big-is-beautiful orthodoxy. On the contrary, we believe that in a modern capitalist economy, businesses of every size, along with government agencies, research universities, and other nonprofit organizations, play essential roles. Still, it is important for any discussion of the economics of firm size to recognize, as we do in chapters 4, 5, and 6, that on virtually every meaningful indicator, including wages, productivity, environmental protection, exporting, innovation, employment diversity and tax compliance large firms as a group significantly outperform small firms, and not just in rich nations but in virtually all economies. Moreover, it turns out that small firms are not, as their defenders would have us believe, the font of new jobs. To be sure, they create lots of jobs, but they destroy almost as many when so many of them fail.

These truths should have simple but important implications for public policy. As we explain in chapter 12, economic policies, including taxation, regulation, and spending, are systemically biased in favor of small firms in most nations around the world, thanks to a mix of nostalgia, misconceptions, and political pressure. We propose that instead, policy makers should embrace firm size neutrality and abolish small business preferences, including government procurement preferences, regulatory exemptions, small business financing programs, and tax benefits that favor small firms.

Innovative, high-tech startups do not remain startups for long. Successful startups either grow into large firms themselves or are acquired by existing large firms that are capable of scaling up the startup's innovative technology or technique. This means that if government is to help any small firms, its focus should be on startups that have the desire and potential to get big, not on nurturing Ashley's and Justin's efforts to open a local pizza shop.

To be sure, public policy should not be blind to genuine problems caused by monopoly or oligopoly or abuses by particular firms. But that does not mean embracing a crude approach to competition policy that simply sees big as bad. In chapter 11, we argue that a well-informed approach to competition policy must be based on the understanding that there are a number of different kinds of industries, including network industries, economies of scale industries, innovation industries, and global industries that all need large scale to maximize productivity and innovation.

We agree that the undue influence of large corporations in politics is a matter of serious concern. But the threat should be addressed by political reform, including campaign finance reform and the "countervailing power" provided by parties and other centers of social and economic power, not by the crude weapon of antitrust law wielded by single-minded Justice Department lawyers. Moreover, reforms to combat special-interest corruption should target not only large firms but also small firms and their powerful special-interest trade associations.

The United States became the world's leading industrial nation in the nineteenth and twentieth centuries on the basis of a commonsense approach like this. Federal, state, and local governments subsidized infrastructure monopolies, including canals, railroads, interstate highways, and municipal water and electrical systems and telephone systems. To prevent them from exploiting their pricing power, infrastructure monopolies, unless they evolved into competitors, as cable and telephone companies and rail and trucking did, have usually been publicly owned, like highways, or organized as privately owned, publicly regulated utilities. Antitrust legislation was not allowed to prevent the formation of efficient, competing oligopolies in increasing-returns industries, including the automobile industry, steel and oil in the past, and computers, search engines, and online platforms today. At the same time, as we discuss in chapter 9, the history of attempts in the United States to rig markets to protect small producers has been a history either of failed and abandoned policies (anti–chain store laws, anti–branch banking laws) or waste (most of the subsidies for less efficient small businesses).

As in the past, American prosperity will depend on growing economic dynamism driven by technological innovation, while sharing the gains more widely. That will require a flourishing innovation ecosystem in which for-profit enterprises of all sizes, from tiny startups to global corporations, together with government at all levels and academic institutions, play important and complementary roles. And perhaps most important, as we discuss in chapter 13, this will require a new orientation to federal policy, what we term "national developmentalism," in place of the failed global neoliberalism that now rules Washington economic policy making. National developmentalists recognize the critical need for an active development state that partners with companies (often big ones, but also small innovative ones) to help them innovate, be more productive, and compete globally.

The generational reaction against big government and cartelized industries in the late twentieth century was healthy insofar as it helped create public support for the creative destruction of the early information age. Nearly half a century later, however, the small-is-beautiful worldview has degenerated from refreshing iconoclasm into stifling bipartisan orthodoxy. Ritualized denunciation of what Governor Bobby Jindal called "big anything" prevents Americans from thinking seriously about solutions for America's growing economic challenges that require a healthy big business sector.

As Samuel Florman wrote, "*Smallness*, after all, is a word that is neutral—technologically, politically, socially, aesthetically, and, of course, morally. Its use as a symbol of goodness would be one more entertaining example of human folly were it not for the disturbing consequences of the arguments advanced in its cause." Indeed. Small enterprises have an important place in the American system. But to flourish in the twenty-first century, we must learn again that big can be beautiful, too.[58]

2   Why Business Got Big: A Brief History

What a difference two centuries make! According to the 1810 census, the United States had a population of slightly more than 5 million people, of which only 6.1 percent lived in urban areas.[1] In 1816 the list of the twenty-five largest companies was dominated by financial institutions: twenty-three banks, one insurance company, and one manufacturing company, which made textiles. Of 2,087 companies with state or federal charters, 280 were in the financial sector and only 141 in manufacturing, the second largest sector. Of the 141 manufacturing firms, 91 were in Massachusetts and 34 in New York.[2]

By 2016 the US population had grown to 324 million—roughly sixty-five times the population in 1810. And almost 81 percent of the population was now urban.[3] The ten largest US companies in terms of revenue were nonfinancial firms: Walmart, ExxonMobil, Apple, Berkshire Hathaway (the conglomerate led by investor Warren Buffett), McKesson (a pharmaceutical distributor), UnitedHealth (a health insurer), CVS, General Motors, Ford, and AT&T.[4] The largest bank, JP Morgan Chase, was twenty-third and was the only bank in the top twenty-five, not counting the government-controlled mortgage company Fannie Mae.

In growing big, America has grown prosperous. In 1900 the typical American household spent 43 percent of its income on food and 14 percent on apparel; thanks to technology-enabled productivity growth in agriculture and textile manufacturing, the percentages by 2003 had plummeted to 13 percent for food and 4 percent for apparel, and for the first time in history the average American household now spends more on food outside the home at restaurants than on food prepared at home.[5]

Indeed, more advanced technology has allowed fewer workers to produce more goods for more consumers at lower prices. As a result, between 1920 and 2009, the portion of the labor force that worked in factories, farms, or mines plummeted from 60 percent to 13 percent.[6]

What made America rich? Not markets alone, but the interaction of markets and machines. The modern economy is first and foremost a machine economy, one in which machinery, powered by sources other than human and animal muscle, has partly replaced human brawn and, more recently, human brainpower. The chief contribution to growth has been increasing productivity based on technological progress that favors large enterprises, not atomistic competition among many small firms to whittle down prices here and there. Big business has flourished in the machine age because machines enabled economies of scale and scope. As technology got better, by and large firms got bigger.

Much of the focus on firm size evolution was initially on manufacturing, in large part because the revolution in industrial mechanization in the second half of the 1800s enabled the growth of much larger manufacturing firms and factories. The economic historian Alfred Chandler documented how technology enabled new economies of scale and scope.[7] Likewise, John Blair found that plant and firm size began to increase after the late 1800s.[8] He found that manufacturing plants with more than 1,000 employees increased their employment share in US manufacturing by 9 percent between 1914 and 1937.[9] Likewise, Saul Sands found that average plant size increased between 1904 and 1947.[10]

The benefits of scale were not limited to material factors such as the size of blast furnaces or the length of assembly lines. In *The Theory of the Growth of the Firm*, first published in 1959, Edith Penrose provided a list of managerial economies of scale:

Managerial economies are held to result when a larger firm can take advantage of an increased division of managerial labour and of the closely allied mechanization of certain administrative processes; make more intensive use of existing managerial resources by the "spreading" of overheads; obtain economies from buying and selling on a large scale; use reserves more economically; acquire capital on cheaper terms; and support large-scale research.[11]

In the preindustrial economy, almost all business firms were single-unit enterprises operated by a few workers and a single owner. In what John Kenneth Galbraith called the modern "bimodal economy," small owner-operated firms continue to exist, and indeed constitute the great majority. But the most productive, science-based, capital-intensive industries are dominated by giant companies employing thousands or tens of thousands of workers, with establishments spread across regions or countries and run by a professional managerial bureaucracy. While purchasing some goods and services from smaller suppliers, large firms produce many other goods and services within the firm. Because of the partial substitution of arm's-length commercial transactions by in-house production, Galbraith called the oligopolistic corporate sector "the planning sector," referring to the internal planning of these huge private bureaucracies.[12]

In the last few decades, as information technology (IT) has allowed more and more services to be automated and achieve the economies of scale that mechanical technology earlier made possible for farming and manufacturing, more services have begun to be provided by large, highly efficient firms. Amazon.com is displacing mom-and-pop retailers because it is incredibly efficient, using robotic warehouses and low-cost Internet ordering. Using Internet delivery of movies, Netflix replaced tens of thousands of mom-and-pop video stores. Large banks such as USAA have no branches and rely extensively on Internet banking. By selling books in electronic format, Amazon and Apple are replacing tens of thousands of small, local bookstores, making us all wealthier in the process, at the cost of transitional costs for displaced workers.

The progress of technology and the growth of big business continue to be intertwined, despite the widespread contemporary belief that technological innovation is eliminating the advantages of scale. In his 1942 book *Capitalism, Socialism, and Democracy*, the economist Joseph Schumpeter coined the phrase "creative destruction" for technology-enabled economic transformations:

The opening up of new markets, foreign or domestic, and the organizational development from the craft shop to such concerns as U.S. Steel illustrate the same process of industrial mutation—if I may use that biological term—that incessantly revolutionizes the economic structure from within, incessantly destroying the old one, incessantly creating a new one. This process of creative destruction is the essential fact about capitalism.[13]

The creative destruction Schumpeter described included the destruction of small, inefficient craft producers by larger, efficient mass production corporations. In this chapter we tell the story of how business and America grew big and rich together.

How Business Got Big

Economic historians often date the first Industrial Revolution to James Watt's "invention" (actually, improvement) of the steam engine in the 1770s. But it took decades before steam engines, developed to pump water from British coal mines, were incorporated into steamships and locomotives and steam-powered factories. And it took even longer for the United States and other nations to build the railroad infrastructure that made it possible to fully reap the gains from steam-era technology.

In many countries railroads were state-owned or state-controlled public utilities. In the United States, railroads were usually privately owned but subsidized by cities, states, and the federal government, by means of money or land grants. The toxic interaction of political boosterism and private ambition in the nineteenth century led to massive overbuilding, redundancy, and bankruptcies in the railroad industry. It also spawned widespread political corruption and episodes of bloody labor strife, when railroad companies sometimes called in the National Guard and federal troops to suppress striking railroad workers. To this day, titans of the railroad era—Vanderbilt, Jay Gould, Leland Stanford—are remembered as the archetypal brutal and corrupt "robber barons."

But along with tainted reputations, the railroad companies bequeathed a valuable legacy to the American economy not only by laying down the foundations for national mass production for national markets connected by iron rails but also by pioneering the large-scale modern corporation. As the multiple regional and localized rail systems consolidated after the 1870s to gain network efficiencies, it meant that the sheer scale of railroads and the impossibility of their close supervision by their nominal owners necessitated the development of the new profession of the corporate manager. It was not an accident that many industrial innovators, including Andrew Carnegie and Thomas Edison, got their start in the railroad industry. At the same time, the need on the part of railroad companies to raise enormous amounts of money stimulated the rapid development of investment banking and the stock market in America. This made it easier to scale up capital-hungry manufacturing enterprises.

Perhaps the greatest contribution of the railroads to the growth of scale in American industry and commerce was their creation of regional and national markets. Before the railroad, almost all firms were small because it was expensive to ship a product more than a few dozen miles and it was virtually impossible to provide a service that was not face-to-face. But once a community had access to a railroad line, this spurred the creation of larger manufacturing firms.[14]

However, almost until the end of the nineteenth century, railroad corporations were by far the largest firms in the United States. Even in 1890, when the assets of American manufacturing ($6.5 billion) were almost as large as those of American railroads ($10 billion), only a few manufacturing firms had more than $10 million in assets, while the ten largest railroad companies each had assets worth more than $100 million.[15] The rise of corporate leviathans other than railroad companies had to await the introduction of newer technologies, including advanced and cheap steel, electricity and electric motors, and the internal combustion engine.

As technology made size more efficient, firms got bigger, in part through organic growth, but often by mergers. Indeed, there were three major waves of mergers in the United States: in the 1890s to 1900s, the 1920s, and the 1950s to 1960s.

The first wave was initially thwarted and then enabled by state and federal law. The US Constitution permits the federal government to charter corporations, such as the short-lived First and Second Banks of the United States. But in the first half of the nineteenth century most corporations were chartered by state governments by special statutes for particular, narrow purposes, usually related to transportation (turnpikes, railroads, canals) or utilities (municipal water supplies). So-called special incorporation by statute gave rise to scandals involving bribes of legislators or extortion of companies by politicians. In the aftermath of the canal and railroad bubbles of the 1830s and 1840s, which left many state governments with fiscal crises, American states followed the example of Britain in adopting "general incorporation" statutes permitting any eligible company to incorporate without any action by the legislature.

However, corporations were still prevented from owning stock in other corporations until 1889, when New Jersey allowed any company chartered in the state to own stock in the corporations of any other state. This permitted truly national firms to take the form of multistate holding companies; an example is US Steel, created in 1901 by the financier J. P. Morgan.

The passage of the Sherman Antitrust Act in 1890, intended to thwart the trend toward consolidation, inadvertently enabled it. The federal courts interpreted the Sherman Act to forbid cartels but to permit mergers. For example, in *Addyston Pipe and Steel Company et al. v. United States* (1899), the Supreme Court ruled that an attempt by six cast-iron pipe companies to rig bid prices for pipes sold to municipal water companies was harmful. Nearly a century later the scholar George Bittlingmayer made the case that the conditions of the cast-iron pipe industry at the time made collusion by the suppliers reasonable, to maintain capacity during slack periods of demand in a highly volatile market in which market prices had to be high enough to allow firms to recover their high fixed costs.[16] In this case as in others, eliminating the ability of firms—whether through collusion or merger—to recoup their high fixed costs by means of market power would not necessarily have led to greater production and falling prices. It might instead have led to widespread insolvencies and even declining production. So the response of the bid-rigging conspirators who were thwarted by the *Addyston* decision was to merge to form a single company, US Cast Iron Pipe and Foundry.

During this period Germany, Japan, Britain, and other leading nations were more tolerant than the United States was of cartels, which allowed medium-sized and small firms to coordinate prices and pool their resources for some purposes but not others. In countries such as the United Kingdom, this lenience toward cartels enabled industrial firms to coordinate without merging, preventing them from gaining the scale they needed to take advantage of modern industrial technologies. Many European manufacturers have continued in the craft mode of production, unable to reap the substantial benefits of mass production technologies that only large corporations possessed.

In the United States, however, the combination of the prohibition of cartels and a permissive attitude toward mergers and acquisitions produced what the historian Naomi Lamoreaux has called the first great merger movement of 1895–1904.[17] In a single decade, 1,800 enterprises—most of them in the manufacturing industry—were consolidated into only 157 firms. By 1904, one or two giant firms, usually put together by merger, controlled at least half the output in seventy-eight different industries. In 1896 there were fewer than twelve firms worth $10 million; by 1904 there were more than 300.

Lamoreaux studied ninety-three consolidations. Forty-two resulted in firms that controlled at least 70 percent of their respective industries while seventy-two created firms that controlled at least 40 percent. Among the former were General Electric, created by the merger of eight firms, which controlled 90 percent of its market; American Tobacco, a single company formed from the merger of 162 firms, which controlled 90 percent of its market; International Harvester, created from four firms, which controlled 70 percent of its market; and DuPont, formed from sixty-four firms, with a 65 to 75 percent market share. Companies that dominated 40 percent or more of their markets included United States Steel, Otis Elevator, Eastman Kodak, National Biscuit Company (Nabisco), National Candy, and a cigar company, National Stogie.[18]

This consolidation wave that created corporations of an unprecedented scale came as a shock to many Americans. In 1901 the economist John Bates Clark wrote, "If the carboniferous age were to return and the earth were to repeople itself with dinosaurs, the change that would be made in animal life would scarcely seem greater than that which had been made in business life by these monster-like corporations."[19] In documenting the emergence of the large managerial corporation, Alfred D. Chandler argued that before 1940, these changes were almost certainly opposed by a majority of Americans.[20]

The leviathan corporations spawned by the great merger wave existed in a fragmented American financial system with nearly 30,000 tiny "unit banks" that were protected from competition by state and federal laws and unable to get big. In the absence of entities like Germany's universal banks, corporations of necessity turned both to the stock market and to investment bankers such as J. P. Morgan. In return for raising vast sums of money from shareholders, investment bankers such as Morgan put their own agents on corporate boards, in the manner of European universal banks.

Having begun his career in the railroad industry, Morgan orchestrated the mergers that created General Electric, American Telegraph and Telephone (AT&T), the Pullman Company, Nabisco, and International Harvester, culminating in the creation in 1901 of US Steel, the first billion-dollar company. The initial capitalization of US Steel at a billion dollars was twice that of the US federal budget, and the $480 million that Morgan paid for Carnegie Steel made Andrew Carnegie the richest person in the world.[21] Owing to the unprecedented size of this new corporation, financiers on Wall Street referred to it simply as "the Corporation."

Companies engaged in both vertical integration (to control multiple stages of production, from the acquisition of raw materials to marketing the finished products) and horizontal integration (the merger of similar firms). Horizontal mergers designed to eliminate competition and create monopolies with pricing power could hurt consumers. But horizontal mergers in increasing-returns sectors that led to productivity-enhancing investment could benefit consumers by allowing goods to be produced much more cheaply.

This increase in size occurred not just at the enterprise level but also at the establishment level as factories got big to take advantage of the revolution in mechanized production. By 1920 there were more than 10,000 manufacturing plants with more than 500 workers that accounted for more than two-thirds of manufacturing output. The value of physical capital per plant doubled from 1880 to 1900 and doubled again from 1900 to 1920.

Machinery and the Growth of Big Business

For generations, many populists have claimed that big businesses are less efficient than small firms and exist only because of mergers and acquisitions and similar legal and financial machinations. From this perspective, big firms owe their size to predation, not innovation or efficiency. But firms did not get bigger because their founders and shareholders were greedier or less honest than small-town business owners. Rather, new production, communication, and transportation technologies let establishments grow to hitherto unprecedented size. The larger the factory or the corporation, the more efficient it could become and the more it could drive down costs, put its competitors out of business, and grow even more. And the better the transportation and communication networks, the easier it was for these efficient large firms to penetrate distant markets and take market share from smaller, local firms. The cost reductions resulting from factory operations and the geographic concentration of production overwhelmed made-to-order and small-volume production in industry after industry, where this was permitted by law.

However sordid and selfish the motives of the industrialists and financiers who promoted the mergers of the 1895–1905 period may have been, the results frequently were falling prices for consumers. For example, between 1893 and 1899, the American Tobacco Company lowered the wholesale price of its cigarettes from \$3.02 per thousand to \$2.01 per thousand, while its costs fell from \$1.74 per thousand to \$0.89.[22]

New technology enabled price declines, which in turn enabled increases in manufacturing firm size from 1850 to 1960. Because of the high fixed costs for much of the new equipment, such as steam engines, larger firms had an easier time amortizing these costs.[23] This is why Jeremy Atack, Robert A. Margo, and Paul W. Rhode found that machine horsepower per employee in firms with more than 1,000 employees was almost ten times as large as the horsepower per employee in firms with up to five employees.[24] As one of their studies described it:

For the majority of industries in every census year that he examined, Atack found efficiency advantages to large scale production—economies of scale—relative to small-scale production—artisan shops. Atack accounted for the persistence of small establishments by noting that many served markets that were protected from competition from more distant competitors by high shipping costs. Improvements in internal transportation and the diffusion of new technologies, such as steam, however, caused the market share of small establishments to erode over time.[25]

In other words, large establishments were more productive because they used more powered machinery and benefited from a greater division of labor.

Nor was this a phenomenon unique to the United States. History makes it clear that the simultaneous emergence of large industrial firms dominating the same sectors at nearly the same time in radically different societies can be explained only in terms of technological and organizational efficiency, not as a result of political corruption in particular countries of the kind blamed by populist adherents of the small-is-beautiful school. Alfred Chandler, Jr., and Takashi Hikino have demonstrated remarkable parallels in the patterns of industry concentration in the United States, Britain, Germany, France, and Japan in the period from 1912 to 1918.[26] In each of these different industrializing countries, industries characterized by the need for high investment in machine-based technology were far more concentrated than other, less capital-intensive and technology-based sectors.

In Britain, for example, between 1909 and 1970 the share of all net manufacturing output of the hundred largest firms grew from 16 percent to 45 percent.[27] In imperial Germany, Marcus Biermann found that as geographic markets opened up, there was a "stark shift in employment and firm share from small and medium firms towards larger firms."[28] Between

1882 and 1907 railroad volume in tons tripled, while the average capacity of ships increased 429 percent between 1877 and 1912 and exports almost doubled. On top of that, the rise of the telephone and telegraph made it easier to coordinate geographically distance production and markets. As a result, average firm size in German manufacturing increased 78 percent and the share of employment in small firms decreased from 45 percent in 1882 to 19 percent in 1907, while the share of employment in the largest firms increased from 37 percent to 57 percent.

This is why in industries with increasing returns to scale we see similar increases in firm size across nations. For example, during World War I the 200 largest industrial enterprises in the primary metals industry—a classic technology-based, capital-intensive sector—accounted for the following percentages of assets in the industry as a whole: 29 percent (United States), 35 percent (Britain), 49 percent (Germany), 36 percent (France), and 21 percent (Japan). At the other extreme, the lumber industry in each of these countries was characterized by minimal levels of asset concentration by the top 200 firms: 3 percent (United States), 0 percent (Britain), 1 percent (Germany), 1 percent (France), and 3 percent (Japan). In the case of furniture, an old-fashioned craft industry, the top 200 firms had less than 1 percent of the total distribution of assets in all five countries.[29] This was also the case sixty years later: a 1972 study showed that the trends and level of industrial concentration were similar in all industrial economies.[30]

When Chandler studied 379 manufacturing companies with more than 20,000 employees in 1973, which were then divided roughly equally between the United States and abroad, he discovered that the ratios were amazingly similar: twenty-two transportation equipment companies in the United States and twenty-two abroad, twenty electrical machinery companies in the United States compared to twenty-five abroad, twenty-four chemical companies in the United States compared to twenty-eight abroad, and fourteen petroleum companies in the United States compared to twelve abroad. In industries in which there were few or no increasing returns to scale, so that most firms were small, foreign markets also mirrored the US market. Among manufacturing companies with more than 20,000 employees, there were only seven textile companies in the United States and only six abroad, only three tobacco companies in the United States and only four abroad, and only seven stone, clay, and glass companies in the United States and only eight abroad among the largest manufacturing firms. As a rule, mergers or growth became a source of long-term global competitive advantage where economies of scope and scale were sizable (e.g., agricultural equipment, steel, electrical devices, chemicals) but were more ephemeral in industries that did not need significant scale (e.g., cigars). This important point has been ignored by many critics of big business in the past and the present.

All of this confirmed Chandler's argument that firms at the "center" of the economy, characterized by increasing returns to scale, tend to be both large and, if successful, long-lasting, compared to the smaller firms on the "periphery" of the economy, in which size produces few productive advantages.[31] Indeed, attempts to create large, vertically or horizontally integrated firms in industries that were not characterized by increasing returns to scale often produced miserable and short-lived failures. GE and Ford Motor Company flourish today, while United States Leather, National Wallpaper, American Glue, National Starch, Standard Rope and Twine, and the American Cattle Company are long forgotten.[32]

Firms did not get bigger because their owners acquired a new taste for wealth and power, although many so-called robber barons certainly enjoyed both. Nor can the growth of large industrial and commercial enterprises be explained in terms of the unique local politics or legal systems of particular nations, important as those factors have been. When they industrialized, the United States and France were republics with universal suffrage for white male citizens; Britain was a constitutional monarchy with limited suffrage; Germany and Japan were authoritarian monarchies. Their legal systems were as different as their political systems, with different corporate laws and different treatment of cartels and competition. And yet similar patterns of concentration emerged in dissimilar nations in similar industries.

The reason is clear: new technology allowed establishments to grow to hitherto unprecedented size and drive down costs, put competitors out of business, and grow even more. The cost reductions resulting from large-scale factory and firm operations overwhelmed made-to-order and small-volume production in industry after industry, in country after country.[33]

Innovation Cycles and Firm Size

Because of machine-driven economies of scale, following the wave of consolidation in technology-based industries such as oil, steel, automobiles, and electricity between the 1880s and 1920s, the structure of the American economy was remarkably stable until the last quarter of the twentieth century. According to Chandler, in both 1917 and 1973, twenty-two of the largest 200 firms were in the petroleum industry, and many of them were the same firms in both time periods.[34] Likewise, in both 1917 and 1973, five of the biggest 200 corporations were in the rubber industry and four were the same (Goodyear, Goodrich, Firestone, and Uniroyal). Machinery companies—many of them the same—accounted for twenty of the 200 biggest firms in 1917 and eighteen in 1973. In transportation equipment and food products there were similar continuities.[35]

Automobile manufacturing became the dominant industry of the twentieth century, consuming vast amounts of steel, glass, rubber, and gasoline and reshaping both infrastructure and the commercial and residential sectors. In the 1970s one-sixth of American business firms were involved in automobile manufacturing, distribution, service, or operation.[36]

However, the history of developed economies is not a story of continual progress and stability but of successive waves of major innovations separating what economists in the tradition of Schumpeter call "techno-economic paradigms." Early in the life cycle of a techno-economic paradigm, there are many small, innovative companies of the kind now called startups as entrepreneurs swarm to take advantage of the new technological opportunities. This long wave pattern is familiar from the history of the automobile industry. In 1895, there were 125 automobile startups; by 1915 there were 350.[37]

As the techno-economic paradigm matures, the few firms that survive the savage Darwinian competition tend to prevail, and in many cases they stay on top for decades or generations. Markets become oligopolistic or monopolistic. Big firms focus on incremental improvements in the technologies or procedural innovations established in the earlier wave of breakthrough innovation. This is why by 1926 the number of new entrants into the US auto industry had fallen to fewer than ten and why it remained below thirty-five through the 1950s. The product technology had become relatively mature as water-cooled internal combustion engines defeated air cooled engines, steam engines, and electrically powered cars. At the same time, economies of scale dramatically increased, thanks to process innovations such as Henry Ford's assembly line.[38] And by the 1960s the American car market had been winnowed down to essentially the "Big Three"—Chrysler, Ford, and GM.

As a techno-economic paradigm ages, firms are tempted to substitute financial engineering for further productivity-enhancing innovation, which, absent new technological breakthroughs, has become difficult. This occurred in corporate America from the 1970s to the 1980s, contributing to the competitive decline of the US Big Three automakers.

But policy can help or hurt in this stage. The Celler-Kefauver Act of 1950, which authorized antitrust prosecution for the merger of firms in related businesses, inadvertently triggered a wave of conglomerate mergers among companies in unrelated lines of work. These mergers diverted management from concentrating on its core business and prevented the increases in scale that would be needed in the 1970s as the US economy faced stiff new global competition. Because antitrust law now made it much harder for companies to gain scale with horizontal or vertical mergers, managers seeking to grow their companies through acquisitions increasingly sought conglomerate mergers, which were allowed. Among the 148 firms that were in the top 200 corporations in both 1950 and 1975, the mean number of lines of business that a firm engaged in grew from 5.2 to 9.7.[39]

Between 1950 and 1978, Beatrice Foods made 290 acquisitions and W. R. Grace made 163. The latter, originally a chemical company, acquired Hostess Twinkies snack cakes, Mexican restaurants, sports teams, fire extinguisher makers, banks, and western wear makers, among other firms. RCA purchased Random House, a publishing house, Hertz Rent-a-Car company, Banquet Foods, which made frozen meals, a carpet company, Coronet, and a company that made golfing attire.[40]

It took another twenty-five years before this massive government-induced misallocation of resources began to be undone. The "takeover artists" and "corporate raiders" of the 1970s and 1980s such as Carl Icahn and Michael Milken targeted poorly performing conglomerates to get a one-time boost in stock price and used techniques pioneered by the conglomerates themselves, which by the 1970s increasingly financed their own takeovers of other firms with debt. In US manufacturing the debt-to-equity ratio between 1965 and 1970 rose from 0.48 to 0.72.[41]

Unlike the merger waves of the 1890s to 1900s and the 1920s, which created many dynamic firms that lasted for decades, the conglomerate merger wave boosted profits without boosting productivity or innovation. What saved the US economy from a future of rearranging existing assets through unproductive mergers was not only the attacks by the corporate raiders, coupled with a relaxation of antitrust rules starting in the 1980s, but also the most recent industrial revolution, based on digital technologies such as the computer and the Internet.

During the 1980s and 1990s, the temporary coexistence of a great number of tech startups with a few giant, familiar "old economy" companies such as Ford and Procter & Gamble and ExxonMobil led many to believe that the information era would inaugurate an age in which small firms would replace the lumbering dinosaurs of the past. The *Economist* wrote, "The biggest change coming over the world of business is that firms are getting smaller. The trend of a century is being reversed. ... Now it is the big firms that are shrinking and small ones that are on the rise. The trend is unmistakable—and businessmen and policy makers will ignore it at their peril." In *Business Week* in 1993, John Byrne argued that large corporations would be supplanted by "the virtual corporation," a "temporary network of independent companies, suppliers, customers, even erstwhile rivals linked by IT to share skills, costs, and access to one another's markets."[42] He quoted the head of a consulting firm as saying that such a change was "inevitable." Another author, John Case, writing in *Inc. Magazine*, observed:

As a group the *Fortune* 500 had been growing steadily ever since the list was created in 1954. By 1979 their total sales amounted to 58% of America's gross national product, up from 37% 25 years earlier. They employed more than three-quarters of the manufacturing work force, up from half. Ah, well. Times change. Today almost any upstart seems able to outsmart Sears or Macy's or IBM. And today, small business matters—a lot.[43]

But by the 2000s it had become clear that the startup phase of the IT revolution had been a normal and predictable transitional phase. Just as dozens of automobile startups gave way to the Big Three by the mid-twentieth century, so most of the startups of the digital era perished or were absorbed by a few victors. By the early twenty-first century, tech oligopolies, such as Google, Apple, Microsoft, and Facebook, dominated their markets in the same way that "old economy" firms, such as Nabisco and GM, had long dominated theirs, and in so doing they created enormous consumer value through scale and network efficiencies.

Moreover, in each successive wave of industrial innovation, the possible scale of production has expanded, along with enabling technology. In the age of steam, the railroad and telegraph made possible a continental market in the United States. But steam-era factories had to be sited near coal seams or else canals or rivers that could bring the coal for their steam engines. This explains the concentration of steam-powered factories in Pittsburgh and the midwestern United States, the British Midlands, and the Ruhr in Germany.

The technologies of the next industrial era made possible truly national production across several regions. The corporate headquarters could be located in a finance and services center such as New York, while plants could be located near markets or in states with favorable tax and labor laws. The telephone, and later the facsimile (fax) machine, made it possible for headquarters to monitor far-flung operations. In the same period, personal inspection was facilitated by passenger airline travel after World War II, which made it possible for executives to travel anywhere in the United States in a day or less. Multinational corporations existed in this era, but they tended to be separate national enterprises sharing a brand, not integrated production chains. Truly transnational production was enabled by the technologies of the most recent industrial revolution, including the Internet, fiber-optics, and advanced computing and software systems.

In the 1960s containerization lowered the prices of ocean transport, particularly on long routes.[44] Also, the rise of air transport has meant that an increasing share of high-value, low-weight products can be easily traded. As a result, the value of air-shipped trade grew from almost nothing in 1950 to nearly 30 percent of all international shipping in 1998.[45] This meant that it became more economical for larger factories to serve larger geographic markets. Combined with the liberalization of trade after the Cold War, the use of "carrot"-like subsidies and "stick"-like in-market production requirements by mercantilist nations, and the competition of former communist and protectionist nations for corporate investment, the new technology allowed truly global companies to emerge and evolve.

In 1969, Harry Magdoff and Paul M. Sweezy, leading economists of the "monopoly capital" school associated with the neo-Marxist journal *Monthly Review*, correctly predicted that global economic integration would lead to global concentration, "with all major industries in all capitalist countries dominated by a few hundred giant corporations."[46] In 1975 the economist Stephen Hymer wrote:

Suppose giant multinational corporations (say 300 from the US and 200 from Europe and Japan) succeed in establishing themselves as the dominant form of international enterprise and come to control a significant share of industry (especially modern industry) in each country. The world economy will resemble more and more the United States' economy, where each of the large corporations tends to spread over the entire continent, and to penetrate almost every nook and cranny.[47]

In 1986 the economist Joseph Bowring similarly predicted, "It is expected that the evolution of a more integrated world economy will produce an evolution of the world industrial structure similar to the development of core and periphery within the US; not all core firms may make the transition successfully."[48] What the economist Peter Nolan has described as "the global business revolution" following the Cold War has indeed produced a wave of consolidation on a planetary scale, comparable to the waves of consolidation of national industries in the United States, Britain, Germany, and other industrial countries a century earlier.[49] By the time the worldwide recession began with the financial crash of 2008, many global industries were dominated by a few large corporations. One hundred percent of the large jet airliner industry was divided among two firms, Boeing and Airbus. Two-thirds of the glass bottles in the world were made by two firms, Owens-Illinois and Saint Gobin. Half of the world's cars were made by four companies, GM, Ford, Toyota-Daihatsu, and DaimlerChrysler. Microsoft held 90 percent of the market for personal computer operating systems.[50] In 2007 the top two firms controlled 86 percent of the global market in the financial information industry and 77 percent in electronic games, while three firms accounted for 71 percent of legal publishing.[51] A similar pattern occurred in many supplier industries. In 2008, three firms—GE, Pratt and Whitney, and Rolls-Royce—dominated the world market for jet engines. Sixty percent of tires were made by three multinational corporations, Bridgestone, Goodyear, and Michelin.[52] As Nolan has observed:

By the early 2000s, in the high value-added, high technology, and/or strongly branded segments of world markets, which serve mainly the middle and upper income earners who control the bulk of the world's purchasing power, a veritable "law" had come into play: a handful of giant firms, the "systems integrators," occupied upwards of 50 percent of the whole global market.[53]

In addition to the rise of global oligopolies as a result of growth, mergers, or alliances, another trend was transnational production. By the early twenty-first century, more than a third of the total trade of US multinationals was intrafirm trade or transnational production by a multinational enterprise with suppliers in multiple nations.[54] The Apple iPhone became the epitome of a product with components from all over the world. Apple iPhone 6 models included components from China, the United States, Japan, South Korea, Taiwan, Germany, France, Italy, the Netherlands, and Singapore. While many supply chains were regional or global, most major multinationals continued to be rooted in a single nation-state—most often the three most populous developed industrial nations with the biggest internal markets, the United States, Japan, and Germany.[55]

Multinational globalization was controversial, both in developing nations and in developed nations. A larger share of gains from global growth went to some select investors and executives, while low-wage competition from developing nations meant either joblessness or downward pressure on wages in former industrial areas of the US Midwest and "old" Europe. Furthermore, the pattern of global production was manipulated by mercantilist states such as those of East Asia, especially China, which used elaborate and unfair industrial policies to try to capture as much as they could of high-value-added global supply chains. As in the past, corporate forms and market structures were shaped by the interaction of politics and purely commercial decisions.

The growth in firm size has not been limited to transnational corporations in the digital era. Firm and establishment size have grown in the domestic economy, too, in part because IT has allowed firms to link more operations inside their firms. In 2006 the United States passed a milestone: for the first time in history, a majority of the workforce was employed in firms with at least 500 workers. That number has continued to rise. According to the US Census Bureau's Statistics of US Businesses database, firms with 500 or more employees accounted for 45.5 percent of private employment in 1988, but by 2011 this number had risen to 51.5 percent. Thus the median private sector employee today works for a firm with 500+ employees.

From 1992 to 2012, firms with fewer than 100 employees lost share in terms of number of firms (down 0.08 percent), sales (down 25 percent), and number of employees (down 12 percent, from 38.2 percent of workers to 33.8 percent). Even larger declines are evident for firms with fewer than 50 employees. Their share of total firms fell 5 percent and their share of employment fell 11 percent (from 31 percent to 28 percent).[56] In contrast, firms with more than 2,500 employees increased their share of firms by 17 percent, while their share of sales increased by 20 percent and their share of employees increased 16 percent.[57] And the really big firms (more than 10,000 employees) saw their share of employment increase by 27 percent.

Between 1990 and 2011, total private employment grew by 17.5 million, or 19 percent. While firms with 500 or more employees accounted for 42 percent of employment in 1990, they accounted for 65 percent of this gain. Firms with between 50 and 499 employees accounted for 28 percent of jobs in 1990 but for only 19 percent of the growth. And smaller firms accounted for 30 percent of jobs at the beginning of the period but for only 16 percent of the growth.[58] Most of this change in firm size share occurred in the 1990s, with little change in shares in the 2000s. However, since the global recession of 2008–2009, small and mid-sized firms lost a greater share of jobs than large firms and were slower to recover.

Similar trends are evident in the share of self-employed workers. Unincorporated self-employed persons declined from 20 percent of full- and part-time workers in 1948 to 9 percent in 1987, a decline of 56 percent. Much of this decline was attributable to a large drop in self-employed farmers. The share of self-employed workers in all other industries declined 26 percent. Only two industries saw an increase in self-employment, mining (presumably small-scale wildcatters and prospectors) and transportation and public utilities.[59] One recent trend has been the emergence of "gig" workers who use Internet platforms such as Uber or Task Rabbit to do work. One study estimated there were only about 600,000 of these kinds of workers in 2015. In any case, even with the emergence of these workers, many who only work through Internet platforms, the share of the workforce that is self-employed has continued to fall, to less than 7 percent by 2016.[60]

Whatever the benefits and costs of economic growth are judged to be, one thing is clear. From the steam era to the information age, in a growing number of industries technological innovations have enabled a long-term trend toward ever larger firms. The trends in firm size and firm startups are the subject of the next chapter.

3 Understanding US Firm Size and Dynamics

In light of widespread complaints that US firms are becoming monopolistic behemoths, it might come as a surprise to learn that the average US enterprise employs just 20.2 workers and the average establishment even fewer (an enterprise or firm consists of the entire company, while an establishment is a separate operation).

However, these size patterns differ significantly by industry. Some industries are inherently small. The five smallest industries in terms of *firm* size are fishing, hunting, and trapping (3.1 workers), building construction (5.5), real estate (5.9), funds, trusts, and other financial vehicles (6), and repair and maintenance (6.1). The industries in table 3.1 all had average *establishment* sizes of fewer than three employees in 2012. The vast majority of small establishment industries have few opportunities to get more efficient through size, by means of economies of scale. For example, a commercial photography firm of 1,000 workers using the same techniques would likely be less efficient than the average-sized photography firm of three workers.

Moreover, most small firm industries are engaged in local production, selling the lion's share of output locally (think of barber shops, dry cleaners, real estate appraisers, auto repair services). In fact, just 6 percent of employment in the 100 industries with the smallest average firm size is in traded industries (mostly in fishing and sound recording and production).[1] Thus, when policy makers advocate for small business, they are mostly favoring local businesses without national or global competitors, which would exist regardless of government favors. Someone will dry clean our clothes even if dry cleaners don't get tax subsidies.

At the other end of the size distribution are industries in which the average firm in 2012 had more than 1,000 workers, including hospitals,

Table 3.1

US industries with an average establishment size of three employees or fewer, 2012

Independent Artists, Writers, and Performers	Other Marine Fishing
Shellfish Fishing	Footwear and Leather Goods Repair
Interior Design Services	Record Production
Offices of Real Estate Agents and Brokers	Mobile Food Services
Lessors of Miniwarehouses and Self-Storage Units	Commercial Photography
Home and Garden Equipment Repair and Maintenance	Offices of Real Estate Appraisers

Source: US Small Business Administration, Firm Size Data (Table 2. Number of Firms, Establishments, Receipts, Employment, and Payroll by Firm Size [in Receipts] and Industry), https://www.sba.gov/advocacy/firm-size-data (accessed March 10, 2017).

Table 3.2

US industries with an average establishment size of more than 400 employees, 2012

Guided Missile and Space Vehicle Manufacturing	Casino Hotels
General Medical and Surgical Hospitals	Poultry Processing
Guided Missile and Space Vehicle Propulsion Unit and Propulsion Unit Parts Manufacturing	Light Truck and Utility Vehicle Manufacturing
Professional Employer Organizations	Aircraft Manufacturing
Colleges, Universities, and Professional Schools	

Source: US Small Business Administration, Firm Size Data (Table 2. Number of Firms, Establishments, Receipts, Employment, and Payroll by Firm Size [in Receipts] and Industry), https://www.sba.gov/advocacy/firm-size-data (accessed March 10, 2017).

department stores, casino hotels, nuclear power generators, and airlines. These are industries in which economies of scale and scope enable larger size. For example, companies such as Macy's, Sears, and Target benefit from a nationwide network of stores. Airlines such as American, Delta, and United benefit from a large network of airline routes so flyers can more easily get from point A to point B. Industries with average establishment sizes of more than 400 workers see similar economies of scale (see table 3.2).

Large-firm industries are more likely to sell output outside the nation; that is, they occur in traded sectors. In the approximately 100 industries with an average firm size of more than 175 workers, the share of jobs in traded sector industries was approximately 60 percent. These include industries such as aircraft, tire, motor vehicle, and guided missile manufacturing.[2]

Trends in Firm and Establishment Size

From 1997 to 2012, average firm size increased 6.6 percent, from 19 employees to 20.2, up from 17.6 in 1987 (see figure 3.1). But this trend masked considerable differences among industries. The average number of jobs in manufacturing firms fell 22 percent, with jobs in apparel manufacturing firms down 35 percent, jobs in textiles down 34 percent, and jobs in computer and electronic products down 23 percent. Likewise, construction firms have gotten slightly smaller. But overall average size would have increased even more had employment not shifted to sectors that employed on average fewer workers per firm. So while services gained employment and their average establishment size increased, their average firm size was much smaller than that of manufacturing firms.

We see similar patterns with the change in size of establishments (see figure 3.2). From 1997 to 2012 the number of workers in the average establishment increased by 2 percent, but this increase masked considerable intersectoral difference, with manufacturing declining and others

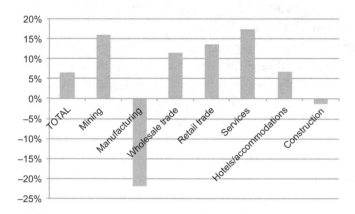

Figure 3.1
Change in Average Firm Size by Industry, 1997–2012 (Employees)
Source: US Census Bureau, Statistics of US Businesses Annual Data Tables 1997 and 2012, https://www.census.gov/programs-surveys/susb/data/tables.html.

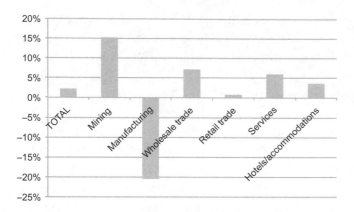

Figure 3.2
Change in US Establishment Size by Industry, 1997–2012
Source: US Small Business Administration, Firm Size Data (Detailed Industry Data),
https://www.sba.gov/advocacy/firm-size-data (accessed March 10, 2017).

increasing. Establishments with fewer than 500 employees accounted for 10 percent fewer jobs in 2009–2010 than in 1998, while establishments with more than 500 employees accounted for 20 percent more. There were only two industries in which large establishments lost share: farming, fishing, and hunting and manufacturing. But large construction establishments accounted for 51 percent more jobs than in 1998–1999 and transportation and warehousing accounted for 42 percent more, while information technology (IT) accounted for 27 percent more.[3]

The perception that firms are getting bigger on average is accurate. True, the share of employment in establishments employing more than 10,000 fell from 16 percent in 1974 to 13 percent in 2006. But this loss was all in manufacturing. In services the share increased from 12.5 to 17 percent. Likewise, the largest 1 percent of establishments employed 58 percent of service workers in 1974 but 62 percent in 1997.

Shrinking Manufacturers

While overall firm size is getting bigger, manufacturers have been getting smaller since the late 1960s. The average manufacturing plant employed around twenty workers in the first two decades of the 1900s, but this figure had tripled by the end of World War II, in part because of the adoption of the assembly line and mass production technology in many discrete goods industries (cars, airplanes, appliances, electronics) and process industries (pulp and paper, chemicals, steel) (see figure 3.3) But since 1967 average manufacturing plant size has fallen, dipping below 1925 levels in 2012.

We see the same trend for average manufacturing firm size, which fell from around eighty workers in 1972 to around fifty in 2007.[4] The same dynamics can be observed in most other industrial nations. In Italy the share of manufacturing workers in plants with more than 100 workers declined from 43 percent in 1961 to 29 percent in 2007, in France from 61 percent in 1962 to 52 percent in 2001, and in Germany from 69 percent in 1962 to 60 percent in 2001.[5]

Some of the decline may be due to higher productivity in manufacturing than nonmanufacturing. In other words, manufacturers can produce as much or more with fewer workers. But this can't be the whole explanation, in part because manufacturing productivity has grown faster than nonmanufacturing for more than a century. Rather, new, more flexible production technologies which emerged in the 1960s that allow manufacturing firms and establishments to produce shorter production runs appear to play a key role. In a world where manufacturing meant expensive investments in specialized tooling and machining to make specific parts (e.g., a car door panel), firms had incentives to have very long production runs, necessitating large factories. Changing tooling to make a different part was

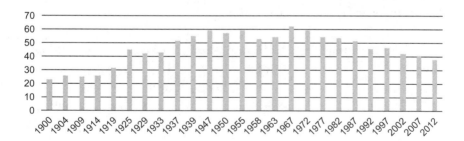

Figure 3.3
Trends in Average US Manufacturing Plant Size (Employment)
Source: US Census Bureau, Statistical Abstracts of the United States (various years, 1900–1987), https://www.census.gov/library/publications/time-series/statistical _abstracts.html (accessed March 22, 2017); US Census Bureau, Economic Census: Manufacturing (various years, 1992–2007), https://www.census.gov/programs -surveys/economic-census/data/tables.html (accessed March 22, 2017).

time consuming and expensive. Moreover, when coordination between different plants and suppliers was difficult (using paper-based forms and telephone communications to coordinate), it was easier to consolidate all production within a massive facility, as exemplified by Henry Ford's Rouge River plant, where coal and iron ore went in one end and cars came out the other end.[6]

But with the development of flexible production technology in the 1960s, first numerically controlled (NC) machine tools and then computer-numerically controlled (CNC) machine tools, followed by the availability of computer-aided design tools, firms could lower the costs of shorter production runs. And with the emergence in the 1970s of electronic data interchange (EDI) systems and then in the 1990s of Internet-based systems, it became more economical to link specialized plants together in extended production networks. The rise of just-in-time production networks meant establishments didn't need to be huge to enable coordination.

Global competition has also led to reduced manufacturing establishment size. With the increased ease and effectiveness of global coordination systems, it became much easier to develop global supply chains, with commodity-based, mass production activities moving to low-wage nations to take advantage of cheap labor (and government subsidies). The establishments most likely to move were the larger ones making more standardized goods.

Nonmanufacturing Firms Getting Bigger

While manufacturing firms have been getting smaller, establishments and firms in most nonmanufacturing industries have been getting bigger. The average service sector establishment increased from twelve employees in 1977 to eighteen in 2014, with firms increasing from thirteen employees in 1977 to twenty-one in 2014.[7] Professional services, education, health care, arts, accommodations, other services, and administrative and waste management firms all got bigger, as did mining (by 16 percent), wholesale trade (11 percent), retail trade (14 percent), and hotels/accommodations (7 percent). The changes since 1963 were even more dramatic, with all sectors other than manufacturing seeing increased establishment size: hotels grew 545 percent, construction grew 500 percent, and retail trade grew 355 percent.

In the late 1990s it was widely believed the Internet would do for services what computer technologies had done for manufacturing: empower small firms. Now mom-and-pop firms could access a world market with just a broadband connection and a website. But by the same token, big firms also got access to the mom-and-pop firms' customers with their broadband connections and better web pages.

The result has been that IT has enabled greater economies of scale for many service industries, in part by letting these firms serve larger regional markets and reducing transport costs between facilities. The internet in fact, enabled firms to get larger. Many services, among them retail, banking, insurance, law, accounting, and securities services, that were once tied to local economies can now be conducted at a distance. IT has enabled an increasing share of information-based services to be physically distant from the customer (e.g., e-banking) or more consolidated (e.g., back office operations) while remaining functionally close.

From 1997 to 2012 the average warehouse and storage company increased in size by six times (from fifteen employees to ninety-eight) as technology enabled warehousing to consolidate and regionalize.[8] With the emergence of big box retailers with powerful IT systems to coordinate ordering and inventory management, and more recently online commerce, retail firms got bigger, including electronics and appliance firms, such as Best Buy (33 percent more workers); building material and garden equipment companies, such as Home Depot (19 percent), home and furnishing companies, such as Ikea (10 percent); sporting goods and book and music companies, such as Barnes & Noble (15 percent); clothing retailers, such as Old Navy (35 percent); and general merchandise stores, such as Amazon.com (35 percent). In part because of the increased use of technology and increases in demand, firms in health care got bigger, with nursing homes up 8 percent, ambulatory health care services up 14 percent, and hospitals up 47 percent. Banks saw an average establishment size increase of 30 percent. And with the continued spread of national lodging chains, the average size of accommodation firms grew by 12 percent.

But some industries shrank. The securities, commodity contracts, and other financial investment and related activities industry fell 27 percent, while the size of insurance carriers shrank by 6 percent. Moreover, in some industries, while technology enabled larger firms, it meant smaller establishments. That occurred in banking, for example, where the widespread use of automatic teller machines allowed branches to employ fewer people. Banks are getting bigger, but average employment in commercial bank branches declined from about twenty employees in 1988 to thirteen by 2004.[9]

One result is the spread of large, multi-establishment corporations into markets that once were more heavily populated by mom-and-pop stores. From 1977 to 2013, US employment rose by 72.3 percent, while the number of firms rose by just 47.9 percent. In other words, firms were getting bigger. Much of this can be explained by consolidation, as firms could use technology to more easily manage multiple business locations. This is why the number of US establishments rose by 61.4 percent, less than employment growth. In other words, new firm formation lagged.

Why Have New Firm Startup Rates Fallen?

With the tepid and long recovery from the global recession of 2008–2009, a cottage industry has emerged in identifying the reasons for slow growth. One popular answer is the decline in new business formation. It is almost impossible to read business publications without being bombarded by warnings that small firms are starting at anemically low rates, which is keeping America's growth in the slow lane.

In 2012 Barry Lynn and Lina Khan warned that "the share of the working-age population that is self-employed has been declining since 1994. ... Overall, between 1994 and 2009, the share declined nearly 25 percent."[10] This is correct, but the trend goes back much further. Self-employment rates fell from 9.1 percent in 1965 to 6.8 percent in 2005.[11]

But it was not until 2014 that alarm over dwindling new business formation got widespread media attention, when a Brookings Institution report by Ian Hathaway and Robert Litan found that new business starts had "declined in all fifty states and in all but a handful of the more than three hundred and sixty US metropolitan areas during the last three decades."[12] As their report shows, the trends are clear (see figure 3.4).

Other studies joined in raising the alarm. In 2015 Jason Wiens and Chris Jackson of Kauffman Foundation wrote: "New businesses represent a declining share of the business community. ... New firms represented as much as 16 percent of all firms in the late 1970s. By 2011, that share had declined to 8 percent."[13] The next year, John W. Lettieri and Steve Glickman of the

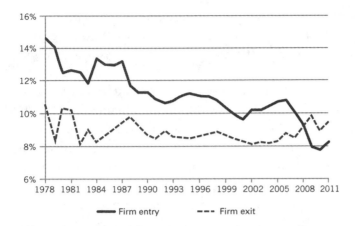

Figure 3.4

Change in US Firm Entry and Exit

Source: Ian Hathaway and Robert E. Litan, "Declining Business Dynamism in the United States: A Look at States and Metros," Economic Studies at Brookings (Washington, DC: Brookings Institution, May 2014), https://www.brookings.edu/wp-content/uploads/2016/06/declining_business_dynamism_hathaway_litan.pdf.

Economic Innovation Group wrote that "the U.S. economy has steadily become less entrepreneurial over the past 30 years. That decline turned into a rapid collapse following the Great Recession, when the economy produced hundreds of thousands fewer new businesses than it did in previous recovery periods, marking a lost generation of new enterprise."[14]

This decline is seen by many as a crisis of major proportions. Hathaway and Litan warn that the US business sector is getting "old and fat" and that "nothing less than the future welfare of America and its citizens is at stake."[15] Lettieri calls this "the fundamental challenge of our time."[16] Lynn and Khan agree: "The founding generation was right: as America's entrepreneurs go, so goes America's prosperity and democracy."[17] Gallup CEO Jim Clifton warns that "this economy is never truly coming back unless we reverse the birth and death trends of American businesses."[18] And John Dearie, executive vice president of the Financial Services Forum, warns that "this is nothing short of a national emergency."[19]

We disagree. In our view, the only important question is what is happening to "Schumpeterian" entrepreneurship—the creation of technology-intensive businesses that can get big—not the total number of new small businesses of all kinds, many of them founded merely so that the owner can fulfill personal lifestyle goals. From this perspective, contemporary alarmism over dwindling startups and self-employment is misguided and can even be dangerous, if the mistaken diagnosis leads to harmful prescriptions.

Why have startup rates declined? Few seem to know. According to Hathaway and Litan, "The reasons explaining this decline are still unknown,"[20] though a later report from them suggests a few causes, such as slow population growth and increased firm size.[21] But by and large, the cause of the decline has remained a mystery. This has not stopped advocates from using the alleged problem to justify their preferred public policies.

The Kauffman Foundation proposes increasing the number of immigrants, removing regulatory barriers, making the tax code simpler, and increasing education levels.[22] But immigration for the last two decades—the very period of "entrepreneurial" decline—has been at record highs. Why would it help to add even more immigrants, particularly ones with low levels of skills and education? The tax code is arguably more complicated than it was twenty years ago, but not by much. Besides, any small business can plunk down a few bucks for an easy-to-use tax preparation software package, such as TurboTax. More education? A greater share of Americans are going to college and graduating than ever before, to the point that more than 15 percent of American adults have more education than they need for their job.[23]

The free market conservatives of the Heritage Foundation blame high taxes, just as they tend to blame high taxes for a variety of economic woes.[24] But tax rates are lower today than they were in the 1980s. At the other end of the political spectrum, the progressive liberal Roosevelt Institute blames the decline on increased corporate concentration and profits.[25] But, as we show in chapter 11, this does not appear to be the case.

The National Federation of Independent Business warns that small businesses are "burdened by an ever-growing pile of regulations."[26] But new firm formation declined from 1980 to 1992, when Ronald Reagan and George H. W. Bush were in the White House and pushing a deregulatory agenda. It continued to decline after 1994, when the Republicans gained a majority in the House and began to implement their Contract with America to reduce regulatory burdens. Moreover, if regulation is really the problem, why did states with business climates as different as California and Texas have large and similar declines in new business starts?[27] According to the Kauffman

Foundation rankings, California, a state hardly known for regulatory reticence, outperforms Texas in new firm formation.[28]

Another theory holds that big banks are refusing to lend to creditworthy borrowers. Barry Lynn and Lina Khan write, "The effects of the radical consolidation in the banking industry that began in the 1980s are equally dramatic. Relatively few bank officers today have the leeway and local knowledge to lend to established local businesses, much less new ventures."[29] But as we note in chapter 10, research shows that bank consolidation has helped as banks are better able to spread risk. However, some have argued that the Sarbanes-Oxley and Dodd-Frank legislation has made it harder for firms to go public and for banks to lend to small business. But that is a different issue from saying that large banks per se are behind the decline in startups.

Donna Kelley, a professor of entrepreneurship at Babson College, blames millennials, describing them as slackers who have a preternatural fear of failure.[30] If so, it suggests that colleges are failing our students, as the number of college entrepreneurship classes has increased twenty times over the last thirty years.[31] Moreover, Britt Hysen, the editor in chief of *MiLLENNiAL* magazine, claims that "60 percent of Millennials consider themselves entrepreneurs, and 90 percent recognize entrepreneurship as a mentality."[32] While some blame millennials, others blame the boomers for being too numerous and too old.[33] However, using a regression model of firm entry by state, Hathaway and Litan convincingly rebut this explanation.[34]

By far the favorite explanation for the decline of startups is that swelling, sclerotic monopolies are thwarting innovative entrepreneurs. Lynn and Khan write, "The single biggest factor driving down entrepreneurship is precisely the radical concentration of power we have seen not only in the banking industry but throughout the U.S. economy over the last thirty years."[35] In his *Atlantic* article, "America's Monopoly Problem: How Big Business Jammed the Wheels of Innovation," Derek Thompson writes that the decline "has coincided with the rise of extraordinarily large and profitable firms that look like the monopolies and oligopolies of the 19th century."[36] Stacy Mitchell of the Institute for Local Self-Reliance writes, "The decline of small business and entrepreneurship is owed, in significant part, to anticompetitive behavior by dominant corporations which routinely use their size and market power to undermine and exclude their smaller rivals."[37] The argument of modern champions of the antimonopolist tradition is simple: concentration went up and startups went down, so the former caused the latter.

To paraphrase former senator Patrick Moynihan, who famously said "Everyone is entitled to his own opinion, but not his own facts," we don't disagree with the small firm startup alarmists' facts, or at least with most of them. We disagree with what they mean. We see the decline in small businesses like Justin and Ashley's independent pizza parlor as a good thing, reflecting the growth of more efficient and more innovative larger firms.

Moreover, we want to advance a more nuanced argument that the decline in new firms is not so simple. It's one thing to assert that fewer Justins and Ashleys are opening up pizza parlors or dry cleaners. It's quite another to assert that there are fewer Sergeys (Brin), Larrys (Page), and Jeffs (Bezos) starting the next Google or Amazon. The first is true, the second much less so.

Should we be concerned that "entrepreneurs" like Justin and Ashley are starting fewer small firms? On the face of it we shouldn't be, because as we show in the next chapter, large firms outperform small firms on virtually every economic indicator. But if their decline was due to some problem with the business environment or a decline in entrepreneurial drive, then maybe we should be worried, since this might also hamper high-growth startups.

Why Did Startups Decline?

So why have the Justin and Ashley startups declined? The "business startup sky is falling" narrative implies that if we get more new businesses, the economy will grow faster. But what if the economy's performance has affected the rate of new business formation, rather than the other way around? A Federal Reserve Bank of Cleveland study finds that the rate of aggregate demand, largely after the Great Recession, influences firm startup rates. The authors write: "We find that cyclical factors have contributed to recent low levels of self-employment. ... Decreasing demand leads to an increase in exit from entrepreneurship but has countervailing effects on entry."[38]

In other words, slower economic growth has reduced the opportunities for new firms. We see this in the fact that the twenty metro areas with the highest rates of new firm formation were all in faster-growing "Sunbelt" states while the twenty with the lowest rates were all in slower-growing "rust belt" states.[39] As the US economy over the last three decades has come to more resemble the rust belt than the Sunbelt, it shouldn't come as a surprise that there are fewer new firms.

But slower US growth is not the only factor. To understand the decline, it's important to look at startups by industry. When you do that it becomes evident that not all industries have seen declines. While almost 100,000 fewer new firms formed in 2011 than in 2003, in about 40 percent of 290 industries more firms formed in 2011 than in 2003. For example, mining startups increased 30 percent, largely because of the oil and gas shale boom. Educational services startups increased 11 percent as new technology offered new market opportunities. Startup rates in professional, scientific, and technical services; information (e.g., software, telecom, broadcasting); and health care and social assistance industries remained unchanged.

Moreover, some industries that saw declines were ones that felt the impacts of the global recession particularly acutely. The collapse of the construction industry after the housing bust meant that construction startups fell 26 percent and real estate and rental and leasing fell 13 percent. Why start a new construction firm when home building is in tank? Similarly, with the financial crises and the bankruptcy of multiple financial services firms, why start a new firm in the financial services industry, where startups fell 29 percent?

And in some industries where the rate of startups did fall, concentration ratios actually fell or were stable, suggesting that excessive market power favored by antimonopolist narratives was not the cause. For example, in "other services," startups fell by 24 percent, but the C4 and C8 ratios (the share of sales in industry by the top four and top eight firms, respectively) fell 1 percent. In the wholesale trade and arts, entertainment, and recreation industries, startups declined 16 percent and 14 percent, respectively, but C4 and C8 concentration ratios were unchanged.

In manufacturing, where new firm formation was down 20 percent from 2003 to 2011, the decline was not due to big manufacturers taking market share and crushing the new guy, as evidenced by the average C4 and C8 concentration ratios in manufacturing increasing by less than one percentage point. The most likely reason manufacturing startups fell is because stiff international competition from nations such as China, much of it unfair and based on mercantilist policies such as currency manipulation, intellectual property theft, and government subsidies, made it hard for budding US entrepreneurs to break in.[40] Why start a manufacturing firm if you are likely to face predatory competition not from big US firms but from Chinese competitors backed by their state? Unfair foreign competition, coupled with the absence of a national US competitiveness policy, is a major reason why inflation-adjusted US manufacturing output fell more than 10 percent in the 2000s, with over 65,000 manufacturing establishments closing their doors.[41] And when output is falling, that is hardly a good time to start a new manufacturing firm.

Between 2000 and 2014 (China joined the World Trade Organization in 2000), the number of small manufacturing establishments (one to four workers) in the United States fell by 14 percent, while the number of large establishments (1,000+ workers) fell by 42 percent. One reason for the difference was the slow movement of smaller firms into the large size class. In 1980, 110 establishments with more than 1,000 workers were three years old or less. That figure fell every decade, to just eighteen establishments by 2014, a decline of 84 percent. In contrast, the growth of younger small establishments fell between 52 and 62 percent. At the firm level, the share of manufacturing workers employed by firms employing 5,000 or more workers fell from 46 percent in 1977 to just 15 percent in 2005.[42]

Notwithstanding the stiff headwind from competition, a few manufacturing sectors saw an increase in new firm formation, but these sectors were mostly ones that produced products less subject to import competition. For example, bakery and tortilla manufacturing startups expanded by 17 percent, "other food manufacturing" by 14 percent, and beverage manufacturing by 74 percent (in part because of the expansion of craft beer and healthy drink products such as Honest Tea).[43] But if the antimonopoly story is right and decreased competition was the cause of fewer startups, we should have seen declining new firm formation in the beverage industry since the C4 and C8 concentration levels increased by ten percentage points over the last decade.

To be sure, the assertion that larger firms are crowding out startups is valid in some sectors. The fact that technology has enabled larger and more efficient firms in many nonmanufacturing sectors means there are fewer opportunities for small and new firms. This is why David Audretsch has argued, "The likelihood of new-firm survival should be lower in industries exhibiting greater scale economies."[44] This is not about predation but about space for new firms in any particular industry.

We see this trend in some industries, especially retail trade. Retail industry startups fell 16 percent from 2003 to 2011, but not because large firms abused their market power to kill startups. Rather, technologies such as software-enabled logistics systems and web-based e-commerce enabled the average retail firm to get larger, meaning there was less market space for startups unless they had something truly unique to offer or local convenience.

For example, it was once not too hard to open a book or music store. When one of us was younger, he used to take a trip after school to the local record store, Pauls (owned by Paul), to sample the latest 45s. Now we get our music from iTunes and Pandora. This is why book and music store startups fell 58 percent from 2003 to 2011, while the total number of establishments shrank by one-third.[45] At the same time, the market share of the largest four firms increased from 48 percent to 66 percent. But these changes came about because of technology and efficiency, not predation. Large specialty bookstores such as Barnes & Noble, and then later in the decade online retailers such as Amazon.com, and the rise of e-book sellers such as Apple's iTunes store and Amazon's Kindle, meant that more people bought books and music at large brick-and-mortar stores and at online stores because they could save money and have a wider choice of products.

We have seen the same dynamic with hardware stores. Forty years ago someone who was good with tools might think of opening a hardware store. Today they would likely think twice about doing so since big box stores such as Home Depot and Lowes serve this market very well, having gained market share from small, independently owned hardware stores. But they didn't gain it by predation and unfair practices that crushed the little guy. They gained it by providing a much wider selection of products at a significantly lower price. The typical Home Depot store is around 105,000 square feet (almost the size of two football fields), more than ten times larger than the typical neighborhood hardware store.[46] And the big box stores stock upward of 25,000 different products, significantly more than the neighborhood stores do.[47] This volume lets them be much more efficient, with sales per square feet of store two-thirds higher than at neighborhood stores and 25 percent more per employee.[48]

This story has played out in many retail sectors where large retailers have gained market share by providing goods or services that consumers want at prices they can afford. Owner-operator barbershops have been superseded by Supercuts, coffee shops by Starbucks, donut shops by Dunkin' Donuts, stationery stores by Staples and Office Depot, local pharmacies by CVS and Walgreens. Among the many retail industries that saw increasing average employment size per firm were food and beverage stores (7 percent), furniture stores (10 percent), sporting goods (15 percent), banks (29 percent), electronics and appliance stores (33 percent), and general merchandise stores (35 percent).[49]

These retail giants have tapped into the substantial benefits of scale, which are passed on to customers. Moreover, large retailers compete directly against each other, spurring innovation, technology investment and adoption, and efficiency. Indeed, technological innovation (particularly computer-based supply chain ordering) has enabled size increases. The effects have nowhere been more dramatic than in those sectors that have always been most congenial to individual proprietorships, such as retail, services, farming, and small manufacturing. These were the sectors and the activities most affected, for instance, by the type of "roll-up" strategies pioneered by financiers like Mitt Romney's Bain Capital. In the case of the office-supply retailer Staples, Bain's investment helped propel the company from a one-store operation to a 2,000-store international behemoth. Similar plays resulted in Home Depot capturing a vast proportion of the nation's hardware business, in Best Buy capturing a vast proportion of America's electronics business, and in Macy's capturing a vast proportion of all department store sales. Just one company, Wal-Mart, now has upward of 50 percent of some lines of grocery and general merchandise business—commerce that a generation ago was divided among tens of thousands of family businesses—with shoppers the big beneficiary. And, of course, emerging web-based businesses such as Amazon promise even more competition, efficiency, convenience, and scale.

This transition from local Justin and Ashley stores to chain stores has been going on for more than a century, starting with stores like A&P and Sears, and has occurred largely independently of government policy. If anything, government policy has leaned into this wind, providing big subsidies to the mom-and-pop businesses, and in some communities actively restricting the large stores.

Yet for the antimonopolists, this is a decidedly bad thing. As Thompson writes, "Today, in a lot where several mom-and-pop shops might once have opened, Walmart spawns another superstore."[50] This is supposedly a bad thing because it is stifling "entrepreneurship." But this fetishization of small business misses the point. New business formation is not an end; it is a means. The end is more and better goods at lower prices for consumers, not maximizing the number of owners of small, inefficient businesses.

What Kinds of Firms Are Starting?

To assess whether the overall slowdown in new firm formation is a problem, we also need to look carefully at the types of firms that are being started. As Antoinette Schoar writes,

It is crucially important to differentiate between two very distinct sets of entrepreneurs: subsistence and transformational entrepreneurs. Recent evidence suggests that people engaging in these two types of entrepreneurship are not only very distinct in nature but that only a negligible fraction of them transition from subsistence to transformational entrepreneurship. These individuals vary in their economic objectives, their skills, and their role in the economy.[51]

Justin and Ashley, the owners of the new local pizza parlor, are not likely to be very much like Sergey Brin and Larry Page or Jeff Bezos. Schoar also found that

[The] founders of venture-backed startups in the majority were previously employed at larger technology firms such as Microsoft, Intel, or similar firms. An alternative group of founders of transformational entrepreneurs were serial entrepreneurs who had previously started a high-growth firm. In contrast, almost none of them were running small subsistence businesses before they started a high-growth business.[52]

Nor does there appear to be any correlation between startup numbers and economic growth. A study of entrepreneurship data by Catherine Fazio and coworkers notes that "quantity-based measures of entrepreneurship have little relationship to GDP growth. Yearly fluctuations in counts of firm births appear to hold little relationship to medium-term measures of economic performance."[53]

To be clear: starting yet another small bookstore or pizza parlor is not entrepreneurship; it's small business. In other words, Justin and Ashley are not likely to be Sergey and Larry and Jeff. And what Justin and Ashley do or do not do has little effect on economic growth. If Justin and Ashley don't start that pizza parlor, then Brianna and Jalen or someone else will.

Indeed, using the term "entrepreneur" for someone who opens a conventional small business such as a pizza parlor uses the term in a sense completely different from that of Joseph Schumpeter, the economist who pioneered modern innovation theory. Schumpeter famously wrote,

The function of entrepreneurs is to reform or revolutionize the pattern of production by exploiting an invention or, more generally, an untried technological possibility for producing a new commodity or producing an old one in a new way, by opening up a new source of supply of materials or a new outlet for products, by reorganizing an industry and so on.[54]

He did not say the function of an entrepreneur is to start a business. Only certain kinds of business founders are entrepreneurial. In other words, the startups that really matter are those that are able to exploit market opportunities through technological and/or organizational innovation.[55] As one study of firm formation trends stated, "Poorly performing economies seem to have too many subsistence entrepreneurs and too few high-growth transformational entrepreneurs."[56]

This difference in the kind of new firm startups is why dire claims that the sky is falling on new business formation can exist parallel to claims that we are living in a time of robust innovation and entrepreneurship, with Silicon Valley and other tech hubs throughout the nation enjoying frothy and dynamic innovation. As Silicon Valley venture capitalist Marc Andreessen tweeted, "There's too much entrepreneurship: Disruption running wild!" "There's too little entrepreneurship: Economy stalling out!"[57] A big reason for this contradiction is that the above studies (which are endlessly quoted) don't differentiate between Justin and Ashley, on the one hand, and Serge and Larry and Jeff on the other. The real question is what has happened to the entrepreneurship exemplified by Sergey and Larry and Jeff, and why.

Researchers who have tried to differentiate between the two types are MIT professors Jorge Guzman and Scott Stern. They looked at trends in high growth entrepreneurship for fifteen large states from 1988 to 2014 and found that "in contrast [to] the secular decline in the aggregate quantity of entrepreneurship … the growth potential of startup companies has followed a cyclical pattern that seems sensitive to the capital market environment and overall economic conditions."[58] In other words, while the Justins and Ashleys are starting fewer firms than before, the Sergeys, Larrys, and Jeffs are starting almost the same number. Moreover, Fazio and her colleagues found that when they compared the original "birth dates" of firms that achieved successful exits (defined as an IPO or acquisition at a multiple of the firm's valuation within six years) relative to overall firm births, again, they could find no apparent relationship.[59]

Indeed, in another study Guzman and Stern found that even after controlling for the size of the US economy, the second highest rate of high-growth entrepreneurship occurred in 2014.[60] This research indicates that the entrepreneurial potential (successful startups as a share of GDP) by founding year hit its low point in 1990, peaked in 2000 at almost twice as high, fell after the dot-com bust, and then rose to 2007, fell again with the global recession of 2008–2009, but then bounced back to almost record highs by 2014. As Fazio and colleagues note, "Quantity-based measures document a troubling, three-decade-long decline in the U.S. rate of entrepreneurship. ... Conversely, outcome-based measures indicate that the rate of entrepreneurship is rising. Early-stage angel and venture capital financing of new ventures has been on a significant upswing over the past several years."[61]

The contradiction that Marc Andreessen tweeted about becomes clearer when one digs into the startup data. The studies that warn of a decline in startups rely on Census data that ask people if they started a business, regardless of whether it is "subsistence" or a "transformational" business. This explains why Kauffman's "2015 Index on Startup Activity, State Trends" finds that the two most entrepreneurial states are Montana and Wyoming.[62] Real high-tech powerhouses such as California and Massachusetts rank just fourteenth and thirty-fourth respectively. As Fazio, et al. write, this "mismatch between index rankings and top hotspots of entrepreneurial activity (like Silicon Valley and Kendall Square) signals strongly that, to the extent that trends in entrepreneurial growth potential are being captured, they have been swamped by the effects of more local or regional businesses."[63]

Technological Cycles and High-Growth Startups

As Guzman and Stern note, the number of truly entrepreneurial, high-growth startups is a small fraction of the size of the number of startups overall. But despite their relatively small size, they play an oversized role in the economy in bringing new innovations to the market. For many of these startups either produce technology (e.g., Tesla) or use new technology to create new business models (e.g., Uber), or both (e.g., Google). This means that the rate of technology-based startups is in part a function of the overall rate of technological innovation. As Acs and Audretsch write, "Fundamental changes in technology often result in shifts in the firm-size distribution."[64]

As we have observed earlier, these fundamental changes do not proceed evenly but rather in waves, with some periods being more active than others. In fact, technological innovation appears to follow a pattern of repeating S-curves, with waves of technology emerging and then plateauing before the next new wave. This is what Joseph Schumpeter argued when he wrote that "each of the long waves in economic activity consists of an 'industrial revolution' and the absorption of its effects."[65] He went on to state, "These revolutions periodically reshape the existing structure of industry by introducing new methods of production—the mechanized factory, the electrified factory, chemical synthesis, and the like."[66]

Schumpeter's key insight was that innovation is not a regular process bringing steady incremental improvements but rather a discontinuous process that leads to waves of innovations. He noted that "these revolutions are not strictly incessant; they occur in discrete rushes which are separated from each other by spans of comparative quiet. The process as a whole works incessantly, however, in the sense that there is always either revolution or absorption of the results of revolution, both together forming what are known as business cycles."[67] One reason technology changes in waves is because the prior technology system establishes firmly committed ways of doing things that are not easily disrupted. Existing systems must become exhausted before institutions look to whole new approaches.

Proponents of Schumpeterian technology long-wave theory postulate five waves to date: (1) the first Industrial Revolution, launched by the steam engine in the 1780s and 1790s; (2) the second revolution, of iron, in the 1840s and 1850s; (3) the third revolution, based on steel and electricity, in the 1890s and 1900s; (4) the fourth revolution, based on electromechanical and chemical technologies, in the 1950s and 1960s; and (5) the fifth revolution, based on IT and communications technology, that emerged in the 1990s and peaked in the last few years. According to this long-wave periodization theory a sixth wave will emerge, but not before an intervening period of relative stagnation perhaps as long as twenty years; a period we appear to be in now.

This may explain why John Haltiwanger, Ian Hathaway, and Javier Miranda find that the high-tech entrepreneurship rate fell from 55 percent in 2000 to 38 percent in 2011.[68] They write,

In the post-2000 period, the high-tech sector is experiencing a process of economic activity consolidation, away from young firms and into more mature firms. The high-tech sector looked different than the rest of the private economy did during the 1990s, when the share of young firms was declining in the overall economy but rising in high-tech. In the early 2000s, entrepreneurial activity in the high-tech sector began declining sharply during what is well-known as the dot-com bust.[69]

But rather than be seen as a serious flaw in the US innovation system, certainly at least part of this decline reflects the fact that as technology systems become more mature, the number of new entrants generally falls. As techno-economic paradigms mature, the most successful startups based on the latest "general-purpose technology" tend to eliminate most of their competitors and dominate an industry, on a national or global scale. Despite what the "big is bad" proponents claim, firm size is largely determined by the economics of production, and that is determined in part by the nature of production technologies. As Blair has stated, "It is technology which largely determines the relationship between the size of plant and efficiency."[70] The pace of entrepreneurial, technology-based startups is therefore related to the phase of the technology long-wave cycle.

Audrestch argues that technology cycles create either entrepreneurial regimes in which new technology opportunities emerge and business models are not yet set, or routinized regimes thereafter when the business models are more set and a few firms emerge as the winners. He writes that in the entrepreneurial regime,

New entrants have a greater likelihood of making an innovation and ... are less likely to decide to exit from the industry, even in the face of negative profits. By contrast, under the routinized regime the incumbent businesses tend to have the innovative advantage, so that a higher portion of exiting businesses tend to be new entrants. Thus, the model of the revolving door is more applicable under technological conditions consistent with the routinized regime, and the metaphor of the forest, where the new entrants displace the incumbents—is more applicable to the entrepreneurial regime.[71]

In summary, new-firm startup activity tends to be substantially more prevalent under the entrepreneurial regime, in which small enterprises account for the bulk of the innovative activity, than under the routinized regime, in which the large incumbent enterprises account for most of the innovative activity.

We see this technology-driven dynamic in the disk drive industry in North America, in which the number of new firms increased from just a couple in the early 1960s when the technology was invented to around eighty-five in the late 1980s. But as the technology began to stabilize and economies of scale got larger, coupled with stiff foreign competition, the number fell to around twenty-five in the mid-1990s.[72]

Likewise, in the 1980s and 1990s there were numerous entrants in the computer industry, as such companies as Compaq, Dell, Gateway, Leading Edge, Apple, HP, IBM, AT&T, NCR, and others tried to become key players. But as computer innovation slowed and scale economies increased, fewer startups emerged. In the computer and peripheral equipment manufacturing sector, startups fell 45 percent, while the industry actually became less concentrated, with the C4 and C8 ratios declining 7 percent and 8 percent, respectively, largely owing to foreign competition.

We see this pattern in manufacturing. Francisco Louçã and Sandro Mendonça studied the largest 200 manufacturing firms from 1917, 1930, 1948, 1963, 1983, and 1997, or a total of 543 distinct firms for the entire period. They found that only twenty-eight firms were present in all six years—"persistent giants," Louçã and Mendonça call them—that were largely founded at the turn of the twentieth century or resulted from mergers during that century.[73] The persistent giants included such firms as Alcoa, Amoco, CocaCola, DuPont, Deere, Procter & Gamble, Ford, and GM. But more than half of firms appear only once. The number of new firms entering the top 200 was constant over time but the rate changed, with peaks in 1930 (eighty-eight firms) and 1997 (eighty) but lower numbers in the middle periods of 1948 (sixty-two); 1963 (seventy-two), and 1983 (forty-two).[74]

Using a Schumpetarian long-wave model in which technological change is cyclical, with strong periods and weaker ones, Louçã and Mendonça found that peaks of firm entry into the top 200 are associated with periods of technology transition from one wave to another. It is during these transition points, marked by the emergence of combinations of radical innovations, that new technology systems replace older ones. If this is true, it suggests that today's relative decline in startups and firm churn could be more related to the stage in the long-wave cycle we are in, with more entry likely to emerge in another decade or so as the sixth wave begins its take-off phase.

In some industries, innovations, often based on federally supported R&D, emerge, often producing a swarm of entrants seeking to capitalize on the opportunities. We see this today as companies such as Tesla (electric cars) and Google (self-driving cars) are getting into the auto business. Indeed, in industries where technology is still evolving and has not matured, we see more startups as entrepreneurs take risks to try to find new opportunities in new markets. For example, startups in the pharmaceutical and medicine manufacturing industry are up 38 percent over the last ten years as entrepreneurs try to capitalize on biotech innovations such as genetic tools. Likewise, startups in the engine, turbine, and power transmission equipment sector are up 87 percent, in large part because of innovations in renewable energy and natural gas power.

In other proverbial "buggy-whip" industries, entry declines because the product is superseded by technological change. For example, startups fell 47 percent from 2003 to 2011 in the magnetic and optical media industry, largely as magnetic tape and CDs were replaced by electronic storage. Similarly, with the rise of cloud computing and the maturing of the data processing and hosting industry, startups fell by 47 percent. Indeed, the last years of the 1990s led to a flourishing of startups as tens of thousands of firms competed to be one of the winners that would emerge. But the market would naturally not support tens of thousands of firms, so there was a shake-out. For example, scores of companies competed to be the dominant Internet search firm but only a few, among them Google and Microsoft, survived.

This suggests that those who blame the slowing rate of innovation on the decline of startups have the causal direction backward. Startups declined because innovation slowed, providing fewer opportunities for new entrants to pursue. Restoring the pace of technological innovation, in part by reversing the budget cuts for federal R&D and expanding tax incentives for business investments in innovation, will help create the opportunities that will lead to increased startups.

In summary, technology is the key driver of firm size. In manufacturing, flexible production technologies are enabling efficiencies with smaller firm size. In nonmanufacturing sectors, IT is enabling greater efficiencies with larger firm size. And because of that, in many of these sectors there is simply less space for the cycling in and out of small startup businesses that was so prevalent before the 1990s. To the extent that larger, more efficient firms are using technology to gain market share and displace many small, inefficient startups, many of them doomed to quick failure; regardless, we should be celebrating this change, not bemoaning it.[75]

Moreover, to the extent there is any decline in real entrepreneurship, of the kind that produces technology-driven, fast-growing startups, much of that is explained by where the contemporary economy is located in the Schumpeterian long-wave cycle. If a new cycle emerges, perhaps sometime toward the end of the 2020s, we are likely to see a resurgence of tech-based entrepreneurship.

II The Advantages of Size

4   The Bigger the Better: The Economics of Firm Size

Suppose that there is a size class of firms that outperforms another size class on virtually every indicator of economic and social performance, including job creation, wages, worker benefits and safety, environmental protection, productivity, workforce diversity, unionization, tax compliance, and business social responsibility. You might expect this size class to be embraced and favored by most people across the political spectrum. You would be wrong, because it is large firms that outperform small firms.

Any claim that small is beautiful and big is ugly should be based on facts, not ideology, self-interest, or emotion. And the facts are eminently clear that on virtually every measure, big business is superior to small. As Todd L. Idson and Walter Y. Oi wrote in in their review of the relationship between firm size and economic factors:

A worker who holds a job in a large firm is paid a higher wage, receives more generous fringe benefits, gets more training, is provided with a cleaner, safer, and generally more pleasant work environment. She has access to newer technologies and superior equipment. ... The cost of finding a job with a small firm is lower. The personal relation between employee and employer may be closer, but layoff and firm failure rates are higher, resulting in less job security.[1]

This pattern is clear in every industrial economy. Another scholar, Joachim Wagner, who looked at small firms in Germany, concluded the following:

Wages are lower, non-wage incomes (fringes) are lower, job security is lower, work organisation is less rigid, institutionalized possibilities for workers' participation in decision making are weaker, and opportunities for skill enhancement are worse in small firms compared to large firms. The weight of evidence, therefore, indicates that, on average, small firms offer worse jobs than large firms.[2]

Still another study looking at US small businesses found that "most surviving small businesses do not grow by any significant margin. Most firms start small and stay small throughout their entire lifecycle. Also, most surviving small firms do not innovate along any observable margin."[3]

A World Bank study of developing nations concludes that while:

> MSMEs [micro, small and medium sized enterprises] tend to have higher rates of job growth in developing countries, larger companies provide more sustainable jobs, are typically more productive, offer higher wages and more training, and support a big multiple of the direct jobs they provide through their supply chains and distribution networks (which in particular provide opportunities for the poor).[4]

The report goes on to note that on net job creation MSMEs don't outperform large firms because more MSMEs "exit the market."

In short, on virtually every measure, large businesses perform better than small. This is not meant to denigrate small "Main Street" businesses. Most small business owners take risks, work hard, and contribute to their communities. But we should not let sentiment get in the way of reality. Economic prosperity will be determined principally by large firms, not by small firms, and least of all by the vast majority of small firms whose owners do not intend them to grow beyond a few employees.

Economic Factors

Wages

For most working-age people, labor income (wages or salary) is the major source of income. And virtually every study shows that big firms pay more than small firms. Even Walmart, the retail giant that progressives love to hate,[5] pays its retail workers on average 25 percent more than the industry average.[6] One study found that "working in a store with 500+ employees pays 26 percent more for high-school educated and 36 percent more for those with some college education, relative to working in a store with fewer than ten employees.[7] So if you are advising your children where to work—in a big corporation or a small company—advise them to go big if they want to maximize lifetime earnings.

This difference is not new. As far back as 1890, when the US Census Bureau first started collecting the data, large manufacturers paid their workers more than small ones.[8] This pattern has held over time and across nations. Indeed, it is as consistent a finding as anything in economics. One review of the literature concluded, "Our bottom line is that the size-wage differential appears to be both sizeable and omnipresent."[9]

A study from the early 2000s showed that firms with more than 500 workers in the US pay 28 percent more than small firms. In 2015 workers employed by large firms earned on average 54 percent more than workers in companies with fewer than 100 workers.[10] And this is true across sectors. For example, workers employed at large US hog farms earn 38 percent more than workers at average-sized hog farms.[11] Similarly, as a 2014 study from researchers at Stanford and the University of Michigan found, large chain retailers like Walmart "pay considerably more than small mom-and-pop establishments. Moreover, large firms and large establishments give access to managerial ranks and hierarchy."[12] And large firms give bigger increases to their workers: "Staying an additional year in a large firm brings an estimated average of 3.4% increase in salary in large firms but only 2.6% in small firms."[13] This pattern is repeated around the world. In Germany, average wages in firms with one to nine employees are about half those in large firms.[14] Even after controlling for industry to reflect the fact that some industries with larger firms pay more and for differences in level of education of workers between firms, big firms still paid 14 percent more in the United States and 8 percent more in Canada.[15]

Small firms are also much more likely to employ low-wage workers. A 2007 study by The Urban Institute found that "Low-income workers are disproportionately likely to work in smaller firms. Although 20 percent of all workers are employed in firms with fewer than 10 workers, such firms employ 42 percent of low-wage workers and 35 percent of low-wage workers in low-income families with children." Large firms with over 500 workers employ just 28 percent of low wage workers, but 44 percent of all workers.[16]

The wage gap is even larger in many developing nations. Indian firms with five to forty-nine workers paid their workers just 22 percent of what firms with more than 200 workers paid. Indonesian workers at small firms made 32 percent of the salaries of workers in large firms, in the Philippines 35 percent, in South Korea 50 percent, in China 60 percent, and in Thailand 72 percent.[17] As a World Bank study concludes, "Large firms offer more stable employment, higher wages and more non-wage benefits than small firms in developed and developing countries, even after controlling for differences in education, experience and industry."[18] So for developing nations in particular, boosting living standards requires boosting firm size.

Is age the determining factor rather than size? Do new firms pay better than older firms? No. The average new firm paid its workers 72 percent of the average wage in the firm's first year, and even four years later their wages were still below the average.[19]

The data lead to a clear if controversial conclusion: if policy makers want to improve wages, they should focus their efforts on helping both existing large firms and the minority of small firms that are capable of significant growth.

Benefits

In the United States, workers in large companies receive 85 percent more supplemental pay (e.g., overtime and bonuses), 2.5 times more in the value of paid leave and insurance (e.g., health insurance), and 3.9 times more in retirement benefits (and more than 5 times more in defined benefit plan contributions) than workers in firms with fewer than 100 workers.[20] For example, few small retailers match their employee's 401k contributions, if they even provide plans. But Walmart provides a 6 percent company match after one year on the job.[21] Large firms (100 or more employees) are almost twice as likely to offer paid life insurance and disability insurance as smaller firms.[22]

In 2011, before the passage of the Affordable Care Act, more than 97 percent of firms with more than 200 employees offered health insurance to their workers, compared to fewer than 50 percent of businesses with three to nine workers. This is why 36 percent of workers employed in firms with fewer than ten workers were uninsured, in contrast to fewer than 15 percent of workers employed by large firms.[23] In the case of benefits, new businesses and startups are not more generous than old ones. On the contrary, as Scott Shane points out, "Studies show that older businesses are more likely to offer a pension plan or health insurance coverage to their employees."[24]

Small firms are far less likely to give their workers time off when they or their partners have a baby. In 1997, 95 percent of medium-sized and large establishments provided their workers maternity and paternity leave coverage, but only half of small establishments did the same. As a Bureau of Labor Statistics study concluded, "The contrast was stark, with larger establishments offering a full range of formal leave plans designed to provide time off for vacations, sickness, funerals, and other personal commitments and smaller establishments providing time off only for holidays, or ... basing time-off policies on individual performance."[25] In fact, the average number of paid vacation days at large firms is between 20 to 40 percent higher than at small firms.[26]

Large firms are also more likely to provide wellness benefits than small firms. Fifty-three percent of firms with more than 5,000 workers offered weight loss programs such as Weight Watchers versus 16 percent of small firms, and 57 percent of large firms offered health coaching versus 24 percent of small firms. Large firms are significantly more likely to offer free health risk assessments, on-site exercise facilities, smoking cessation programs, and weight loss programs.[27]

This may be why the share of workers who voluntarily quite a job at a large establishment (one with more than 5,000 employees) is about 40 percent the rate at small establishments.[28]

Productivity
Some critics of big business argue that the reason big firms pay their workers more is that they have market power and use that to charge higher prices, at least some of which they pass on to their workers in the form of higher wages while the rest is funneled to shareholders.

In fact, large firms pay more because they are on average more productive. One 1978 study of US manufacturing firms sought to determine whether large firms were more productive than smaller firms and, if so, whether that was the reason they were more profitable. The study found that on average, the four largest firms in any industry had profits 57 percent higher than the other firms in the industry.[29] But these higher profits did not come from squeezing their suppliers, charging higher prices, or paying lower wages. Rather, the four largest firms in any industry enjoyed labor productivity rates on average 37 percent higher than the remainder of the industry. They passed on at least some of the gains to their workers, with average wages 15 percent higher than in the rest of the industry. And this advantage was experienced at all levels of workers, not just top managers. In fact, production workers in the largest four firms made on average 17.2 percent more than production workers in the rest of the industry.[30]

Why are big firms more productive? One reason is that they use more capital equipment to drive efficiency. Capital intensity is positively related to productivity and firm size.[31] A 1988 national survey of 10,000 manufacturers found that technology use is positively correlated with plant size.[32] Likewise, larger banks were significantly more likely to adopt ATMs when they were first developed in the early 1980s.[33]

But the willingness of large firms to spend money on equipment and software to drive productivity is just one factor. Even when this factor is controlled for by measuring total factor productivity, larger firms are still 16.6 percent more productive than smaller firms.[34] This may be because of more economies of scale in production or because larger firms are simply better managed and operated.

Local Economic Benefit

Many small business advocates like to claim that small business deserves a privileged position because it does more to support local communities. The American Independent Business Alliance urges consumers to "Shop Small" and shift 10 percent of their spending to local independent firms because "community-serving businesses are the backbone of local economies, civic life, local charities, and wealth creation for millions of citizens, as well as a training ground for future generations of entrepreneurs."[35]

At one level they are right. One study found that local retailers returned 52 percent of their revenue to the local economy, compared with 14 percent for national retailers. Local restaurants spent 79 percent of revenue in the local economy, compared with 30 percent for franchises and national chains.[36]

But this is zero-sum thinking. If one region gets to keeps more of its spending in its region by preferring small, locally owned firms, by definition that means other regions will get less. But if all other regions do the same, it will mean less spending for the first region. The very reason why regions, like nations, trade is because it leads to higher productivity and incomes, thanks to specialization or increasing returns to scale.

These communitarian small business advocates are actually advocates for their local community at the expense of the broader national community. Moreover, they don't even advocate for the local community. As one study of buy-local movements found, the focus was on local business owners, not on the well-being of low-income individuals in the community.[37] And buy-local policies are not even associated with more local growth. As one study found, "In downturns, single-establishment firms reduce employment more than non–locally owned companies."[38]

Job Creation

When it comes to jobs, it also turns out that the dominant narrative is largely wrong, as we demonstrate in chapter 5. The main reason that small businesses create more jobs is that they also destroy more jobs. When we look at net job creation, we find that big business is at least on par with small businesses and that over the last two decades large companies have created more net jobs than small businesses.

R&D and Innovation

Small business advocates tout the claim that small firms rather than large are the innovators. Indeed, they often argue that small firms make up for lower productivity with more innovation. As David Audretsch writes, small business defenders argue that "the dynamic contributions made by small firms far offset any static efficiency losses."[39] If this were true, it might compensate for small businesses' sub-par performance on wages and productivity. But as we discuss in chapter 6, this is not the case. A couple of data points for now: while small firms account for 49 percent of US employment, they account for just 16 percent of business spending on R&D, while firms of more than 25,000 workers account for 36 percent.[40] Likewise, small firms account for 18.8 percent of patents issued, while the largest firms account for 37.4 percent of patents.[41]

Exports

Exports enable a nation to afford needed imports. Nations with anemic export strength suffer either through high trade deficits or a weaker currency or both, in the case of the United States. Large firms export more than small firms. A review of studies on the relationship between firm size and export intensity found that the lion's share found a positive relationship.[42] A study of German firms found that the share of output going to exports increased with firm size.[43] A study of South Carolina firms showed that "the larger the firm, the higher the likelihood that it will choose to engage in exporting." In the United States, small firms (fewer than 500 employees) employ 49 percent of workers but account for just 34 percent of exports.[44]

Moreover, from 1997 to 2007 exports by small firms grew 3 percent more slowly than exports from large firms.[45]

Social Factors

Even if big business's economic benefits to consumers and workers eclipse those of small business, it might still be the case that small business outperforms big business on social factors, such as business social responsibility and environmental protection. In fact, big business outperforms small business on almost all social factors.

Environmental Protection

Many advocates decry big corporations for their impact on the environment, seeing them as rampant polluters. We see the tragic pictures from Bohpal in India when a Union Carbide plant sustained a chemical gas leak that killed thousands of local residents. We were horrified by the *Exon Valdez* oil spill in Prince William Sound, Alaska, and Americans watched for months as oil spewed into the Gulf of Mexico from the BP oil rig. There is no doubt that some large companies have put profits before environmental stewardship. And there is no doubt that in many more polluting industries, such as chemical production, big firms account for most production. But that's not the point. The point is that within any particular industry, does big business pollute more than small business per unit of output? And on this point, the research shows they pollute less.

A wide array of studies finds that large firms invest significantly more in pollution control than small firms, in part because they are subject to more stringent regulations and enforcement. Not only do some environmental regulations exempt small firms but regulators are more likely to enforce environmental regulations at large, multiplant firms than at small firms.[46] This makes sense, as regulatory budgets are fixed and it can take nearly the same time to inspect a large firm as a small one. Moreover, large corporations are more likely to be in the public eye when it comes to their environmental behavior and to suffer reputational harm if they do something bad.

This is why one study noted that "environmental expenditure is more feasible to large companies due to a combination of greater economies of scale in the provision of the services and the greater likelihood of both image benefits and regulation enforcement on large firms."[47] And it is why a study of compliance with the US Clean Air Act found that factories belonging to multi-unit firms (e.g., large corporations) spent $185 and $477 more on pollution control capital expenditures and operating costs than smaller firms, for every $10,000 more of value added.[48] The largest plants spent approximately four times more on air pollution control per unit of output than the smaller plants. One reason is that large firms have environmental compliance departments staffed with experts whose job it is to keep their company from getting hauled into court or being on the front page of the *New York Times* for a violation. One study found that larger firms in the agricultural chemical sector are better able to address strict regulatory requirements.[49] Indeed, many small businesses don't even think about the environment. As a study of UK small firms concluded, "The typical SME is ill-informed and unwilling to take action unless threatened by strong external forces such as prosecution or customer demands. Worse still, many foresee no threats or advantages to their companies from the environment."[50]

Cybersecurity
With all the attention regarding cybersecurity and hacking, with high profile breaches and attacks at large corporations such as Target, surely large firms have worse cybersecurity than small firms. In fact, small firms that are online (only 54 percent had a website in 2015)[51] are less secure with regard to the Internet.[52] This makes sense as larger firms can devote the internal and external resources to ensure that their computer and Internet systems are secure. Two-thirds of small firms with websites manage their sites solely with internal resources, with 40 percent of owners doing it themselves. Forty-two percent report cybersecurity as one of the biggest IT challenges they face, 44 percent report being the victim of a cyberattack, but just 21 percent report that they have a high understanding of the issue.[53]

Tax Compliance
Enron. Tyco. Sophisticated corporate tax avoidance schemes with exotic names like double Dutch Irish. Certainty compared with smaller firms, corporations must cheat more on their taxes. But before considering this, it's important to recognize the distinction between tax evasion, which is illegal, and tax avoidance, which is legal. To be sure, many large corporations

are rich enough to be able to hire the best accounting talent to help them engage in complex tax avoidance schemes, the lion's share of which are legal and pass muster with the IRS. In these cases, it is incumbent on government to close the loopholes it believes are a problem.

But even with regard to these legal schemes, publicly traded firms are less likely to engage in sophisticated tax avoidance schemes than nontraded firms, and the former are on average larger than the latter.[54] One reason is that the 1,500 or so largest Subchapter C corporations that are subject to the corporate income tax are for the most part subject to annual and even continual audits, which clearly serves to limit aggressive tax avoidance, not to mention tax evasion.[55] This is why larger firms disclose more information on risks to investors than do smaller firms.[56]

Contrast that with the many small businesses that operate in substantial part on a cash basis, where the level of underreporting income can be quite high. As one study of business tax evasion notes, "Many self-employed people deliberately choose this organizational form over working as dependent employees, in order that they can evade taxes."[57] In Italy, unincorporated companies pay only about 45 percent of the tax they are legally required to pay.[58] In the United States, individuals underpay tax on business income by around $345 billion a year.[59] According to Jane Gravelle, a tax policy expert for the Congressional Research Service, the underreporting rate for proprietorship income is 57 percent, contrasted with a rate of less than 20 percent for large and medium-sized corporate businesses.[60] In other words, small businesses report only 43 percent of their actual income, compared to the 80 percent reported by medium-sized and big business. And 61 percent of small businesses understate their income; that is, they lie.

One study of small business tax avoiders found that many rationalized it on the grounds that tax evasion by small firms is a subsidy "that equates to direct subsidies to farmers or bail-outs to various international businesses." They believed they deserved such a subsidy because "a small business person is key to a healthy economy."[61] Others said that if they didn't cheat, they might have to go out of business. Exactly! Cheating lets low-productivity, "zombie" businesses stay in business, hurting the rest of us. On top of this, the fact that small business tax scofflaws seldom have to pay significant penalties if by some slim chance they are audited (about a one in 200 chance) has made tax avoidance part of the culture for many small businesses.[62] In this they are enabled by shady small accounting firms that know that if they don't at least turn a blind eye to evasion, they will lose the business.[63]

Risk of Layoffs

Surely, given all the press about rapacious CEOs with nicknames like "Chainsaw Al" Dunlap and "Neutron Jack" Welch, big corporations must be more likely to lay off workers to pad their profits. But this is not the case. In fact, small firms show less loyalty to their workers. One study found that both the quit rate and the dismissal rate of workers in German companies declined as firm size increased.[64] Workers employed by larger Austrian firms had a lower risk of being laid off than those employed by small firms.[65] Likewise, Canadian firms with fewer than twenty employees were almost five times as likely to lay off their workers as companies with 500 or more employees.[66]

It is no different in the United States. When 50 percent of jobs created by new firms, which are mostly small, disappear in five years, the odds of losing one's job are quite high.[67] As one study concluded, "Small-firm jobs are less stable. Workers in these jobs have shorter tenures, are more likely to quit or to be fired, and are more likely to experience a future spell of unemployment."[68] Another study using data from between 1978 and 1984 found that firms with fewer than 100 workers were almost three times more likely to permanently separate their workers than firms with more than 2,000 employees.[69] More recent data show that every year between 2000 and 2012, establishments with more than 250 workers had a lower share of layoffs and discharges than smaller firms. In 2015, small establishments with 1 to 249 employees had a four times higher rate of employee discharge than establishments with 5,000 or more employees.[70] Small establishments pay 20 percent more in federally required unemployment insurance taxes because they lay their workers off more and must pay higher experience-rated unemployment taxes.[71] If unemployment insurance taxes were fully experience-rated, instead of capped, small firms would pay even higher unemployment taxes. So "Chainsaw Al" is actually much more likely to be a small mom-and-pop employer.

Worker Safety

Workers at smaller firms are more likely to be injured on the job. Firms with fewer than 100 employees pay 9 percent more in workers' compensation insurance payments than bigger firms, reflecting their higher claims on the system.[72] We see this in many industries, including coal mining[73] and construction.[74] The rate of work injury in small utilities is almost four times higher than in large firms. In cable and telecommunications firms the rate is almost three times higher, and in information technology firms it is twice as high. Small trucking firms have higher rates of accidents than large firms, including unsafe driving violations, hours of service compliance, vehicle maintenance violations and crashes.[75] Overall, in goods-producing industries the rate of worker injury is 25 percent lower for firms with over 1,000 employees than for firms with ten to forty-nine employees.[76]

Unionization and Worker Training

What about unionization rates? Aren't large companies vociferously anti-union, able to afford expensive and sophisticated anti-union campaigns? To be sure, a growing share of US corporations has taken actions to avoid unions, but large companies are still more likely to be unionized. For example, in Canada, 50.2 percent of large firms are unionized compared to only 27.4 percent of small firms.[77] One study of unionization rates in Pennsylvania found that rates ranged from 22 percent of manufacturers with over 1,000 employees to between 12 and 13 percent of manufacturers with fewer than 100 employees.[78]

Large firms also invest more in workforce training. In Germany, 60 percent of small firms had no connection to apprenticeship programs, while only 12 percent of large firms had no connection.[79] Likewise, the probability that a firm pays for further training for its workers increases with firm size, from 24 percent in the smallest firms to 93 percent in the largest. In the United States, new employees received far more hours of both formal and informal training in establishments with more than 500 workers than in smaller ones.[80] Across the OECD countries, large firms train on average 63 percent of their workers, compared to just 39 percent for small firms.[81]

Employment Diversity

With respect to racial and gender diversity, large businesses are more diverse than small, both because they have professional human resource departments that are more aware that employment bias can hurt firm performance and because they are more likely to be under scrutiny for their hiring practices. As one study concludes, "There are other reasons to expect establishment size to foster racial and gender heterogeneity: Organizational size is positively related to sophisticated personnel systems, formalization, and job differentiation, which contribute to diversity in firms."[82]

One reason US larger firms are more diverse is because federal contractors with more than fifty employees are required to use affirmative action plans when hiring, but small firms are exempt.[83] In addition, small firms with fourteen or fewer employees are exempt from Title VII of the 1964 Civil Rights Act, which prohibits employment discrimination based on race, color, religion, sex, and national origin, and companies with fewer than 100 employees are exempt from reporting requirements.[84]

Moreover, large corporations are more likely to be under public scrutiny for hiring practices. This is why Jonathan Glater and Martha Hamilton wrote in the *Washington Post*, "At many of the nation's large corporations, affirmative action is woven into the fabric of the companies."[85] A study from the late 1990s by the labor economist Harry Holzer found that African Americans constituted 13.3 percent of the workforces of employers of more than 500 employees but only 7.9 percent of the workforces of companies with fewer than ten employees.[86] In large part this was because most small businesses are owned by whites, who can be reluctant to hire nonwhites. Small firms did employ a larger share of Hispanics, but even accounting for this, large firms with more than 1,000 workers had a smaller share of white workers than small firms, by four percentage points.[87]

Large firms also employed a higher share of women than small firms, by approximately three percentage points (48 percent to 45 percent), and employed a higher share of veterans (8 percent more) than did small firms.[88] And don't look to "entrepreneurs" for gender parity: in the United States the rate of female business ownership is 60 percent that of the male rate, and it is even lower across other OECD nations.[89] In sum, large corporations' workforces are more diverse than small business's workforces.

Business Social Responsibility

To listen to small-is-beautiful advocates, big corporations are interested only in profits and not in giving back to society, while small businesses are grounded in and committed to their local communities. In fact, the situation is more complicated than that.

One study found that both large firms and small firms have higher levels of charitable giving than middle-sized firms.[90] The hypothesis is that small firms give because they are close to their community and local customers, while large firms give more because they are under more scrutiny than medium-sized firms.

However, other studies find that big business outperforms small and middle-sized companies. As one study of business social responsibility concluded: "The first and most important conclusion we draw is that most small businesses do not recognize specific social responsibility issues. ... [Most have] never thought about it."[91] Indeed, most studies on the topic find that small business focuses less on business social responsibility than does large business.[92] This is in large part because "small business managers themselves argue that they have no time or resources to dedicate to social responsibility."[93] Another study of business managers found that the larger the corporation, the more the manager believed that business social responsibility in factors such as environmental protection and corporate philanthropy was important for the corporation's sales and market share.[94]

Moreover, in line with the "follow the money" principle, large corporations are vastly more likely to be targeted for action by social activists, whether it's boycotts, demonstrations, stock proxy efforts, or some other form of pressure. When was the last time a small mom-and-pop business was targeted for action by an organization like Common Dreams?[95] Did the *Guardian* newspaper publish a list of small companies and their giving levels in the UK? No, it focused on large companies.[96] And this pressure does lead large corporations to respond because for most of them, sales depend at least in part on their reputation and "visibility." For example, as economist Kevin Cochrane writes, Walmart donated $1.6 billion to local charities and causes in 2016. To match this as a share of their sales, the typical small retailer would have to donate about $4,000 a year to local causes.[97]

It's also easy for big business critics to forget that most of the assets held by charitable foundations in America came from corporate wealth. Carnegie, Ford, Rockefeller, Gates, Hewlett, Pew, Sloan, and Smith Richardson are just a few of the foundations endowed out of the profits of large corporations. In fact, of the largest 100 charitable foundations by assets in the United States, 78 were capitalized by individuals who owned or managed large corporations.[98]

Inequality

Finally, what about inequality? Aren't big corporations with their often extravagant CEO salaries and stock options the cause of much of the growth in income inequality? Thomas Piketty thinks so, writing that "the primary reason for increased income inequality in recent decades is the rise of the supermanager."[99] Likewise, former Obama administration economic officials Jason Furman and Peter Orszag argue that over the past two decades, large firms have gained market power, which allows them to pay even higher compensation to their top workers.[100]

A study of UK and US firms by Holger Mueller and coauthors found results that would seem to support the Piketty argument. In the UK, as firms get larger, inequality between the top three categories of occupations and the bottom increases.[101] The authors of that study found, for example, that moving from the 25th to the 75th percentile of the firm-size distribution raised the wage associated with job level 9 (the highest level) by 280.1 percent relative to the wage associated with job level 1 (the lowest level).[102] They also found that wages in high-skill occupations 6, 7, and 9 all increased with firm size increases.

However, several factors suggest we should be careful in how we interpret these findings. First, the Mueller study focused only on relatively large firms, not on the smallest. In fact, 60 percent of the firms in their sample were publicly traded, and the average firm size was over 10,000 workers. The vast majority of UK firms are small, so understanding trends in firm-based inequality requires looking at all size classes.

Second, it's not clear how much of this has contributed to the growth of inequality. The authors point out that since 1986, employment in the largest 100 US firms has grown by 53 percent. But at the same time, total US employment has grown by 33 percent.[103] So certainly some of the growth in top incomes in large firms has contributed to the growth, but not all.

Moreover, Jae Song and coauthors in another NBER study note that dispersion between high-wage and lower-wage firms appears to hold in all size classes; it's not a matter of big versus little only.[104] In other words, it's not just big firms that are contributing to inequality. In fact, new research from the US Bureau of Labor Statistics finds exactly that: the ratio of compensation for the top 5 percent of earners compared to the bottom 10 percent was no different between small establishments (one to forty-nine workers) and large establishments (500 or more workers).[105]

Song and coauthors found that much the income inequality from work income can be explained not by highly paid managers getting more than lower-paid workers within the same firm but between firms.[106] In other words, the ratio of pay between the highest-paid and lowest-paid employee within individual firms has remained more or less constant, but pay in some firms increased faster than pay at others, increasing the pay of those at the top. The authors write: "Although individuals in the top one percent in 2012 are paid much more than the top one percent in 1982, they are now paid less, relative to their firms' mean incomes, than they were three decades ago. Instead of top incomes rising within firms, top paying firms are now paying even higher wages."[107] In other words, as some firms have grown in size, productivity, and sales, they have been able to pay all their workers more, including the ones at the top.

In addition, large companies appear to pay their clerical and production workers more than small business, but their higher-paid professional workers tend to be paid the same, an outcome anyone concerned with helping the working and middle class should applaud. In 1995, according to the Bureau of Labor Statistics, establishments with 50 to 499 workers paid their professional and administrative workers 2 to 3 percent less than the largest establishments (2,500 or more workers), and their attorneys and engineers were even better paid. But small firms paid their clerical workers 6 percent less, their maintenance workers 27 percent less, and their material movement workers 42 percent less.[108]

While Mueller and coauthors found that larger firms pay their more skilled workers more than smaller firms, this appears to be a reflection of greater human capital and more skills. They write, "Our results support the notion that high pay disparities within firms are a reflection of better managerial talent."[109] They go on to note that "controlling for firm size, we find that higher pay disparities are associated with better operating performance, higher firm valuations, and higher equity returns."[110]

Moreover, some research suggests that large corporations actually reduce income inequality. The University of Michigan business professors Gerald Davis and Adam Cobb found that between 1950 and 2006 there was a strong negative correlation (−0.8) between the annual change in the share of the US labor force employed by the top 100 largest US corporations and income inequality. In other words, when their share decreased, income inequality increased.[111] They argue that these relationships are causal as large corporations tend to employ more middle-income workers, compared to either firms like investment banks at the top or small mom-and-pop companies at the bottom. As Gerald Davis writes, "Small is beautiful ... if you love inequality."[112]

Amid the adulation of small business owners, it is easy to forget that on average, they make considerably more than the average worker. Business-owning households make almost three times as much, on average, as non-business-owning households (one study showed $127,702 compared to $45,177).[113] As Scott Shane writes, "The average net worth of a business-owning household was $984,307, as compared to $190,023 for the average non-business owning household."[114] A Federal Reserve Bank study on small business owners concluded, "More wealthy individuals are small business owners than poor individuals.[115] According to the Tax Policy Center, the top 1 percent of pass-through businesses earned 50.8 percent of all such income, and the share going to the top 0.1 percent was 22.8. The bottom 60 percent received just 13.4 percent of such income.[116]

Furthermore, new research suggests that it is not managers of firms that constitute the largest share of the "one percenters" but professionals and financiers. Gallup economist Jonathan Rothwell finds that 6 percent of the one percenters (the top 1 percent of earners) are in the financial services industry, 7 percent are lawyers, 7 percent are doctors, 4 percent are dentists, and 7 percent work in hospitals.[117] In fact, 21 percent of dentists are in the top 1 percent of earners, while 31 percent of physicians and surgeons are in the top 1 percent. Even 15 percent of college presidents are one percenters. In contrast, workers in the software, Internet publishing, data processing, hosting, computer systems design, scientific R&D, and computer and electronics manufacturing represent just 5 percent of workers in the top 1 percent of income earners. As Jonathan Rothwell writes, "There are five times as many top 1 percent workers in dental services as in software services."[118] And while there are no large dental corporations, there are plenty of large software corporations. Overall, Rothwell finds that managers in nonfinancial firms account for just 29 percent of the top 1 percent of earners, and a nontrivial portion do not work for large corporations.[119]

Steven N. Kaplan and Joshua Rauh come to similar conclusions. When looking at the top 0.01 percent of income (adjusted gross income) they find that in 2004, nonfinancial executives represented just 3.98 percent of the individuals in this income bracket, up slightly from 3.66 percent in 1994.[120]

They write, "In 2004, nine times as many Wall Street investors earned in excess of $100 million as public company CEOs. In fact, the 25 highest paid hedge fund managers combined earned more than all five hundred S&P 500 CEOs combined."[121] Moreover, there are more than three times the number of top earners from finance and law than from nonfinancial occupations, and the former earn five times more than the latter. So, if you want to find the biggest causes of income inequality, look to the successful hedge fund manager, not the typical CEO.

Even if all of the other advantages of big firms are conceded, the small-is-beautiful school can fall back on the familiar claim that small business is the engine of job creation. As we will see in the next chapter, under close examination the evidence for even this popular claim falls apart.

5 Small Business Job Creation: Myth Versus Reality

Cognitive scientists refer to something called the "truth effect," which occurs when people believe something simply because it is widely repeated. This is the case with regard to the claim that small businesses are the font of job creation.[1] Ever since David Birch wrote in the late 1970s that small businesses are the job creators, this assertion has taken on mythic proportions, to the point that it is no longer even questioned. President Obama's budget summed up the view: "Small businesses are the engine of job growth in our economy."[2]

This is mostly wrong. But that does not stop small-is-beautiful advocates from continually making the claim. Indeed, job creation is their ace in the hole. Even if small businesses lag large businesses on every other performance indicator, small business advocates can always assert that at least small firms create the lion's share of jobs. With too many workers still unemployed or underemployed, even after almost a decade of recovery since the global recession of 2008–2009, the claim that the secret to job creation is multiplying the number of small firms is a powerful card to play. But it is a myth.

The Origin of the Small Business Job Creation Myth

Where did this small business jobs myth start? For most of the postwar period, economists believed that large companies created most of the jobs. But this was in part because, in the absence of longitudinal data on individual firms' employment levels, economists simply counted the number of jobs in each size class in one period and subtracted the number of jobs in the same size class in a prior period to see which size firms created the most jobs. The problem was that this assumed that the firms in one size class in the current period were the same firms as in the previous period. So if a firm had 200 workers in the initial time period but grew to 600 workers in the later time period, it would look as though big firms had created 600 jobs while small firms had lost 200.

This was clearly not the right way to measure job growth. In 1979 MIT professor David Birch decided to study individual firm employment records from Dun & Bradstreet. Birch purported to show that between 1969 and 1976, more than 80 percent of jobs were created by businesses with fewer than 100 employees and more than two-thirds by firms with fewer than twenty workers.

Unlike most economic studies, this became big news. No longer could economists and policy makers simply assume that large corporations were the big job generators. Very quickly the new conventional wisdom became that small firms were biggest generators of jobs. Now a host of small business preferences, from tax breaks to regulatory exemptions to procurement favors, could be justified, not by the old-fashioned argument that small proprietors are the pillars of a democratic society but because small businesses are the most important job generators, the backbone of the economy.

Since Birch's initial research, some economists have found similar results, but many others have criticized his conclusions, finding different results. Still others have added the wrinkle that it is not small firms that are the big job generators but new businesses. This controversy notwithstanding, Birch's claim has been endlessly repeated, like an urban myth, getting larger and larger, even being garbled into claims that small business is responsible for *all* job creation.

Why Small Business Is Not the Main Source of Jobs

Birch's research has been criticized on a number of grounds. Birch himself said that his earlier results were a "silly number" and that he could "change that number at will by changing the starting point or the interval."[3] Some have criticized his work for a "regression to the mean" bias. In other words, a number of firms classified as large in the base period are more likely to have experienced a recent transitory increase in employment that made them large, meaning that these are precisely the firms that are more likely to contract in the next year, making it look as though large firms lose jobs. Likewise, some firms that are classified as small in the base year may have recently contracted, and because of regression to the mean are more likely to expand in the next year.

Other studies found less compelling or even contradictory results. In an attempt to replicate Birch's work, the economist Catherine Armington found that from 1976 to 1982, small firms were responsible for 56 percent of new jobs, a far cry from over 80 percent and much closer to their actual share of total jobs.[4] Other studies found that large firms created the most jobs. Looking at job creation in manufacturing from 1973 to 1988, the economists Steven J. Davis, John Haltiwanger, and Scott Schuh found that larger firms were more likely to create jobs.[5] According to a 2010 study by Haltiwanger, Ron S. Jarmin, and Javier Miranda, large firms more than a decade old with more than 500 workers employed 45 percent of private sector workers and accounted for 40 percent of job creation.[6] And a study by American Express and Dun & Bradstreet found that mid-market firms with revenues between $10 million and $1 billion were responsible for 92 percent of the net new job creation from 2008 to the end of 2014.[7]

More recent research has drilled down and found that it is not small firms per se that create most jobs, only new ones. Haltiwanger, Jarmin, and Miranda found that after controlling for firms' age, "the negative relationship between firm size and net growth disappears and may even reverse sign as a result of relatively high rates of exit amongst the smallest firms."[8] In other words, it is not the size of the firm that matters in job creation, it is the age. Just as young children grow faster than adults, young firms grow faster than mature ones.

Nevertheless, a widely cited study for the Kauffman Foundation, a foundation devoted to supporting entrepreneurship, finds that all net job growth comes from firms less than one year old—in other words, startups.[9] But the problem is that these new firms also destroy jobs as many go out of business soon after they start. As Ryan Decker and coauthors write, "Most business startups exit within their first ten years, and most surviving young businesses do not grow but remain small."[10] And Jonathan Leonard writes, "The obvious pattern, and one that has been largely ignored in previous studies, is that small establishments account for most net job loss just as surely as they account for most net job gain."[11] In other words, lots of new firms hire workers, but most proceed to lay them off soon, when they go out of business. This is why Haltiwanger and his colleagues at the US Census Bureau find that the median net employment growth for young firms is "about zero."[12] According to the Small Business Administration (SBA), just one-third of new businesses survive to their tenth year.[13] Indeed, Zoltan Acs writes, "Some industries can be best characterized by the model of the conical revolving door, where new businesses enter but where there is a high propensity to subsequently exit from the market."[14]

One study concluded that the smallest firms generate a slightly greater share of new jobs than their share of overall jobs (35.1 percent relative to a 27.2 percent employment share), though "there is stronger evidence that the smallest firms also generate a disproportionate share of gross job destruction (33.9%, relative to the 27.2% employment share)."[15] This is why the correlation between the startup rate and the failure rate across industries at the three-digit industry code level is 0.77. In other words, industries that have the highest rates of firm startup also have the highest rates of firm failure.[16] Davis, Haltiwanger, and Schuh rightly point out that "a common confusion between net and gross job creation distorts the overall job creation picture and hides the enormous number of new jobs created by large employers."[17]

We see this in the fact that from 1993 to 2010, small firms with one to nineteen employees were responsible for 29 percent of gross job creation in the United States but only 15 percent of net job gains. In contrast, firms with more than 500 employees were responsible for 26 percent of gross job gains but 38 percent of net job gains. (Firms with 20 to 99 employees and firms with 100 to 499 employees were responsible for 23 percent each.)[18] In fact, overall gross job gains per month were twenty-seven times more than net job gains, reflecting the enormous amount of churn in the labor market, particularly among small and new firms. Decker and coauthors find that that when only continuing firms are considered (leaving out firms that start and then die), from 1992 to 2005 large firms (more than 500 employees) created more jobs at every age than did firms overall. For example, in their eighth to ninth year of existence, large firms created jobs almost three times faster than all firms of the same age (4.5 percent growth versus 1.8 percent). Moreover, for firms older than sixteen years, small firms with fewer than fifty employees actually lost jobs, while large firms continued to grow.[19]

According to the logic of small business advocates, society should favor firms when they are small, but as soon as they add their 501st employee, they become the object of indifference or even derision. This is as perverse and unhealthy as the attitude of parents who hope that their children will never grow up.

Perhaps the biggest indictment of the small-is-beautiful view when it comes to jobs is the simple fact that in the United States small firms' share of output and employment over time have been declining for decades. The share of sales accounted for by small firms declined from 57 percent in 1958 to 50 percent in 1982, while the share of workers employed in small firms in 1986 was slightly less than in 1958.[20] More recently, since April 1990 private employment has grown by 17.5 million, or 19 percent. About 65 percent of these jobs were in firms with 500 or more employees in 1990, even though at the beginning of the period these large firms employed just 42 percent of workers. Just 19 percent were in firms with between 50 and 499 employees, and 16 percent were in smaller firms.

Far from becoming more important to the US economy, small firms are becoming less important. In fact, from 2000 to 2014, the share of employment in firms with fewer than 500 employees actually fell, from 53 percent to 51 percent. Moreover, the Bureau of Labor Statistics reports that "since its employment low in October 2009, employment in firms with less than 50 workers grew at an annualized rate of 0.8 percent through March 2011. In comparison, employment large firms grew at an annualized rate of 2.1 percent after reaching a low point in February 2010."[21] This is hardly evidence of the increased importance of small firms. In fact, according to the 2011 US Census Bureau's *Statistics of U.S. Businesses*, firms with zero to four employees accounted for only 5.2 percent of all employment.[22]

In contrast, firms with 500+ employees, while constituting only 0.3 percent of all firms, accounted for 51.5 percent of all employment. Most of this employment came from the very largest of firms: those with more than 10,000 employees, while constituting only 0.016 percent of all firms, accounted for 27.8 percent of all employment.[23]

Finally, research shows that employment change in large firms is a larger driver of the unemployment rate than employment change in small firms. According to Giuseppe Moscarini and Fabien Postel-Vinay, "The differential growth rate of employment between large and small US firms is strongly negatively correlated … with the contemporaneous unemployment rate."[24] In other words, when firms with over 1,000 workers add more workers than firms with workers with fewer than fifty workers, the unemployment rate goes down (the correlation is –0.52). And the converse is true as well. This is why research shows that while small firms create more jobs during periods of high unemployment, they create fewer during periods of full employment. And it is why Moscarini and Postel-Vinay write, "The conventional wisdom that 'small businesses are the engine of job creation' finds some empirical support in our data only at times of high unemployment. ... This statement clearly fails in tight labor markets."[25]

Likewise, Zoltan Acs and Catherine Armington looked at the rate of firm formation between 1993 and 1998 in 394 US metropolitan areas and found that those metro areas that had higher per capita income growth in the prior year had more firm formation in the next year.[26] In other words, firm formation was the result of growth, not the cause. And the cause often was the growth of large, export-oriented firms that brought more money into the local economy for spending on small, local dry cleaners, carpenters, and restaurants. In other words, large firms are the driver, small firms the result. Moreover, the authors suggest that one reason why small firms grow more in recessions is that small firms benefit from high unemployment, as that relaxes hiring constraints. In other words, workers who otherwise would want to work at large corporations that pay more and have better benefits now have no other choice but to work at small firms.[27] The authors go on to note, "This picture corroborates only in part the common wisdom that small businesses are the engine of job creation: small firms appear to create more jobs as a fraction of their employment only when unemployment is high."[28] The authors found the same dynamics in Canada, Denmark, France, and the UK. For this reason, Scott Shane writes, "Many studies have shown than in places with more unemployment, and in time periods when unemployment is increasing, people are more likely to go into business for themselves than at other times and in other places."[29] For example, between January and December 2009 the number of self-employed Americans remained constant even as the unemployment rate increased from 7.7 percent to 10 percent.

The Startup Jobs Myth

But what about startups, the supposed source of American economic renewal? It turns out that most startups don't actually create that many jobs either. As Shane shows, "Only 1 percent of people work in companies less than two years old, while 60 percent work in companies more than ten years old."[30] A study of UK startups found that of the more than 560,000 firms estimated to have employed fewer than twenty persons in 1982, 10 percent had gone out of business by 1984, and 88 percent still had fewer than twenty employees at that time. Only 2 percent of the 1982 cohort grew beyond twenty employees during the two years following their startup.[31]

The majority of small companies actually shed jobs after their first year. One study found that among small companies in their second, third, fourth, and fifth years of business, more jobs were lost to bankruptcy than were added by those still operating (see figure 5.1). This is why the mean number of workers per firm actually goes down every year after a firm is born. According to the SBA, the mean number of workers in a new firm in its first year is 3.07. But by year 5 this figure declines to 2.36, and to 1.94 in year 11.[32] Or, as the SBA puts it, "Employment gains from growing businesses are less than employment declines from shrinking and closing businesses."[33] During the depths of the 2008–2009 recession, small businesses were adding an average of nearly 800,000 new jobs a month. But they were shedding an even larger number of jobs per month—about 971,000. In short, small firms create lots of jobs, but they also destroy lots of jobs. In light of increased concern about employment instability, this certainly can't be a good thing, at least for the workers, half of whom lose their jobs.

Statistics that claim to show that small businesses are responsible for the lion's share of job creation frequently rely on data in figure 5.1. New firms by definition cannot lose employees from the previous year, and any employees on the payroll are credited as "jobs created." By contrast, if a firm in its second year goes out of business, this is counted as negative job growth. From 2000 to 2013, only very young and very old firms showed positive net job growth.

The fact that young and adolescent companies don't on net create many jobs cannot be blamed on regulation and high taxes; if anything, as we discuss in chapter 12, small business is pampered and protected when it comes to the taxes and regulatory burdens bigger firms face. Rather, most small business owners have no desire to grow their firms. Nearly three quarters of individuals who start a business want to keep their businesses small.[34] Surveys show that the lion's share of people who start businesses do so not because they want to be a rich entrepreneur, something that takes

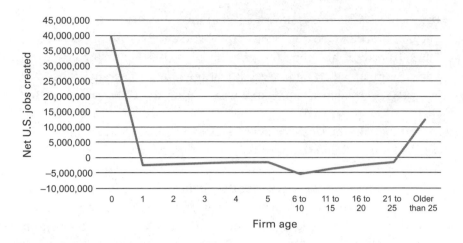

Figure 5.1
Net Jobs Created by Firm Age, 2000–2013
Source: US Census Bureau, Business Dynamics Statistics (Longitudinal Business Database, Firm Characteristics Data Tables, Firm Age by Firm Size, 1977 to 2014), https://www.census.gov/ces/dataproducts/bds/data_firm.html (accessed March 17, 2017).

enormous dedication and hard work to achieve; rather, most don't want to work for a boss.[35] As Shane found, "One study of a representative sample of the founders of new businesses started in 1998 showed that 81 percent of them had no desire to grow their new businesses."[36]

Another study found that 50 percent of small business owners did not start their business principally to make money.[37] A Federal Reserve Bank study by Pugsley and Hurst noted the following:

When asked about their ideal firm size, the median response of new business owners is that they desire their business to only have at most a few employees. This is not surprising given that the overwhelming majority of small business owners in the US are skilled craftsmen (e.g., plumbers, electricians, painters), professionals (e.g., lawyers, dentists, accountants, insurance agents), or small shopkeepers (e.g., dry cleaners, gas stations, restaurants).[38]

This, combined with the fact that so many new firms fail within ten years, is why Shane has found that it takes forty-three startups to end up with just one company that employs anyone other than the founder after ten years.[39] And on average, that surviving startup will have just nine employees. As Shane points out, "From 1992 through 2008, the 4 percent of small businesses that had 50 to 499 employees created 30 percent of all net jobs, whereas the 79 percent of small businesses with fewer than 10 employees created only 15 percent."[40]

To the extent policy should focus on new business, the focus should be on those that want to and can get big. Recent evidence suggests that only a tiny subset of businesses is responsible for most of job creation. Dane Stangler found that just 5 percent of companies in the United States create two-thirds of new jobs in any given year.[41] However, though they tend to be more accurate than studies that claim that small firms create the most jobs, studies that celebrate the role of "high-impact" firms also suffer from several problems.

First, the definition of high-growth companies is based in part on job creation. So a company that is highly productive and that significantly expands sales while lowering prices and increasing wages is likely to be excluded from the universe of high-growth firms because it didn't create as many jobs as a less efficient labor-intensive firm. As the author of an SBA-funded report on high-impact firms writes, "Many of the earliest definitions were based solely on revenue growth. A limitation of this approach is that it does not take into account employment change. This is an important policy consideration for government."[42] The troubling implication is that productivity is not an important consideration.

The second and more serious limitation of studies of high-impact firms relates to how these firms are defined. High-impact companies are defined as firms whose sales double in size over a four-year period. But by definition it is easier for a small pizza shop to double in size than it is for a large company like Apple to double in size. Not surprisingly, therefore, research shows that these "high-impact" firms are mostly small firms. The SBA-funded study found that the average growth of high-impact companies with more than 500 workers was around 125 percent, whereas it was 375 percent for the smallest firms (one to nineteen) employees. It's not that hard for a firm with three employees to grow to fourteen. (The average size of companies that started with one to nineteen employees was 2.7 at the beginning of the period and 14.4 at the end.) But it's a lot harder for a firm with 5,000 workers to grow to 17,000 in four years. (For firms with more than 500 workers, the average size was 4,466 at the beginning of the period and 10,102 at the end.)[43]

Logically, we should be indifferent to whether a company doubles in size from twenty to forty workers or grows from 10,000 to 10,020 workers. In fact, because of the superior performance of large firms, we should be decidedly in favor of the latter. Nonetheless, even with the biased definition the SBA employs, companies with more than 500 employees were still responsible for creating 43 percent of jobs created by high-impact companies.[44]

Most Small Firms Are Dependent on Big Firms

In the natural world, "capstone species"—large animals or plants—help to shape an environment in which many smaller organisms can flourish. On the North American prairie, bison cleared spaces for prairie dogs and grasses by grazing and wallowing. In tropical rain forests, giant trees provide support for vines and shade for smaller, shade-loving plants. Like capstone species, in many sectors big firms provide "ecosystem services" to much greater numbers of small and medium-sized companies. Large corporations are customers for complex webs of smaller suppliers. Their spending benefits yet other firms, as does the spending of their large number of more highly paid employees. And large firms can help innovations scale up, by buying them from startups or buying the startups. In advanced industrial economies, many small firms and big firms are mutually interdependent partners in a common productive enterprise, not natural enemies engaged in a battle to the death. Moreover, whether America thrives in the global economy is not whether a clothing shop on Main Street sells more pants. It is whether companies that export goods and services and compete in tough international markets do well; whether companies that drive productivity in their operations through the introduction of new technology do well; and whether high-growth entrepreneurial companies, especially ones that develop and commercialize innovations, do well. While they may have Main Street suppliers, these are not Main Street companies. They are "Industrial Street" and "Office Complex Street" companies, the former being manufacturing firms, particularly those competing in international markets, and the latter being technology-based nonmanufacturing companies

Why does job creation or loss by large firms have a bigger effect on the unemployment rate than similar changes by small firms? One reason is, as we showed in chapter 3, that larger firms are more likely to sell goods and services outside of the geographic area they are located in. It's important to understand the difference between what regional economists refer to as local-serving and export-serving businesses.

Let's consider the Maytag appliance factory that closed in Newton, Iowa, a few years ago. In a *60 Minutes* segment about the suffering of local, small businesses in Newton caused by the closing (the washers and dryers were to be made in Mexico), the host, Scott Pelly, bemoaned the fact that these small companies weren't getting help: "Three years after the beginning of the Great Recession, with interest rates the lowest they have ever been in history, banks are lending less money to the engines that create jobs."[45]

This misses the point. Maytag was an export-serving business, meaning that it shipped products outside the local labor market. Though a small share of the washers and dryers coming off the assembly line were sold to local Newton residents, the vast majority were sold to customers throughout the nation or even the world, who sent money back to Maytag, who paid some of it to its local workers and contractors.

In contrast, the local Newton restaurants, dry cleaners, clothing stores, and barbershops are local-serving, as the lion's share of their output is sold to Newton residents, including Maytag workers. If one of these local-serving small Main Street restaurants had gone out of business, it would have had no effect on the output of the Maytag factory. Moreover, another restaurant would more or less automatically have expanded or emerged to meet local demand.

But the Maytag factory closure had an immediate negative impact on the local-serving businesses, whose customers (Maytag workers, their suppliers, and the suppliers' workers) had much less money to spend locally on meals, haircuts, dry cleaning, and other needs and desires. Conversely, if Newton, Iowa, were to attract a large "exporting" company to occupy the abandoned Maytag facility, the health of Newton's small businesses would immediately revive.

So what determines whether America thrives, including impacts on the unemployment rate, is not whether a clothing shop on Main Street sells more pants. It is whether companies that export goods and services and compete in tough international markets do well. As noted, while some small firms export, big firms are more likely to export.

The majority of US businesses are local-serving. These include 219,986 doctors' offices, 166,366 auto repair facilities, 151,031 food and beverage stores, 115,533 gas stations, 111,028 offices of real estate agents and brokers, 93,121 landscaping companies, 75,606 nursing homes, 36,246 furniture stores, 28,336 veterinary offices, 15,666 travel agencies, 4,571 bowling alleys, 2,463 amusement arcades, 858 radio networks, and 26 commuter rail systems. When looking at the forty largest four-digit code industries in terms of share of small businesses (with twenty employees or fewer), which collectively constitute two-thirds of all small businesses, all but two industries (consulting services and computer system design) are primarily local-serving, such as restaurants, physician offices, auto repair, insurance agents, and so on.[46] In this regard it doesn't matter for job creation whether a large firm or a small firm satisfies this demand; some firm will because consumers have money to be captured.

Many other small firms are dependent on large firms as their customers or business partners As Bennett Harrison has written, "Many du jure independent small companies turn out in varying degrees to be de facto dependent on the decisions made by managers in the big firms on which the smaller ones rely for markets, for financial aid, and for access to political circles."[47] We see this, for example, in the fact that Boeing, the leading aerospace company, spent $5 billion with US small business suppliers in 2016, representing approximately 50,000 jobs.[48] In Europe, for example, 56 percent of small businesses in Denmark are dependent on large firms, with 55 percent dependent in Norway, that is, they are part of a larger enterprise group.[49]

Finally, at the end of the day, this entire jobs debate hinges not only on what the data show but also on whether one thinks that job creation comes from the supply side or the demand side. Small business advocates John Dearie and Courtney Geduldig point to the supply side when they write, "In the seven other years over the period, older firms also contributed to job creation. But start-ups contributed an average of 3 million new jobs every year. In other words, without new businesses and the jobs they create, net job creation in all but seven years between 1977 and 2005 would have been negative."[50]

But this is inaccurate. To understand why, we need only remember that innovation, productivity, and exports are supply-side factors. In other words, while the level of demand in an economy can affect these factors, the major drivers are internal factors within firms—the level of R&D, the level of investment in capital equipment, the development of better business models, and the like. But when it comes to job creation for an entire economy, the determining factors are on the demand side. The key word here is "entire." The mistake that most small business advocates make when they say that small business is needed for its job creation prowess is that they conflate macro with micro factors. This is a fallacy of composition.

Let's assume for the moment that the US economy is closed with no trade. Then all the companies sell all their output to US businesses or consumers. Let's also assume that in the current year, more young people enter the labor force than retire. Now, absent job creation, there will be unemployment because there are now more workers. Do we want to ensure that policies encourage Justin and Ashley to start a new pizza parlor to employ some of those young people? Maybe we should even give Justin the pizza "entrepreneur" a tax incentive so he will take the risk of starting the company in the hope it is successful and he will be able to employ some of those young people.

Or do we want the Federal Reserve Bank to lower interest rates a few basis points, spurring a bit less saving and a bit more spending and investment? As that spending and investment flow through the economy they create more demand, which creates more production, which in turn creates demand for more workers. The young new entrants to the labor market are hired and the economy is back to full employment, at which point the Fed raises the interest rate back to its old equilibrium rate (the rate that balances inflation and unemployment).

In this model it doesn't matter whether the firms are small or large; firms of any size respond to the demand and hire the new workers. So there is simply no need for favorable policies to help small business in order to create jobs. In fact, as we argue in chapter 12, such policies are downright harmful to economic growth.

6   The Myth of the Genius in the Garage: Big Innovation

The most celebrated commercial of the information age is "1984," the ad that introduced the Apple Macintosh computer in its only airing on January 22, 1984, during the Super Bowl. Filmed by the director Ridley Scott, the ad begins with scenes that evoke dystopian science fiction, such as George Orwell's novel *1984* and Fritz Lang's movie *Metropolis*. As uniformed workers march through tunnels, a female sprinter in full color, chased by police, runs up to a giant screen depicting a droning black and white Big Brother figure and shatters the screen by hurling a hammer at it. Next a voiceover narrates scrolling text: "On January 24th, Apple Computer will introduce Macintosh. And you'll see why 1984 won't be like '1984.'"

The advertisement captured the *Zeitgeist* of the early information age. Drawing on the cultural revolution of the 1960s and the suspicion of authority that spread in the 1970s, "1984" symbolized what many saw as a break between the old, dying industrial era dominated by big corporations and big government and a postindustrial, libertarian new age that would blend the individualism of the Age of Aquarius with up-to-date technology such as the personal computer (PC). As Stewart Brand, creator of the *Whole Earth Catalog*, wrote, "Technology was a tool for expression. It expanded the boundaries of creativity and, like drugs and rock, could be rebellious and socially transforming."[1] And unlike the managers of the old-line industrial corporations, emerging tech entrepreneurs such as Steve Jobs of Apple and Bill Gates of Microsoft became culture heroes.

A third of a century has passed since "1984" startled American television viewers. In that time, startups such as Apple and Microsoft, and newer companies such as Google and Facebook, have grown into corporate giants themselves, most of them run by professional managers. From today's perspective it is clear that there was no transition from an industrial, corporate economy to a postindustrial, entrepreneurial economy, only from one kind of industrial corporate economy to another. Far from replacing the centralized firms of the smokestack era with a decentralized landscape of "electronic cottages" inhabited by burgeoning numbers of the self-employed, the information age has witnessed the development of global corporations and supply chains of unprecedented scale—and the continuing decline of self-employment in the United States and similar economies.

Most of all, today's perspective allows us to see that the origin myth of the information age—the overthrow of sclerotic, hide-bound, giant corporations by scrappy, brilliant tinkerers building the future in their garages— is just a myth. Steve Jobs, Bill Gates, and others deserve credit for their brilliant success in commercializing new technologies. But most of those technologies had been invented in the laboratories of giant corporations, many of them working for the US military or civilian federal agencies on contract. The tech revolution of our time owes far more to teams of scientists and engineers working in well-funded corporate labs than to college dropouts tinkering in garages.

From the Alto to the Apple Macintosh

Before there was the Apple Macintosh, there was the Alto. And before there was Apple, there was Xerox PARC. On March 1, 1973, the first Xerox Alto was unveiled. The Alto was the first PC to combine a graphical user interface with a handheld mouse and other features that became standard elements of PCs a decade later. By the end of the decade, roughly 1,500 Altos were in use.

In 1976, Steve Jobs and Steve Wozniak cofounded Apple computer, a venture that grew out of the Homebrew Computer Club, a group of computer hobbyists that met in Silicon Valley. Initially Apple sold PCs named Apple I and Apple II. A key moment in the history of the young company came in 1979, when the twenty-four-year-old Jobs persuaded Xerox to allow Apple staff to tour the Xerox PARC facility in Silicon Valley in return for Xerox's acquisition of stock in Apple. Taking part in the second tour, Jobs was reportedly amazed by the Alto, seeing the commercial potential of the device. According to Larry Tesler, a Xerox engineer who demonstrated the use of the new "windows" and other features of the Alto, "He was very excited. Then, when he began seeing the things I could do onscreen, he watched for about a minute and started jumping around the room, shouting, 'Why aren't you doing anything with this? This is the greatest thing. This is revolutionary!'"[2]

In 1981 Xerox brought out a version of the Alto called the Xerox Star, but the concepts pioneered by Xerox and others were commercialized best by Apple, which released the first Macintosh PC in 1984, following the poor sales of the Apple Lisa, which came out in 1983. And just as the Apple Mac was inspired in part by the Xerox Alto, so the Apple LaserWriter drew on the laser printer technology developed by Xerox.

It would be wrong to accuse Apple of simply copying ideas from PARC. Even before the PARC visit, the designers of the Macintosh intended it to include a number of features, such as bitmapped screens, that later appeared in the Mac. Furthermore, Apple modified the pioneering design of the Alto in numerous ways that made the Macintosh both cheaper and easier to use. And, of course, Apple also pursued a business and marketing strategy that proved to be more successful than those of its rivals, including Xerox, which was hamstrung by unimaginative management that failed to see the commercial potential in these innovations. In the late 1970s and early 1980s, Apple promoted its computers through computer stores, magazines, and schools and encouraged software developers to write their own programs.

Xerox PARC itself developed concepts that originated at other institutions. One was the Augmentation Research Center (ARC) of the Stanford Research Institute (SRI). ARC's founder, Douglas Engelbart, was a radar technician serving in the US Army when he read an essay that changed his life, "As We May Think," by Vannevar Bush, published in the *Atlantic* in July 1945.[3] At the time Bush was the director of the federal Office of Scientific Research and Development, and played a critical role in developing the atomic bomb.

Bush envisioned a device he called the Memex that would permit individuals to share text and pictures and serve as the basis for a collective memory. Following the war, Engelbart graduated with a Ph.D. in engineering and joined SRI in 1957. In 1962 he published an essay titled "Augmenting Human Intellect: A Conceptual Framework." With funding from the Defense Advanced Research Projects Agency (DARPA), Engelbart created his own lab at SRI, the ARC, to develop what he called the oN-Line System (NLS).

Engelbart showcased his lab's work at what is now called "the Mother of All Demos," a presentation at a San Francisco conference of the Association for Computing Machinery/Institute of Electrical and Electronics Engineers (ACM/IEEE) on December 9, 1968. In ninety minutes Engelbart and his colleagues, including some at remote sites communicating by wireless technology, demonstrated many of the features of what became the PC: the mouse, windows, graphics, hypertext, and even video conferencing. Vannevar Bush's dream of the Memex had been realized.[4]

When Xerox founded PARC in 1970, the lab hired veterans of ARC. The first director of the PARC Computer Sciences Division was Robert Taylor, who as the director of the Information Processing Techniques Office of DARPA had funded Engelbart's work at ARC. Taylor hired engineers and scientists from the DARPA and ARC networks.[5] In turn, many PARC veterans went on to play leading roles in Silicon Valley in the late twentieth century.

The history of the tech industry provides many other examples of giant firms and corporate research labs responsible for breakthroughs that were developed and commercialized by others—including veterans of the same institutions. For example, after presiding over the development of the transistor at AT&T's Bell Labs, William Shockley in 1957 founded his own semiconductor company in Mountain View, California, called Shockley Semiconductor Laboratories. Rebelling against his authoritarian style, eight of the young technicians he had recruited—the "traitorous eight"—quit and formed their own company, Fairchild Semiconductor. Fairchild produced spin-offs, including Intel, which became known as "Fairchildren." One of the eight was Gordon Moore, who became a cofounder of Intel and is best known for Moore's law, which predicted the regular doubling of the number of transistors per integrated circuit. Another, Eugene Kleiner, cofounded the Silicon Valley venture capital firm Kleiner Perkins Caulfield & Byers, which made early investments in such companies as AOL, Amazon, Google, Netscape, and Sun Microsystems.[6]

If Silicon Valley has a birthplace, it is 367 Addison Avenue, Palo Alto, California. In 1939 this bungalow was home to two young electrical engineers, both graduates of Stanford, Dave Packard and Bill Hewlett, when they founded the partnership Hewlett-Packard (HP). In the garage they assembled their first products, audio oscillators, selling eight to Walt Disney Studios to test sound systems in movie theaters scheduled to run the first stereophonic movie, *Fantasia*. But it was World War II that gave HP a real boost, as it produced radio, radar, sonar, and other supplies for the US military. After incorporating in 1947, HP became the world's largest producer of electronic measuring devices, as well as a major producer of computers, calculators, and printers.[7]

But there was more to the success of HP than the genius of two young electrical engineers with access to a garage. The historical marker at the HP Garage makes this clear. Under the heading "Birthplace of Silicon Valley" the historical marker reads:

This garage is the birthplace of the world's first high-technology region, "Silicon Valley." The idea for such a region originated with Dr. Frederick Terman, a Stanford University professor who encouraged his students to start up their own electronics companies in the area instead of joining established firms in the East. The first two students to follow his advice were William R. Hewlett and David Packard.

Writing in the *Harvard Business Review*, Gary P. Pisano and Willy C. Shih coined the term "the industrial commons" for an industry-specific network that can include, among other things, "R&D know-how, advanced process development and engineering, and manufacturing competencies related to a specific technology."[8] Long before it had a name, an industrial commons existed in Silicon Valley based on productive interactions among startups, big firms, university research departments, government agencies, and venture capitalists.

To be sure, the "innovation in a garage" story is partly right. Startups do play an important role in innovation, particularly early in the emergence of whole new technologies. But the story and its proponents assume that startups are the source of virtually all innovations and moreover that a startup can no longer be innovative once it gets big. In this perspective, while HP might have developed some important innovations in the 1930s and 1940s, or Apple in the 1980s and 1990s, by the time these firms become giants they had to have lost most of their ability to innovate and become dependent on new garage innovators, which they simply bought up. As we will see, this is just plain wrong.

Firm Size and Innovation

Economists have studied the relationship between firm size and innovation for over a century. Joseph A. Schumpeter's 1911 book, *The Theory of*

Economic Development, focused on the entrepreneur as the driving force for innovation. He wrote, "The typical entrepreneur is more self-centered than other types, because he relies less than they do on tradition and connection and because his characteristic task ... consists precisely in breaking up old, and creating new, tradition."[9]

But writing thirty years later, after the emergence of dedicated corporate research labs and what Alfred Chandler called the "managerial corporation," Schumpeter viewed the large corporation as central to innovation. In *Capitalism, Socialism, and Democracy*, first published in 1942 he said, "Technological progress is increasingly becoming the business of teams of trained specialists who turn out what is required and make it work in predictable ways."[10] He went on to observe that innovation by individual inventors and entrepreneurs "is already losing importance and is bound to lose it at an accelerating rate. ... Innovation itself is being reduced to routine. Technological progress is increasingly becoming the work of trained specialists who turn out what is required to make it work in predictable ways."[11] Schumpeter argued that by focusing on price gouging by monopolies, traditional economists ignored the case of the innovative firm, which could recoup spending on R&D by using its market power to charge a price higher than marginal cost. According to Schumpeter, "There cannot be any reasonable doubt that under the conditions of our epoch such superiority is as a matter of fact the outstanding feature of the typical large-scale unit of control."[12]

In 1952 John Kenneth Galbraith agreed with Schumpeter, with whom he had studied at Harvard. Writing in *American Capitalism*, he said, "The modern industry of a few large firms is an excellent instrument for inducing technical change. It is admirably equipped for financing technical development and for putting it into use. The competition of the competitive world, by contrast, almost completely precludes technical development."[13] Among leading contemporary economists, William J. Baumol emphasized the extent to which competition among oligopolistic firms based on innovation, not prices, is the major driver of technological progress. He compared this oligopolistic competition to an arms race "that participants cannot easily quit."[14]

In contrast to the crude simplicities of Econ 101, in which competition among numerous small firms in conditions of technological stasis drives down prices for consumers, in what might be called Econ 201, or modern industrial economics, competition among a small number of large firms drives technological innovation. History does not bear out the claim that large, oligopolistic corporations are inevitably less dynamic and innovative than small firms. On the contrary, as Joseph Bowring has written, "Core firms are not pitiful, helpless giants fated to topple and rot into ... senescence; their competitive advantages have made them virtually indestructible."[15]

For more than a century, then, a rich body of academic economic and historical scholarship has treated oligopolistic competition among large firms in imperfectly competitive markets as the norm in modern industrial economies. And yet this scholarship is all but unknown to policy makers and the educated public. The fault lies largely with the mathematical turn taken by neoclassical economics departments in the second half of the twentieth century. In 1939 John Hicks, one of the founders of modern mathematical economics, observed that it was difficult if not impossible to produce elegant mathematical models of oligopolistic markets:

If we assume that the typical firm (at least in industries where the economies of large scale are important) has some influence over the price at which it sells ... [it] is therefore to some extent a monopolist. ... Yet it has to be recognized that a general abandonment of the assumption of perfect competition, a universal adoption of the assumption of monopoly, must have very destructive consequences for economic theory.

Faced with a choice between complex reality and elegant equations that assumed competitive equilibrium, Hicks advised the academic economics profession to ignore reality in order to save the equations:

It is, I believe, only possible to save anything from this wreck—and it must be remembered that the threatened wreckage is the greater part of general equilibrium theory—if we can assume that the markets confronting most of the firms with which we shall be dealing do not differ very greatly from perfectly competitive markets. ... We must be aware, however, that we are taking a dangerous step, and probably limiting to a serious extent the problems with which our subsequent analysis will be fitted to deal.[16]

The academic economics discipline has largely taken Hicks's advice. Galbraith compared the emphasis of academic neoclassical economics on small firms in competitive markets to a

description of the United States which, by assuming away New York, Chicago, Los Angeles and all other communities larger than Cedar Rapids, was then able to describe the country as essentially a small-town, front-porch community. Only an assumption very important to economics, as it is conventionally taught, would justify such a questionable defense.[17]

Galbraith noted the mystical American belief in competitive markets: "For competition, with us, is more than a technical concept. It is also a symbol of all that is good. We wouldn't survive under a regime of competition of classical purity—with an economy rigorously so characterized we should have succumbed not to Hitler but to Wilhelm II—but we must still worship at its throne."[18]

Schumpeter's argument that firms with temporary monopolies would have both the resources and the incentive to innovate was challenged by the economist Kenneth J. Arrow, who argued that innovation would be greater in more competitive markets.[19] But as the Obama Council of Economic Advisers reported, "Allowing firms to exercise the market power they have acquired legitimately can maintain incentives for research and development, new product introduction, productivity gains, and entry into new markets, all of which promote long term economic growth."[20]

The Rise and Fall of the Corporate Research Lab

Ironically, neoclassical economics predicts that in a truly competitive economy there would be little or no R&D. It is much cheaper for companies to copy another firm's innovations than to invest in expensive innovation. In other words, the company that chooses to fund breakthrough R&D cannot be certain it will recoup enough of the gains from its initial investment if other companies can copy it through reverse engineering and other means. So in a completely competitive and free market with no patent and other intellectual property protection it is quite possible that no companies would spend money on risky long-term innovation, in part because profit rates would be at the cost of capital, leaving little or no resources to invest in R&D.

History bears out what economic theory predicts. Modern economic progress depends largely on the commercialization of technological innovation that originates in systematic early-stage research. Since the nineteenth century, early-stage research has been undertaken chiefly by three types of institutions—research universities, government labs, and corporate research labs—and funded by two main sources—government spending and corporate profits. And in the last half century some high-tech startups, funded by venture capital, have played a key role as well.

This approach to technological innovation was pioneered in the late nineteenth century by imperial Germany. The modern research university in the United States, starting with Johns Hopkins and then others, is modeled on imperial German precedents. Indeed, two universities founded as research universities along German lines, MIT and Stanford, have played a disproportionate role in technological progress. With its Kaiser Wilhelm Institutes, imperial Germany also pioneered the government research laboratory, which in the United States includes laboratories associated with the Department of Energy and the Department of Defense, among others. After the Civil War, the United States pioneered the state technical universities (e.g., North Carolina State University, Ohio State University), most of which were established by federal land grant funds.

Corporate research labs were also pioneered by the German chemical industry in the late nineteenth century and soon copied by many nations in the first half of the twentieth century. Throughout the twentieth century, most of the breakthrough technological innovations in the private sector originated with companies that were funded by government either directly or indirectly (through tax incentives, grants, or contracts) or with companies that enjoyed some modicum of market power. IBM's development of much early computer technology with Department of Defense funding is an example of the former. Bell Laboratories benefited from the legal monopoly in the United States held by its parent company, AT&T.

However, it was not until the 1920s and 1930s that the main sources of innovation in the United States changed from being based largely on technical tinkering and trial and error by mechanics and inventors to a science-based approach in which innovation followed from a more fundamental understanding of underlying processes. Since then the research labs of large corporations, sometimes supported by the federal government, have become the major source of technological innovation.

With the growth of a more formal, laboratory-based system of R&D, R&D expenditures and the number of scientists and engineers employed in industrial research exploded. Growing by 300 percent between 1921 and 1938, industrial research was one of the largest forty-five occupations by employment in 1937. Industrial laboratories increased from fewer than 300 in 1920 to more than 2,200 in 1938 to almost 5,000 in 1956, with many, like Bell Labs, conducting extensive basic research. At the same time, annual expenditures on industrial research ballooned from $25 million to $175 million.[21]

As a result, the locus of innovation switched from individual inventors tinkering, like Edison and Bell, in their garages to scientists working in corporate labs. Reflecting this switch was the distribution of patents: in 1901, 20,896 patents were issued to individuals in the United States, and only 4,650 went to corporations. The proportions were more even in the 1930s, but in 1953 individual inventors received only 40 percent of patents, and of the 60 percent of patents that went to firms, two-thirds originated with a company's research personnel.[22] By 1980 corporations were obtaining about five times more patents than individuals. As a result, in the mid-twentieth century, a few large corporations dominated private R&D. In 1974, 126 companies with more than 25,000 employees performed three quarters of all industrial research; of these companies, four were responsible for 19 percent of industrial R&D.[23]

Big companies were responsible for major technology breakthroughs. Synthetic materials derived from hydrocarbons became the foundation of new products and industries. Standard Oil of New Jersey led the way in developing synthetic rubber during World War II, and seemingly miraculous new materials flowed from the corporate laboratories of giant firms like DuPont and Dow: nylon, polyester, Formica, latex paint, Kevlar armor, Fiberglas, Lucite, Plexiglas. In the private sector, only immense corporations with steady profits that went in part to fund cutting-edge research could have made and commercialized these discoveries. Henry Kressel and Thomas Lento have described the importance of corporate laboratories in the genesis of the information and communications technologies (ICT) revolution:

For example, the UNIX operating system and its offshoots and the software languages C and C++ were developed at Bell Labs in Murray Hill, New Jersey. Relational databases and reduced instruction set computers were invented at IBM Yorktown Labs, New York. Semiconductor devices and integrated circuit manufacturing were developed at Bell Labs, Western Electric, and RCA Labs (later Sarnoff Corporation).[24]

As Michael Mandel has observed, most Nobel Prize winners in science and technology have worked for universities and very large corporations. The last time the founder of a startup won a Nobel Prize (in physics) was in 1909; the prize went to Guglielmo Marconi, the pioneer of radio. Since then, two colossal corporations, AT&T and IBM, have won all the Nobel Prizes awarded to companies.[25]

The Decline and Fall of the Corporate Research Lab

As the historian Eric Hobsbawn has written, "It is often assumed that an economy of private enterprise has an automatic bias towards innovation, but this is not so. It has a bias only towards profit."[26] This view is borne out by the shift by many US corporations in recent decades from early-stage research to later-stage, more incremental development and, for some, to various forms of financial engineering, which can yield higher short-term profits. Among the casualties of this shift has been the classic corporate research lab.

Increased competitive pressures have led to less corporate expenditure on basic and applied research (as opposed to product and process development), exactly as economic theory would predict. As one MIT study found, more competition, including from low-wage, mercantilist nations such as China, reduced US business R&D expenditures.[27] Couple that with pressure from Wall Street to focus on short-term profits, not long-term breakthroughs whose benefits, however useful for society, are not always captured by the business making the investment, and we see a shift away from what Clayton Christensen calls disruptive innovation to safer sustaining innovation. One of the few exceptions to the trend of declining corporate R&D expenditure on basic science is found in the pharmaceutical industry, for the simple reason that their future is impossible without new drugs, which require early-stage research (patent protections also give pharmaceutical companies some chance to recoup the costs of expensive R&D). As in-house corporate laboratories have declined in importance, large firms in many industries have adopted the model of partnering with or acquiring small startups.[28]

As a share of revenue, US corporate R&D has remained relatively steady, falling just slightly since 2000. But because the economy is getting more innovation-based and the United States should be specializing even more in innovation as globalization deepens, one would have expected corporate R&D to increase as a share of GDP. Moreover, Ashish Arora, Sharon Belenzon, and Andrea Patacconi observed that the number of publicly traded companies whose researchers published in scientific journals had declined by two-thirds to a mere 6 percent between 1980 and 2015.[29] The authors concluded, "Large firms appear to value the golden eggs of science (as reflected in patents) but not the golden goose itself (scientific capabilities)."[30] According to them, firms that engage in more research have lower stock values.[31]

Under pressure from shareholders, many firms have eliminated or spun off their research efforts. Under pressure from the activist investor Nelson Peltz, for example, DuPont merged with Dow and cut R&D.[32] Bell Labs virtually disappeared after AT&T spun it off after AT&T was broken up. In 2002 Xerox PARC became an independent subsidiary that has replaced basic R&D with research on demand for clients. IBM Research still exists, and has produced major innovations such as the artificial intelligence system Watson, but even it faces pressures as IBM revenues and profits decline.[33] Apparent exceptions to the trend prove the rule. Because Microsoft was somewhat insulated from competitive pressures, it was able to invest $6 billion to $12 billion per year in R&D from 2002 to 2016.[34] The fact that Google is a closely held corporation insulated from shareholder pressure with robust profits may explain its willingness to engage in "moonshot" projects, such as self-driving cars. Although even Google appears to have cut back on some of these projects with longer and more speculative outcomes.

While firms may do less basic and early stage applied research than in the past, they continue to fund R&D, with the largest global corporations leading the way. According to Peter Nolan, Jin Zhang, and Chunhang Liu, "The increased focus on core business among the world's leading systems integrators and subsystems integrators has enhanced the efficiency of R&D expenditure, allowing benefits from economies of scale and scope."[35]

A New Age of the Individual Entrepreneur?

The decline of the classic mid-twentieth-century corporate research lab is one factor in the contemporary revival of small-is-beautiful thinking in the area of innovation. Another is the association of innovation in the popular mind and the media with a few entrepreneurs in the tech sector, such as Steve Jobs and Mark Zuckerberg. Because of this, in the last couple of decades there has been ongoing debate over which Joseph Schumpeter was correct about innovation—Schumpeter I, who ascribed innovation to individuals, or Schumpeter II, who believed that the future of innovation lay with the research teams of "trustified" capitalism.

When Schumpeter published *The Theory of Economic Development* in 1911 (Schumpeter I), individual entrepreneurs such as Thomas Edison, Andrew Carnegie, and John D. Rockefeller were the drivers of innovation and growth. But when he wrote *Capitalism, Socialism, and Democracy* in 1942 (Schumpeter II), it was large managerial corporations such as ATT, GM and DuPont with dedicated R&D labs that drove innovation. This change over time does much to explain the evolution of his views on the firm size sources of innovation.

In other words, the relative importance of small and large firms in innovation is time dependent. One reason why there was a revival of Schumpeter I theories after the late 1980s was that as the IT revolution took off, it enabled a swarm of entrepreneurs—people like Michael Dell, Larry Ellison, Bill Gates, or Steve Jobs—to strike out and form new companies. But as the technology has matured there has been shaking out and consolidation, to the point that the balance has shifted back toward the large firm. This is why by the mid-2000s only about 7 percent of new company startups in the United States were in high-tech industries and only about 3 percent of business founders considered their new businesses to be "technologically sophisticated."[36]

But with the cutbacks in corporate funding for earlier-stage, more risky research and the seeming flowering of small, innovative startups, is it still true that big firms are innovative? The dominant narrative would suggest no: these corporate giants have become sluggish, risk-averse copiers. The entrepreneur Sam Hogg speaks for most when he writes, "Startups require innovative entrepreneurs, and that typically isn't in a job description for a large company. Big companies hire people when the workload demands it, not when they can come up for air and think about innovation."[37]

But this narrative, as widely touted as it is, is not true. Scholarly research shows that large corporations continue to play a leading role in innovation. To be sure, some research has found that some small businesses are more innovative per dollar of revenue than large firms. A Small Business Administration (SBA)–funded study found that "small businesses develop more patents per employee than larger businesses, with the smallest firms, those with fewer than 25 employees, producing the greatest number of patents per employee."[38] Another study found that "small patenting firms are roughly 13 times more innovative per employee than large patenting firms."[39] Still another found that "small firms with at most 290 employees obtained on average 1.2626 patent citations per dollar of R&D stock, while large firms obtained 0.5712; thus, small firms obtained on average 2.2104 times more citations per dollar of R&D stock than large firms."[40]

But studies claiming to find that small firms are more innovative are actually looking at a small subset of firms. Among firms that obtain patents, small businesses do produce more patents per employee than large firms. But that doesn't stop the SBA from misleadingly stating that small firms produce thirteen times more patents per employee than large firms.[41] Note the omission of the word "patenting" before the words "small business." Also note that the top 1.5 percent of patenting firms, all large firms, are responsible for 48 percent of all patents from 1999 to 2008. In 2011, 108,626 utility patents of US origin were granted. Just fifty US companies getting the most patents (all large corporations) were responsible for over 30 percent of these patents. The reality is, only a tiny fraction of the nation's 6 million small firms patent or innovate.[42] This is not to say that some small technology-based firms are not highly innovative. But to assume that small always equates with innovative or entrepreneurial is not accurate.

One reason for this poor performance is that very few new businesses have any intention or capability to innovate. As Scott Shane writes,

Most new businesses don't intend to do something innovative enough to alter the market they are in. Data from the Entrepreneurship in the United States Assessment indicates that only 2 percent of new business founders expect their new companies to have a substantive effect on the markets in which they operate, and 91 percent expect to have little or no impact on those markets.[43]

Shane goes on to note that

almost all new businesses produce the same products and services as existing businesses, and almost none of them provide a product or service that their founder views as unique. Even among some of the best start-ups—the Inc. 500 firms, which are the fastest growing private companies in the United States—only 10 percent offer a product or service that other companies do not offer.[44]

Another study found that

within the first four years of business, only 2.7 percent of the businesses in the sample had already applied or were in the process of applying for patents. Copyright and trademark usage is slightly higher but still most firms do not innovate at least according to these crude observable measures. ... Nearly 85 percent of small businesses did not acquire a patent, trademark or copyright during their first four years of existence.[45]

This study also found that just between 6 and 8 percent of new businesses had developed any proprietary business practices or technology during their first few years of business.[46]

Studies touting the superiority of small firms thus need to be interpreted with care. First, while small technology companies in some industries may be more innovative dollar for dollar than large firms, the real question is the share they contribute to overall innovation. On this measure, it is small. For example, one study found that while small technology firms patent more per employee than large firms, they were responsible for just 6.5 percent of patents from 2002 to 2006.[47] In other words, while small technology firms may be more efficient at innovation, collectively they do much less of it than large firms. In fact, one firm, IBM, received more patents than all the 504 small firms in the study combined. When looking at small firms that had received more than 15 patents in five years Nolan and coworkers found that a number of firms fell out of the database. Six percent of small firms became large firms, while 17 percent had merged or been acquired. Most of the remaining small firms that dropped out did so because they fell below the fifteen-patent threshold, while another 4 percent dropped out because they became troubled or declared bankruptcy. Among the top 700 firms in 2003, the top seventeen were responsible for 25 percent of all R&D expenditures, the top thirty-three for 40 percent, and the top 300 for 80 percent.[48]

Moreover, while small firms account for 49 percent of US employment, they account for just 16 percent of business spending on R&D, while firms of more than 25,000 workers account for 36 percent (see figure 6.1).[49] Likewise, they account for 18.8 percent of patents issued, while the largest firms account for 37.4 percent of patents.[50] Average R&D spending per worker increases with company size (not controlling for industry), with firms with five to ninety-nine workers spending around $790 per worker and large firms with 5,000 or more workers spending around $3,370 per worker.[51]

When Adams Nager and coworkers at the Information Technology and Innovation Foundation surveyed almost 1,000 US scientists and engineers involved in filing triadic patents (patents filed in the United States, Europe, and Japan), they found that approximately 75 percent of materials science and IT patents and 60 percent of life science patents were filed by firms with more than 500 employees.[52] Countering the popular narrative that

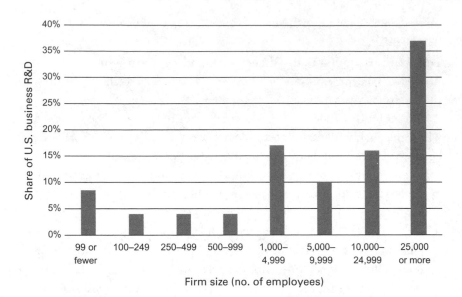

Figure 6.1

US Business R&D by Firm Size

Source: National Science Foundation, "Business Research and Development and Innovation: 2012," NSF 16-301 (Arlington, VA: NSF, October 29, 2015) (Table 21. Percent of R&D by Firm Size), https://nsf.gov/statistics/2016/nsf16301/#chp2.

large firms are sluggish copiers and small firms the true innovators, small or medium-sized firms with 500 or fewer workers in the sample accounted for only around 30 percent of patents, yet they employed 48.4 percent of workers. As the innovation scholar Luc Soete has found, "Inventive activity seems to increase more than proportionately with firm size."[53]

Other research suggests that even among firms that patent, the assumption that small firms are more innovative is not that simple, in part because of the focus on patents as a measure of innovation. In a 1996 paper, Wesley M. Cohen and Steven Klepper found that R&D and firm size are closely related. In other words, large firms invest more in R&D as a share of sales.[54] Like other scholars, Cohen and Klepper found that the number of patents and innovations produced per R&D dollar declined with increasing firm size. But they argue that this is not due to inefficiency, bureaucracy, and lack of drive but rather reflects a mismeasurement of innovation outputs. Large firms engage in "cost spreading," in which the benefits from one innovation are spread across more units and products, leading to a greater overall level of innovation per unit of R&D. They write, "Not only does cost spreading provide the basis for explaining the R&D-size relationship, it also challenges the consensus that has emerged from the R&D literature that large firm size imparts no advantage in R&D competition."[55] Further, "By applying the fruits of their R&D over a larger level of output, larger firms not only have a greater incentive to undertake R&D than smaller firms but they also realize a greater return from their R&D than smaller firms."[56]

More recently, in 2016, business professors Anne Marie Knott and Carl Vieregger explain how previous studies got the data wrong.[57] Historically, innovation scholars have relied on product or patent counts as a proxy for innovation output. But doing so overemphasizes product innovation and underestimates process or incremental innovation—innovation activities that large firms engage in more but rarely involve a patent filing. But the recent development of the National Science Foundation's Business Research and Development and Innovation Survey allowed them to better analyze incremental and process innovation. They estimate that a 10 percent increase in the number of employees increases R&D by 7.2 percent and that a 10 percent increase in firm revenues increases R&D productivity by 0.14 percent. Their conclusions show that large firms invest more in R&D activities and enjoy higher returns on innovation output per dollar invested in R&D.

One reason why some studies have found less R&D per employee or sales among large firms is that smaller firms are newer and are more R&D-focused because they are not producing as much. In other words, in young firms a larger share of the effort is devoted to developing a product because they don't have a product. This is perhaps why a study of more than 1,000 European enterprises of all sizes from 2002 and 2005 found that after the age of the firms was controlled for, large firms were about 14 percent more likely to be involved in innovation (product and process) than small firms. And small firms that were young and middle-aged were two and a half to three times more likely than large firms *not* to be involved in any innovation.[58] These results held when a number of factors such as industry, country, and ownership type were controlled for.

This pattern has been found to be true in many nations. For example, as one study of innovation in Japan found, "Japanese SMEs [small and medium enterprises] spend comparatively little on innovation. While Japan as a whole spends a lot on R&D in comparison with other developed economies, its SMEs do not."[59] Another study found that EU nations with smaller average firm size, such as Italy and Spain, have corporate R&D spending that is about half the EU level as a share of GDP. The authors conclude that "economies geared to small-scale production may be ill prepared to appropriate the full benefits of the current phase of massive and rapid technological change."[60] OECD data on thirty-three nations that compared the percentage of large firms that introduced a new product to the percentage of small firms that did so found that in no nation were small firms more likely to introduce a new product. In fact, the advantage for large firms ranged from double in Australia to almost six times higher in Spain and Poland (see figure 6.2). This is one reason why a study of 1,053 enterprises from twenty-six countries in the years 2002 to 2005 found a positive and statistically significant relationship between firm size and innovation.[61]

Moreover, if startups are the driver of innovation, how do small business defenders explain that California and Massachusetts—home of Silicon Valley and Route 128, respectively—had below-average rates of new firm formation?[62] As Shane writes, San Francisco and Boston metro areas "aren't

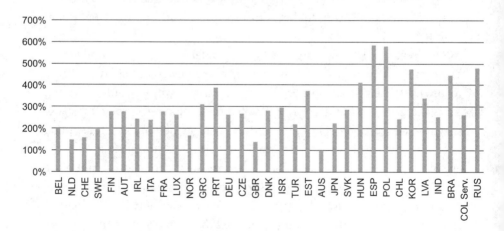

Figure 6.2
Ratio of Share of Large Firms to Share of Small Firms Introducing New Products, 2010–2012

Source: OECD, *OECD Science, Technology and Industry Scoreboard 2015: Innovation for Growth and Society* (Paris: OECD Publishing, October 19, 2015) (Table 4.5.3. Firms Introducing Products New to the Market, by Firm Size, 2010–12, October 2015), http://dx.doi.org/10.1787/sti_scoreboard-2015-en.

anywhere close to the number one metro area in terms of per capita firm formation; that honor goes to Laramie, Wyoming. San Francisco comes in at number 121 out of 394, with about 40 percent the per capita business formation rate of Laramie," with San Jose coming in even lower at 165.[63]

Another problem is that it is misleading to generalize about the relationship between firm size and innovation across industries. One 1987 study of four decades of innovation in the UK found a U-shaped pattern, with the greatest innovation carried out by the smallest and biggest firms.[64] But this ignores the unique characteristics of particular industrial sectors. As Giovanni Dosi and coworkers noted in 2011, "Innovative firms are likely to be rather small in industrial machinery; big firms prevail in chemicals, metal working, aerospace and electrical equipment, while many 'science-based' sectors (such as electronics and pharmaceuticals) tend to display a bimodal distribution with high rates of innovation of small and very large firms."[65]

Finally, one reason the research on firm size and innovation is somewhat ambiguous is that small firms play a more important role in some industries than in other industries, and at different times. In other words, a healthy innovation ecosystem depends on a mix of firm sizes. As Zoltan J. Acs and David B. Audretsch found in one of the definitive studies on the issue, "The greatest difference between the large- and small-firm innovation rates, implies that the correct answer is: It depends on the particular industry. For example, in the tire industry, the large-firm innovation rate exceeded the small-firm innovation rate by 8.46, or by 8 innovations per 1,000 employees."[66] They found that in industries characterized by higher levels of capital intensity, "innovation tends to be greater in large firms than in small firms."[67] For example, in the US electric utility industry most of the research is conducted by large generation companies, especially if they are part of a larger holding company.[68] Interestingly, electric utility R&D declined precipitously (by 78.6 percent) after US electricity markets were restructured to make them more competitive, more evidence of the inverted U-shape of innovation and competition (see chapter 11). An older (1974) study found that "larger pharmaceutical firms were 'better' at innovation than smaller firms."[69] Likewise, a 1980 Federal Trade Commission report concluded: "It is questionable whether smaller firms could support an R&D program on a scale similar to that of General Electric. Without the support of a multiplant operation such as General Electric, it is doubtful that various large, specialized research programs on lamps and lighting would be undertaken in the private sector."[70] We see this in agricultural biotechnology. As a report from the US Department of Agriculture notes, "In the crop seed and animal breeding sectors, the emergence of biotechnology was a major driver of consolidation. Companies sought to acquire relevant technological capacities and serve larger markets to share the large fixed costs associated with meeting regulatory approval for new biotechnology innovations."[71]

Other research has found that "small firms prevail in the early stages and innovation tends to concentrate in larger firms as industries evolve towards maturity."[72] We saw this in the 1990s when many small firms emerged and competed to be the winners in IT. But only a few firms could emerge as winners, and the ones that did continued to invest in innovation to improve their products and services and gain advantage in related activities. The study concluded, "The question is no longer whether size positively or negatively affects innovation but under what circumstances may small firms enjoy an innovation advantage over large ones (and vice versa)."[73] This is why Frederic M. Scherer's warning that "the search for a firm size uniquely and unambiguously for invention and innovation is misguided" is such good advice.[74]

According to some, however, big firms are the natural enemies of small, innovative startups. Big companies, it is asserted, can present a take-it-or-leave-it ultimatum to smaller innovative firms: either merge with us or be destroyed. Barry C. Lynn writes, "In such an environment, independent firms find it ever harder to keep it that way; just ask the founders of Tom's of Maine, Ben and Jerry's, Niman Ranch, Honest Tea, or Stonyfield Farm, all of which have been forced to sell out to bigger companies."[75]

In at least one of these cases, Lynn is mistaken. When one of us asked Seth Goldman, the cofounder and "TeaEO" of Honest Tea, why he chose to partner with Coca-Cola, he said this:

Honest Tea was not "forced" to sell out to a big company. Rather, we chose to partner with Coca-Cola as a way to put our growth on a faster track. ... It had taken us 10 years to get into 15,000 retail accounts, and we had sold a cumulative $120 million over those first ten years. In the next six years, we expanded into more than 100,000 accounts, and we sold a cumulative $880 million. So there were some powerful incentives (and rewards) for us to sell to Coke, but we certainly weren't forced to do so. ... Moreover, Honest Tea's ability to raise capital from investors was dependent on the belief that at some point we would be able to sell to a larger company which would give a return to our investors. Now that I have the benefit of hindsight, I would not have chosen a different outcome for the brand.[76]

In the case of Honest Tea, partnering with a large corporation allowed an innovative startup with deeply held progressive values and behaviors to get its healthy products in front of many times more American consumers. And it sent a clear message to other budding entrepreneurs: if you can succeed in building a successful company, you can put its growth on steroids by partnering with a larger company. This is something progressives should be cheering, not decrying.

In conclusion, it should be no surprise that despite the publicity that rewards the rare successful tech startup, most small businesses are not innovative. Few of them want to be. In a 2011 study, Erik Hurst and Benjamin Wild Pugsley found that most small businesses do not intend to grow or innovate.[77] Most small business owners cited nonpecuniary reasons, such as being their own bosses or having flexible schedules, as their motives for starting a company; only 41 percent had a new business idea or sought to create a new product.[78] Only 15 percent of new businesses surveyed planned "to develop proprietary technology, processes, or procedures in the future."[79] This is not to say that tech startups and small R&D-intensive firms are not important to driving innovation, but to privilege small over large when it comes to innovation is a fundamental mistake.

7 Small Business in a Big World

What if we told you that if we know a single statistic about a country, we can tell you whether its per capita income is in the top, bottom, or middle of global rankings? And what if we told you that, knowing only that one statistic, we could also guess with considerable accuracy what the country's overall economy is like and even in what region of the world it is probably located?

There is such a tell-all statistic. It is the percentage of the population that is self-employed. The poorer a nation is, the more of its people are self-employed. In 2016, 6.4 percent of unincorporated Americans were self-employed.[1] In Burundi, the share that is self-employed or in family businesses is 89.9 percent. In 2016 the per capita income in Burundi (purchasing power parity) was $800, while it was $57,300 in the United States.[2]

As a rule, the richest regions are those in which self-employment is lowest, while the poorest are those with the most self-employed inhabitants. Self-employed workers amount to 7 percent of the workforce in North America and 10 percent in the European Union, 22 percent in Latin America and the Caribbean, 36 percent in sub-Saharan Africa, and 41 percent in Southeast Asia.[3] The reason, as we noted in chapter 4, is simple: as a rule, the smaller the firm, the lower the productivity level.

Here's another fun trick. If we know the percentage of self-employment in a country, we can also accurately guess what kinds of things that country exports. High-value-added manufactured goods dominate the exports of countries with low levels of self-employment, while low-value-added commodities such as raw materials and agricultural products and services such as tourism dominate the exports of nations with high levels of self-employment.

According to the World Bank, the poorest countries are Malawi, Burundi, the Central African Republic, and Niger, and their exports are such items as tobacco, uranium and thorium ore, tea, sugar, coffee, cotton, hides, wood, spices, and precious stones. Now let us look at the major exports of the three largest advanced industrial capitalist countries, the United States, Japan, and Germany: machinery, electronic equipment, aircraft, spacecraft, vehicles, oil, medical equipment, iron and steel, plastics, organic chemicals, engines, pumps, and pharmaceuticals. Rich countries export mostly high-value-added manufactured goods. Poor countries export mostly low-value-added commodities, much of them harvested or made by hand using primitive, labor-intensive methods instead of modern machinery.

Specializing in tourism is another guaranteed route to poverty. In 2015, tourism as a percent of total exports was 10.9 percent in the United States, 3 percent in Germany, and 3.5 percent in Japan but 52 percent in Albania, 55.3 percent in Jamaica, 55 percent in Montenegro, and 73.4 percent in the Bahamas.[4]

There is also a positive correlation between the share of firms that are small and income inequality. Davis and Cobb find that the most equal nation in their sample of fifty-three nations, Denmark, had about one quarter of its workers employed in its largest ten firms. In contrast, in the least equal nation, Colombia, the largest firms employed fewer than 1 percent of workers. Overall there is a negative correlation (–0.47) across nations between income inequality and the share of workers employed in large companies.[5]

What about new business startups? According to a World Economic Forum report examining the share of startup firms, Uganda is number one, Thailand two, Brazil three, and Cameroon four.[6] These countries are hardly economic powerhouses.

What explains this striking correlation among five seemingly unrelated factors: self-employment rates, per capita income, the composition of exports, income inequality, and startup rates? The answer is big business—to be more precise, medium to large to colossal firms in industries characterized by increasing returns to scale. While poor, undeveloped countries are dominated by small famers, producers, and peddlers, often in the informal sector, in the advanced technological nations of North America, Europe, and East Asia big firms are responsible for disproportionate shares of output and employment.

The modern economy is a "bimodal economy," to use Galbraith's phrase. It can be divided into industries with constant or diminishing returns, in which the cost of each additional good or service produced is the same as the previous one (think massages), and industries characterized by increasing returns to scale, in which, mainly for technical reasons, the average cost of producing the ten thousandth unit is less than the first (think automobiles). In some digital industries, such as software, the second unit is cheaper than the first by a very large margin because the second one is largely free to produce (it is copied by a computer). Increasing-returns industries tend to be in traded sectors while constant- or diminishing-returns industries such as massage therapy tend to belong to nontraded sectors.

Before the Industrial Revolution, which began in the eighteenth century, the tradable sector was small and negligible, limited to a few luxury items such as spices and silks, which were consumed only by rich elites. Everything else—tools, clothing, food—was made or grown at home or nearby. Industrialization is the process by which more and more goods and services that once were produced locally by human and animal power are produced by machines (including computers) using sources of energy other than human or animal muscle, shifting many of those goods and services from the nontraded sector to the traded sector (whether they are in fact sold abroad or not, they can be). Because the most efficient firms in increasing-returns industries are usually of substantial size, during the process of economic development the number of self-employed workers and mom-and-pop businesses declines, particularly in traded sectors, and the number of wage earners working for medium-sized to large firms expands. So does public sector employment, because rising prosperity permits higher tax revenues with less pain and an expansion of the functions of government.

As large, more efficient firms gain market share, they provide better opportunities for workers. This is why richer nations also have relatively less self-employment.[7] As firm size increases so do incomes for more individuals, many of whom switch from suboptimal "entrepreneurship" to working for wages. This may also explain the recent increase in contingent or gig work since the global recession in Europe and the United States. Much of the focus on the growth of the gig economy has been on the new platforms, such as Uber and Task Rabbit, but it may be that one reason more workers are using work-finding apps to become "1099 workers" (self-employed workers) is because other, higher-quality employment opportunities are lacking.

As a nation industrializes and labor and resources shift from the traditional small firm sectors to the innovative large firm sectors, the country gets richer, because of—and not in spite of—the growth of big business. And the information technology (IT) revolution is enabling a wider variety of service industries to also become increasing-returns-to-scale industries and to become traded. A case in point is banks, which for centuries were mostly local and nontraded. People banked with local banks. Today, with "fintech" and e-banking, banking can be done anywhere in the nation and even across borders. Internet-based banking is like manufacturing, with increasing returns to scale, but even more so, and it enables distance consumption. We see this IT transformation occurring in a host of industries—news, insurance, travel services, retail, law, and several others—where technology is providing increasing returns to scale and making them tradable, just as most of manufacturing has long been. That is why, as we showed in chapter 3, the average nonmanufacturing industry in the United States is seeing increasing average firm size.

Firm Size around the World

American politicians love to talk about American exceptionalism. But the general pattern of American economic development is very similar to that of other advanced industrial nations in Europe and East Asia, characterized by the same coevolution of technological innovation and business on an ever-larger scale. After all, technology tools largely determine firm size, and those tools are available around the globe.

But that's not to say that other factors don't impinge. Given the trends in technology, one might expect that, like the United States, other advanced nations would in fact be seeing increased firm size. But while firm size has been increasing in the United States, in some regions it has been shrinking. In Europe, the average firm size declined from seven workers per firm in 2005 to 6.2 in 2013 (see figure 7.1).[8] Portugal went from 15.7 workers per firm in 1986 to 9.1 in 2008 and in no sector did firm size increase, while the share of workers who were self-employed increased by a factor of ten.[9] Likewise, the share of employment in small firms in China grew from around 22 percent in 2004 to 32 percent in 2009.[10]

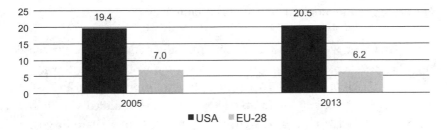

Figure 7.1

Change in Average Firm Size in the United States and the EU-28

Sources: US Small Business Administration, Firm Size Data (Table 1. Number of Firms, Establishments, Employment, and Payroll by Firm Size, State, and Industry) (database), https://www.sba.gov/advocacy/firm-size-data (accessed February 11, 2106); and Eurostat, Structural Business Statistics—Main Indicators (Number of Enterprises) (database), http://ec.europa.eu/eurostat/web/structural-business-statistics/data/database (accessed February 2, 2017).

What explains firm size changes in a nation? There are two factors: the growth effect and the mix effect. The mix effect refers to changes in the mix of jobs between industries. The growth effect refers to overall trends. In virtually every nation, manufacturing firms are larger than nonmanufacturing firms. So as jobs shift to services, the effect should be to reduce overall average firm size. But the growth effect also plays a role; for example, IT is allowing a range of service firms to gain scale. In countries where firm size is getting smaller, some of this is the result of fewer manufacturing jobs, but much of it appears to be related to the growth effect, whereby average firm size other sectors is not getting larger or are even shrinking.

Why have service firms gotten smaller in some nations but bigger in the United States? Several reasons can be adduced. One may be efforts by nations to "demonopolize" industries that had been nationalized. Another may be policies explicitly favoring small firms while taxing and regulating large firms. In South Korea, for example, the share of output from large firms fell from 72 percent in the early 1970s to around 50 percent in 2006, while the share of employment in small and medium-sized enterprises (SMEs) increased from 80 percent in 2000 to 87 percent by the early 2010s.[11] As we will discuss, Korea has enacted a vast array of policies, including explicitly charging its competition authority to create a "competitive environment" for SMEs, that made it harder for large firms to grow.

Around the World Small Firms Are Less Productive

This stagnant or even declining firm size in many nations matters because big firms are on average more productive than small firms. One way to estimate this difference is look at their share of employment and GDP. In the early 1990s, out of fourteen OECD nations studied, in all but Spain, small firms' share of employment exceeded their share of GDP[12] In other words, small firms' workers produced less. In the UK, small firms accounted for two-thirds of jobs but just 30 percent of GDP.[13] Workers in very large firms in the UK are more than twice as productive as workers in businesses with one to nine workers.[14] Large Finnish firms (more than 1,000 employees) had 13 percent higher total factor productivity than small firms (fewer than fifteen employees), when the type of industry was controlled for.[15]

Bart van Ark and Erik Monnikhof show that large firms are more productive than small in France, Germany, Japan, the UK, and the United States.[16] In Canada, productivity in plants with 100 or fewer employees was 62 per cent of the industry average, but it was 165 percent in plants with 500 or more employees.[17] These differences persisted even after other characteristics were controlled for, such as foreign control, export intensity, unionization, and age.[18] Even when researchers controlled for industry and age, large firms were still 10.5 percent more productive. One study of Japan found that all of the decline in growth in Japan leading to Japan's so-called "lost decade" was the result of SMEs not increasing their productivity, something large firms continued to do.[19] Indeed, from 1980 to 2000, total factor productivity growth continued to grow for large firms but either stagnated or fell for SMEs. In a combined 18 European nations, firms with 250 or more employees are 80 percent more productive than firms with fewer than ten employees (see figure 7.2).

What about in the developing world? After all, it has become an article of faith in the international development community that multiplying the number of small, even micro, firms will help developing nations escape poverty. But a World Bank study of seventy-six nations found no evidence that SMEs support growth or reduce poverty.[20] Another study of ten African nations found that small and large firms created similar numbers of net jobs, but the jobs in larger firms paid persistently higher wages.[21] This is because large firms are more productive than small ones.

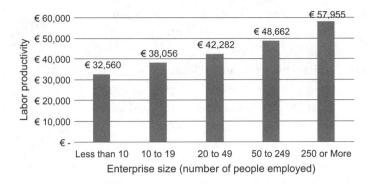

Figure 7.2
Labor Productivity and Enterprise Size in the European Union, 2014
Source: Eurostat, Structural Business Statistics Overview, Labor Productivity by Size of Enterprise (database), http://ec.europa.eu/eurostat/statistics-explained/index.php/Structural_business_statistics_overview.

Large firms in Asia are also more productive than small firms. In India, firms with five to forty-nine workers were just 10 percent as productive as firms with more than 200 workers; productivity for smaller firms in relation to larger firms was 19 percent in Indonesia, 21 percent in the Philippines, 22 percent in South Korea, 42 percent in Thailand, and 46 percent in Malaysia.[22] We see the same dynamic in Africa, where larger firms are more productive than smaller ones,[23] and in Turkey.[24]

This explains why a predictable way to determine how rich an economy is is to look at the share of workers in large firms. The larger share of a region's employment in large firms, the richer it will be. This is also why residents of US states with a higher share of jobs in small businesses have on average lower incomes. In fact, there is a –0.27 correlation between the share of jobs in a state in firms with fewer than twenty employees and the state's per capita income. For example, per capita income in Montana is just $39,800, with the share of jobs in small firms over 31 percent. Massachusetts enjoys a per capita income of $62,900 and only 16 percent of its jobs are in small firms.[25]

The same pattern holds true across nations. In general, high-income countries have a much higher share of jobs in big companies.[26] Moreover, small business growth appears to be negatively, not positively, related to growth. Scott Shane found that "removing the effect of all other factors that differ between countries, the rate of new firm formation in a particular year has a negative effect on a country's real per capita GDP in the following year."[27] Moreover, "The countries that have had consistently faster economic growth had declining rates of new firm formation over time from 1975 to 1996."[28] This is why data on new business formation in forty-four countries from 2000 to 2004 show that developing countries have a much higher rate of new business creation than developed countries.[29] Higher rates of new firm formation are a sign of poverty, not wealth, because they reflect the paucity of real economic opportunities at firms that are sophisticated and able to be highly productive.

Firm size is also one reason why Canada is poorer than the United States. The smaller average firm size in Canada accounts for approximately 20 percent of the gap in Canada-US sales per employee overall and 48 percent in manufacturing.[30] While average firm size in the United States increased, the average size of firms in Canada fell from 17.5 employees in 1984 to 15.3 employees in 1997, with most of the decline coming from large firms getting smaller.[31] This decline caused average sales per employee in Canada to fall by $1,700. If the United States had the same firm size distribution as Canada—which, as we will see in chapter 10, the populist left in America desires—US per capita GDP would be $1,800 lower.[32] If the United States had the same firm size distribution as Europe, US productivity would be $2,060 lower. That is the small business "tax" these nations pay.

Explaining Firm Size Differences between Nations

Why does this distribution of firm sizes differ so widely between nations? One factor is whether a nation has a greater share of firms that are on average larger, such as manufacturing firms. Nations with more manufacturing firms tend to have higher average firm sizes, all else being equal. Likewise, R&D-intensive industries tend to be larger, and so nations with a larger share will (all else being equal) have larger than average firms.[33] But these factors do not appear to play a large role in explaining differences between nations.

One factor in national firm size appears to be population size and the size of market access. A larger population means larger markets, so more firms are able to achieve economies of scale using mass production technologies. Indeed, there is a positive 0.45 correlation between the population of twenty-nine OECD nations[34] and the share of jobs in firms with more 250 workers and a negative 0.2 correlation between population size and share of jobs in firms with fewer than 51 workers. Likewise, better access to foreign markets through trade agreements and other market opening measures should enable greater firm size, as would improvements in transportation networks and communication networks. If firms can reach more markets through better physical transportation or through information transfer on broadband networks, they will likely be larger.

Higher per capita income also plays a role. Higher incomes not only increase market size, they make it more likely a person will want to be a wage worker rather than a subsistence entrepreneur. Many studies have found this relationship. Examining the period of 1900–1970, Robert E. Lucas, Jr., found a strong positive relation in the United States between average firm size and GNP per capita.[35] Likewise, in a study of more than thirty countries, Markus Poschke found that richer nations have more large firms and fewer small firms.[36] Rich nations also have relatively more managerial jobs.[37] In short, as nations get richer, their firm size generally increases, as was the case in most East Asian economies over the last forty years, including Indonesia, Japan, South Korea, and Thailand.[38] Small firms are more prevalent in poor countries in part because poor countries provide smaller markets for needed economies of scale. So having a large share of small firms should not be seen as a sign of success, something that policy makers should build on. Rather, it should be seen as a sign of underdevelopment. A high level of self-employment in a country means there are not enough good full-time jobs, so many people are forced to obtain low incomes by working for themselves.

Culture also plays a role. In his book *Trust: The Social Values and the Creation of Prosperity*, Francis Fukayama argues that strong family ties are bad for the formation of larger firms because they make it harder for individuals to trust non-family members. For example, the large number of small firms in Southern Italy stems in part from a culture in which family is trusted but outsiders are not. This may be why numerous studies have found that nations with a population that showed higher levels of trust of non-family members had a statistically significant greater share of economic output in larger firms.[39] Higher levels of trust also let managers delegate to a broader range of individuals with greater assurance that they will act in the interests of the firm.[40]

The regulatory and legal climate also plays a role. Several studies have found that nations with stronger property rights, including intellectual property rights, have larger firms.[41] The argument is that "an efficient legal system eases management's ability to use critical resources other than physical assets as sources of power, which leads to the establishment of firms of larger size. It also protects outside investors better and allows larger firms to be financed."[42] This is also true at the subnational level. For example, Mexican states with more effective legal systems have larger firms because states with better legal systems reduce the risk firm owners face, leading them to increase investment.[43] Nations with better-developed financial markets also have larger firms. One study found that firms in industries more dependent on outside financing are larger in nations where financial markets are more developed.[44]

Policies to Keep Businesses Small

A major reason firms are smaller in some nations is that governments actively want small firms and have a broad array of policies that tilt toward smaller firms, including weaker regulatory requirements, tax preferences, and subsidies. When policy rewards smallness and penalizes bigness, smallness is the result.

In most nations, governments exempt small businesses from regulation or subject them to lesser requirements. The European Commission's official policy is to size discriminate, stating: "Being SME-friendly should become mainstream policy. To achieve this, the 'Think Small First' principle should be irreversibly anchored in policy making from regulation to public service."[45] In France a number of regulatory requirements apply only to businesses with fifty or more employees. In Portugal, firms with fewer than workers have access to workers whose wages are subsidized by public funds and who receive priority for worker training subsidies. Also, the more workers, the higher the fines are for violations of labor law. The exemptions for small firms are even stronger in many developing nations. For example, in Brazil, most of the labor inspections are focused on large, formal firms, not on small informal firms.[46]

Many countries also protect small-scale mom-and-pop stores through barriers to entry, zoning laws, and restrictions on the size of stores. For example, Argentina has an array of policies to favor small, less-productive grocery stores.[47] Larger firms are forced to "donate" food to neighborhood associations and face price controls and import limits. Regulations limit the size of stores and the maximum number of stores any one firm can operate in an area. Some regions even require hardship pay increases for working in large stores.

Worried that French consumers will buy too many books on Amazon. com and reduce sales at small bookstores, France's minister of culture has described Amazon.com's free shipping of online orders as "a strategy of dumping."[48] And a bill recently unanimously approved by France's lower house of Parliament would effectively force online booksellers to sell at higher prices than brick-and-mortar stores by banning any seller from applying discounts to the cover prices of books that are shipped to readers. The McKinsey Global Institute has found the same kind of small retailer protections in Brazil.[49] In Japan, laws limiting the entry of large supermarkets and providing incentives for small retailers to stay in business explain the country's high share of low-productivity family retailers.

Most nations require large firms to pay higher taxes. In Mexico, from 1998 until 2013, firms with sales below 2 million pesos (about $125,000 in 2008) paid a flat tax of about 2 percent of their sales and were exempt from payroll income and value-added taxes. Firms above the 2 million pesos threshold were subject to a 15 percent value-added tax, a 38 percent income tax, and a 35 percent payroll tax.[50] In Indonesia, firms above a certain size are required to pay 10 percent value-added tax. In South Korea, small companies pay a 10 percent corporate tax while large ones pay a 22 percent tax.

Many nations have special tax incentives that either apply only to small business or are more generous for them. In South Korea, only small firms are eligible for a 5 percent tax credit for expenditures on industrial or advanced office equipment. The UK provides a new enterprise tax allowance but only to small firms. In Canada, small firms are eligible for an R&D credit 75 percent greater than that for large firms. China has recently introduced an additional round of special tax cuts for small businesses, including a tax rebate scheme for small businesses.[51]

In most nations, small businesses also benefit from subsidized loans, direct grants, lower fees for government services, and set-asides for obtaining government contracts. South Korea requires banks to lend to small firms, resulting in an overabundance of debt. In 2012, 78 percent of bank lending went to SMEs, compared to about 25 percent in the United States.[52] In addition, public financial institutions such as the Korea Finance

Corporation and the Small and Median Business Corporation provide loans directly to SMEs. Only 21 percent of loans made to SMEs were not guaranteed or collateralized by government.[53] The government also operates 1,300 SME programs and forty-seven support measures covering taxes, marketing, and employment.

Many governments simply give small businesses cash. While the European Commission restricts state aid to business, it exempts many small firms.[54] European governments can give direct aid to small fishers, farmers, coal-mining companies, shipbuilders, steel companies, and synthetic fiber firms, but not to large ones. The European Commission wants to reduce "competition-distorting handouts to national champions, and instead support measures which contribute to boosting growth and creating jobs."[55] This means they want to give money to small business. This is one reason why in France, "There are over 250 different grants and subsidies ... available to individuals for starting up a personal enterprise or small business."[56]

Many nations prop up small firms because they do not want to suffer the economic disruption coming from job loss and because policy makers do not trust the market to create jobs. So they in essence enable inefficient small companies to continue to be inefficient. But this simply keeps more productive firms from gaining market share. Korea is a classic case in point. Because of deep societal aversion to employment disruption, the Korean government perpetuates an array of policies to limit firms from going out of business. The *2012 Global Innovation Index* ranks Korea 120th in the cost of redundancy of dismissal of employees.[57] The government promotes a range of domestic policies to shelter small firms from competition. Its National Commission on Corporate Partnership is charged with "designating suitable industries for SMEs."[58] For example, it ruled that medium-sized restaurant companies cannot open new stores within 150 meters from small eateries that earn less than 48 million won ($42,800) in annual revenue.

The situation in South Korea demonstrates how size discrimination limits growth. SMEs account for 87 percent of jobs, compared to just 44.4 percent in the US.[59] The lavish benefits and regulatory exemptions SMEs enjoy mean that few firms want to grow. Of the millions of SMEs in South Korea in 2002, only a paltry 696 had graduated from SME status by 2012. And their labor productivity in manufacturing is less than a third that of large companies and 45 percent in services. Massive government favoritism toward small firms lowers labor productivity below what it would be if workers were distributed randomly between low, medium, and highly productive firms. In contrast, in the United States the actual distribution raises productivity by 50 percent over what it would be if less productive firms had the same market share.[60]

The consequences of a tilted playing field are similar in many nations. In France, firms with fifty or more employees face substantially more regulation than firms with fewer than fifty. An NBER study by Luis Garicano, Claire LeLarge, and John Van Reenen finds that as a result, many French firms intentionally stay under the magic fifty-worker threshold, and that this lowers French GDP by as much as 5 percent of GDP, with workers bearing most of the cost.[61] A related cause of this lower growth is that by reducing wages, these regulations encourage "too many agents with low managerial ability to become small entrepreneurs rather than working as employees for more productive entrepreneurs."[62]

In Portugal, the expansion of discriminatory regulations meant that the average firm size declined by almost 50 percent from 1986 to 2009, and because these firms are less productive than larger firms, growth stagnated.[63] Likewise, studies show that small firm preferences keep firms small in India,[64] Italy,[65] and Japan.[66]

These policies not only keep more efficient larger firms from gaining market share, they stifle the growth of small businesses into large ones, since they are loathe to lose their cushy preferences. This hurts growth by diverting output from more productive larger firms to less productive smaller ones. This is why one study found that "policies that reduce the average size of establishments by 20% lead to reductions in output and output per establishment up to 8.1% and 25.6% respectively, as well as large increases in the number of establishments (23.5%)."[67]

These small firm preferences are even extensive in many developing nations and even more damaging given their already low levels of per capita income. India is emblematic. Post-independence Indian economic policy was heavily influenced by "small is beautiful" thinking. Embracing this mentality, coupled with pressures from unions for featherbedding and protections against productivity improvements, India's government passed laws limiting the size of certain enterprises, in the quixotic pursuit of job creation. In the 1970s, Prime Minister Indira Gandhi reserved approximately 800 industries for the small-scale sector. Investment in plant and machinery in any individual unit producing these items could not exceed $250,000.[68] For example, pencil makers could grow no larger than fifty employees, which resulted in India having one of the world's most inefficient pencil industries. As Gurcharan Das writes, "Thus, large Indian firms were barred from making products of daily use such as pencils, boot polish, candles, shoes, garments, and toys—all the products that had helped East Asia and China create millions of jobs. Even after 1991, Indian governments were afraid to touch this holy cow."[69] One result of this tragic legacy is that by 2005, while 52 percent of China's manufacturing workers were employed by large firms, just 10.5 percent of India's were.

Though these "permit raj" policies have largely been abandoned, India still seeks to protect its fragile small business flowers from big business. In India, various regulations on manufacturers kick in at various firm size levels, depending on the type of regulation, such as health, social security, and labor protection. The Industrial Disputes Act, which significantly limits the ability of firms to lay off workers, applies only to companies employing 100 or more workers, which must get permission from the government to lay off workers and give twenty-one days' notice if they are going to change leave, wages, and hours.[70] Likewise, the Indian government prohibited Wal-Mart from selling directly to consumers; it could only sell to retailers, which then resold their purchases to customers. If you want to buy a set of sheets or some socks for your child, you don't go to Wal-Mart; you go to your local corner shop, which resells to you what it bought from Wal-Mart, at a markup. The study found that Indian states with more flexible labor market regulations have a higher share of employment in large firms.[71]

Most developing nations have made the same mistakes. One study found that large firms in Pakistan, South Korea, Ghana, and Sierra Leone had costs of between 10 and 26 percent more than small firms because of tax policy differences, while costs for large firms in Ghana, Sierra Leone, Tunisia, and Brazil were 20 to 27 percent higher because of labor regulations.[72] These distortions reduced GDP by between 6 and 18 percent. Hsieh and Kienow found that in India and China, small manufacturers have a significantly larger share of the market than they would if the goal was to maximize productivity.[73] They argue, "It is harder for a more productive firm to grow but also easier for a less productive firm to survive in India than in the United States."[74]

Moreover, in the developing world large numbers of small firms are not subject to regulatory and tax obligations because they operate in the informal economy (what could be more accurately termed *the illegal economy*). For example, in Brazil most of the labor inspections are focused on large formal firms, not small informal firms.[75] As the World Bank writes, informality provides "unfair advantage to noncompliant firms, thereby distorting the allocation of resources."[76] Luis Videgaray Caso, Mexico's Secretary of Finance and Public Credit, writes, "The informal workforce reduces productivity and thereby diminishes economic growth."[77] The McKinsey Global Institute found: "One reason for Mexico's weak productivity growth overall is that more than half of non-agricultural workers are employed in the informal sector; indeed, informality is growing due to the high regulatory cost of establishing a formal business and lax enforcement."[78] Informality is a drag on growth, not a progressive force.[79]

The international development community has not helped matters by latching on to fads such as supporting microbusinesses and the informal economy. For example, the European Commission writes: "In many developing countries, the expansion of the private sector, notably micro-, small- and medium-sized enterprises, is a powerful engine of economic growth and the main source of job creation."[80] Under Goal 8 of the UN Sustainable Development Knowledge Platform to encourage sustainable growth, one of the means is to "encourage the formalization and growth of micro, small, and medium-sized enterprises."[81] And the World Bank "promotes small and medium-sized enterprise (SME) growth through both systemic and targeted interventions."[82] The irony of these policies is that they are resulting in the exact opposite of their intention: the holding back of development. The result of this fixation on small business has been slower productivity and per-capita income growth.[83]

The lesson should be clear. If the goal is to advance global development, particularly in low-income nations, the focus should be on size neutrality at minimum. Ill-advised national policies to prop up, subsidize, or protect small firms in the name of job creation or social inclusion work against achieving the long-term goals of economic development and improved living standards.

III Politics and Policy

8   A Republic, If You Can Keep It: Big Business and Democracy

Following the conclusion of the Philadelphia convention of 1787 that created the US federal Constitution, according to Maryland delegate James McHenry: "A lady askcd Dr. Franklin, Well Doctor what have we got a republic or a monarchy. A republic replied the Doctor if you can keep it."[1]

Since the late nineteenth century, many Americans have believed that the rise of big business is a threat to the American republic. As we have seen in earlier chapters, the antimonopoly school is actually a combination of two different traditions.

One strand, associated with the legacy of Thomas Jefferson, William Jennings Bryan, and Louis Brandeis, is producer republicanism—the deliberate protection and promotion of an economy dominated by small producers for its alleged social and political benefits, by means of government obstruction of market forces if necessary. In this variant of the antimonopoly tradition, markets characterized by monopoly and oligopoly, perhaps even productivity growth itself, are bad because they tend to replace the majority of self-employed proprietors, on whom republican government is alleged to depend, with a new majority of wage earners or "wage slaves," dependent on the tender mercies of large employers, the welfare state or charity. As the contemporary admirers of Brandeis Barry Lynn and Phillip Longman admit, "In this tradition, breaking up monopoly has little to do with promoting efficiency or better deals for consumers, and everything to do with protecting political equality, self-government, and democratic institutions."[2] Brandeis himself argued, "The doctrine of the separation of powers was adopted ... not to promote efficiency but to preclude the exercise of arbitrary power." The way to "save the people from autocracy," he said, is precisely by building "friction" into the system.[3] He continued: "There cannot be liberty without industrial independence and the greatest danger to the people of the United States today is in becoming, as they are gradually more and more, a class of employees."[4]

The other strand of the antimonopoly tradition, associated first with Adam Smith's classical economics and now with today's neoclassical economics, claims to defend the interests of consumers, not producers, large or small. But in crude versions of neoclassical economics, all industries are assumed to be atomistic industries, with no economies of scale or network effects, made up of many small firms, which are "price-takers" rather than "price-makers." In this variant of the antimonopoly tradition, monopoly and oligopoly are bad because they are threats to the interest of the consumer in purchasing goods from producers with the lowest possible profit.

While the producer republican tradition was willing to sacrifice consumer welfare to the alleged interest of the republic in maintaining a large number of small producer-citizens, most in the market fundamentalist wing of the antimonopoly tradition have claimed there is no need to choose between consumer welfare and producer independence. In a free market undistorted by political favoritism toward particular firms, most firms should be small and the competition among them should lead to lower prices for consumers.

In one respect, the distance between market fundamentalists and producer republicans is narrow: they both are willing to sacrifice improvements in material well-being for "freedom." Brandeis spoke for many civic republicans when he argued that with an economy of large firms, "We may have all these things and have a nation of slaves."[5] Friedrich Hayek, the patron saint of market fundamentalists, agreed, writing, "Personally, I should much prefer to have to put up with some such inefficiency than have organized monopoly control my ways of life."[6] So for both, "freedom" trumped prosperity. Brandeis feared that big business would take away freedom, Hayek, big government.[7]

Producer republicans and market fundamentalists, then, both worry that the growth of big business will undermine democracy. But producer republicans worry that democracy is undermined when most citizens work for other people rather than for themselves as small farmers, artisans, or shop owners. Market fundamentalists have no objection to wage labor. Their focus is on the citizen, not as a producer but as a consumer and a taxpayer who is threatened by "crony capitalist" collusion among businesses and governments, which can lead to both higher prices and higher taxes. Minimizing opportunities for political corruption for private benefit, not maximizing the numbers of the self-employed, is the objective of the market fundamentalist wing of the small-is-beautiful school.

In this chapter we address both arguments about the relationship between the scale of business and the health of democracy. In our view, producer republicanism has been anachronistic for generations. If gig workers and other part-time workers along with contract workers are defined as wage earners, then the overwhelming number of adult citizens in the United States and similar advanced industrial democracies are and will remain "wage slaves" from the perspective of producer republicanism. There is not the slightest chance that a majority of Americans, Canadians, Germans, Britons, French, Japanese, and South Koreans will once again be self-employed owners of small, independent enterprises, barring a global cataclysm that causes a reversion to preindustrial conditions. What is more, it is likely that the ratio of the truly self-employed in advanced economies will continue to decline as productivity advances and technology enables large firms to continue to invade remaining pockets of small-scale, labor-intensive jobs, such as those of travel agents, taxi drivers, and real estate agents. Either twenty-first-century democracies are democracies in name only or the claim of producer republicans that democracy requires a self-employed majority must be rejected.

With the market fundamentalist strand in the small-is-beautiful antimonopoly tradition, we share concern about the illegitimate capture of government by businesses for their own private ends. But we differ with the conventional wisdom about "crony capitalism" in two ways.

To begin with, corruption is corruption, whether it is caused by big firms or small firms. A republic can be killed by army ants as well as by elephants. Breaking up big corporations into lots of smaller units does not eliminate the threat of political corruption by special interests as long as trade associations and lobbies representing the selfish and antisocial goals of many small producers can intimidate or bribe politician and officials. If political corruption is the concern, it should be dealt with directly, by campaign finance reforms and other measures that reduce the illegitimate influence of all special interests—including small businesses and nonprofit advocacy groups.

Furthermore, market fundamentalists of the political right, sometimes joined by anticorporate progressives, often mistakenly denounce as "crony capitalist" policies of government support for innovation and industry that are legitimate and necessary in dynamic, advanced industrial economies embroiled in intense competition with other nations and that are taken for granted by most of the nations with which the United States competes for global markets.

The Roots of Producer Republicanism

The ideology of producer republicanism has its roots in Enlightenment ideas about "republican liberty," inspired by ancient Greek and Roman political thought. Many Anglo-American republican theorists in the seventeenth and eighteenth centuries defined "liberty" not as "license," or the absence of interference, but as "nondomination," or independence from arbitrary power.[8] In this view, the citizens of a republic had to have a minimum of economic independence, to reduce the possibility that they could be intimidated by tyrannical individuals or factions.

According to Aristotle, "The real difference between democracy and oligarchy is poverty and wealth. Wherever men rule by reason of their wealth, whether they be few or many, that is an oligarchy, and where the poor rule, that is a democracy."[9] He preferred a mixed constitution with a large propertied middle class rather than a property-less rabble. In the ancient Roman republic, the "proletarians" were the lowest class of citizens. Unable to support themselves as independent farmers or small business owners, proletarians were forced to labor for others in return for wages. Their lack of property and their poverty, it was thought, made them susceptible to ambitious demagogues like Sulla and Caesar. The decline of small proprietors and the rise of a large, wage-earning proletariat, therefore, was simultaneously seen as a disaster for individual proletarians and a danger to the constitutional republic.

American republicans inherited the classically inspired European republican tradition's contempt for "wage slavery" or "wages slavery." Working-class "labor republicans" in the nineteenth-century United States sometimes quoted the seventeenth-century English republican Algernon Sidney's *Discourses Concerning Government*:

The weight of chains, number of stripes, hardness of labor, and other effects of a master's cruelty, may make one servitude more miserable than another; but he is a slave who serves the gentlest man in the world, as well as he who serves the worst; and he does serve him if he must obey his commands and depend upon his will.[10]

In his political tract "Commonwealth of Oceana" (1656), the English republican theorist James Harrington argued that a constitutional and accountable "commonwealth" could be created and sustained only in a society in which farmland was widely distributed among citizen-farmers: "Equality of estates causeth equality of power and equality of power is the liberty not only of the commonwealth, but of every man."[11] Harrington credited an act of Henry VII that prevented landowners from evicting tenants who held twenty or more acres with creating "the yeomanry, or middle people" on whom British liberty depended.

The British colonists who rebelled and created the United States were deeply influenced by this tradition of agrarian republicanism. In 1776 John Adams wrote, "Harrington has shown that power always follows property. ... The only possible way, then, of preserving the balance of power on the side of equal liberty and public virtue, is to make the acquisition of land easy to every member of society; to make a division of land into small quantities, so that the multitude may be possessed of landed estates."[12]

In an 1859 address before the Wisconsin Agricultural Society in Milwaukee in which he defended free labor against slave labor, Abraham Lincoln took it for granted that for most Americans, wage work would continue to be merely a youthful stage, to be followed by ownership of a farm or small business:

The prudent, penniless beginner in the world, labors for wages awhile, saves a surplus with which to buy tools or land, for himself; then labors on his own account another while, and at length hires another new beginner to help him. ... If any continue through life in the condition of the hired laborer, it is not the fault of the system, but because of either a dependent nature which prefers it, or improvidence, folly, or singular misfortune.[13]

In the same speech, however, Lincoln looked forward to the progressive mechanization of agriculture, perhaps without realizing that, by allowing a few individuals to grow more than enough food for the whole society, technology would eventually render most family farms obsolete: "It is to be hoped that the steam plow will be finally successful, and if it shall be, 'thorough cultivation'—putting the soil to the top of its capacity—producing the largest crop possible from a given quantity of ground—will be most favorable to it."[14]

More than a century ago in the United States and similar nations the industrialization of agriculture, by leading to larger, more productive farms and creating a wage-earning majority, caused a crisis for producer republicanism. For those in the producer republican tradition, higher prices were worth the guarantee of a "yeomanry" of many self-employed Americans, who underpinned the democratic experiment. Indeed, Alexis de Tocqueville warned that the growth of manufacturing industry and wage labor could undermine American democracy: "For if ever permanent inequality of conditions and aristocracy are introduced anew into the world, one can predict that they will enter by this door."[15]

In our view, this theory of democracy (or, to use the older term, republicanism) was indeed relevant in the agrarian era. But in an advanced technological economy, the link between collective self-government and individual economic independence is necessarily severed because most citizens are not self-employed small producers. This does not mean that concerns about the effects on democratic government of high inequality and wealth and lack of economic independence on the part of most citizens are unjustified. But these challenges cannot be addressed in the modern world by the classical republican solution of making most citizens small yeoman farmers, artisans, or shopkeepers.

During the millennia that preceded the industrial era that began in the nineteenth century, most people, apart from a remnant of hunter-gatherers, were farmers, often unfree farmers bound to an employer or an estate as slaves or serfs. Rulers derived revenue from agriculture, either directly, in the form of tributary payments of crops or livestock, or indirectly, in the form of taxes. Long-distance trade was minor and dominated by luxury goods such as spices and silk, which were taxed by rulers through whose territories or sea-lanes traders had to cross. Technological innovations were so few and far between that a citizen of Cicero's Rome transplanted to George Washington's Virginia would have been surprised by little other than muskets and wind-up watches and clocks.

In the agrarian era, given the limited importance of trade and innovation, the surest way to enrichment was conquest of arable land and the farm laborers attached to it. The more acres and the more peasants you controlled, the more revenues you obtained—and also the more soldiers you could afford. More soldiers allowed you to conquer more farmland, and so on. For this reason, premodern empires—usually controlled by monarchs but sometimes by city-states, such as Athens and republican Rome—tended to expand, amoeba-like, absorbing ever more acreage and ever larger populations, until they met a stronger military force or ran into the natural barriers of mountains or oceans.

In that system, most people were pawns of parasitic warlords. Here and there, in the ocean of agrarian despotism, were sometimes to be found islands of collective self-government. Usually these were in territories in which natural defenses made it difficult for foreigners to conquer them—the mountains of Greece and Switzerland and northern Italy, the marshes of Venice and the Netherlands. The natural defenses also made it unnecessary for the communities—usually city-states with contiguous or nearby farmland—to maintain standing armies of professional soldiers who might decide to overthrow the government and install one of their own as tyrant.

In these small agrarian city-states the idea of the republic was born. An idealized image of the classical Greco-Roman polis or city-republic was passed on to America's founders by Renaissance and early modern humanists. The republic rested on the self-reliant, armed citizen, the adult male head of a household. Because he was economically independent, deriving his family's income from a farm he owned (possibly worked by slaves or serfs) or a small business, the citizen-proprietor could not be bribed to support corrupt politicians or would-be military dictators. And because he belonged to the citizen militia, which substituted for a professional military, he was ready at any moment to take up arms to defeat invaders or internal tyrants.

In the United States, Thomas Jefferson and the school of political economy of which he was the patron saint were guided by agrarian republican ideology. For them, the American experiment was a test of whether agrarian republicanism was possible in what Montesquieu called "an extended republic," not just an isolated city-state. Although Jefferson himself was a rich slave plantation owner, he hoped to create a society of yeoman farmers. Jefferson's grand scheme for agrarian America involved the Northwest Ordinances, which banned slavery from the region of the present-day Midwest; the purchase of the Louisiana Territory, which he hoped would provide farmland for new small family farms for generations; the abolition of primogeniture and entail laws, which would forbid feudal estates of the British aristocratic kind in the United States; and the delay, as long as possible, of large-scale American industrialization and urbanization. Jefferson's yeoman republic would be limited to whites. Jefferson hoped that black Americans could be "colonized" or repatriated to Africa.

The United States never realized the Jeffersonian ideal of the yeoman republic. Regional upper classes, from southern plantation owners to New England traders and merchants, dominated the politics of the early American republic. The plantation South, lorded over by an oligarchy of slave owners with large plantations, made a mockery of Jeffersonian agrarian republicanism. The citizen-soldier was something of a myth as well. George Washington depended on European mercenaries and allies for his victory over the British, and professional soldiers frequently outperformed volunteers in subsequent American wars.

Nevertheless, something like the Jeffersonian agrarian utopia was realized in the Midwest and a few other areas in the late nineteenth and early twentieth centuries. Producer republicanism in America was doomed not by political factors but by technology-driven productivity growth, which led to the eclipse of small producers in agriculture and manufacturing by large, well-capitalized firms.

Many thinkers in the small-is-beautiful antimonopoly tradition have resisted this conclusion. At every stage of industrial development, including the present, some idealists have hoped that the new technology—if not the old—would not only be compatible with a decentralized society based on small-scale production but would actively bring about its reemergence.

In 1812, former president Jefferson wrote to a Polish acquaintance, Tadeusz Kosciuszko: "We have reduced the large and expensive machinery for most things to the compass of a private family; and every family of any size is now getting machines on a small scale for their household purposes."[16] But the age of iron and steam produced colossal railroad companies, steam-powered factories, and expensive agricultural combines.

In the early twentieth century, the progressive intellectual Lewis Mumford hoped that what Mumford called the "neotechnic" era—the second industrial era, based on electricity, radio, telephony, and the internal combustion engine—would witness the withering away of large-scale production and a flourishing of high-tech village life. As he wrote in his jeremiad, *The Pentagon of Power:*

There was no reason whatever to make a wholesale choice between handicraft and machine production: between a single contemporary part of the technological pool and all the other past accumulations. But there was a genuine reason to maintain as many diverse units in this pool as possible, in order to increase the range of both human choices and technological inventiveness.[17]

Instead, electric conveyor belts plus trucking made possible the construction of even larger factories on greenfield sites. The geographic scope of centralized corporations expanded as passenger air travel allowed trips from headquarters to facilities hundreds or thousands of miles away in a day. And vast shopping malls and suburbs sprang up at the intersection of interstate highways, to the horror of Mumford and other proponents of small, walkable, human-scale "garden cities."

In the late 1960s, Stewart Brand and his *Whole Earth Catalog* followers envisioned a similar blossoming. He wrote that "personal power is developing power of the individual to conduct his own education, find his own aspiration, shape his own environment and share his adventure with whoever is interested."[18] Armed with new tools, catalog readers could reestablish themselves as independent artisans and farmers.

The failure of Mumford's electric cottage society and Brand's intentional communities to evolve did not prevent the futurist Alvin Toffler from predicting that the third industrial revolution, based on information and communications technology (ICT), would produce "the electronic cottage" in his 1980 book *The Third Wave*.[19] Technology would liberate workers from vast, faceless corporations, allowing them to be connected "entrepreneurs." While telecommuting has risen slightly, the global trend, as we have seen in earlier chapters, has been toward even larger continental and global corporations and far-flung supply chains united by container shipping and the Internet, with ever-greater concentrations of wealth and income among entrepreneurs, executives, and professionals clustered in a small number of immense "world cities."

To those developments, adherents of the antimonopoly tradition may reply that, while technological innovation may have permitted the growth first of national and then of transnational firms, technology in itself did not require it. Society, driven by corporate interests supposedly, crafted this result.

While it is true that technology does not directly determine any legal or political outcome, this view fails to take into account the transformative effects on society and the economy of technology-driven productivity growth. A simple thought experiment illustrates this point.

Suppose that, in the twentieth-century, antimonopolists had achieved all of their legislative goals for the American economy. Suppose that the Justice Department had wielded antitrust laws far more aggressively to break up all large and medium-sized companies. Suppose that small companies had received even greater subsidies and protections than they have received to date.

Would most Americans still be small farmers or small craftsmen? The answer is no—as long as the victorious antimonopolist regime permitted labor-saving technology. In our imaginary America run by the intellectual disciples of Brandeis and Mumford, technological productivity would not have manifested itself in larger, more efficient enterprises, thanks to the constant smashing of companies larger than a certain size by the all-powerful antitrust division of the Justice Department. But the mechanization of agriculture and manufacturing still would have led those sectors to shed labor, even if those sectors were artificially divided among numerous small, less efficient firms rather than a few large efficient companies. Tractors still would have replaced field hands; robots still would have replaced assembly-line workers.

The neo-Jeffersonians might have achieved their goal of ensuring that most or all companies were small—but productivity would have doomed their goal of ensuring that most citizens were small farmers or manufacturers. Even in the alternative universe in which the antimonopoly tradition had prevailed in law and politics, by the twenty-first century only a minority of Americans would have been needed to produce most or all food and manufactured goods. Even if corporate agribusiness had been outlawed, a relatively small number of highly productive family farms would have been able to produce more than enough food for the entire US population, driving most other farm families out of business.

The only way to avert this outcome would have been to go beyond mandating size limits for farms and companies and to ban the use of labor-saving modern technology altogether. The entire United States would have had to freeze its technology and standard of living at the early industrial level while the rest of the world moved on. Tiny religious subcultures like the Amish and the Hasidim could have managed to do this. But the consequences for a continental nation-state that chose to arrest productivity growth, in an age of cold wars and world wars, would have been much more severe. Among other things, there would have been no American arsenal of democracy to help defeat the Axis powers and enable the democracies to prevail in the world wars and the Cold War.

A related way to avoid the problem of productivity-driven gluts would have been to abandon production for sale entirely. Perhaps most Americans could have become subsistence farmers, growing food only for their own use and using high-tech craft machinery in a garage or barn to make their own furniture, clothing, and appliances. But even if a subsistence economy began with the highest technology available, technological stagnation would soon set in, because self-sufficient family compounds would lack both the incentives and the resources to invest in further technological development.

If technology-driven productivity growth had not been frozen or abandoned to gradual decay, then what would become of the majority of Americans no longer needed to grow food, make things, or mine energy and raw materials? A universal basic income would not have been an option. The Jeffersonian utopia is not socialist, and taxing the minority of highly productive yeomen to let everyone else lead lives of leisure goes against the logic of small-producer republicanism.

Perhaps most workers outside the high-tech, low-employment production sector would become self-employed providers of services to their fellow citizens—nannies, home health aides, caterers, tutors, and so on. But from a strict classical republican viewpoint, these individuals would still be proletarians dependent on wage income and thus unfit for civic life. This would be true even if they incorporated themselves as small businesses, called themselves "entrepreneurs," and reclassified the skills they sold in the labor market as "human capital." The nightmare of classical republican theorists—an insecure wage-earning majority instead of a small-producer majority that owns productive assets—could not be escaped by the mere semantic trick of reclassifying insecure wage earners as small producers.

Our conclusion is that small-producer republicanism is an intellectual, economic, and political dead end. In a modern society, most citizens will not be owners of their own farms or businesses. Most citizens will be wage earners who derive most or all of their income from selling their labor in exchange for employment, and most soldiers will be highly trained professionals who make up a small percentage of the population.

Because agrarian republicanism is irrelevant in an industrial or service economy, we must either abandon the term "republicanism" or redefine it to give it a meaning other than that which agrarians like Thomas Jefferson and his intellectual predecessors and successors gave it. And we must focus on ways to increase the economic security and independence of wage earners other than helping them to exit the wage labor market to become small business owners. In practice in the United States, as in similar societies, we have done both things in the nineteenth and twentieth centuries. We have redefined the term "republic" to include nation-states like the United States whose populations dwarf those not only of the republican city-states of antiquity but also those of most premodern kingdoms and empires.

And there is widespread support, across the political spectrum in Western democracies, for policies that bolster the security of wage earners who remain wage earners all of their lives. The social democratic left supports policies to increase the bargaining power of workers in negotiations with employers over wages and working conditions—policies including a high minimum wage, universal social benefits instead of employer-based benefits, making it easy to form and maintain labor unions, and macroeconomic policies that privilege full employment. On the right there are proposals to lessen the burden of taxation on workers and to increase household savings as a financial cushion. Proposals to limit immigration to create tight labor markets and raise wages have traditionally been associated with the labor left and the populist right. While they disagree, sometimes vehemently, over the means, most mainstream conservatives, centrists, and progressives share the goal of converting a low-income, insecure "precariat" into a numerous and contented "middle class" (the term used in the United States for a wage-earning proletariat with adequate incomes and opportunities for home ownership and savings).

To the conversation about how to ensure that the wage-earning majority in modern industrial democracies has adequate incomes and benefits, antimonopolists of the small-is-beautiful school have nothing to offer other than hoping that more people will start their own small businesses. As we have seen earlier in this book, large corporations pay better and provide better benefits than small, undercapitalized firms. Encouraging individuals to quit working for others and go into business for themselves is a prescription for failure for the majority of small business founders. It is also a formula for insecurity and disappointment for small business workers, who earn less and enjoy more precarious attachment to their employers.

If we do not count wage earners in the gig economy who are reclassified as "independent contractors," then no more than about one in ten Americans at most will be self-employed, either now or in the foreseeable future. Preventing the wage-earning majority from being underpaid and insecure "wage slaves" is important. But it cannot be done by multiplying the numbers of small farmers, craft workers, and shopkeepers. In a modern, high-tech economy, the theory of small-producer republicanism is anachronistic and the policies it inspires are irrelevant.

The Market Fundamentalist Tradition

While producer republicans fear that big business will turn formerly self-reliant republican citizens into wage slaves at the mercy of employers, market fundamentalists are more concerned that big businesses will enter into an unholy alliance with big government and in the process succeed in enriching themselves at the cost of the freedom of citizens and the pocket-books of taxpayers.

The claim that "the corporations" control government at all levels is commonly made in the United States. The case would seem to be undeniable, if corporate spending on lobbying and campaign donations is considered in isolation from other political spending and if it is assumed that lobbyists and donors usually get their way. But these assumptions are unrealistic. When all sources of financial influence on politics are considered, it is clear that big business competes for influence with individual wealthy donors, nonprofit organizations, and trade associations representing small business. Nor is it the case that big business always gets its way. Indeed, on many issues, from corporate tax reform to infrastructure investment and immigration reform, the corporate sector has experienced repeated defeat in American politics.

Let us begin with campaign finance and lobbying. In 1907 Congress banned corporations from donating to federal political campaigns. In 1947 Congress then prohibited both unions and corporations from making independent political expenditures to help federal political candidates indirectly. But in 2010, in *Citizens United v. Federal Election Commission*, the Supreme Court ruled that both unions and corporations could spend unlimited amounts to help candidates as long as their expenditures were "independent" of parties and candidates.

The biggest winners of the campaign spending arms race begun by *Citizens United* have been not corporations but rich individuals. By February 2016, nearly half of the money that went into Super PACs—41 percent—came from only fifty "megadonors" and their relatives, led by Tom Steyer, a former hedge fund manager who contributes to environmentalist organizations and Democrats.[20]

Megadonors are an elite within an elite. According to Open Secrets, in the 2016 election only 0.52 percent of the US population made political contributions large enough to be itemized—$200 or over. This one-half of 1 percent of the population was responsible for 70.4 percent of all individual contributions to federal candidates, parties, and PACs.[21] Some of these megadonors made their money in the corporate sector, as founders of startups or in some cases as CEOs; others come from finance or real estate; a substantial number inherited their money. It is hard to make a case that their motive for massive political spending is to win benefits for particular industries, much less particular companies or banks. On the contrary, studies show that many of them are motivated by ideology and partisanship, and in most cases they are motived by a desire to improve society.

The partisan preferences of individual megadonors are not typical of the US population. The politics of the American donor class skews in a libertarian direction—liberal on social issues, libertarian in economics. The average megadonor is far more likely than the average American voter to oppose higher taxes on the rich, support high levels of immigration, and favor cutting middle-class entitlements including Social Security and Medicare.[22] But the self-interest of the rich, as a class, in policies like abolishing estate taxes and lowering capital gains and income tax rates is different from the particular objectives of particular corporations and particular industries, which typically involve matters of industry-specific regulation and business-related tax breaks.

What about lobbying by corporations and other economic interest groups, rather than individuals? According to Maplight, most of the top ten spenders on lobbying from 2008 to 2016 were not individual corporations at all but trade associations, with the US Chamber of Commerce at the top, followed by the National Association of Realtors, the US Chamber of Commerce

Institute for Legal Reform, and Apparel for All. Two corporations—General Electric and Boeing—came in fourth and ninth place, respectively. But the rest are trade or professional associations, including the Pharmaceutical Research & Manufacturers of America, the American Medical Association, the American Hospitals Association, and the National Cable & Telecommunications Association.[23] Of the top sixteen business PACs, five represent small business (National Association of Realtors, National Beer Wholesalers, National Auto Dealers Association, National Association of Insurance and Financial Advisors, and Credit Union National Association).[24]

Some of the industries represented by trade associations with deep pockets are dominated by large firms because they are increasing-returns industries, like pharmaceuticals and cable and broadband. But the top spender, the US Chamber of Commerce, represents many small firms, and the number two lobbying spender, the National Association of Realtors, represents a highly fragmented industry in which the typical realtor's office is local and employs only a few people. For its part, the American Medical Association has long represented the interests of physicians working alone or in small partnerships, who until recently accounted for most doctors.

Lobbying expenditures, like campaign donations, probably exaggerate the influence of large companies and minimize the actual influence of small businesses. Much of the influence of small business arises from geography. In every congressional district and every state there are family farmers, franchise owners, automobile dealers, realtors, and others whose support politicians cannot ignore. In contrast, the headquarters and production facilities of major national and global corporations are found in a relatively small number of places. Every American state has family farmers and realtors; far fewer have automobile or aerospace manufacturers. Local businesses and their employees and suppliers provide the small business lobby with an unpaid auxiliary army whose influence is exercised through the ballot box rather than by means of campaign contributions. As Charles Brown, James Hamilton, and James Medoff write, "As a lobbyist for the National Federation of Independent Business (NFIB) put it in assessing the impact of these political resources: 'Small business is a terrifically effective lobbying force. There are more of us. Our members are personally involved in their businesses; they aren't managers. Our people make up the vast majority of the moderate-to-conservative, politically active people back home.'"[25]

Moreover, while large firms sometimes lobby for what economists call rent-seeking activities, which divide the economic pie rather than grow it, so too do small firms. For example, the National Federation of Independent Business's lobbying agenda features three main rent-seeking issues: cutting the tax rates of the wealthy (e.g., cutting the top marginal tax rate and repealing the estate tax), repealing the Affordable Care Act, and eliminating regulations.[26]

To imagine that if the economy was made up just of small "yeoman" businesses, they would not lobby for programs to protect their economic interests, is to ignore political realty. Small car dealers would still lobby to prohibit large car manufacturers from selling directly to consumers. Small dairy farmers would still lobby for subsidies and trade protection. Organic food growers would still lobby to raise food prices by limiting the use of biotechnology-based crops.

In contrast, a not insignificant share of big companies' political lobbying is for actions to benefit not only them but also society, such as more spending on infrastructure, education, and scientific research, where all too often average voters don't care or resist such spending as they don't want to pay more in taxes. On these kinds of issues corporations' interests and society's overlap. An example is the lobbying agenda of the Business Roundtable (BRT), the leading trade association of large corporations in America. To be sure, it calls for lower taxes and regulatory reform (using more cost-benefit analysis), but it also pushes for policies to rebuild infrastructure, improve education and training, support clean energy and fight climate change, and strengthen cybersecurity.[27] And while action in these policy areas would help BRT members, it would also help the republic.

How effective are expenditures on campaign contributions and finance? According to a recent academic study, resources account for less than five percent of the difference between lobbying efforts that succeed and those that fail.[28] Major changes in public policy, such as the Affordable Care Act, tend to occur only when a president or party makes the reform a signature issue for political reasons. The political scientist Frank Baumgartner, one of the study's coauthors, explains: "Sixty percent of the time, nothing happens. … We see a pattern of no change, no change and no change—and then some huge reform."[29] As a general rule, special interests are most likely to succeed in influencing small, technical issues of little interest to the general public—a regulation here, a tax credit there—and are least influential when it comes to major issues of concern to voters. This rule can be illustrated in one area of public policy after another.

The American corporate sector, for example, has long supported "comprehensive immigration reform" that would include an amnesty for the roughly 11 million illegal immigrants already resident in the United States, in addition to increases in the number of legal immigrants. Notwithstanding the consensus in favor of these policies by corporate America, attempts at comprehensive immigration reform in 2006–2007 and again in 2013–2014 were doomed by grassroots voter opposition. For example, an obscure college professor, David Brat, defeated Republican House majority leader Eric Cantor in the 2014 Republican primary for Virginia's seventh congressional district. Brat was unknown and Cantor was one of the most powerful, best-funded members of Congress. But Brat rode populist conservative opposition to Cantor's pro-employer immigration policies to victory, in an election in which a sitting House majority leader was defeated by a primary challenger for the first time since 1899.

Corporate tax reform is another area in which policies favored by a broad spectrum of the business community have repeatedly failed to gain support in Congress. Most economists agree that corporate taxes are inefficient, causing the "deadweight loss" associated with elaborate schemes for tax avoidance. Because they are ultimately paid by individuals—shareholders, corporate employees, or consumers—corporate taxes should be reduced and made up for by increased direct taxes on individuals that do not incentivize wasteful tax-avoiding behavior by firms. Despite support from the business establishment and most academic economists, attempts to lower or eliminate corporate taxation have been successfully opposed to date not only by progressives and populists animated by anticorporate sentiment but also by the small business lobby, which holds corporate tax reform hostage to cutting individual taxes on high earners.[30]

If there is an exhibit A in the case that corporations are not all-powerful in Washington, D.C., it is provided by the controversy over the Ex-Im Bank (Export-Import Bank). Most leading industrial nations support their manufacturers' efforts to export by providing low-interest loans, loan guarantees, and other forms of aid to the purchasers of manufactured exports in other nations, including foreign governments and foreign firms. America's Ex-Im Bank dates back to the New Deal era of the 1930s and has long enjoyed the support of both parties in Congress and has been reauthorized every few years.

In 2015, populist conservatives and libertarians in Congress, who demonized the Ex-Im Bank as a form of illegitimate "crony capitalist" welfare for corporations, prevented its reauthorization. Nearly half a year passed before Congress finally reauthorized the institution. Whatever one's view of this particular institution—we believe it is effective and needed—the controversy over the Ex-Im Bank makes it clear that business does not automatically get its way in Washington, D.C., or even within the Republican Party, traditionally known as the pro-business party.

It is not our purpose to argue that special-interest spending does not influence public policy, sometimes to the detriment of the public interest. But large firms are simply one of many kinds of special interests, in addition to small producers represented by powerful national trade and professional associations, nonprofit organizations such as universities and single-issue advocacy groups, and individual megadonors. If the goal is to get money out of politics, then the focus should be on comprehensive and direct campaign finance and lobbying reform, not on breaking up large firms.

Our purpose in this chapter has not been to minimize the very real tensions between big business and democratic government but to direct attention to practical rather than irrelevant ways to deal with them. Whether the evil is the warping of public policy by special interests or the need to strengthen the economic security of ordinary citizens, the answers do not include antitrust, punitive restrictions on large businesses or small business subsidies and other favors.

Blaming outcomes in American politics on special interests—be they large corporations or small businesses—diverts attention from the very real ideological and class divisions within the American body politic. It is comforting to believe that all ordinary Americans are in fundamental agreement about what government should do, and only the behind-the-scenes machinations of special interests motivated by greed can explain the failure to act in the public interest.

But Americans do not agree on the public interest and never have. That is why there are two major parties instead of a single uncontested party that wins every election by unanimous acclamation. The great debates over US foreign policy and the size and structure of the welfare state and taxation and immigration are debates that divide Americans along ideological and class lines. Corporations and trade associations have no particular influence on these great debates; when they do intervene, as they have done in the cases of corporate taxation and immigration policy, they have often been defeated. The greatest successes of economic lobbies tend to be in specialized areas of public policy of little broad interest to voters. This kind of limited "corruption" is a nuisance, but it is not an out-of-control cancer that will destroy the American republic.

The talk of special interests subverting the will of a unified people seems even more irrelevant in light of the class conflict that is reshaping politics on both sides of the Atlantic and manifested in such phenomena as Brexit and the election of Donald Trump. The gap is growing between college-educated professional and business elites in national establishments, on one side, and working-class majorities on the other. Compared to the tumultuous class war being waged through the ballot box, the question of whether this firm gets that tax credit is minor indeed, on the grand scale of things. Needless to say, if business really were all-powerful, nothing like this kind of class war politics would exist, because the all-powerful, business-friendly establishment would have suppressed it.

In time, the outcome of today's trans-Atlantic political upheaval is likely to be some sort of "settlement" that answers the legitimate demands of populists while maintaining a high degree of autonomy for productive business. The newer deal of the twenty-first century will not resemble the New Deal of the twentieth in its details. But like that earlier settlement, the next social contract within the United States and similar societies will aim to provide adequate income and economic security to the wage-earning majority, not to radically shrink the number of wage earners while expanding the number of self-employed small producers. Some small businesses will have important roles to play as suppliers, among other things, in the dynamic economies of the future. But democracies in which most citizens are self-employed small proprietors have passed into history along with the agrarian republic, never to return.

9   The Strange Career of Antitrust

History, it is said, is written by the winners. But that has not been true in the case of the history of American business that the American public thinks it knows. In popular discourse, the history of antitrust in the United States is treated as a melodrama pitting good Davids against evil Goliaths. In the late nineteenth century, so the story goes, American capitalism and democracy were threatened by the rise of "trusts" (large firms), the instruments of sinister "robber barons." Democracy was saved by the Sherman Antitrust Act of 1890 and by "trust-busters" like President Theodore Roosevelt who stood up to big business on behalf of small business and ordinary Americans. Nevertheless—so the popular story goes—today the control of the US economy by monopolies is a growing danger that must be prevented by thwarting corporate mergers, breaking up large firms, and rigging markets to favor small firms.

The tendency to mistrust big and favor small has a long tradition and is reflected in many aspects of American political institutions. One is competition policy, which in the United States is defined as what it is against: "antitrust." The historian Richard Hofstadter has observed, "Antitrust must be understood as the political judgment of a nation whose leaders had always shown a keen awareness of the economic foundations of politics."[1] The very term "antitrust" is peculiar because it refers to a particular form of business organization—the trust—which became obsolete around the time of the Sherman Antitrust Act of 1890.

Other nations use the term "competition policy." But that is not a perfect synonym for the antitrust tradition in the United States, which has always had two, somewhat contradictory goals, reflecting the division of the American antimonopoly school among producer republicans and market fundamentalists. For the producer republicans, the purpose of antitrust policy should be to maximize the number of small producers—at the price, if necessary, of efficiency and consumer well-being. For market fundamentalists, however, the purpose of antitrust should be to maximize short-term efficiency and consumer well-being by maximizing competition.

These rival conceptions of antitrust policy have always existed in tension with each other. From the passage of the Sherman Antitrust Act in 1890 until the 1930s, the champions of antitrust policy were chiefly to be found among the producer republicans. Their social base was among small merchants, small bankers, and other small business owners threatened by competition from large enterprises. The less industrialized South and parts of the Midwest were the regional bases of twentieth-century producer republicanism. Among the tools they supported to limit competition that threatened small enterprises were federal antitrust law, unit banking laws, anti–chain store laws, and resale price maintenance laws. The purpose of these policies was to rig markets artificially to favor small firms and banks and penalize large ones. Although it invoked the rhetoric of Jeffersonian producer republicanism, the twentieth-century producer republican movement was anything but populist. It served the interests of elite local southern and midwestern retailers and bankers while reducing the access of local workers and farmers to cheaper goods and cheaper credit. Imagine Mr. Potter in Frank Capra's *It's a Wonderful Life* protecting himself not from the Bailey Brothers Building and Loan but from Chase Manhattan Bank.

Beginning in the 1930s, the emphasis of US antitrust policy shifted from protecting small producers from competition posed by larger and more efficient firms to freeing the economy from what Thurman Arnold, the head of Franklin Roosevelt's Antitrust Division of the Justice Department, called the "bottlenecks of business."[2] Meanwhile, after World War II advocates for small business sought low-interest loans, tax breaks, and other subsidies, such as those provided by the Small Business Administration, created in 1953, instead of the older agenda of small-producer protectionism, such as anti–chain store laws. As the small business lobby focused on subsidies and regulatory exemptions, the emphasis of antitrust policy shifted from protecting producers to protecting consumers.

What might be called, with apologies to C. Vann Woodward, the strange career of antitrust in America is the subject of this chapter and the next. This chapter discusses the rise and fall of the producer republican school of antitrust. The next discusses the evolution of antitrust policy from the mid-twentieth century to the present day.

Small Producer Protectionism

The antitrust regime established by the Sherman Antitrust Act of 1890 cannot be viewed in isolation. Nor can the familiar story of antitrust as a rational reaction to abuses of power by large corporations stand up to scrutiny. In reality, American antitrust policy has been simply one of a number of policies of small producer protectionism devised in the nineteenth and twentieth century to protect small, inefficient firms from larger, more efficient firms by privileging the small firms and penalizing the big ones, in the process punishing American consumers and workers, who are forced to pay higher prices or interest rates. The intended beneficiaries of small producer protectionism in the United States have included small banks, small farmers, small manufacturers, and small retailers.

Small manufacturers. Between the Civil War and World War I, the federal courts prevented the Balkanization of the US economy by striking down many state laws that discriminated against out-of-state or "foreign" corporations. But state legislatures, with the occasional assistance of the US Congress, used other methods to try to counteract the advantages that large enterprises derived from scale. Both the federal and many state governments prevented railroads from offering discounts to high-volume shippers or charging lower freight rates for long hauls than for shorter ones. The enforcement of antitrust laws by the Justice Department and the Federal Trade Commission was yet another version of small producer protectionism.

Small retailers. The owner-operators of local general stores and drugstores enlisted the power of the state and federal governments to tax and regulate larger regional and national chain stores. So-called fair trade laws, such as the Robinson-Patman Act of 1936 and the Miller-Tydings Act of 1937, also sought to protect small retailers from competition with larger, more efficient firms, to the detriment of consumers. Local automobile dealers also benefited from small producer protectionism through bans on automakers selling cars directly to the public. With the repeal of prohibition, federal law protected small alcohol wholesalers

by banning direct sales to retailers from producers, a provision that
largely exists today.

Small banks. In Canada, Britain, and other English-speaking countries,
   branch banking created a financial system dominated by a few national
   banks in the nineteenth century. In the United States, however, most
   states had laws preventing branch banking across state lines—or even
   among cities in the same state. The result was a pattern, unique to
   the United States, of thousands of tiny, undercapitalized "unit" banks
   owned by members of the local gentry. Their fragility caused bank pan-
   ics to continue to exist, long after branch banking had eliminated pan-
   ics in Canada and elsewhere. In the financial realm, small producer
   protectionism took the form of first state, and then federal, deposit
   insurance, as an alternative to branch banking. Only in the late twentieth century was America's archaic and inefficient system of unit banking reformed, but compared to other nations America still suffers from
   too many small banks.[3]

In popular memory, many of these policies are associated with the
progressive-liberal tradition in American politics. In few areas is the public
perception of American history so at odds with the reality. The truth is that
for much of the twentieth century the rise of large, modern industrial and
commercial enterprises was viewed as inevitable and desirable across the
political spectrum from organized labor and most progressives on the left
to the pro-business right. His reputation as a "trust-buster" to the contrary,
Theodore Roosevelt, like his cousin Franklin D. Roosevelt, wanted to regulate modern corporate capitalism in the public interest, not turn back the
clock to the premodern society of small producers and shopkeepers. Ronald
Reagan began his career of commentary on public policy issues as a spokes-
man for the wonders of mass production and modern consumerism on
behalf of one of America's largest corporations, GE.

If large-scale industrial capitalism was so uncontroversial, where did
the opposition come from? Part of the answer stems from people's natural
unwillingness to accept change. For the economic changes of this era were
profound. As the business historian Roland Marchand writes, "It was the
strong tradition of localism, the awareness of community as expressed geographically in the small town, that the new power of the giant corporation
had disrupted."[4]

But geography also supplies part of the answer: the American periphery of the time, the South, West, and Midwest. Most of the twentieth-
century patron saints of today's American small-is-beautiful school were
born and raised in the South (Louis Brandeis of Kentucky, Woodrow Wilson
of Virginia and Wright Patman of Texas) or the West (Thurman Arnold
of Wyoming). And support for small-producer protectionist policies was
concentrated in agrarian states, not industrial, urban states. These peripheral regions resented the rise of large "eastern" corporations that sought
through greater efficiency to take market share from the peripheral petty
bourgeoisie. But knowing that they couldn't very well frame their case as
one of one group of capitalists against another, they pitted it as David and
Goliath, just what we see in the global economy of today in which many
peripheral nations—India, Indonesia, various African nations—rail against
the perfidies of "northern" big business seeking to take market share from
their local petty bourgeois producers.

The major disagreement about the legitimacy of large-scale enterprise
in the last century has not been between left and right but between the
industrial core of the Northeast and the Great Lakes region and the agrarian and commodity-exporting periphery of the South and the West. From
the Civil War until after World War II, the United States was in effect two
economies—a modern industrial economy in the northeastern-midwestern
core and a traditional agrarian, natural resource economy in the periphery.
The former exported industrial products to the latter in exchange for food,
fiber, and minerals. With the coming of the railroad and telegraph, the
expansion of national corporations and markets from the northeastern-
midwestern core threatened local elites whose income and status came
from their ownership of general stores, small-town banks, mid-sized farms,
or other local businesses. It was these local elites who stood to lose—not the
workers or farm laborers of the southern and western periphery, who stood
to gain—and who provided the social base for the defense of the small
and provincial against the large and national. It is no coincidence that
as patterns of urbanization and industrialization in the South and West
caught up with those of the older industrial states after World War II, the
public and the politicians in those regions lost interest in the once influential small producer protectionist agenda. In the age of the newly industrialized Sunbelt, crusades for antitrust, unit banking, and fair trade laws
were anachronisms left over from the vanished age of agrarian populism.

At that point, small businesses shifted their emphasis to small business subsidies like those provided by the Small Business Administration, while the mission of antitrust policy changed to protecting consumers, not small producers.

These fights to protect powerful local business elites united small producers in many industries. During debates in the House of Representatives about the Sherman Antitrust Act in 1890, Congressman William Mason of Illinois declared that large firms (the "trusts") may have reduced prices, "but if the price of oil, for instance, were reduced to one cent a barrel, it would not right the wrong done to the people of this country by the 'trusts' which have destroyed legitimate competition and driven honest men from legitimate business enterprise."[5]

Like the small business owner, the traveling salesman was another fixture of the preindustrial economy whose livelihood and status were threatened by the rise of national retail firms and manufacturers that marketed their own products, enabled in this enterprise by the spread of the railroad. P. E. Dowe, a representative of an association of traveling salesmen, lamented that many could no longer hope to work for others and then go into business for themselves: "The history of this country gives examples of poor boys who became great men, beginning at splitting rails, tanning hides, driving canal horses, etc. ... Trusts have come, however, as a curse for this generation and a barrier to individual enterprise. What will be the prospects for our children? God-Almighty alone knows."[6]

"Who is this small or independent businessman—the independent producer and the independent distributor?" The rhetorical question was asked by Millard E. Tydings, US senator from Maryland, in 1938:

Why, he is an American institution. He is just as much a part of the life of every community as its church or schoolhouse. He knows when there is sickness in the neighborhood, when there is a wedding, a death, or a birth. ... He is local business with a heart, and often too much heart for his own good. ... I see this great humane and worthy institution, this bulwark of democratic Government—the small independent businessman.[7]

In a 1949 antitrust case, Supreme Court Justice William O. Douglas wrote in dissent:

... There is the effect on the community when independents are swallowed up by the trusts and entrepreneurs become employees of absentee owners. Then there is a serious loss in citizenship. Local leadership is diluted. He who was a leader in the village becomes dependent on outsiders for his action and policy. ... Clerks responsible to a superior in a distant place take the place of resident proprietors beholden to no one.[8]

The civic-minded leader of the village to whom Douglas referred? The independent gas station owner.

For Mason, the small oil producers were the "honest men" who were "driven from legitimate business enterprise" by larger, more efficient and corrupt competitors. For Dowe, the independent traveling salesman rather than the corporate representative was the symbol of republican virtue. For Douglas, the health of the republic required gas station operators to be owners, not corporate employees or franchise holders. For all of them, the goal of antitrust policy was to preserve the existence of inefficient small producers—at the expense, if necessary, of technologically driven productivity and consumer welfare.

Reformers and the Trusts

In American politics, this kind of producer republicanism peaked around the turn of the twentieth century. In 1890 Congress passed the Sherman Antitrust Act, which purported to outlaw "every contract, combination in the form of trust or otherwise, or conspiracy, in restraint of trade or commerce among the several States, or with foreign nations."

Then in 1892 the People's Party or Populist Party was founded in Omaha, Nebraska. With its strongest support in the agrarian South and the Great Plains states, the Populists, alone or in fusion with other parties, campaigned for reforms, including government ownership of railroads and telegraphs, the abolition of national banks, and an income tax that would have fallen chiefly on the millionaire industrial capitalists. Their Omaha Platform declared: "We meet in the midst of a nation brought to the verge of moral, political, and material ruin. Corruption dominates the ballot-box, the Legislatures, the Congress, and touches even the ermine of the bench."[9]

In 1896 the Populists supported the Democratic candidate for president, the charismatic orator William Jennings Bryan, whose support for adding silver to gold as the basis of the US currency was intended to produce inflation, thus reducing the debts of farmers to creditors, many of them in the East. In 1896, Bryan was defeated by Republican William McKinley in the first of three elections in which he was the Democratic nominee. Alarmed by populist radicalism, conservative elites in the one-party Democratic South used devices like poll taxes and literacy tests to purge almost all blacks and many poor whites from the voting lists until the civil rights revolution of the 1960s. The young progressive thinker Walter Lippmann in 1914 described William Jennings Bryan as "the true Don Quixote of our politics," at odds with "the economic conditions which had upset the old life of the prairies, made new demands on democracy, introduced specialization and science, had destroyed village loyalties, frustrated private ambitions, and created the impersonal relationships of the modern world."[10]

Lippmann's contempt for Bryan and Bryanism was widely shared among the metropolitan progressives of his time. As Nicholas Lemann has observed,

The dominant line of liberalism, in the past century, has been in the tradition they favored, based on the conviction that the age of small economic units had ended, and the way to tame the formidable power of the corporation was to have equally large forces on the other side. These could take various forms—a vast, centrally organized labor movement, or new kinds of federal regulation, or even centralized economic planning—but the common thread was the idea of one great liberal power center.[11]

By the late nineteenth and early twentieth centuries, the advantages of large firms were widely recognized by leading American economists. John Bates Clark observed that large industrial companies were "the result of an evolution, and the happy outcome of a competition so abnormal that the continuance of it would have meant widespread ruin. A successful attempt to suppress them by law would involve the reversion of industrial systems to a cast-off type, the renewal of abuses from which society has escaped by a step in development."[12] The economist and leader of the progressive movement Richard T. Ely agreed that "owing to discoveries and inventions, especially the application of steam to industry and transportation, it became necessary to prosecute enterprises of great magnitude."[13]

Welcoming industrial efficiency if not industrial capitalism, most American socialists, labor activists, and progressives accepted the inevitability of large-scale enterprises and viewed industrial combination as a necessary development on the way to a superior social order. Socialists in the Marxist tradition shared Marx's contempt for "the idiocy of rural life" and welcomed the emergence of large-industrial concerns. In the long run the giant corporations would be socialized, they believed. In the short run, former small producers such as craftsmen and small farmers and shop owners would be forced to join the wage-earning class, swelling the ranks of the proletariat. According to the *Socialist Campaign Book of 1900:*

It is but natural that a squeezed pig should squeal. The shopkeeper and the manufacturer coming out of the bankruptcy court would endeavor to enlist public sympathy, but the march of progress cannot be stopped because the unfit are eliminated. The industries are becoming still more consolidated, and the gates of economic opportunity are one by one closed to the middle class. The laboring class opens its ranks and tries to give the newcomer a place.[14]

Non-Marxist socialists also viewed the rise of the trusts as a positive development. For Eugene V. Debs, the five-time presidential candidate of the Socialist Party of the United States, the rise of large corporations made it easier to nationalize industry: "Monopoly is certain and sure. It is merely a question of whether [there] will be collectively owned monopolies, for the good of the race, or whether they will be privately owned for the power, pleasure and glory of the Morgans, Rockefellers, Guggenheims and Carnegies."[15]

William Dean Howells in his utopian novel *A Traveler from Altruria* and Edward Bellamy in *Looking Backward* envisioned a gradual and peaceful transition from big business capitalism to big government socialism. Bellamy's novel inspired a network of Nationalist Clubs, whose publications declared: "The combinations, trusts, and syndicates, of which the people complain, demonstrate the practicability of our basic principle of association. We merely seek to push this principle a little further and have all industries operated in the interest of all by the nation."[16] The democratic socialist Jack London praised the mechanization that big manufacturers were driving, proclaiming, "Let us not destroy these wonderful machines that produce efficiently and cheaply. Let us control them. Let us profit by their efficiency and cheapness. Let us run them by ourselves. That, gentlemen, is socialism."[17] The radical economist Thorstein Veblen favored large-scale industry but wanted financiers to be expelled by "a practicable Soviet of technicians."[18] In 1933 the socialist Stuart Chase published *Technocracy: An Interpretation.*[19] In 1921 Chase and Veblen had joined the Technical Alliance, which, renamed Technocracy Inc., promoted the short-lived technocracy movement during the Great Depression. The technocracy movement presaged NAFTA by sixty years, proposing an integrated North American production system dominated by large corporations and massive public works projects.

The American labor movement favored industrial consolidation for a different reason. It would be easier for unions to bargain with large, centralized companies than with many small firms, and large technology-based firm would produce more profits, which union members could share. Union members in the industrial states often sided with industrial capitalists against southern and western agrarian populists, whose farmer-friendly policies, such as a low tariff, threatened the industries in which they worked.

Samuel Gompers, the president of the American Federation of Labor, told his associates that organized labor should be more concerned with the well-being of poor and landless farm workers than with family farmers.[20] In a 1907 speech titled "Labor and Its Attitude toward Trusts," Gompers declared that the trust was "the logical development of the present economic era. With the invention of good artificial light, of machinery and power, and their application to industry, came the modern industrial plants. With their advent and development the day of individual workman and individual employer passed, never to return."

Gompers went on to say,: "Organized labor has less difficulty in dealing with large firms and corporations today than with many individual employers or small firms." He criticized corporations for abuses and courts for siding with employers against labor unions. But he dismissed antitrust as a panacea: "For the consumer to shout 'down with the trusts' because he finds his pocket-book affected is no more reasonable than the cry of 'smash the machines' which was once heard from wage-workers whose means of livelihood were threatened during the period of adjustment in certain trades while machinery was replacing hand labor."[21]

The progressive movement of the early twentieth century was divided on the issue of scale in business. One wing was represented by Theodore Roosevelt, who called for a "new nationalism" in a speech in Osawatomie, Kansas, in 1910. When it came to protecting consumer interests, the method preferred by many US progressives since the early twentieth century has been the regulation of corporations, not their pulverization by means of antitrust decrees.

In *The Promise of American Life* (1909), the founding editor of the *New Republic*, Herbert Croly, wrote: "The new organization of American industry has created an economic mechanism which is capable of being wonderfully and indefinitely serviceable to the American people" as long as it was supervised and aligned with the national interest.[22] For Croly, the purpose of regulation was not to "level the playing field" by penalizing big firms to help small firms. On the contrary, Croly wrote approvingly, "the regulation of the large corporation is equivalent to the perpetuation of its existing advantages," to the extent that these depended on "abundant capital," "permanent appropriation of essential supplies of raw materials," "possibilities of economic industrial management," and other advantages that were foreclosed to smaller firms.[23]

Today Theodore Roosevelt is often remembered only as a trust-buster. This is a distortion of history, since he distinguished between "good" and "bad" trusts and preferred federal licensing and regulation of corporations to the adversarial methods of antitrust litigation. In his 1905 Annual Message to Congress Roosevelt declared:

I am in no sense hostile to corporations. This is an age of combination, and any effort to prevent all combination will be not only useless, but in the end vicious, because of the contempt for law which the failure to enforce law inevitably produces. We should, moreover, recognize in cordial and ample fashion the immense good effected by corporate agencies in a country such as ours, and the wealth of intellect, energy, and fidelity devoted to their service, and therefore normally to the service of the public, by their officers and directors. The corporation has come to stay, just as the trade union has come to stay. Each can and has done great good. Each should be favored so long as it does good. But each should be sharply checked where it acts against law and justice.[24]

Roosevelt insisted that business "cannot be successfully conducted in accordance with the practices and theories of sixty years ago unless we abolish steam, electricity, big cities, and, in short, not only all modern business and modern industrial conditions, but all the modern conditions of our civilization."[25] The historian Martin J. Sklar notes that "Roosevelt's position was not that of 'Trust-Buster' but of 'Trust-Muster'—he would muster the trusts into the national service."[26] As the legal scholar Daniel A. Crane notes: "By 1912, Roosevelt was staking a position against any trustbusting at all. Far from honoring his "trustbuster" moniker, Roosevelt argued for just the opposite—the legality of large combinations of capital, nonetheless subject to pervasive governmental regulation."[27]

Although his administration had brought the antitrust case against Standard Oil, TR privately regretted the decision of the Supreme Court in 1911 to break up the company:

I do not myself see what good can come from dissolving the Standard Oil Company into forty separate companies, all of which will still remain really under the same control. What we should have is a much stricter governmental supervision of these great companies, but accompanying this supervision should be a recognition of the fact that great combinations have come to stay and that we must do them scrupulous justice just as we exact scrupulous justice from them.[28]

Roosevelt sought to shift competition policy from the courts to an expanded federal Bureau of Corporations, whose decisions would be shielded from judicial review, on the grounds that "a succession of lawsuits is hopeless from the standpoint of working out a permanently satisfactory solution."[29]

The Progressive Party Platform of 1912 reflected the views of Roosevelt, its presidential candidate. According to the platform,

The corporation is an essential part of modern business. The concentration of modern business, in some degree, is both inevitable and necessary for national and international business efficiency. But the existing concentration of vast wealth under a corporate system, unguarded and uncontrolled by the Nation, has placed in the hands of a few men enormous, secret, irresponsible power over the daily life of the citizen—a power insufferable in a free Government and certain of abuse.[30]

The solution was not antitrust—a word that does not appear in the Progressive platform—but regulation: "We therefore demand a strong National regulation of inter-State corporations." The discussion of the Sherman Act treated competition policy solely as a matter of policing the conduct of corporations, not their scale: "We favor strengthening the Sherman Law by prohibiting agreement to divide territory or limit output; refusing to sell to customers who buy from business rivals; to sell below cost in certain areas while maintaining higher prices in other places; using the power of transportation to aid or injure special business concerns; and other unfair trade practices."[31]

In addition, the Progressive Party called for the federal government to help large corporations become more competitive, including by export promotion efforts of the kind later carried out by the Export-Import Bank of the United States (EXIM) and the Overseas Private Investment Corporation (OPIC): "The time has come when the Federal Government should co-operate with manufacturers and producers in extending our foreign commerce. ... In every way possible our Federal Government should co-operate in this important matter." The Progressives also called for "the establishment of industrial research laboratories to put the methods and discoveries of science at the service of American producers." Ironically, agencies like these are often denounced today as examples of corrupt "crony capitalism" by twenty-first century populists and progressives who falsely claim to be the heirs of TR the "trust-buster" and the Progressive Party of a century ago.[32]

But while socialists, unionists, and nationalists like Herbert Croly and Theodore Roosevelt welcomed large industrial firms under certain conditions, the progressive movement of the early twentieth century also included a group influenced by the antimonopoly tradition. In politics they were represented by William Jennings Bryan, Woodrow Wilson, and, later, Wright Patman. Among intellectuals, their leading proponent was Louis Brandeis.

Brandeis grew up in a prosperous Jewish immigrant family in Louisville, Kentucky, and although he made his career in the Northeast, his world-view was that of a member of the southern merchant-gentry class. Brandeis started his legal career in the 1890s defending small firms against large firms, and developed a distinct animus toward large corporations.[33] For him the only reason firms sought bigness was to exploit monopoly power and the only way they attained bigness was through cheating. As the economic historian Thomas K. McCraw writes, "Early in his career, Brandeis decided that big business could become big only through illegitimate means. By his frequent references to the 'curse of bigness,' he meant that bigness itself was the mark of Cain, a sign of prior sinning."[34] Moreover, Brandeis went to great pains to try to paint small firms as being as efficient as large ones, declaring in testimony before the US Senate in 1911, for example, that "a corporation may well be too large to be the most efficient instrument of production and of distribution."[35]

Woodrow Wilson at times sounded like Theodore Roosevelt in his acknowledgment of the benefits of big business: "Modern business is no doubt best conducted upon a great scale, for which the resources of the single individual are manifestly insufficient." Wilson denounced "retro-reformers" who wanted "to disintegrate what we have been at such pains to piece together in the organization of modern industrial enterprise."[36] But, like Brandeis, Wilson was a product of the southern gentry elite and shared its suspicion of Teddy Roosevelt's centralizing, corporation-friendly New Nationalism. Brandeis influenced Wilson's alternative, the New Freedom, which put greater emphasis on states' rights and decentralization. In 1912, Brandeis, advising Wilson during the presidential campaign, dismissed Roosevelt's belief in regulating large enterprises, writing: "We believe that no methods of regulations ever have been or can be devised to remove the menace inherent in private monopoly and overweening commercial power."[37]

Daniel A. Crane has observed: "A striking and often misunderstood fact about the 1912 election is that, although all four major candidates generally agreed that something needed to be done about the trusts, only two of them—the conservative Taft and the progressive Wilson—thought that anything like antitrust law, as we currently think of it, was the solution. The two other candidates—Roosevelt and Debs—favored either regulation taking the place of antitrust or complete nationalization of industry."[38]

From World War I to the New Deal: The Triumph of Associationalism

In 1914, President Wilson signed the Clayton Antitrust Act, which created the Federal Trade Commission and sought to toughen the antitrust regime created by the 1890 Sherman Act. But the mobilization of the US economy by the federal government under the Wilson administration during World War I created a degree of national regimentation far beyond anything proposed by Theodore Roosevelt. Following the war, the antimonopoly tradition sank to a low ebb. The Republican presidential administrations of the 1920s, including Herbert Hoover both as president and as commerce secretary, favored allowing a high degree of interfirm cooperation in the interest of efficiency under the name of "associationalism." Most leaders of the era understood that large corporations were permitting the United States to emerge on the global stage as a leading economy and a great power. Between the two world wars, the US government tolerated the participation of American corporations in transnational cartels beyond US borders.[39]

In this era both antitrust enforcers and the courts were generally willing to accept large firms, in part because they believed that firms needed scale for efficiency. As the innovation policy scholar David Hart notes, in the formative period from the Sherman Act to the New Deal, antitrust was characterized by the establishment of judicial supremacy and laissez-faire thinking.[40] He writes, "The Act is perhaps best read as an effort to recreate the norms of self-governing markets under the watchful eye (and perhaps iron fist) of the Department of Justice and the Federal Courts, without pre-judging the specific organizational forms that would evolve in those markets or worrying much about their consequences."[41] Likewise, William H. Page argues that during this period, "The goal of government intervention [was] the restoration of a competitive market rather than the establishment of fair outcomes."[42] And the courts were focused on abusive behavior to attain or retain market share, not possession of significant market share itself. The Supreme Court wrote in the *Alcoa* case of 1945, "The successful competitor, having been urged to compete, must not be turned upon when he wins."[43] As applied by the courts, antitrust law enforcement in the early twentieth century frequently fell heavily on small businesses, which were charged with collusion, and on labor unions (which won limited exemptions from antitrust laws in the Clayton Act of 1914).

Although he was a Democrat, Franklin D. Roosevelt was closer in his public philosophy to his distant cousin Teddy Roosevelt than to Wilson, whom he served as assistant secretary of the Navy. As president from 1933 to 1945, FDR presided over shifting coalitions with different views of the legitimacy of large-scale private enterprise.

In a speech he delivered at the Commonwealth Club in San Francisco during his 1932 campaign for the presidency, a speech written with the help of Adolph Berle, who with Gardiner Means developed the idea of the separation of ownership from control in modern public corporations, FDR expressed skepticism about antitrust policy: "In retrospect we can now see that the turn of the tide came with the turn of the century. ... In that hour, our anti-trust laws were born. The cry was raised against the great corporations. ... If the government had a policy it was rather to turn the clock back, to destroy the large combinations and to return to the time when every man owned his individual small business." "This was impossible," FDR told his audience. Like his cousin, FDR preferred regulating large corporations to breaking them up:

We did not think because national government had become a threat in the eigh-teenth century that therefore we should abandon the principle of national govern-ment. Nor today should we abandon the principle of strong economic units called corporations, merely because their power is susceptible of easy abuse. In other times we dealt with the problem of an unduly ambitious central government by modifying it gradually into a constitutional democratic government. So today we are modifying and controlling our economic units.[44]

During what historians call the First New Deal, Brandeisian progressives and Bryanite populists were marginalized. Organized labor as well as progressive nationalists like Adolf A. Berle, an influential member of FDR's Brains Trust, supported the Agricultural Adjustment Act and the National Industrial Recovery Act (NIRA). The NIRA, modeled on government-brokered employer-labor relations during World War I, sought to raise mass purchasing power in the Great Depression by allowing industries to cartelize, on condition that they shared higher profits in the form of both wages and benefits with their workers.

In 1934, Adolfe Berle warned President Roosevelt that Brandeis, then a Supreme Court justice, and his allies were turning against the New Deal, which they saw as too favorable to big business:

His idea was that we were steadily creating organisms of big business which were growing in power, wiping out the middle class, eliminating small business and putting themselves in a place where they rather than the government were controlling the nation's destinies. He added that he had gone along with the [New Deal] legislation until now; but that unless he could see some reversal of the big business trend, he was disposed to hold the government control legislation unconstitutional from now on.

Berle told FDR, "His view, if ever stated, would command wide popular support. But as long as people want Ford cars they are likely to have Ford factories and finance to match."[45]

Berle was right to warn FDR against Brandeis. In 1935 a unanimous Supreme Court, to which Brandeis then belonged, struck down the NIRA as unconstitutional; in 1936 it struck down the Agricultural Adjustment Act. The latter was revived with slight modifications in the Agricultural Adjustment Act of 1938. The NIRA, however, remained dead. Following the waves of producer republicanism that produced the Sherman Antitrust Act and the Clayton Act, a second wave was rolling toward Washington, D.C.

Wright Patman and the Chain Store Wars

With the development of the railroad, mass production factories, and a more sophisticated accounting system, by the turn of the twentieth century larger retail stores organized into national chains emerged. By the 1920s, national chains included what would become a number of familiar names, including A&P, Woolworth, Kroger, and J. C. Penney. For many small farmers, the rise of national retail companies was a welcome development, liberating them from the tyranny of the local rural merchants. Following the establishment by the US Post Office of rural free delivery (1896) and parcel post service (1913), southern and midwestern farmers found alternatives to local merchants in the form of mail-order houses. The Amazon.com of its day, Sears, Roebuck was the most important. Farmers would wait with excitement for the latest edition of the Sears, Roebuck catalog because it gave them choice. These new national retailers weakened the exploitative monopolies of the local gentry families who controlled the general store, the unit bank, and much of the farmland. Chain stores improved and diversified American diets by carrying refrigerated meat and dairy products and preserved foods. They made shopping less time-consuming, particularly to the benefit of women. And A&Ps in urban areas provided an alternative for African Americans, who were charged high prices by independent stores.

But the chain stores threatened the local monopolies of general stores and drugstores owned by local elites, particularly in rural areas. A&P, the nation's largest retail chain, was demonized by populists in the 1920s and 1930s in the same way that Walmart and other "big box" stores were vilified by populists in the 1990s and 2000s for putting out of business "Main Street" stores. During the Great Depression, when local stores lost market share at rapid rate, political attacks on chain stores escalated.

The battle over resale price agreements was first raised in the 1911 Supreme Court case, *Dr. Miles Medical Company v. John D. Park and Sons Company*. Miles, a seller of drugs, sold only through contracts that prevented druggists from discounting the price of the product. Favored by small local businesses, which feared being undercut by chains that could engage in discount pricing, the policy was challenged as a violation of the Sherman Act by a larger wholesaler, Park, who wanted to sell at a discount. The Court ruled against such resale price agreements. As a result, small merchants went first to state legislatures and then Congress for protection. Brandeis railed against the decision (this was before he was on the court), writing that "prohibition on price-maintenance imposes upon the small and independent producers a serious handicap."[46]

A "fair trade" law passed by California in 1931 was copied by nine other states, including New York and Illinois, by 1935. Around the same time, fifteen other states enacted resale price-fixing legislation that prevented the chains from offering discounts.[47] In *Jackson* (1931), the Supreme Court upheld an anti–chain store law passed by the Indiana legislature that imposed higher taxes on chain stores, and later upheld a similar Georgia law. Between 1931 and 1940, twenty-two states adopted anti–chain store tax laws that survived court tests.[48] But not all did. The Court struck down a Florida law targeting chain stores in *Liggett* (1933), in a decision in which Brandeis wrote a passionate dissent. Former governor of Louisiana Huey Long, then a US senator but still the dominant Louisiana politician, declared: "I would rather have thieves and gangsters than chain stores in Louisiana."[49]

Another southern populist, Wright Patman, became the national leader of the anti–chain store movement in the 1930s. Born in a log cabin in East Texas in 1893, Patman was elected to the House of Representatives in 1928 in a campaign in which he denounced the "money barons of the East" and declared his opposition to "monopolies, trusts, branch banking and excessive and discriminating freight rates."[50] An agrarian populist in the William Jennings Bryan tradition, Patman in 1934 authored a self-published tract, *Bankerteering, Bonuseering, Melloneering*.

In Congress, Patman served as a front for lobbyists representing small distributors. What became the Robinson-Patman Act of 1936, which outlawed various kinds of discounts that advantaged large chain stores, was drafted by H. B. Teegarden, the general counsel of United States Wholesale Grocers, and backed by that lobby, along with the National Association of Retail Druggists.[51] Patman's nationwide speaking tour the following year, 1937, was paid for in part by McKesson & Robbins, a drug wholesaler that was financing the anti–chain store campaign to gain support of independent drug stores, all the while secretly assembling its own retail drug store chain. Patman's patron, the president of McKesson, had adopted the name David F. Coster to conceal his earlier life as Philip Musica, a convicted gunrunner, smuggler, and bootlegger; the revelation of his crimes in 1938 led to his suicide.[52]

In 1937, mom-and-pop operations won another victory with the Miller-Tydings Act, which amended the Sherman Antitrust Act to allow contracts to prescribe minimum prices for the resale of products sold in interstate commerce, essentially making *Dr. Miles* moot. This was intended to pre-vent volume discounts by chain stores. But the passage of the Robinson-Patman Act and the Miller-Tydings Act marked the peak of the influence of the anti–chain store movement. Consumer groups and labor unions joined retail chains to fight back. The Roosevelt administration and leading Dem-ocrats in Congress, among them House Speaker Sam Rayburn, distanced themselves from Patman. In 1938 the Texan populist introduced a bill to impose a federal tax on chain stores, declaring: "A democracy of opportu-nity and the freedom of individual initiative cannot survive in competition with the unnatural and inherent economic and financial advantages of the chains."[53] Despite Patman's increasingly inflammatory rhetoric—"Let's keep Hitler's methods of government and business in Europe"—the bill died in committee in 1940.

In addition, states and localities, pressed by small retailers, pushed for other legislation to protect them, including Sunday closing laws (to limit competition with mom-and-pop stores whose owners took Sunday off), licensing of florists to keep big chains from selling flowers, and laws curb-ing advertising of prices. As Stanley C. Hollander wrote in 1980, "The list of all such laws is almost infinite."[54]

After World War II, retail chains and supermarkets became such a famil-iar feature of the new suburban middle-class lifestyle that the once passion-ate crusade against chain stores faded from memory. In 1951 the Supreme Court in *Schwegman Bros. v. Calvert Distillers* gutted the Miller-Tydings Act, and in 1976 the act was formally repealed. The Robinson-Patman Act remains on the books but is only rarely enforced. Patman remained in Con-gress until his death in 1976, but in 1975 he was stripped of his chairman-ship of the US House Committee on Banking and Currency as younger Democratic reformers overthrew the old seniority system that benefited reactionary members from what was then the one-party South.

The goal of Brandeis, Patman, and other producer republicans was to maximize the number of small, independent proprietors, if necessary through price-fixing "fair trade laws" and punitive antitrust laws that arti-ficially raised prices for consumers. The Brandeis-Patman approach is not accurately described as "populism" because it served the interests of the relatively affluent and politically powerful petty local bourgeoisie in small-town America, not wage earners and farm laborers and small family farmers whose lives were dramatically improved by the low prices offered by large manufacturing companies and national retail chains, just as their lives are improved today by large efficient retailers.

Antimonopoly and the South

One of the ironies of the antimonopoly tradition is that the rhetoric of the small business owner as the backbone of democracy was deployed most vigorously in the twentieth century in the least free and most hierarchical part of the United States, the American South.

In the South, the rhetoric of the antimonopoly tradition was employed to defend, among other things, the small-scale local monopolies of the rural "furnishing merchant." Between Reconstruction and the New Deal of the 1930s, the old slave plantation system was replaced by the crop-lien system. Under the crop-lien system, farmers, many of them tenants of landlords, would sign away the rights to the future sales of their crops to local merchants as collateral for loans of seed and tools. During this era, there were alliances or even mergers among the petty local despots in the South, the rural merchants and the large landowners. Merchants often used their profits from exploiting local farmers to invest in local land, becoming major landowners themselves. In other cases, landlords opened up general stores for their tenants and neighbors.

According to one contemporary observer, the rural store keeper "was all things to his community. ... His store was the hub of the local universe. It was the market place, banking and credit source, recreational center, public forum, and news exchange. There were few aspects of farm life in the South after 1870 which were uninfluenced by the country store."[55] In the words of one study, "The rural merchant of the Cotton South was a monopolist who held a local, territorial monopoly over credit. As a monopolist he exploited his customers by charging exorbitant prices." The terms on which the merchants made loans to farmers were highly exploitative. The "cash price" offered to farmers who could pay in cash was usually much lower than the "credit price," which sometimes translated into an interest rate of 40 or 60 percent.[56]

The southern country merchants, while fleecing local farmers and laborers, damaged the southern economy. The merchants pressured their debtors to grow more cotton and fewer crops of other kinds, reducing the diversification of the southern agrarian economy. The southern journalist Henry

Grady observed in 1899: "When [the farmer] saw the wisdom of raising his own corn, bacon, grasses and stock, he was NOTIFIED that reducing his cotton acreage was reducing *his line of credit*."[57] This overreliance on cotton worsened the impact on the regional economy of the boll weevil infestation of the early twentieth century and reinforced the dependency of many farmers.[58]

In the early twentieth century, in US counties in which an elite of landowners had disproportionately large landholdings, there were fewer banks and credit was costlier, according to a study whose authors conclude: "The evidence suggests that elites may restrict financial development in order to limit access to finance, and they may be able to do so even in countries with well-developed political institutions."[59]

Unit banking laws protected small local banks from competition by outlawing branch banking among states and sometimes among cities within a single state. As we have seen, the small-town unit bankers and the furnishing merchants were sometimes the same individuals. When the McFadden Act of 1927 sought to require states to provide the same branching rights to national banks that were provided to state banks, congressional opposition came largely from counties in which landholdings were concentrated in a local elite and in which bank credit was expensive.[60]

Far from defending freedom and democracy for ordinary Americans against plutocracy, the antimonopoly tradition served the selfish economic interests and social prestige of the "local notables" or petty oligarchs of rural and small-town America, particularly in the South and Southwest and Midwest. The very regions—such as the South—that were the most supportive of anti–chain store and unit banking laws that preserved local monopolies for local oligarchs also tended to be the regions of the country most hostile to laws protecting African Americans, organized labor, women's rights, anticensorship reforms and sexual and reproductive rights. Those reforms all enlarged individual freedoms but threatened the provincial elite's domination of the social order. When they spoke of freedom, the antimonopolists of the Brandeis-Patman school did not mean political and civil freedom for nonwhite Americans, or the economic freedom for consumers to buy goods at the lowest price from the greatest number of producers or distributors, or the freedom of borrowers to obtain credit at the lowest possible rates. No: when the Brandeisian antimonopolists of the first half of the twentieth century spoke of freedom, they meant freedom from competition that could undermine the income and social status of small-town merchants and small-town bankers.

What Thomas K. McCraw has written of Brandeis applies as well to Patman and other champions of the producer republican tradition:

In the last analysis, Brandeis's emphasis on bigness as the essence of the problem doomed to superficiality both his diagnosis and his prescription. ... It meant, finally, that he must become in significant measure not the "People's Lawyer" but the mouthpiece for retail druggists, small shoe manufacturers, and other members of the petite bourgeoisie. These groups, like so many others in American history, were seeking to use the power of government to redress or reverse economic forces that were threatening to render them obsolete. And in Brandeis they found a great advocate.[61]

10 Brandeis Is Back: The Fall and Rise of the Antimonopoly Tradition

In the middle of the twentieth century, the emphasis of US antitrust policy shifted from protecting small producers to protecting consumers. As we saw in the previous chapter, in the first half of the twentieth century antitrust was only one of a number of methods of artificial political protection of small producers, many of them located in the rural South and Midwest and threatened by national competitors in the Northeast. Along with antitrust, the arsenal of small-producer protectionism included unit banking laws, which privileged local banks; anti–chain store laws, which protected owner-operated general stores from competition with national chain stores; and resale price maintenance legislation, which limited the ability of large retailers to offer discounts. Unit banking laws lasted until the late twentieth century, but the rest of the producer republican agenda was moribund by World War II. Its champions, among them Wright Patman and Louis Brandeis, seemed like throwbacks to an earlier era of agrarian populism in the increasingly industrialized and urban America that developed after 1945. Already in the late 1930s the Antitrust Division of the Department of Justice under Robert Jackson and Thurman Arnold was changing the focus of federal antitrust policy away from small-producer protectionism to protecting consumers and rival businesses from the alleged dangers of excessive market power and market concentration. Arnold declared that the sole test of antitrust policy should be, "Does it increase the efficiency of production or distribution and pass the savings on to consumers?"[1]

This new strain in the antimonopoly tradition displaced the older producer republican strain. For a generation after World War II, US antitrust policy was dominated by the Harvard school of antitrust, also known as the "structure-conduct-performance" (S-C-P) school, which ignored the benefits of scale in many industries and indiscriminately treated large firms and high market shares as bad. For them, markets in which a single firm or a few firms controlled more than a certain percentage of production were automatically suspect, not so much because small firms got hurt as because such markets were alleged to lead to allocative inefficiency, consumer harm (e.g., higher prices), and increased inequality. As a result, their goal, as David Hart has written, was to "establish market structures for ideal performance."[2]

In the last third of the twentieth century, the simplicities of the Harvard school came under attack from two rival schools. One was the Chicago school of economics and its more mainstream variants, both of which were even more extreme than the Harvard school in their religious faith in markets. However, the most accurate and impressive criticism of postwar antitrust policy came not from the Chicago school but from the branch of institutional economics known as evolutionary economics or innovation economics. Economists in this tradition—Schumpeter, Galbraith, Baumol— argued that imperfect competition among large oligopolistic firms in such sectors as manufacturing was a positive good that promoted technological progress, not a dangerous deviation from free market purity. And in a world economy dominated by global oligopolies based in particular nations and often helped by home governments, for one country to pulverize its leading firms inadvertently could lead to the capture of both home markets and foreign markets by the national champions of rival countries. As we will see below, this happened in the United States owing to overly aggressive antitrust policy.

These overlapping critiques of mid-century antitrust policy persuaded administrations of both parties, beginning with the Reagan administration in the 1980s, to adopt more nuanced and balanced approaches to antitrust policy that continue to this day, focusing less on market structure and more on business conduct and looking beyond short-term effects on prices and profits to longer-term effects on efficiency and even occasionally innovation. But as we note in the next chapter, a small but vocal school of neo-Brandeisians now seeks to turn back the clock in US competition policy.

Thurman Arnold and Antitrust Policy

As the administration of Franklin Roosevelt came to the end of its first term and faced setbacks from Congress and the Supreme Court, the critics of big business within the administration started to assert themselves. The anti-monopoly tradition found a champion inside the Roosevelt administration in Robert H. Jackson, who soon headed the Justice Department's Antitrust Division in 1938–1939. Jackson was born on a farm in rural Pennsylvania, which he later described nostalgically as "socially classless" and "the nearest to Paradise that most of us ever know."[3]

His successor, Thurman Arnold, born in rural Wyoming, sometimes also sounded like a producer republican from the agrarian periphery. In 1961, in his seventies, he told a correspondent, "This process [of consolidation] repeated in industry after industry during the period between the first World War and the depression created a system of absentee ownership of local industries which made industrial colonies out of the West and South, prevented the accumulation of local capital and siphoned the consumers' dollars to a few industrial centers like New York and Chicago."[4] But in his 1937 book, *The Folklore of Capitalism*, Arnold mocked trust-busting campaigns as "entirely futile but enormously picturesque."[5] According to Arnold, the problem was not the size of large corporations but their behavior: "There can be no greater nonsense than the idea that a mechanized age can get along without big business."[6]

Partly in response to the threat of populists such as Louisiana governor and senator Huey P. Long, the Roosevelt administration tilted toward the antimonopolists during the second New Deal of 1935–1936. The federal government broke up public utility holding companies and in 1936 passed an undistributed profits tax inspired by the mistaken theory that large corporations were prolonging the Great Depression by hoarding cash instead of giving it to workers in the form of wages or to shareholders as dividends.

In 1937 the United States experienced a sharp recession. Most economists view the "Roosevelt recession" as an avoidable mistake, the inadvertent result of federal policies with contractionary effects: an increase in bank reserve requirements, which caused banks to reduce lending; the first collection of Social Security payroll taxes, which reduced take-home pay; and the end of a bonus for World War I veterans. Reducing the federal deficit by 2.5 percent, these measures caused a downturn in an economy that still had not fully recovered.[7]

Unfortunately, this accurate Keynesian explanation of the 1937 recession was rejected by Roosevelt. In his memoirs, Robert Jackson wrote that

Roosevelt "knew that there were evils in the suppression of competition and that there were evils in competition itself, and where the greater evils were he never fully decided."[8] Having sided with supporters of big business and public-private collaboration in his first term, Roosevelt now refused to accept partial responsibility for the economic downturn and ignored the small group of Keynesians who understood the dynamics of aggregate demand. Instead he listened to Jackson, Benjamin Cohen, Arnold, and other "antitrusters" who had opposed the government-industry-labor partnership of the first New Deal. This group favored the erroneous theory that the Great Depression had been caused not by a collapse of aggregate demand triggered by a financial crisis but rather by monopolies and oligopolies hoarding money and creating artificial "bottlenecks." Arnold shared this view, mocking the Keynesian theory of inadequate aggregate demand: "The cause of spending to prime the pump is the destruction of a free market, and at the same time it is the reason why such spending never does prime the pump according to expectations." The problem, according to Arnold, was not a lack of demand but "economic toll bridges" caused by inadequate price competition among firms.[9] More competition, the theory went, would lead firms to reduce prices, and spur demand, which would in turn spur hiring.

During its brief ascendancy in the late 1930s, the antimonopoly school won a few symbolic victories, including Roosevelt's endorsement of its mistaken theory in his April 29, 1938, message to Congress on curbing monopolies: "Managed industrial prices mean fewer jobs. It is no accident that in industries, like cement and steel, where prices have remained firm in the face of falling demand, payrolls have shrunk as much as 40 and 50 percent in recent months." Unwilling to concede that the problem was inadequate aggregate demand rather than the perfidy of big business, Roosevelt asked Congress to give more resources to the Antitrust Division and also to fund a study of the effect of concentration on the economy.[10]

Ironically, one of the few people ever to read the resulting 1941 congressionally mandated *Report on the Concentration of Economic Power* was the hero of the free market libertarian right, Friedrich von Hayek. In his 1944 manifesto *The Road to Serfdom*, Hayek quoted the report, which argued that "the superior efficiency of large establishments has not been established." Hayek, like today's anti–big business libertarians, denied that there was any tendency toward oligopoly in increasing-returns industries and blamed the idea that there was on "the influence of German socialist theoreticians."[11]

Under Arnold, the Justice Department focused on preserving small competitors and insulating them from "coercion" by their suppliers and from competition from larger firms. One area of special emphasis was distributional restraints. In an era when larger chain stores were emerging, Arnold believed big retailers were undermining the freedom of action of independent dealers. A majority in Congress held this view as well, as evidenced by the passage of the Robinson-Patman Act of 1936, which attempted to protect small businesses from cost-based pricing by their suppliers. The big retailers' price reductions were not the kind the New Dealers wanted to get the economy moving.

His mission, as Arnold saw it, was to break up large firms or discipline them with consent degrees under the theory that somehow this would be the shock therapy needed to get the economy out of the Great Depression. Under his leadership the Antitrust Division grew twenty-seven times, from eighteen lawyers to 500. As Senator Elizabeth Warren (D-MA) has admiringly noted, "In Arnold's five years running the Division, those lawyers brought almost as many cases as there had been in the previous thirty-five years. Antitrust law was real—and American corporations knew it."[12]

With the approach of World War II, however, trust busting fell out of favor, given the need of the federal government to mobilize large industrial corporations to be what FDR termed the "arsenal of democracy." FDR removed Thurman Arnold from the Antitrust Division by the expedient of appointing him to the US Court of Appeals for the District of Columbia Circuit, a post from which he resigned after only two years to become a lawyer and lobbyist.

Antitrust and the Economists after 1945

After World War II, large national, and in many cases, multinational corporations emerged in many industries and often gained considerable market share. There was a growing concern among followers of the Brandeisian tradition that firms in some industries had become too powerful and too concentrated. These large firms came to be seen as retarding entry and innovation rather than driving growth.. The focus of antitrust policy shifted from protecting small firms to policing "oligopolies."

With the establishment of the Small Business Administration (SBA) in 1953, subsidies replaced protectionist measures such as fair trade laws and anti–chain store laws as the preferred method for American politicians to bestow favors on small businesses.

In addition to multiplying subsidies and tax breaks for small firms, Congress expressed concern about increasing market concentration in the two decades after 1945. Adolf Berle and Gardiner Means predicted in their 1932 book, *The Modern Corporation and Private Property,* that, based on the growth in large corporations from the first three decades of the 1900s, the largest 200 firms would hold all corporate wealth by 1970. In fact, as Elaine Tan writes, "The largest 200 and 500 corporations held 38.85% and 50.08% in 1946 respectively, and kept their share in tandem until a peak in 1968, when the top 200 share dropped steadily, losing more than a third of their share by 1997. In contrast, the biggest 500 corporations saw only a gentle decline from 54.64% in 1968 to 50.14% in 1997."[13]

To check the feared growth of big business, the Celler-Kefauver Act of 1950 sought to strengthen the Clayton Antitrust Act of 1914, which itself amended the 1890 Sherman Antitrust Act. The Celler-Kefauver Act empowered the federal government to thwart competition-limiting vertical mergers, in addition to the horizontal mergers that had been the focus of previous antitrust laws. The high-water mark of political concern about concentration was the 1968 submission of the Neal Report, a task force report commissioned by President Lyndon Johnson.[14] It recommended enactment of a "concentrated industries act" and a "merger act" that would mandate deconcentration of any "oligopoly industry" and limit conglomerate mergers.

Much of this policy action was inspired by the prevailing school of antitrust policy in the postwar era. This was a time in which highly mathematical, neoclassical economics displaced other, more pragmatic and empirical approaches in academic economics departments. The dominant paradigm in antitrust policy became the structure-conduct-performance paradigm devised at Harvard University by Edward S. Mason in the 1930s and 1940s and developed by his student Joe S. Bain Jr. and others. In the highly deterministic theory of the Harvard school, market structures in radically different industries could be modeled by the same methods and using the same variables. This view, best characterized by Carl Kaysen and Donald F. Turner, was that market power per se is harmful and therefore should be illegal.[15] The focus of analysis was on market structure rather than on business conduct as the source of adverse economic performance. Because they argue that market forces, including technological innovation, are insufficient to challenge the entrenched power of a dominant firm, the S-C-P school emphasized structuralist solutions, such as aggressive merger enforcement and the breakup of large firms. Even George Stigler, who subsequently abandoned this school, was sympathetic when he wrote, "An industry which does not have a competitive structure will not have competitive behavior."[16]

The S-C-P approach gave a veneer of economic scientism to Brandeisian prejudice against big business. Something like Brandeis's view of "the curse of bigness," detached from the earlier small-producer protectionist agenda that included unit banking and anti–chain store laws, became, if not dominant, at least highly influential in the period from the 1930s to the 1970s. In the 1948 case of *United States v. Columbia Steel Co.*, 334 US 495, Justice Douglas wrote, "No monopoly in private industry in America has yet been attained by efficiency alone. No business has been so superior to its competitors in the processes of manufacture or of distribution as to enable it to control the market solely by reason of its superiority."

The Harvard school influenced federal case law in this era. The Supreme Court in *United States v. Von's Grocery Co.* in 1966 rejected a merger that would have produced a firm with just 7.5 percent of the relevant market because of "threatening trends toward concentration." A few years earlier, in *Brown Shoe Co., Inc. v. United States* (1962) the court declared that Congress intended the Clayton act "to promote competition through the protection of viable, small, locally owned businesses."[17] In 1963, Adolf Berle, the veteran New Dealer and rival of Brandeis and Arnold, criticized the result:

The court found that the four largest shoe manufacturers, including Brown, produced 23% of the nation's shoes, and Brown was third largest, and also that there was a "trend toward concentration." Brown and Kinney together would control 7% of retail shoe stores, and 2.3% of all retail shoe outlets of all kinds. Monopoly thus was not even remotely involved.[18]

From the era of Thurman Arnold to the 1970s, US antitrust enforcers took a very Brandeisian view of the economy, prosecuting a wide array of firms for having supposed market power. But in many cases this aggressive antitrust enforcement was blind to either important technological innovations that were reshaping market conditions or rising international competition. Indeed, in their zeal to limit market power, US antitrust enforcers imposed real damage on a number of important firms and industries, and in so doing seriously set back the US economy, the effects of which continue to be felt to this day. As historian John Steele Gordon writes:

> Those with the hammer of antitrust in their hands have had a record of doing at least as much harm as good. Often their timing has been nearly surreal. Standard Oil was broken up just as Royal Dutch Shell was beginning to provide true competition. In 1948, the very year that television really took off in this country with the debut of the 'Texaco Star Theater,' with Milton Berle, Hollywood studios were forced to change several practices. The purpose was to lessen their stranglehold on popular visual entertainment; the result was to move power in Hollywood from the Samuel Goldwyns to the Barbra Streisands. I am not sure that is progress.[19]

Over the course of several decades, aggressive antitrust enforcement significantly weakened, and in some cases helped kill, a number of leading American technology companies. As Lynn and Longman write approvingly, "Antitrust enforcers weren't content simply to prevent giant firms from closing off markets. In dozens of cases between 1945 and 1981, antitrust officials forced large companies like AT&T, RCA, IBM, GE, and Xerox to make available, for free, the technologies they had developed in-house or gathered through acquisition."[20] They praise such actions as opening up patents to other companies: "Over the thirty-seven years this policy was in place, American entrepreneurs gained access to tens of thousands of ideas—some patented, some not—including the technologies at the heart of the semiconductor."[21] Lynn elsewhere notes that "a study done in 1961 counted 107 judgments just between 1941 and 1959, which resulted in the compulsory licensing of 40,000 to 50,000 patents."[22]

In some cases compulsory sharing of trade secrets—mostly ones, it should be noted, developed fairly through hard work and investment—no doubt helped spur innovation, at least in the short term. But this overlooks two serious problems. The first is the absurdity of having a nation's industrial policy carried out not by the Commerce Department or another agency tasked to promote long-term national productivity growth and export success but by the Justice Department, in adversarial settings dominated by lawyers and academic economists, on the basis of government litigation or threats of government litigation.

Praise for the Justice Department as the promoter of innovation through compulsory sharing of intellectual property also overlooks the very severe damage that this policy did to leading US technology companies, along with the benefits to foreign companies at enormous cost to American economic development, innovation, and job creation.

The AT&T case is a case in point. After inventing the transistor at its Bell Labs facility, the company faced pressure from antitrust regulators to license that technology. And so in 1952 AT&T licensed the technology for a small fee to thirty-five companies. At one level this spurred innovation, as it helped emerging companies, such as Texas Instruments and the predecessor of Intel, Fairchild. But because of government pressures AT&T also licensed this technology to foreign companies, including Sony, which was the core advantage Sony needed to propel itself to global leadership, in the process taking market share from the leading US consumer electronics firms of the time. At the time, no one in the US government could conceive that a company like Sony could pose a competitive threat to US companies.

RCA is another case of unintended damage done by antitrust policy. As Gordon writes, "Perhaps the best example of the harm antitrust has sometimes done to our economy is RCA."[23] Because RCA had a dominant share in the emerging color television industry, achieved by its own internal research and development, the Department of Justice required RCA to share its patents with US companies for free, stating, "By this criminal indictment, we seek to restore competition in this significant industry so that all competitors of RCA can compete with it at every level from the research laboratory to the sale of end products."[24] As an article in *Time* magazine noted, "In what the department considers 'a stroke of industrial statesmanship,' an agreement was reached on a color TV patent pool."[25]

The Justice Department required RCA to provide its valuable patent portfolio to US competitors at no cost. However, RCA was allowed to license the patents to foreign companies for the usual royalty arrangement. Because RCA had long relied on licensing revenue, it now was essentially forced to license its technology to foreign firms, in this case predominantly Japanese firms who were seeking, with little success to break into the color TV market. As James Abegglen, a leading technology historian, has written, "Unwittingly, RCA actually assisted the Japanese by selling them whatever technology licenses they required. It was a highly profitable exercise. ... Clearly ... Japan was dependent on foreign sources for virtually all of the technology employed even to the stage of color television. ... RCA licenses made Japanese color television possible."[26] But without the criminal indictment by the US Department of Justice, RCA would in all likelihood not have licensed its crown jewels to foreign companies, and very well could have survived to this day as a global, leading TV producer.

Armed with this valuable technology, produced through years of research and engineering costing RCA billions of dollars, the Japanese TV manufacturers, which were protected from foreign competition by the Japanese government, soon took over the US market, and an industry invented in America was destroyed. The Japanese government understood the remarkable gift RCA, under pressure from the US government, gave Japanese TV makers. Indeed, when RCA CEO David Sarnoff visited Japan in 1960, he was awarded the Order of the Rising Sun for his contributions to the Japanese electronics industry.

What was the real cost to consumers of this RCA "monopoly"? One study found that it raised the price of televisions by just 2.26 percent.[27] This was despite the fact that most of the product and process innovations in the TV industry came from RCA because RCA had the scale and scope to be able to invest in innovation. As one study of radio producers at the time, including RCA, found, "Firms that were larger and had prior radio manufacturing competence innovated far more than other firms, and pursued more challenging innovations including more mechanization innovations, confirming cost-spreading models of innovation incentives."[28] Indeed, the two leading producers of radios, RCA and Philco, produced more process innovations (e.g., innovations related to how to produce TVs) than any other firm in the industry. As Margaret Graham notes in her history of RCA, "If RCA was no longer entitled to claim licensing revenues for maintaining the whole state of radio-related research, the obvious question for the company was which kind of research should it continue to support, and at what level?"[29] The answer was there would be less research funding and the research would be much less risky. In summary, as Gordon writes, "To protect an American industry from the dominance of one company, antitrust had killed off the entire industry. That's a bit like using a guillotine to cure a headache."[30]

Oblivious to the possibility that its actions might end up driving out of business a US technology leader, the government went after other leaders, including AT&T, Xerox, Kodak, and IBM. Indeed, nearly a hundred of

America's most innovative companies were forced to give away their patents, over 50,000 of them, by 1960.[31] A 1954 consent decree put Eastman Kodak on notice that its attempt to protect its film-processing technology would be heavily constrained. One effect of the FTC's intervention was to allow Japan's Fujifilm to enter the US market for film essentially unimpeded by a competitive response.

A decade later, in 1969, the Antitrust Division sued IBM. As Gordon writes, "With 65 percent of the market at that time, IBM was the eight-hundred-pound gorilla of the computer industry. But by the time the case was finally abandoned as unwinnable, in 1982, the next oversize anthropoid of computing, Microsoft, was already shipping its software and IBM was headed into the worst decade of its existence."[32] A few years later the Federal Trade Commission filed suit against Xerox, accusing it of monopolizing the office copier business, with the head of FTC's Bureau of Competition stating that he would be "dissatisfied if Xerox's market share isn't significantly diminished in several years."[33]

And indeed, Xerox soon did lose half its market share, but mostly to Japanese firms, in large part because Xerox was forced to provide its Japanese competitors with "written know-how, including drawings, specifications and blueprints for existing and subsequent machines. It made an estimated 1,700 patents available to its competitors."[34] As former Boston Consulting Group consultants Mark Blaxill and Ralph Eckardt write, "Practically speaking, they forced Xerox to license their patents to the world. The company agreed to license any three of its patents for free, the next three for a maximum royalty of 1.5% and then the entire remainder of its portfolio for nothing."[35] However, the unintended consequence of the FTC's compulsory license was to donate Rochester's technology to the Japanese, who were able to take decades of American investment and innovation and deploy it in their own products for free. Moreover, because Xerox was so afraid of increasing its market share owing to challenges from US antitrust authorities, it did not respond to emerging Japanese competition by lowering its prices. Within a few short years after the consent decree, Xerox's market leadership had withered as Japanese competitors such as Canon, Toshiba, Sharp, Panasonic, Konica, and Minolta each claimed a significant share of the US market.[36]

This aggressive competition policy enforcement, which blithely ignored the threat of global competition to the US economy and jobs in traded-sector firms, had one other pernicious effect. Because companies were so restricted from merging to gain scale and domestic market share, companies turned instead to horizontal mergers in completely unrelated industries. As former deputy assistant attorney general in the Antitrust Division William Kolasky has noted, "In the 1960s the United States experienced a wave of conglomerate mergers, driven in part by overly restrictive antitrust policies toward horizontal and vertical mergers."[37] In *Lords of Strategy*, a history of the business consulting industry, Walter Kiechel writes, "Antitrust law ruled out acquisitions in your own industry. ... So to plow the proceeds back into your company and to keep getting bigger, you often seemed to have only one choice: buy something in an area unrelated to those you were already in."[38] The problem with these kinds of mergers is that they generated little added value through scale economies or synergies, and were largely undone twenty years later. But the damage had been done: companies not able to gain the scale they needed to effectively compete with rising international competitors, often backed by their governments with subsidies and trade protection, instead spent their valuable managerial time and effort on largely worthless mergers.

Unfortunately, this kind of national industry policy in reverse in the name of antitrust continues in the United States. In 2016 the Federal Trade Commission required that the semiconductor maker NXP divest its RF power business as a condition for its $11.8 billion acquisition of US-based Freescale Semiconductor Ltd. While this was done with a focus on the consumer, it opened up the business for acquisition by the Chinese Jianguang Asset Management Co. Ltd. (a company with the financial backing of the Chinese government). Just like that, critical US technology capabilities went to China, thanks to an action undertaken by the US government. This give-away to foreign state capitalism was anything but pro-competition and reflected a lack of understanding of the new nature of global competition in the technology industry, where the Chinese government has a strategy to enable its firms to acquire foreign technology assets to ultimately displace the US technology leaders in the marketplace.[39]

In the last third of the twentieth century, the S-C-P school with its hostility to any and all market power came under attack from two different schools. In part because of the recognition of the damage done to the US economy by the S-C-P school and changing economic conditions, especially increased global competition, the Chicago school was able to gain followers, particularly during the Reagan administration. Adherents of the Chicago school argued that markets were much more contestable and disciplining than the postwar intellectual heirs of Brandeis and Arnold believed, and that government attempts to intervene vis-à-vis antitrust legislation caused more harm than good.

In addition, the Chicago school gave more weight to efficiency than did the populists, who focused more on distributional questions. The Chicago school argued, for example, that if a merger led to increased market power and prices (which reduces allocation efficiency), it still could lead to overall societal welfare if the gains from productivity increased more than the losses from allocation inefficiency. As Robert Bork, a founder of the school, describes it, "The whole effort of Chicago was to improve allocative efficiency without impairing productive efficiency so greatly as to produce either no gain or a net loss in consumer welfare."[40]

Another assault on the structuralist orthodoxy of the Harvard School came from growth-oriented institutional economics, known also as "evolutionary economics" or "innovation economics."[41] Adherents of the innovation doctrine argue that antitrust policy, and merger policy specifically, need to incorporate analysis of longer-term dynamic effects. Joseph Schumpeter explained dynamic efficiency as "competition from the new commodity, the new technology, the new source of supply, the new organization ... competition which commands a decisive cost or quality advantage and which strikes not at the margins of the profits and the outputs of the existing firms but at their foundations and their very lives."[42] In this view, a merger might be justified, even if it results in greater market power, if the increased profits are invested in research and new product development.

Like Schumpeter, John Kenneth Galbraith argued that large firms are essential for modern technological progress: "[A] benign Providence who, so far, has loved us for our worries, has made the modern industry of a few large firms an excellent instrument for inducing technical change." The very market power enjoyed by large firms in markets with limited competition, according to Galbraith, ensured that they could recoup the costs of developing innovations, before the innovations were adopted by competitors. "The net of all this is that there must be some element of monopoly in an industry if it is to be progressive."[43]

To prove his point by counterexample, Galbraith pointed to American agriculture, dominated by family farmers in competitive markets who did not enjoy sufficient profits to allow them to engage in research and development (R&D): "There would be little technical development and not much progress in agriculture were it not for government-supported research supplemented by the research and development work of the corporations which devise and sell products to the farmer. The latter, typically, are in industries characterized by oligopoly. The individual farmer cannot afford a staff of chemists to develop an animal protein factor which makes different proteins interchangeable as feeds."[44] Galbraith noted that as long as large firms were rare, one "could demand prosecution of the offending monopoly under the Sherman Anti-Trust Act with a view to its dismemberment, or, if this latter were impractical as in the case of the utilities, he could advocate public regulation or public ownership."[45] But that was not possible in an economy dominated by large industrial firms: "It is possible to prosecute a few evil-doers; it is evidently not so practical to indict a whole economy." He mocked the Harvard school approach to antitrust: "To suppose that there are grounds for antitrust prosecution wherever three, four or a half dozen firms dominate a market is to suppose that the very fabric of American capitalism is illegal."[46]

In terms of challenging the dogmas of the Harvard school, the innovation school had far less influence on US antitrust policy than the Chicago school of economics, just as it had and continues to have less influence on US economic policy overall. Both the Harvard and the Chicago schools worked within the unrealistic, mathematically modeled universe of neoclassical academic economics. But adherents of the Chicago school, including legal scholar and federal judge Robert Bork, favored a more hands-off approach to market concentration for several reasons, including a belief that any temporary monopolies will soon be corrected by the entry of new competitors, the illogic of punishing firms for success, and a general suspicion of government power and wisdom. The influence of the Chicago school produced a more lenient approach to mergers and concentration under Republican administrations, beginning with the Reagan administration.

When the history of antitrust is reviewed from today's perspective, the most striking thing about it is how ineffectual it has been in achieving either of its two somewhat conflicting goals of producer republicanism and market fundamentalism. More than a century of federal antitrust policy has failed to preserve a society of small producers; at less than 10 percent, the number of self-employed Americans is about the same is it is in other advanced industrial economies. And in many industries, the market fundamentalist objective of preventing one or a few large firms from controlling large market shares has also failed—fortunately so, in many cases, from the perspective of the innovation school. As the historian Philip Cullis notes, "Antitrust might have prevented American industry from becoming dominated by monopolies, but it did little to stem the rise of oligopolies."[47]

The failure of US antitrust policy to eliminate most oligopolies in increasing-returns industries (it did eliminate some, including the entire US TV manufacturing industry) should be a cause for gratitude, not lamentation. Baumol has warned that because of the contributions to economic progress of innovative oligopolistic firms, they should not be

targets for antitrust prosecution simply because their prices are discriminatory or are not close to marginal costs. ... [T]hcy should not be deemed vulnerable to prosecution simply on the claim that their pricing patterns show them to be the possessors of monopoly power. Such a course can easily constitute a major handicap to the steadily growing expenditure on innovation by private industry, which is arguably a mainstay of the U.S. economy's unprecedented growth record.[48]

Adolf Berle's words from 1963 are just as relevant today:

Large corporations are in existence; not many will shrink. Modern conditions being what they are, the largest will tend to prevail in the competitive market. ... Meanwhile, the small units will clamor to the political state for help or protection, or both. The result is likely to be not nineteenth-century competition, but twentieth-century oligopoly. Atomization as a remedy will not do. I doubt if we can bring back the England of the late eighteenth or nineteenth centuries, or that we would tolerate it if it returned.[49]

The innovation doctrine makes it clear that the focus of antitrust thinking should be on the long-term trajectory of product value and price, not just current consumer welfare measured by short-run prices. As Harvard's Michael Porter rightly argues, "Since the role of competition is to increase a nation's standard of living and long-term consumer welfare via rising productivity growth, the new standard for antitrust should be productivity growth, rather than price/cost margins or profitability."[50]

Brandeis Is Back

However, as we have seen, the neo-Brandeisians are back. As we saw earlier, the major heirs of Brandeis following World War II abandoned his support for measures such as anti–chain store laws that protected small producers from competition but retained his conviction that big firms and concentrated markets are social and economic evils. This view informed the Harvard school of antitrust policy, which focused on the structure of industry, with rigid views regarding market share.

Nevertheless, the neo-Brandeisian approach fell out of fashion beginning in the 1970s, largely as a result of the emergence of the conservative Chicago school of antitrust policy, which focused much more than the Harvard school had on efficiency concerns. This view—whether in the conservative Chicago version or the liberal neoclassical economics version—dominated US antitrust thinking until recently. (In contrast, the Schumpeterian school that we favor has had little influence on antitrust policy.)

But now a small but intelligent and articulate school of neo-Brandeisians seeks to turn back the clock, if not to the era of anti–chain store laws and unit banking laws, at least to the heyday of the populist S-C-P era of the 1950s and 1960s, which treated even minor levels of concentration in markets as per se illegitimate and dangerous. Today's new Brandeisianism has found a home in the twenty-first century Democratic Party, which seeks to demonstrate its solidarity with the working class and consumers through its desire to break up big companies.

For many of these neo-Brandeisians, the defeat of the Harvard team by the Chicago team was the result of a conspiracy by corporations and their academic and political puppets to eviscerate antitrust laws. Even worse, relaxed attitudes toward antitrust enforcement are alleged to have caused or contributed to many of the economic and social ills of the present, from higher inequality to slower wage growth and even the global financial crisis of the global recession of 2008–2009.

According to the Yale law school student Lina Khan, writing in the progressive *Democracy Journal:* "America's monopoly problem today largely results from a successful campaign in the late 1970s and early 1980s to change the framework of antimonopoly law."[51] Derek Thompson writes that "antitrust law shifted over the course of the 20th century from principally protecting competition to principally protecting consumers."[52] Today

Brandeisianism has returned, and "many reformers are calling for the pendulum to swing back."[53] Khan writes, "Some policymakers and politicians today are starting to realize that America once again has a monopoly problem."[54] Khan and Sandeep Vaheesen say that "policymakers and the public ought to recognize antitrust as another tool for achieving a more progressive distribution of income and closing the staggering economic disparity we see today."[55] Barry Lynn and Philip Longman write, "What would a True Populist do today? Immediately restore America's traditional antimonopoly philosophy."[56] Nell Abernathy and coworkers of the Roosevelt Institute want to "tame the corporate sector" by reviving "an open markets agenda for the 21st century."[57]

For neo-Brandeisians industry concentration has developed into crisis proportions and breaking up big companies should be the animating goal not just of antitrust policy but of US economic policy generally. In short, when all you have is a hammer, everything looks like a nail. There is almost no economic problem that cannot be laid at the feet of large corporations and a supposed increase in firm size and concentration and cured by the panacea (literally, "cure-all") of antitrust.

Neo-Brandeisians blame income inequality on concentration and claim that breaking up big corporations is the key to boosting incomes for average Americans. The liberal Center for American Progress writes: "Income inequality is rising, middle-class incomes are stagnant, and much of the current economic policy debate is centered on finding ways to counter these trends. A renewed focus on antitrust enforcement could make a significant contribution toward accomplishing this goal."[58] Robert Reich writes that increased concentration has "resulted in higher corporate profits, higher returns for shareholders, and higher pay for top corporate executives and Wall Street bankers—and lower pay and higher prices for most other Americans. They amount to a giant *pre*-distribution upward to the rich."[59]

Lina Kahn blames monopolization for the "fact" that "the vast majority of American workers have seen their hourly wages flatten or decline since 1979."[60] Yet, as we discussed in chapter 4, recent evidence suggests that most of the growth of the "one percenters" is not in corporate managers and CEOs but among the professions: dentists, doctors, lawyers, financers, and the like, most of whom work for small companies or are self-employed. Moreover, according to the US Bureau of Labor Statistics, not only did establishments with more than 500 workers pay their workers 77 percent more than establishments with fewer than fifty workers, but from 2004 to 2016, real, inflation-adjusted compensation for their workers (based on cost per hour worked) grew by almost $4 per hour ($3.88) compared to just $1.45 for establishments with fewer than fifty workers.[61]

Neo-Brandeisians also argue that the modestly declining share of income going to labor is evidence of rent seeking from industry concentration. But as former Obama administration officials Jason Furman and Peter Orszag note, "The decline in the labor share of income is not due to an increase in the share of income going to productive capital—which has largely been stable—but instead is due to the increased share of income going to housing capital."[62] In other words, more of output of society is going to land and building owners. This is a zoning issue, not an antitrust issue. And a war on the landlords would seek guidance from the ghost of single-taxer Henry George, not the ghost of Louis Brandeis.

If our goal is to increase after-tax wages, there are only two ways to do so: increase productivity or change the distribution of income, through government policies of redistribution or by increasing the bargaining power of workers in wage negotiations with employers. Neo-Brandeisians are decidedly ambivalent about the former, productivity growth, because it sometimes leads to job losses. As Lina Khan writes, "One result of consolidation is fewer jobs, as companies routinely lay off thousands of workers after merging."[63] Barry Lynn complains that increased concentration leads to "fewer and lesser jobs."[64] But when companies lay off workers after merging this is almost always because the combined firm needs fewer workers to do the work. Keeping the workers employed by prohibiting the merger would reduce productivity and per-capita income growth since the workers would be doing work that could be done more productively with a merger. Most, if not all, laid-off workers find new jobs and produce additional output for society.

Some neo-Brandeisians concede that big firms give us higher productivity, and hence lower prices and higher real incomes, but dismiss the value of that. The Roosevelt Institute scholar Sabeel Rahman writes, "If consumer prices are our only concern, it is hard to see how Amazon, Comcast, and companies such as Uber need regulation."[65] Others, however, follow Brandeis, who went to great pains to try to paint small firms as efficient as or more efficient than large firms, writing, "A corporation may well be too large to be the most efficient instrument of production and of distribution."[66] Barry

Lynn agrees, dismissing arguments and data about the superior efficiency of larger firms as "metaphysics."[67] Abernathy and coworkers from the Roosevelt Institute writes that firm size is "the product of distinct political and policy choices."[68] To admit that in most cases big businesses benefit from technology-enabled economies of scale would force the neo-Brandeisians to abandon their economic case for antitrust and base their advocacy on producer republican arguments.

Perhaps a world of small, less productive firms with higher prices is fine because we can afford to pay a premium for our craft-brewed beer, organic arugula, free range chickens, and coffee even fancier than Starbucks'.[69] As Thompson writes, "The bigness of business is a result of federal policy, which, in the past three decades, has deliberately made it easier for large companies to dominate their markets, provided that they keep prices down."[70] So low prices are not a goal? Few Americans would prefer to live in India, where mom-and-pop retailers are protected by government against more efficient larger retailers and because of that are about 6 percent as productive as US retailers.

If productivity growth is not to be emphasized, this leaves a second option, redistribution. And there are only two ways to get the money for that: from individuals and from corporations. Increasing taxes on wealthy Americans and using that revenue to reduce the taxes on middle- and lower-income workers (or to expand public services they use, such as health care) could increase the after-tax incomes of the latter. But significant tax hikes on the rich would be opposed by almost all Republicans and some centrist Democrats. And from the point of view of the small-is-beautiful school, redistribution from the rich would be undesirable because it would leave the pre-tax concentration of income and wealth intact.

What about paying for higher redistribution through raising taxes on corporations rather than individuals? How much would the average American benefit if the corporate profit rate was the same as it was in the glory days of the 1950s and 1960s, when antitrust enforcement was much tougher and wage growth much higher? Returning to the profits rate of that era would, at least in the short term, actually make American workers worse off, since corporate profits as a share of GDP were higher then. From 1947 to 1968, corporate profits accounted for 10.3 percent of GDP, while from 1994 to 2015 they accounted for 8.2 percent. To be fair, one reason is because more companies have organized as partnerships and S corporations rather than C corporations to avoid paying the corporate income tax. But even with this trend, income going to "proprietors" (e.g., business owners of non-C corporations) declined from 10.4 percent of GDP to 7.2 percent over the last two decades. So did corporate profits. According to the US Bureau of Economic Analysis the average corporate profit rate from 1965 to 1966 was 13.6 percent, slightly higher than the average profits for 2015 through the third quarter of 2016 (13.3 percent).[71] Yet during the 1960s median wage growth was significantly higher, even with those profit levels.

Let's assume that neo-Brandeisians get their way and break up most large companies into medium-sized ones, and that this somehow reduces corporate profits 25 percent, to 6 percent. Further, let's assume that the resulting decline in business investment from lower profits has no effect on growth and that all the fall in profits goes to price declines. Let's further assume that none of the price declines benefit the top 10 percent (we will assume they pay the old higher prices) but that all the loss of profits hurts the top 10 percent (we will assume that middle-income Americans own no stock whose value would decline from lower profits). So how much would median incomes increase? A whopping—get ready for it—3.1 percent.[72] Not only is this a de minimis amount, it's a one-time effect. The bottom 90 percent would enjoy 3.1 percent higher incomes for the rest of their lives relative to the base case.

One reason for this is that there is just not that much money here. As finance professor Craig Pirrong writes, "In 2015, after-tax corporate income represented only about 10 percent of US national income. Market power rents represented only a fraction of those corporate profits. Market power rents that could be affected by more rigorous antitrust enforcement represented only a fraction–and likely a small fraction–of total corporate profits."[73]

But the negative effects of this would quickly swamp this small static redistributional gain. Firms would be smaller and therefore often less productive. If we assume that the Brandeisians were successful in shrinking the size of large firms so that the United States had the same firm size structure as Canada, US per capita GDP would decrease by 3.4 percent, because on average, smaller firms are less productive than larger firms. But this too is a one-time effect. The negative dynamic effects are likely even larger. Lower profits would reduce investment in R&D and machinery and equipment; according to one study, a cut in profits by $1 would reduce investment by between 32 and 62 cents.[74] This decline would in turn reduce productivity and wage growth. So, it is clear that campaign to reduce the size of large corporations would result in reduced living standards for most Americans.

As an alternative to redistribution, higher wages, whether resulting from a higher minimum wage, more unionization, or tighter labor markets, would be denounced by small businesses that are less able than big firms to respond by investing in labor-saving technology.

The ironies in the archeological excavation of the long-buried antimonopolist tradition in the early twenty-first century are striking. Today's progressive antimonopolists claim they want a return to the golden age of high wages in the decades after World War II. But John Kenneth Galbraith, the leading liberal economist of the mid-twentieth century, thought that the cult of small business was anachronistic. And the labor unions of the New Deal era preferred to negotiate with dynamic industrial oligopolies like the Big Three automakers. Organized labor faced unremitting hostility from the kind of small business owners idealized by today's gentry liberals of the small-is-beautiful school.

Far from being a return to New Deal liberalism, the Brandeisian revival is based on the two strands of the older antimonopoly school that were decisively marginalized by the mainstream New Deal Democrats between the 1940s and the 1970s—producer republicanism and market fundamentalism. Indeed, during the heyday of New Deal liberalism, champions of small firms and "open markets" were more likely to be found on the anti–New Deal right than on the liberal left.

Equally striking, to the eyes of the economic historian, are the parallels between the growth in influence of small-is-beautiful antitrusters on the center left in the late 1930s and in the 2010s. In Franklin Roosevelt's second term, as in Barack Obama's two terms, recovery from a catastrophic global economic collapse continued to be painfully slow. In both cases the incumbent Democratic administration worsened the macroeconomic situation by prematurely trying to balance the budget. In both the Roosevelt and the Obama administrations, this provided an opportunity for members of the antimonopoly tradition to argue for the same erroneous diagnosis of the slow-growth problem—excessive concentration of economic power—and the same mistaken diagnosis—much more aggressive antitrust. In both the late 1930s and the 2010s, this analysis ignored the real problem of inadequate aggregate demand, caused in both cases by a financial panic, not overconcentration (businesses did not abruptly become bigger right before 1929 or 2008).

In the Roosevelt years, wartime mobilization solved the problem of low aggregate demand. And the prosperity of the postwar years was generated in large part by the emergence of a new powerful Schumpeterian innovation wave based on electromechanical technologies, while the ability of workers to share the high profits of industrial oligopolies, with the help of unionization and tight labor markets, spurred wage growth. The explanation of the Great Depression as a result of too much concentration of industry was discredited and relegated to the footnotes of historians. If we are correct, today's neo-Brandeisian school will share a similar fate at some point in the next generation when the next Schumpeterian innovation wave begins to kick in and higher levels of growth result.

11   Has Big Business Gotten Too Big?

As we have seen, a passionate and articulate school of neo-Brandeisians seeks to turn back the clock, if not to the era of anti–chain store laws and unit banking laws, at least to the heyday of the era of the 1950s and 1960s in antitrust policy, influenced by the Harvard structure-conduct-performance school, which treated even minor levels of concentration in markets as per se illegitimate and dangerous. If today's new Brandeisians are to be believed, industry consolidation is rampant and profits are through the roof in America. Senator Elizabeth Warren paints a near apocalyptic picture: "Today, in America, competition is dying. Consolidation and concentration are on the rise in sector after sector."[1] Barry Lynn and Phillip Longman write that "the degree of consolidation in many industries today bears a striking resemblance to that of the late Gilded Age. … In nearly every sector of our economy, far fewer firms control far greater shares of their markets than they did a generation ago."[2] Nell Abernathy and coworkers at the Roosevelt Institute write: "Market concentration in over 600 sectors increased."[3] Jason Furman, head of the Obama White House Council of Economic Advisors declared: "Between 1997 and 2012, market concentration increased in 12 out of 13 major industries for which data are available, and a range of micro-level studies of sectors including air travel, telecommunications, banking, and food-processing have all produced evidence of greater concentration."[4] But as we will see, most of these claims are either not true or not relevant.

Historical Trends in Concentration

Let's start with historical trends. Elaine Tan, in a study of share of the economy by large firms in the United States from 1931 to 2000 found,

"When big business is defined as the largest 200 or 500 non-financial corporations, its share of assets was never as high as it was during World War II, and was declining or stable after the merger wave of the late-1960s."[5] Likewise, the percentage of manufacturing industries in which the top four firms accounted for more than 50 percent of shipments increased only slightly from 1952 to 2007, from 35 percent to 39 percent, hardly evidence of rampant monopolization.[6] The revenue of the largest 200 US corporations as a percentage of total business revenue did grew, but only from 24 percent in 1954 to 29 percent in 2008.[7] These figures include overseas sales, and since large firms are more likely to sell overseas, and since overseas sales have grown faster than domestic sales over the last half century, this increase doesn't necessarily reflect domestic market share.[8] Moreover, the number of mergers under the Hart-Rodino reporting requirement was lower in the 2000s (1,524 per year) than in the prior two decades (2,881 and 2,246, respectively).[9]

It's also important to use the right measures. The Obama Council of Economic Advisers warned that "the majority of industries have seen increases in the revenue share enjoyed by the 50 largest firms between 1997 and 2012."[10] But the C50 ratio (the amount of any particular market captured by the largest fifty firms) is largely meaningless from an anti-trust perspective. If all fifty firms in an industry had equal market share, they would hold just 2 percent. Or the increase could have come from firms with relatively small market share (firms forty-one to fifty) gaining market share from firms fifty-one to one hundred. Moreover, the CEA looked at two-digit industries (e.g., the broadest classification of different industries, such as wholesale trade, finance and insurance, etc.) which are too broad to represent real markets where market power can be exercised. As Carl Shapiro, U.C. Berkeley economist and former member of the Obama Council of Economic Advisers, states, "I don't know any Industrial Organization economist who thinks that's very informative regarding market power. At some broad level, larger firms are having a larger share of economic activity—I think that's true, but that doesn't directly tell us about competition or concentration in markets where market power can be exercised."[11]

To really understand market power and competition it's important to look beyond two and even three digit industries and beyond C50 and even C20 ratios. A more relevant indicator is change in the C4 and C8 ratios at the six-digit industry level. From 2002 to 2012, 59 percent of

792 six-digit-level industries (e.g., flour milling) saw an increase in the C4 ratio, 63 percent in the C8 ratio, and two-thirds in the C20 and C50 ratios.[12] This seems to support the neo-Brandeisians. But on closer look it's not so clear.

First, at the three-digit level, many industries saw no change or even a decline: accommodation and food services (0 percent); arts, entertainment and recreation (0 percent); real estate and rental and leasing (–6 percent); and wholesale trade (–25 percent). Within the twenty-one three-digit manufacturing industries, almost half saw either no increase or a decrease. For example, despite some high-profile mergers, the beverage and tobacco manufacturing industry saw a decrease in the C4 ratio of 14 percent.[13]

Second, it's important to look not just at the direction of change but also at the absolute concentration levels. If industries with low C4 and C8 ratios get slightly more concentrated, that is not a problem. For example, the C4 ratio for the administrative and support and waste management and remediation services industry increased 32 percent between 2002 and 2012. But the share held by the largest four firms increased from just 6 percent to 8 percent, hardly evidence of monopoly power. Likewise, retail C4 increased by 23 percent, but from just 11 percent to 14 percent. In fact, the majority of the C4 increases were in industries that were relatively unconcentrated. Just 16 percent of the industries that saw a rise in the C4 ratio had a C4 ratio higher than 40 percent in 2002, and just 19 percent had a C8 ratio of more than 50 percent.

In addition, increases in concentration often benefit consumers. For example, the fifty largest retail firms increased their market share by 11.2 percentage points. But this meant that more Americans were shopping at efficient, lower priced retailers. As Ryan Decker and coauthors write,

Most of the labor productivity growth in this sector has been attributed to net entry. In many cases, existing firms improve productivity in retail trade primarily through adding new, more-productive retail locations rather than expanding existing establishments. Moreover, much of the exit of low-productivity retail establishments in the US economy has been dominated by the exit of "mom and pop" single-establishment firms.[14]

We see a similar picture in other industries. Between 2002 and 2012, about half of manufacturing industries got more concentrated and half less. But even the concern with the ones that got more concentrated overstates the problem because the issue is what levels of concentration were reached.

Between 2002 and 2012, of 86 four-digit manufacturing industries (such as communications equipment manufacturing), 33 saw declines in their C4 ratio, while the average firm saw its C4 ratio increase by just 8 percent, to 30 percent.[15] Moreover, sixty-one either had a four-firm concentration of 30 percent or less in 2012 or the change from 2002 to 2012 was negative. Thirty-eight saw declines in the eight-firm concentration ratio, with the average ratio going up just 6 percent. But these modest increases in concentration were likely pro-growth as a number of studies find that plants acquired by other firms in the same manufacturing industry experience above-average productivity gains after they are purchased.[16] Robert McGuckin and Sang Nguyin found that plants that were acquired increased their productivity, writing: "acquisition suggests that synergy is a dominant motive for takeovers during the period under study."[17]

The neo-Brandeisian case is in part that concentration leads to higher profits, something the scholarly literature generally finds to be true. One review found that although some studies found that firms with higher market share were less profitable, most studies found they were more profitable.[18] The article estimated that a 1 percent increase in market share led on average to a 0.14 percent increase in profits measured as return on sales. But the key question is whether these profits come from oligopolistic rent seeking or from superior productivity and performance. If it's the latter, then the firms are simply being rewarded with greater sales for superior performance that benefits the economy.

Importantly, the review finds that increases in industry concentration do not lead to an increase in pricing power. The authors write, "The meta-analysis also fails to support market power theory. Price and industry concentration (which can be proxies for market power) do not moderate the impact of market share on profits."[19] In other words, firms with greater market share enjoy higher profits but this does not seem to be a result of market power. For example, a firm that has 3 percent of a market would be more profitable if it had a 6 percent share, even though at 6 percent it would normally still have no market power. The authors suggest that one reason increased size leads to higher profits is because size makes it easier for firms to boost product quality. Moreover, multiple studies have found that mergers increase the combined firm productivity. For example, a report by the US Bureau of Labor Statistics noted: "Mergers are found to have a positive impact upon TFP [total factor productivity] growth, accounting for 0.36 percentage points of total factor productivity growth between census years."[20]

One recent study that has been receiving considerable attention is from economists Jan De Loecker and Jan Eeckhout who attempt to measure the price levels firms charge above the marginal cost of producing each good or service.[21] They found that this markup has gone up over the last 37 years from 17 percent to 67 percent and postulate that much of this increase is owing to increases in market power. But a closer look suggests that something other than market power is at work here. First, they compare markups with overall growth of the market value of firms in the United States, assuming that reflects total net present value of profits. The total amount of profits is not the right measure, however: the rate of profit is. As we note, the rate of corporate profits is essentially the same today as it was in the 1960s when markups were much lower. If markups increased almost four times during this period, surely the rate of corporate profits would have gone up more than a few percent.

Second, they find that markups tend to be higher in smaller firms, which, by definition, have less market power.[22] Third, they find similar markup patterns among industries that have dramatically different concentration ratios. Markups went up considerably in industries such as agriculture, real estate, and arts, entertainment and recreation, all of which have extremely low concentration ratios (the C4 ratio in real estate is just 6.1 percent, 5.4 percent in arts and entertainment, and even lower in agriculture). If market power were really driving this change, markups should not have increased very much, if at all, in these unconcentrated industries. Finally, they release data a few individual firms. It is striking to note that Apple, the most profitable firm in the world, had lower, not higher, markups in 2014 than it did in 1980, while Walmart, the world's largest retailer, had essentially the same levels. While the markup for General Electric increased from 1.45 in 1990 to 1.71 in 2014, its operating margin fell from 22.3 percent to 14.1 percent.[23] A more logical explanation for this finding of increased markups, leaving aside the possibility of faulty methodology, is that the ratio of fixed costs to marginal costs has increased in most industries, particularly as investments in intangible capital (e.g., marketing, software, R&D) have increased significantly.

If the neo-Brandeisians are right that concentration is increasing and enabling more firms to increase profits through market power, then profit rates should be growing faster for large companies than for small since on average large firms have greater market share and potentially market power. In fact, from 1994 to 2013 profits (defined as net income as a share of total receipts) grew 5 percent faster for firms with less than $5 million in revenue than for firms with more than $5 million in revenue and 10 percent faster than for the largest firms, with incomes of more than $50 million.[24] In 2013, corporations with receipts of less than $500,000 enjoyed net income as a share of receipts of 7.1 percent, while the largest corporations, those with receipts of $250 million or more, had a net income of just 6.8 percent. When just the largest corporations, those with more than $250 million in sales, are compared to all the rest, their profits were only slightly higher, 6.8 percent versus 5.6 percent.[25]

But maybe the problem is just with a small share of large firms. Abernathy and coworkers claim that "in 2014 the rate of returns for corporations in the top 10th percentile was five times that of median firms; in 1990, the ratio was two to one. In theory, innovation or improved productivity could be the cause—but the companies capturing greater profits tend to be older, suggesting that the culprit may be a monopoly advantage."[26] In fact, this divergence is likely to be related more to differential growth in productivity than to growth in market power. The OECD found that the most of the leading firms in various industries have continued robust productivity growth since 2000, while the other 90 percent of firms have seen lagging productivity growth.[27] As the OECD report notes, "A striking fact to emerge is that the productivity growth of the globally most productive firms remained robust in the 21st century but the gap between those high productivity firms and the rest has risen."[28] A study conducted under the aegis of the McKinsey Global Institute reports a similar phenomenon.[29] Higher productivity in these leading firms naturally translates into higher profitability. Given this large divergence in productivity performance the real question is why haven't concentration ratios grown even more as the less productive firms lose market share to the global leaders? Clearly this would often be a positive outcome as it would mean higher global productivity.

When it comes to particular industries, the Brandeisian case that higher concentration leads to higher prices often simply falls apart. For example, the industry that has shown one of the highest increases in prices, health care and assistance, saw declining industry concentration over the fifteen years of 1997 to 2012, with the share held by the largest fifty firms declining 1.6 percentage points.[30] Conversely, retail pharmacy concentration has increased while profits have fallen. Yet this doesn't stop Brandeisians from holding up the retail pharmacy industry as an example of the negative effects of concentration. The Institute for Local Self-Reliance praises a North Dakota law essentially banning big pharmacy chain stores, asserting this leads to better consumer outcomes.[31] But if the outcomes are really better, why is there a need for a law banning large pharmacies? Wouldn't consumers just naturally choose the smaller ones? Moreover, if concentration drives up profits, why has the retail pharmacy industry's profitability (i.e., industry average return on assets) dropped 50 percent since the early 1980?[32] Moreover, pharmacy industry productivity grew faster than US productivity growth from 2000 to 2009 than from 1987 to 2000, when the annual value of mergers and acquisitions in the industry was six times higher in the earlier period, setting up the industry for a period of robust productivity growth as larger and more efficient chains gained market share from less efficient smaller companies.[33]

Lynn and Longman complain that Americans face a beer duopoly, writing that "more than 80 percent of all beers in America—are controlled by two companies, Anheuser-Busch Inbev and MillerCoors."[34] Any visit to a liquor store makes it clear that the choice of beers in America has never been higher, even more than in the last half of the 1800s before the emergence of national brewers. The explosion of independent microbreweries, over 1,500 in 2016, gives the lie to the notion of lack of consumer choice.

Robert Reich asserts that, "Antitrust laws have been relaxed for corporations with significant market power, such as big food companies, cable companies facing little or no broadband competition, big airlines, and the largest Wall Street banks. As a result, Americans pay more for broadband Internet, food, airline tickets, and banking services than the citizens of any other advanced nation."[35]

Many readers of Reich might believe his claims. But a cursory examination of the evidence shows he is wrong. US broadband prices are higher than those of some nations but lower than those of at least eight other OECD nations, including the Netherlands and France;[36] no mean feat, insofar as the United States is the second least densely populated nation, which makes deploying broadband wires a lot more expansive than in densely populated nations such as South Korea and Japan.[37] The United States does not even make the list of the top ten countries with the highest cost of food.[38] In part because of the restrictions on large farms in France, the average French consumer pays $336 a month for food, compared to $267 in the United States. Of seventy-five nations, the United States had the seventh cheapest air travel, behind mostly developing nations such as India and Algeria, which have low labor costs.[39] And when it comes to banking, the consulting firm CapGemini finds that average prices in the United States for core banking services are lower than the global average while another study finds that of 11 major developed nations, that US banking costs for consumers are second lowest.[40]

Barry Lynn also argues that big business and mergers lead to higher prices and presumably higher profits.[41] He criticizes a litany of mergers, including Hertz car rental (merging with Dollar and Thrifty) and Safeway (merging with Albertsons), Kraft Foods (purchasing Nabisco), and Procter & Gamble (purchasing Gillette). If he is right that these mergers gave these firms market power, it would seem logical that their profit rates must be exorbitant. In fact, in 2015 their net profit margins were actually lower than the Dow Jones average. The Dow average profit was 9.6 percent, but Hertz (6.6 percent), Safeway (1.6 percent), Kraft (5.7 percent), and P&G (9.2 percent) were all lower.

The Case for Concentration

The neo-Brandeisian argument has morphed into absurdity when even the *Economist* writes, "Slower growth encourages companies to buy their rivals and squeeze out costs."[42] But squeezing out costs is usually about raising productivity, the key to higher prosperity. Indeed, there is a strong case for even more concentration, at least in some industries, because capital-intensive industries, high-wage industries, and industries that do a lot of R&D all have larger firms.[43] Yet neo-Brandeisians ignore important structural differences that can influence competition, including scale economies, network effects, innovation, and global market competition.

Scale Industries
In some industries, firms are big because of economies of scale. Yet, neo-Brandeisians go out of their way to deny the very existence of scale

economies because they know that this reality, more than any other, under-cuts their claim that breaking up big companies would be good for the economy. Matt Stoller, reflects that view when he tweets, "I'm increasingly convinced the biggest con in business history is the notion of 'economies of scale."[44]

Stoller is implying that hundreds if not thousands of economists, opera-tions management scholars, and economic historians are not only inept, but intentionally fraudulent in finding economies of scale in production. Yet, the evidence is overwhelming that Stoller is wrong. In one of the earli-est studies on this, *Perspectives on Experience*, the Boston Consulting Group found that "costs appear to go down on value added at about 20 to 30% every time product experience doubles."[45] This means that "fragmentation of production among many competitors places an extremely high penalty on consumers."[46] More currently, the Obama Council of Economic Advis-ers' issue brief, "Benefits of Competition and Indicators of Market Power," acknowledges scale efficiencies as one reason for a possible increase in con-centration.[47] If marginal costs go down the larger a firm gets, it becomes efficient for the firm to grow in size.

The US government has long recognized the existence and importance of scale economies. A 1980 FTC report on the electric light industry con-cluded that production technology:

would preclude an atomistic industry. A minimum efficient high volume plant would produce from 7 to over 60 percent of the total out-put, depending upon the type of lamp produced. Therefore, one would have to expect four-firm concentration levels ranging from 28 to 100 percent at the product level at least for the products in the widest use.[48]

The report goes on to note that "the importance of plant scale econo-mies precludes the possibility of breaking up the industry into an atomisti-cally competitive market. To produce at minimum cost, only a few firms could operate."[49] In other words if the most efficient electric light factory has to produce at least 10,000,000 bulbs a year, then a fragmented and competitive market composed of firms producing 500,000 bulbs a year each would lead to higher costs and prices. More recent studies have also found scale efficiencies in a number of industries. One study found that most plant and firm acquisitions increase productivity, concluding "the market for corporate assets facilitates the redeployment of assets from firms with a lower ability to exploit them to firms with higher ability."[50]

The banking industry is an example of an industry that benefits from scale economies. Yet neo-Brandeisians will have none of this. Barry Lynn warns, "The total number of banks in America has fallen by some 60 percent since 1981, even as the population has grown substantially."[51] In fact, despite the supposed the rise of banks "too big to fail," the C4 and C8 concentration ratios for commercial banks actually fell between 2002 and 2012, from 29.5 to 25.6 and from 41.0 to 35.8, respectively.[52] Moreover, if one were to create a US banking system from scratch, it wouldn't look like the current one, with its more than 5,000 banks (though that number is down from over 12,000 in 1980.)[53] As discussed in chapter 2, this massive number was a reflection of local bank protectionism, which led states to erect unit banking laws barring banks from opening branches across state lines. As the states relaxed these archaic laws in the 1980s and Congress passed legislation in 1994 eliminating most of these restrictions, smaller banks were bought up by larger, more efficient ones to, take advantage of economies of scale, as the Federal Reserve Bank shows.[54]

But because most other nations never had American-style unit banking laws, they have always had significantly fewer banks per capita. In 1998 Japan had just 170 banks, or one bank for every 747,000 people. Canada, widely viewed as having the safest banking system in the world, had one bank for every 1.16 million residents. The United States has one bank for every 58,000 people. And in 1999 the share of deposits and assets of the five largest US banks was just 27 percent, compared to 77 percent in Canada, 70 percent in France, and 57.8 percent in Switzerland.[55]

But even with the number of banks falling by more than half in the last few decades bank economies of scale have still not been exhausted and the United States still suffers from too many banks. As the Federal Reserve has found, even the largest banks face increasing returns to scale in terms of cost, meaning as they get larger, their cost per customer and dollar deposited goes down.[56] The Fed found, "Our results suggest that capping banks' size would incur opportunity costs in terms of foregone advantages from IRS [increasing returns to scale] in terms of cost."[57] Other studies have found similar results.[58]

Even if neo-Brandeisians were to acknowledge that fewer banks would mean higher productivity, they argue this would mean more restrictive lending policies with big banks being less likely to lend to local, small businesses. But as one study of bank size and lending found, "The declining trend in the importance of small banks has, if anything, increased over-all bank lending rather than reduced it."[59] Likewise, another study found that "greater market share by [large, multimarket banks] is associated with increased competition in small business lending."[60]

Retail also benefits from economies of scale. As one study finds, "much of the increased competitive pressure on small retailers is due to the fact that growing chains face decreasing marginal cost."[61] In other words, when a large store gets larger its costs go down because of scale economies. No wonder small retailers are losing market share; they are less efficient and stock fewer products. Because of its size, Amazon can afford to deploy highly automated fulfillment centers with increasing levels of robotization. Walmart can afford one of the world's most sophisticated software systems for inventory management. And consumers benefit.

Moreover, advances in information technology (IT) are expanding the number of industries that benefit from scale economies. Ten years ago few would have thought that the taxi industry exhibited anything more than modest economies of scale, insofar as most taxi companies were small and local. But the emergence of companies like Uber and Lyft, empowered by software and GPS-enabled smart phones, enabled at least some of the functions in the taxi industry, such as hailing and payment, to benefit from scale economies.

Innovation Industries

Concentration is also a driver of consumer welfare in industries that depend on innovation: regularly bringing to the market new products, services, or business models. Because marginal costs are significantly below average costs in innovation industries, many firms tend to be big and many industries concentrated. In the software industry, for example, it can cost hundreds of millions of dollars to produce the first copy but nothing to produce additional copies.

Firms producing innovative physical products can have also declining marginal costs. For example, it took Boeing almost eight years of development work and an expenditure of more than $15 billion before a single 787 Dreamliner, the first carbon fiber jet airplane, was sold.[62] That $15 billion has to be built into the overhead of every 787 sale. If the market were curtailed for the 787, for example, through unfair government subsidies going to Europe's Airbus and China's Comac, then Boeing would be less able to invest in the next innovative jet airplane. Economists refer to this as increasing returns to scale. While virtually all high-tech industries have this, most low-tech industries do not. A study of more than 1,000 European companies found increasing returns to scale for high-tech firms but, past a certain size, decreasing returns to scale for low-tech ones.[63] This means that in innovation industries, increased firm size and industry concentration mean lower industry-wide costs. Having ten, or frankly even three, aviation firms each investing $15 billion to develop a 787-like jet would be a waste of societal resources, as would having ten firms producing PC operating systems software since all would have to invest considerable amounts in software programming but each would have on average one tenth of the sales compared to just one firm.

Increased firm size and industry concentration also make higher profits possible, in part because sales are higher relative to fixed costs than they would be with many more competitors. But rather than being anti-consumer, these higher returns are a boon to consumers because most innovation companies have to reinvest these profits into the next round of risky innovation if they are stay alive;[64] the next 787 plane, or the next version of the operating system. This is why William Baumol, a leading scholar of innovation economics, writes: "In markets without too much difficulty of entry, an increase in concentration in the longer run may not be ascribable to attempts by firms to achieve monopoly power but, rather, to innovation and the resulting technological changes that make it efficient for output to be provided by firms that are larger than previously was the case."[65]

Neo-Brandeisians regularly see the large market shares and high profits of some technology-based firms as evidence of monopolistic exploitation. But as Baumol points out, "Prices above marginal costs and price discrimination become the norm rather than the exception because ... without such deviations from behavior in the perfectly competitive model, innovation outlays and other unavoidable and repeated sunk outlays cannot be recouped."[66] Indeed, numerous studies of innovation industries have found that increased sales means more R&D.[67] A study of European firms found that for high-tech firms, "Their capacity for increasing the level of technological knowledge over time is dependent on their size: the larger the R&D investor, the higher its rate of technical progress."[68]

We see this same dynamic in the pharmaceutical industry. As the former Congressional Office of Technology concluded, "Pharmaceutical R&D is a risky investment; therefore, high financial returns are necessary to induce companies to invest in researching new chemical entities."[69] Likewise, the Harvard economist F. M. Scherer writes, "Had the returns to pharmaceutical R&D investment not been attractive, it seems implausible that drug-makers would have expanded their R&D so much more rapidly than their industrial peers."[70] This is why the Organisation for Economic Co-operation and Development (OECD) writes that, "There exists a high degree of correlation between pharmaceutical sales revenues and R&D expenditures."[71]

But even though higher profits are the very source of continued innovation, at least for the firms lucky enough to be successful innovators, (the unlucky ones have negative profits) neo-Brandeisians worry about innovation monopolies. But firms in innovation industries are more likely to compete through innovation, making market leadership highly contestable. In other words, firms pursue innovation not just to gain a small share of a stable market but to fundamentally disrupt it: the process of creative destruction. As Joseph Farrell and Michael Katz write, "In network markets subject to technological progress, competition may take the form of a succession of 'temporary monopolists' who displace one another through innovation. Such competition is often called Schumpeterian rivalry."[72] As Schumpeter wrote:

As soon as quality competition and sales effort are admitted into the sacred precincts of theory, the price variable is ousted from its dominant position. ... But in capitalist reality as distinguished from its textbook picture, it is not that kind of competition which counts but the competition from the new commodity, the new technology ... competition which commands a decisive cost or quality advantage and which strikes not at the margins of the profits and the outputs of the existing firms but at their foundations and their very lives. This kind of competition is as much more effective than the other as a bombardment is in comparison with forcing a door.[73]

Schumpeter could very well have had in mind the 1932 Supreme Court case *New State Ice Co. v. Liebmann*. The case revolved around the fact that Oklahoma passed a statute requiring that ice producers be licensed as public utilities. The court rightly overturned the law. But Brandeis defended the statue, seeing ice as a social necessity and writing that the "business of supplying to others, for compensation, any article or service whatsoever may become a matter of public concern." But the development and spread of the refrigerator (with built-in freezers) quickly made this issue moot, as refrigerators went from less than 15 percent of American homes in 1932 to over 80 percent by the early 1950s.[74]

This is why competition in innovation industries is usually more about innovation than about price. According to Baumol:

Oligopolistic competition among large, high-tech, business firms, with innovation as a prime competitive weapon, ensures continued innovative activities, and very plausibly, their growth. In this market form, in which a few giant firms dominate a particular market, innovation has replaced price as the name of the game in a number of important industries. The computer industry is only the most obvious example, whose new and improved models appear constantly, each manufacturer battling to stay ahead of its rivals.[75]

Network Industries

A third kind of industry in which higher concentration often increases welfare are network-based industries. These are also industries in which fixed costs are high but also where the value of investments increases as the size of the network increases. Some examples are transportation (e.g., air travel, railroads), utilities (e.g., electricity, gas, water), and information (e.g., broadband and Internet applications).

Despite the benefits of scale in network industries, neo-Brandeisians decry increased firm size in them. As Abernathy and coworkers write, "Perhaps most alarming is the tech sector, where a combination of network effects, outdated laws, and permissive regulation has enabled a handful of companies to consolidate vast control over key internet services."[76]

But increased concentration in network industries usually works in the direction of innovation and consumer welfare. A case in point is residential broadband, where most US consumers can choose from at least two wireline competitors, cable and telephone company (as well as a satellite provider and multiple wireless providers, though at least with current technology, with either higher prices or lower quality). Neo-Brandeisians decry this duopoly and advocate for more competition, including having government fund and operate the construction of a third wireline network. But using government policy to add more competitors would make consumers and the economy worse off. This is because total costs would by definition increase as three separate networks would have to be built and operated, but each network owner would now capture on average at most one-third of the customers instead of half. So costs would go up and revenue down, making it all but certain that prices would rise even if profits (which are already around the US business average levels) went down. Unfortunately, in part because of federal "universal service" policies that subsidize small inefficient telecommunication and broadband providers, many of these companies are small and have not exhausted scale economy potential. In 2012, there were 3,520 wired telecommunications carriers in the United States, with average employment of just 215 workers.[77]

Another network industry neo-Brandeisians criticize is airlines. Barry Lynn and Phillip Longman write, "In the late 1970s, the Carter administration repealed this body of law, in the name of 'deregulation.' In the years since, airlines have been allowed to consolidate to a degree unknown even to the railroad barons. Today four super-carriers control 80 percent of traffic, and enjoy outright monopoly on many routes."[78] But this overlooks the fact that this more concentrated industry structure provides real value to consumers in the form of more direct flights and better connections. Indeed, the four major domestic airlines coordinate their network of flights to best manage connections. In addition, airline prices increased only about half as fast as the rate of inflation from 1995 to 2015, 29 percent compared to 55 percent.[79] In addition, airline consolidation has had major positive impacts on airline productivity. Between 1997 and 2014, private, nonfarm multifactor productivity increased 19 percent. But airline productivity, in an era of mergers, increased a staggering 74 percent.[80]

In this case as in so many others, the Brandeisians' main objection relates to equity rather than efficiency. As Lynn and Longman write, now airlines "discriminate among people who live in different cities, cutting service and hiking fares to places like St. Louis, Memphis, and Minneapolis, in ways that make it harder to attract and keep business."[81] But in fact, all three of the cities saw airline ticket price increases at or below the national average. (To be fair, since 1995 the average price of airline tickets has increased faster on some routes than others. Fares to or from places like Hawaii and Alaska more than doubled, while fares to or from places like Denver, Milwaukee, and Richmond, Virginia, grew by less than 10 percent, even as inflation increased 55 percent. With market-based pricing and routes and larger airlines there have been winners and losers, but mostly winners.[82]

Railroads are another industry with network effects. Building two rail lines to and from the same place would be a significant waste of societal resources. And when government tried to force the industry into a particular structure while also price regulating it, the US rail industry almost went bankrupt. It was not until the Staggers Act of 1980, when Congress deregulated the industry, that it became healthy. For example, in the almost ten years after the act was passed, industry multifactor productivity more than tripled compared to the period before the act.[83] And as Craig Pirrong writes, "Some segments of the rail market have likely seen increased market power, but most segments are subject to competition from non-rail transport (e.g., trucking, ocean shipping, or even pipelines that permit natural gas to compete with coal)."[84]

We also see industries characterized by network effects on the user side, where the benefit from the product or service is magnified if more people use it. As an Obama administration Council of Economic Advisers' report notes, "Some newer technology markets are also characterized by network effects, with large positive spillovers from having many consumers use the same product. Markets in which network effects are important, such as social media sites, may come to be dominated by one firm."[85]

A good way to think about this is whether people would really like it if the government broke up a company like Facebook, splitting it into two companies, Facebook and Headbook. Half of your friends would be on Facebook and the other half on Headbook. So every time you wanted to post a picture of your kid's birthday party you would have to do it twice. In other words, there is a reason why there is one major social networking firm (Facebook), one microblogging site (Twitter), one major professional networking site (Linkedin), and so on: consumers get much more value by being able to communicate efficiently with a lot of people. Besides, we shouldn't really worry about current concentration levels in Internet-based network industries that provide their services for free because the relevant market from a competition perspective is not the social network or microblog network, it's the advertising market. All these firms compete for advertising dollars and, notwithstanding their size, have little market power in the ad market.

We see the same dynamic in software. Neo-Brandeisians wanted the federal government to break up Microsoft after the Justice Department brought suit against the company in 1998 and claimed that by separating the operating system business from the "Office" market, competitive operating systems would emerge. But breaking up Microsoft would have had negative value for consumers. Who would want two different operating systems, making it difficult for users to share files between people or organizations using different systems? Indeed, the very reason Microsoft was not broken up was because the benefits of network effects for operating system and application programs (e.g., word processing) were clear. This is not to say that competition authorities should not address monopolistic behavior. For example, as part of the settlement with the US government, Microsoft was required to enable competitors in related products (e.g., browsers) to better interface with the Windows operating system. But that is very different from the neo-Brandeisian solution of breaking up digital monopolists and oligopolists.

Industries in Global Competition

A fourth set of industries in which scale improves economic welfare are those facing global competition. Since 1980 global oligopolies have emerged in dozens of industries, usually based in Europe, Japan, and the United States. But as we noted in chapter 2, this is actually the second wave of global consolidation. The first took place in 1918–1939, mainly in the form of international cartels that amounted to 30–40 percent of global trade (about the same as interfirm transfers today). Mergers and cartels at least in increasing returns industries are alternative methods of creating scale economies, although the former is superior. The choice of method reflects national laws. The postwar trend toward mergers rather than cartels reflected the influence of US hostility to cartels and lenience toward mergers on competition policy in Europe and elsewhere. Nevertheless, the tendency toward efficient oligopoly in an industrial economy has been remarkably pronounced, in both eras of industrial age globalization.

Unfortunately, neo-Brandeisians seem oblivious not only to the fact that the United States is now in intense global competition but also to the fact that it is losing this competition, as evidenced by its $500 billion-plus annual trade deficit. The *Economist* writes, "America in particular has got into the habit of giving the benefit of the doubt to big business. This made some sense in the 1980s and 1990s when giant companies such as General Motors and IBM were being threatened by foreign rivals or domestic upstarts. It is less defensible now that superstar firms are gaining control of entire markets and finding new ways to entrench themselves."[86]

Really? US firms are no longer threatened by foreign rivals? In the 1980s and 1990s, the US trade deficit averaged 40 percent less as a share of GDP compared to the period 2000–2015 (1.5 percent vs. 3.8 percent). And then the United States did not face competition from state-directed innovation mercantilist powerhouses such as China, where the government subsidizes and protects national champions, while attacking foreign competitors with unfair domestic practices (e.g., forced technology transfer, intellectual property theft, etc.). In this new global environment, firms in many industries need to bulk up to be able to have the resources to compete effectively at global scale.

Surprisingly, it's the neo-Marxist scholars who present a more accurate picture of competition, recognizing the significant increase in global competition and the concomitant rise of large firms to effectively compete. One article in the socialist *Monthly Review* states:

The giant corporations that had arisen in the monopoly stage of capitalism operated increasingly as multinational corporations on the plane of the global economy as a whole—to the point that they confronted each other with greater or lesser success in their own domestic markets as well in the global economy. The result was that the direct competitive pressures experienced by corporate giants went up.[87]

It goes on to note, "John Kenneth Galbraith's world of *The New Industrial State*, where a relatively small group of corporations ruled imperiously over the market based on their own 'planning system,' was clearly impaired."[88]

Neo-Brandeisians reject this argument. Lynn and Longman write that "the idea entirely ignores all historical evidence. Under the system [Thurman] Arnold pioneered, the American economy prevailed over and ultimately vanquished two rival economic systems, those of National Socialism and, later, Soviet Communism. America became the 'Arsenal of Democracy' during World War II even as the Justice Department was busy slapping domestic monopolies with antitrust suits."[89] The attempt to attribute American economic success during and after World War II to the legacy of Thurman Arnold's Antitrust Division is creative but unconvincing. Let's start with the fact that, as discussed in chapter 10, these neo-Brandeisian policies actually set the stage for the loss of US global competitiveness in a number of industries, including consumer electronics, copiers, and computing.

Second, at that time, far from winning on a competitive playing field, most of the US economic competition was flat on its back, devastated by war in Europe and Asia. And the rigid, state planning system in the Soviet Union could never produce viable competitors. Third, there was relatively little globalization from the 1930s to the 1970s. In the early 1950s exports and imports accounted for just 7 percent of US GDP, compared to 30 percent from 2012 to 2015. Even more important, over the last fifteen years an array of nations, led by China, has embraced an array of aggressive mercantilist policies designed to take global market share away from firms in the United States that go largely unchallenged in the World Trade Organization System.[90]

Take the semiconductor industry, for example, an industry that the United States pioneered and still leads, at least for the present. However, the Chinese government has set a goal to depose the United States from that position and become a world-class player in all major segments of the semiconductor industry by 2030. One Chinese official states that the government intends to have "the visible hand of government join with the invisible hand of the market."[91] The most visible manifestation of that hand comes in the form of government subsidies, specifically National and Regional IC [integrated circuit] Funds, which have already accrued more than $100 billion in assets, with most of the funds channeled from the government through state-owned enterprises (SOEs) into a "private" equity firm so that China can claim that the funds will support "market-based" transactions in accordance with World Trade Organization principles.

A substantial portion of those funds is being used to acquire foreign competitors in the semiconductor industry; in fact, since June 2014 Chinese entities have made seventeen acquisitions across different levels of the semiconductor industry value chain, with the most notable effort being China's Tsinghua Unigroup's $23 billion failed bid for Micron Technologies in July 2015.[92] In this environment, the size of the US market leader, Intel, is one of America's few saving graces, for if any firm has the resources to compete with state-backed firms that can sell below cost for many years and that refuse to follow other global trade rules, it is a firm the size of Intel.

State-backed competition occurs not only in the semiconductor industry. China's 121 biggest SOEs increased their total assets from $360 billion in 2002 to $2.9 trillion in 2010, in part because during the recent financial crisis approximately 85 percent of China's $1.4 trillion in bank loans went to state companies.[93] SOEs account for more than 40 percent of Chinese GDP and 70 percent of China's offshore foreign direct investment (OFDI) activity.[94] In fact, total Chinese OFDI stock grew from $4 billion (USD) in 1990 to $298 billion in 2010 to $1.3 trillion in 2016.[95] As Yasheng Huang notes, China's OFDI is "state-driven and centralized," and it is "probably historically unprecedented for the SOEs to invest on such a massive scale."[96] Nor is China alone in practicing heavy-handed mercantilism designed to challenge US commercial leadership. Brazil, India, Indonesia, Russia, and many other nations are savvy practitioners of this. In this environment, characterized by flaccid prosecution of trade enforcement and a weak, even nonexistent US national competitiveness strategy, including extremely high corporate tax rates, firm size provides at least one potential defense against both fair and unfair foreign advantages.

The Case for Monopsony

While neo-Brandeisians focus mostly on seller power (monopoly), they also worry about buyer power (monopsony). They worry that big companies will unfairly use their market power to hurt business suppliers. As one neo-Brandeisian, Sabeel Rahman, writes, "Despite its low prices, Wal-Mart, for example, has power as a platform: like Amazon, it can leverage its huge consumer base to pressure producers who want their goods on the shelves."[97] Rahman writes that Paul Krugman agrees and states, "Amazon is a different kind of monopoly. It does not extract rents from consumers but rather operates as a monopsony, a company whose buying power allows it to discriminate against suppliers."[98] Rahman concurs:

Amazon is a critical hub through which almost any bookseller or buyer must pass. As a result, Amazon can use its position to unfairly discriminate between publishers, wielding its access to its vast user base as a weapon. It did so with Hachette, refusing to accept pre-orders for the publisher's books because Hachette had demanded the ability to set prices for its e-books.[99]

Amazon was pressuring a publisher, Hachette, so that it, Amazon, could lower prices. It appears that the new call from neo-Brandeisians is: "Side with use and we will make sure that businesses don't lower the prices of things you buy!" Liberal economist Dean Baker gets it right when he writes, "I also don't have much sympathy for the publishers and authors who fear declining incomes due to Amazon's pressure."[100] To be clear, this is not to say that Amazon could not use its market position to act unfairly, but using it to lower prices for consumers is not one of these cases.

While large buyers may be able to pressure suppliers, the result is usually beneficial because it forces them to become more innovative and competitive. Strong buyers are in a better position to require continued cost cutting and innovation on the part of their suppliers, both of which benefit consumers.

More broadly, the goal of competition policy should not be to protect business suppliers but rather to encourage efficiency and competitiveness and to benefit consumers. Yet the Obama Council of Economic Advisers privileged businesses over consumers when it stated: "If an entrepreneur sells its products to downstream firms rather than to end-users, it would benefit from there being a greater number of downstream firms to which it can sell products."[101] In other words, if the government breaks up big retailers like Walmart so that they have less bargaining power, small business suppliers will get to charge higher prices. The only way this cannot have a negative impact on consumers is if neo-Brandeisians believe that the large retailers have complete market power and pass along none of the cost savings from lower supplier prices to consumers, a proposition for which there is no evidence. Moreover, businesses, especially small ones, want an efficient distribution system, not a system that maximizes the number of distributors, because this keeps prices low, which increases consumer demand.

Small Businesses Can Have Market Power

For those in the tradition of Louis Brandeis, market power comes from size. Only big firms can act in anticompetitive and anticonsumer ways. But in fact, some of the most egregious "monopolists" are small firms that collude either through professional rules and guild-like restrictions or with the help of government. By banding together and limiting competition, these small-business-dominated industries hurt consumers and innovation.

A case in point is the optometry industry, which has a long and checkered history of colluding to keep contact lens customers from being able to buy lenses from other, often cheaper sources, such as Walmart and online seller 1800Contacts. By conventional definition, optometrists don't possess market power, since most are small, local practices. Moreover, they don't appear to make supranormal profits that a monopolist might. Nonetheless, the industry has long engaged in anticompetitive behavior to limit the ability of contact lens purchasers to buy contact lenses elsewhere. The industry has this power because it plays a gatekeeper role: customers can't purchase contact lens without a prescription.[102] The industry has used that power to collectively pressure contact lens manufacturers to not sell lenses to lower-cost distributers (particularly online sellers of lenses), making it clear to the manufacturers not toeing the line that optometrists will refuse to prescribe their brand. The collusion was based on professional norms, repeated in blogs and trade journals and at professional conferences, but it had the same effect as a coordinated boycott.

We see this kind of anticompetitive behavior from many industries dominated by small firms: realtors, wine wholesalers, lawyers, car dealers, and others. Car dealers have protected their profits by getting laws passed making it illegal in all fifty states for car manufacturers to sell cars directly to the consumer. Wine wholesalers benefit from laws they support making it illegal for vineyards to sell their wine directly to liquor stores. Lawyers have fought the provision of legal services software. If neo-Brandeisians really want to go after abuse, they should start here, with these unfair practices that benefit relatively well-off professionals and small business owners, for not only do these practices harm consumers directly, they also artificially limit the market share of larger, more efficient firms.

None of this is to say that there are not cases where market power has led to higher prices and consumer harm. Several studies have found that to be the case with US hospitals, which have undergone a consolidation wave in the wake of the rise of managed care. This is why in December 2015 the US Federal Trade Commission announced that it planned to block the combination of two large Chicago-area hospital systems, Advocate Health Care and NorthShore University Health System."[103] But these cases represent the exceptions, and in most cases existing competition authorities provide adequate means for constraining them. The argument of the neo-Brandeisian school that many or most economic problems in the United States stem from rising monopoly—itself alleged to be a result of lax antitrust enforcement since the Reagan years—does not stand up to scrutiny and going down this path would surely lead to negative consequences for US economic competitiveness and growth as well as for consumer welfare and per-capita incomes.

12 Small Business Cronyism: Policies Favoring Small Business

Almost a century ago the journalist Dorothy Thompson wrote: "Two souls dwell ... in the bosom of the American people. The one loves the abundant life, as expressed in the cheap and plentiful products of large-scale mass production and distribution. ... The other soul yearns for former simplicities, for decentralization, for the interests of the 'little man,' ... denounces 'monopoly' and 'economic empires' and seeks means of breaking them up."[1] It is this continued yearning to this day that helps explain why government policy so deeply and consistently favors small business.

Yet the claim that the federal government unfairly favors big business is a staple of rhetoric on all sides of the political spectrum. Rather than supporting hard-working-mom-and-pop small business—Thompson's "little man"—Washington is allegedly in the pocket of big business. For the small-is-beautiful school, the deck is stacked against the small business owner by governments doing the bidding of Big Pharma, Big Tobacco, Big Oil, big banks, big broadband, big you name it. If only small firms could compete on a level playing field, we are told, we'd see vibrant small business and economic growth. Indeed, one survey found that most Americans believed that small business owners had too little political influence while corporate executives had too much.[2]

It's a compelling story, one endlessly repeated by the small business lobby and its fellow travelers. The advocacy group Small Business Majority tells us that "entrepreneurship is essential to ensuring a truly inclusive economy that benefits all Americans. Nonetheless, Washington, when it's able to get anything done at all, persists in pursuing policies that favor large corporations over Main Street."[3] The liberal professor Robert Reich puts it more bluntly: small businesses are "being screwed by big businesses."[4]

If big business is so powerful, why do government regulations, taxation, and spending programs all favor small business? As Alan Viard and Amy Roden write, "Although the House of Representatives has a Small Business Committee and the Senate has a Small Business and Entrepreneurship Committee, the creation of a 'Big Business Committee' would be politically unthinkable."[5] Congressional Research Service economist Jane Gravelle observes, "To question benefits provided to small businesses, especially tax benefits, is as much on the forbidden list as tackling the home mortgage interest deduction."[6] Likewise, Richard J. Pierce writes that to test this assertion that big business has more power than small in Washington, "consider the following question: Would a single member of the House or Senate support enactment of a bill entitled 'The Large Business Regulatory Enforcement Fairness Act'?"[7]

The deck is indeed stacked—in favor of small business. The crony capitalist "size-based" industrial policy that should concern us is the one that lavishes on low-productivity small businesses that pay low wages and provide few or no benefits to their employees lower taxes, subsidies, and regulatory exemptions, to the benefit of their owners but to the detriment of their employees, taxpayers, consumers and national productivity growth. However, as government officials seek to increase productivity-driven economic growth, they have an easy solution that will increase government revenues, create better-paying jobs, and grow the economy: end small business crony capitalism and treat firms of all sizes the same.

The History of Small Business Favoritism

For more than a century, small businesses and their allies have sought to enlist the aid of local, state, and federal governments to hamstring their large competitors while bestowing on themselves all sorts of favors, including lower taxes, exemptions from regulations, and special access to government grants, financing, and contracts. At the end of the nineteenth century, as technologies developed that enabled corporations to gain efficiencies and market share, independent businessmen complained that without government restraint on large firms, they would lose out. In his famous 1945 *Alcoa* opinion, Supreme Court Judge Learned Hand reflected that view when he noted, "It has been constantly assumed that one of [antitrust laws'] purposes was to perpetuate and preserve, for its own sake and in spite of possible cost, an organization of industry in small units which can effectively compete against one another."[8]

But by the 1950s it had become clear that antitrust measures could not stem the tide of bigness. If anything, small firms in even more industries were now threatened by firms that reaped the benefits of scale and the advantages of modern machinery. New technologies and systems such as electrification, air travel, telephony, and the Interstate Highway system enabled more industries to gain the economies of scale once confined to railroads and manufacturing. Indeed, establishment and firm size grew in many other sectors, including hospitality (the first Holiday Inn was established in the 1950s), banking, retail, and other sectors. Big was now everywhere.

Many Americans at the time dreaded the expected emergence of a world with virtually no small businesses. Senator William Proxmire, a Democrat from Wisconsin, wrote, "If you're a small businessman, you're in big trouble and you know it. When you're a butcher, a baker, or a candlestick maker, you may soon be as extinct as the village blacksmith."[9] One not so prescient futurist predicted that private sector consolidation would end in socialism: "The danger that faces us in the further concentration of business into so few units as to imply absence of essential competition, is the take-over by the government."[10]

This fear spurred small businesses and their advocates to mount a rear-guard defense. As William Whyte noted in *The Organization Man*, "Economically, many a small businessman is a counter-revolutionary and the revolution he is fighting is that of the corporation as much as the New or Fair Deal."[11] Small business might not be the future, its advocates argued, but it embodies all that is great about American society. In the case of the Cold War threat from the Soviet Union, small business was seen as a bulwark of American free enterprise. Proxmire wrote, "Only a vigorous small business community can preserve our free competitive enterprise system in the face of these giants."[12] Small business was also the glue that kept communities together and even reduced adolescent misbehavior. Again, Proxmire: "Even if the family retail store were an economically inefficient operation, its contribution to family and community would be a strong enough argument in favor of its preservation."[13]

All of this had an effect. As the liberal economist John Kenneth Galbraith wrote in 1964:

Small business, by contrast [with big business], is regarded with deep affection. Scholars, publicists, and politicians join in stressing its importance and viewing with alarm its prospects for survival. No one seriously argues that the small firm is ordinarily more efficient, more progressive, more responsible, more enlightened, that it pays better wages, or that it sells at lower cost than the large corporation. It is the object of social nostalgia.[14]

With that store of good will, small business turned to the federal government for direct help, including government loans, procurement preferences, and a favorable tax and regulatory system, ignoring the warning from Brandeis that "those asking for help from the government for everything should be deprecated."[15] Nonetheless, their concern was translated into action. In 1940 the Senate established the Special Committee to Study and Survey Problems of Small Business Enterprises, which in 1949 became the Select Committee on Small Business. The House created its own Small Business Committee in 1941. Twelve years later Congress created the Small Business Administration (SBA) "to aid, counsel, assist and protect, insofar as is possible, the interests of small businesses."[16] According to Jonathan Bean, "Congressional sponsorship reflected the vitality of a small business ideology associated with the widely held 'American Creed'—a belief in individualism, equal opportunity, and democracy."[17]

But Congress was just getting started. In the 1950s it started programs requiring federal agencies to set aside contracts specifically for small firms, even if agencies could get the goods or services more cheaply from large firms. As Bean has observed, "By awarding loans and government contracts to a select group of small firms, the agency gave them a competitive advantage over other companies."[18] And, of course, increased government spending that taxpayers were ultimately responsible for.

Since then Congress has regularly passed laws containing special favors for small business. According to one book on small business policy, "By 1981 the U.S. Regulatory Council had identified forty-three regulatory programs whose compliance and reporting requirements varied with the size of the business. As of 1982, the Environmental Protection Agency (EPA) had tiered almost fifty different regulations on the basis of firm size or amount of pollutant released."[19] If this massive favoritism represents neglect by Congress, we can only wonder what congressional solicitude for small business would look like. Indeed, from 1953 to 2017, Congress passed at least sixty-eight pieces of legislation explicitly favoring small business, including the Small Business Prepayment Penalty Relief Act of 1994, the Small Business Job Protection Act of 1996, and the SEC Small Business Advocate Act of 2016.[20]

Before the late 1970s the case for small business favoritism was largely one of fairness: big firms were hurting small firms, so they needed help. As Bean writes, the SBA made arguments "that will sound familiar to students of affirmative action: As a matter of justice, small firms deserved special considerations because they suffered 'institutionalized discrimination' by banks and procurement agencies. ... Since then, few have raised objections to affirmative action for small business."[21]

But fairness was a relatively weak reed on which to build an elaborate discriminatory system. What was needed was an affirmative reason for affirmative action for small business. Fortuitously, the competitiveness challenge to big firms in the 1970s from Japan and Germany coincided with widespread attention to the work of David Birch, who claimed— inaccurately, as we saw in chapter 6—that small business was a jobs engine. Small business advocates could now go to government armed with more than a sob story. Now they could say that they were the real economic engine of America in its competition with Europe and East Asia. This narrative was reinforced by the wave of startups in the tech sector in the 1980s and 1990s. By 2000 all new businesses, no matter how technologically primitive and undercapitalized, had become "startups." A new biotech company was a "startup"; so was a new three-person lawn-mowing business. Only child labor laws prevented lemonade stands from being classified as startups too.

At the same time, the American left was undergoing a transformation from what was essentially a working-class movement to an alliance of upscale whites and minority groups. Based in the professional class and the public and nonprofit sectors, so-called gentry liberals incorporated opposition to large business into their political identities. Whereas the old labor left saw big business as a source of progress as long as big firms could be unionized and regulated in the public interest, the new gentry left saw big business as inherently immoral and antisocial. As the liberal economist Bennett Harrison wrote in 1994, "The Left in many places has also become enchanted with many of the elements of such a program [favoring small firms over big]—although for different reasons. To many, the big firms seemed hopelessly inaccessible."[22]

The result of all of this was that the floodgates of small business crony-ism opened. As Bean writes, "Small business has been transformed from the ugly duckling of the American economy to its 'Prince Charming.' The old Galbraithian notion of 'big (business) is better' has given way in recent years to a 'small is beautiful' philosophy."[23]

The Extent of Small Business Policy Favoritism

Notwithstanding their political popularity, policies that exemplify small business favoritism cause significant economic harm. As we saw in chapter 7, these policies keep the average firm size in an economy smaller than market forces alone would generate, leading to lower productivity, fewer exports, less innovation, and lower wages and reduced benefits. Moreover, small business preferences in regulation, taxation, and contracting benefit the mostly affluent minority of small business owners, to the detriment of the tax-payer and the national economy.

Regulation

Let's start with regulation. In the United States there is a vast array of regu-latory exemptions for small business.

The Clean Air Act exempts small polluters in attainment areas from using best available control technologies that large firms must install.[24] Small firms face lesser reporting requirements for the EPA's Toxics Release Inventory Database. Employers with ten or fewer employees are exempt from most Occupational Safety and Health Administration (OSHA) record-keeping requirements relating to workplace safety, and if a firm with fewer than 25 employees is found guilty of an unsafe work environment, the pen-alty is 60 percent less than what a big company faces.[25] The Small Business Paperwork Relief Act of 2002 means that federal survey requests fall dispro-portionally on large business. The Family and Medical Leave Act, which requires firms to give workers unpaid leave to deal with medical and family care issues, exempts small firms, as does legislation requiring giving workers ninety days' notice before closing a plant.

Most federal and state laws covering discrimination against workers on the basis of race, age, sex, disabilities, pregnancy, and religion have some exemption for small businesses. The Age Discrimination in Employment Act of 1967, which prohibits age discrimination against individuals who are forty years of age or older, does not apply to employers with fewer than twenty employees. Title I of the Americans with Disabilities Act of 1990, which prohibits employment discrimination against qualified individuals with disabilities, does not apply to employers with fewer than fifteen employees. As Richard Carlson writes, as long as a firm "employs no more than fourteen, it can refuse to hire women, Muslims, or disabled persons, and it will not be in violation of federal discrimination law. If it employs as many as nineteen, but no more, it can terminate and refuse to hire anyone over the age of forty."[26] He continues, "An exempt small firm can pay less than the statutory minimum wage, refuse to pay overtime rates, discharge union supporters, and reject collective bargaining regardless of the wishes of its employees."[27] As Carlson writes, "Firms small enough to be exempt from Title VII employ more than 19 million employees, equal to the entire population of the State of New York or more than sixteen percent of the national workforce. The exemption may be one reason why small firms are much less likely than larger firms to hire a representative number of black employees."[28]

Similarly, federal contractors must develop affirmative action programs that are subject to compliance review by the Office of Federal Contract Compliance Programs, but only if they employ fifty or more workers. Congress uses securities law as a way to regulate companies, but relatively few small companies are publicly traded, so this power is used mostly against larger corporations. For example, the Foreign Corrupt Practices Act and Dodd-Frank financial reporting provisions apply only to listed corporations, not to other business forms, most of which are small firms.[29]

The 2010 Affordable Care Act to expand health insurance coverage exempts employers with fewer than fifty full-time employees from having to provide insurance or pay a per employee tax. Small firms are exempt from the information reporting requirements regarding the health coverage they offer and from benefits and coverage disclosure rules.

There are even specific laws that require agencies to favor small business when promulgating rules. Under the inaccurately named Regulatory Fairness Act of 1982, federal agencies must either conduct a full regulatory "flexibility" analysis to design regulations that are more flexible for small business or certify that the proposed rule will not "have a significant economic impact on a substantial number of small entities." The Small Business Regulatory Fairness Act of 1996 seeks to "create a more cooperative regulatory environment among agencies and small businesses that is less punitive and more solution-oriented; and make Federal regulators more accountable for their enforcement actions by providing small entities with a meaningful opportunity for redress of excessive enforcement activities." Under this act the EPA and the Occupational Safety and Health Administration (OSHA) must inform the SBA's chief counsel for advocacy before they even begin to promulgate rules. The counsel then must create a council of small firms that will be affected by the rule so they can raise objections and the agencies must make their proposed changes where appropriate. The act requires agencies to work with the SBA's Small Business Regulatory Enforcement Ombudsman and SBA Small Business Fairness Boards to develop programs to waive or reduce the civil penalties that small entities would pay for violating the rules. Bizarrely, small firms can even have the government pay their legal fees if they bring cases against the federal government related to the enforcement of rules.[30] This is not a mandate to try to simplify federal regulations affecting business of all sizes, something that would likely produce beneficial results. It is pure size favoritism.

There is even an arm of government dedicated to advocating for these differential protections. The SBA's Office of Advocacy is dedicated to enforcing the Regulatory Flexibility Act. The office has even worked to get small businesses making tobacco products exempted from FDA regulations designed to protect the public from the hazards of smoking and to weaken FAA rules governing aircraft repair stations operated by small businesses, because we all know that protecting small businesses is more important than protecting Americans from lung cancer and dying in airplane crashes.

Even where regulations don't size discriminate, small firms benefit from lax enforcement. Becker finds that with regard to enforcement of Clean Air Act regulations, plant size and whether or not it belongs to a multiunit firm has "been shown to be important determinants of who gets regulated when and how intensely, at least in terms of air quality regulation."[31] Another study found that "the probability of inspection for compliance with the Occupational Safety and Health Act rises dramatically with firm size, whether the establishment is in construction, manufacturing, or services."[32]

Moreover, small firms are less aware of their minimal regulatory requirements. One study of 360 US small businesses found that about 40 percent did not fully comply with most regulations. The businesses cited ignorance of the rules as the most common cause of lack of compliance.[33]

If by some chance small businesses are found in violation of regulations, they are often subject to reduced penalties. OSHA may reduce penalties by 60 percent if an employer has 25 employees or fewer, by 40 percent if the employer has 26–100 employees, and by 20 percent if the employer has 101–250 employees. Do we really believe that a worker in a firm with 24 employees deserves a less safe work environment than one with 2,400 workers? Apparently so.

Small firms are also less susceptible to government pressures because they care less about their reputations than do large firms. When a large corporation gets slapped with a government violation, one of the first things it does is hire an expensive public relations firm to limit the damage to its reputation. Small firms, in contrast, can simply reincorporate as different firms. When Congress wants to make an example of a business that has violated the public trust, it is virtually always a large corporation, ideally one with a CEO who flies in on the corporate jet soon after receiving a massive bonus.

Taxation

Not only do small firms face fewer regulatory burdens than large firms, they also face lower tax burdens. But that's not what one might be led to believe from listening to small business advocates. One pro–small business book claims that "businesses organized as pass-throughs that earn income above those levels now pay a tax rate 4.6 to 10 percentage points higher than businesses organized as a corporation."[34] In fact, the US tax code favors small business in four ways.

First, profits from publicly traded companies (C corporations) are taxed twice, once at the corporate level and again when the shareholders accrue capital gains or dividends. In contrast, pass-through firms (e.g., sole proprietorships, partnerships, or LLCs)—the lion's share of which are small—are taxed only once, on the income to the owners. As the tax economist Eric Toder writes, "For businesses that are equivalent in other respects, non-corporate enterprises are taxed more favorably than C corporations."[35] Toder estimates that non-C corporation companies pay approximately 27 percent less in taxes than corporations.[36] The Congressional Research Service estimates that this failure to tax small business income twice amounts to a subsidy worth $77 billion annually.[37]

Second, the US corporate tax code is progressive, with the tax rate on the first $50,000 of income at 15 percent, while on revenue above $18,333,333 it is 35 percent. Small corporations with less than $5 million in receipts are also exempt from the corporate alternative minimum tax.

Third, many tax incentives are structured in ways that only small firms are eligible for or the incentive is more generous for small firms. For example, it is routine for Congress when passing special bonus depreciation rules to limit them to small business, and the maximum amount a firm can expense for capital expenditures was just $139,000 in 2012. In addition, many tax credits are limited in size. For example, the Credit for Employer-Provided Childcare Facilities and Services is limited to $150,000. Only small businesses receive a tax credit for expenses related to removing barriers to access by disabled persons. The Small Business Jobs Act provides tax credits for hiring workers, but only to small businesses.

Gravelle lists many of these tax benefits that either apply only to small firms or are more generous for small firms, including expensing equipment investment, oil and gas percentage depletion, ability to do cash as opposed to accrual accounting, amortization of business startup costs, exemptions from imputed interest rules, completed contract rules, expensing of timber-growing costs, capital gains exclusion of small business stock, expensing of agricultural costs, small life insurance company benefits, special tax for small property and casualty insurance, ordinary loss for small business stock, tax benefits for small refiners, and the tax credit for refueling property. She estimates that the reduced rate on corporate income for small corporations and the other small business tax benefits amount to between $15 and $22 billion of lost revenues annually.[38]

Fourth, the tax code relies largely on self-reporting. As such, and because the odds of getting audited by the IRS is significantly less for small firms than for large, Gravelle writes that "tax compliance is significantly lower in the unincorporated business sector."[39] As Toder writes, "Small businesses, especially those that are paid in cash instead of by check or credit card, have much greater opportunities to avoid tax by underreporting income than larger businesses."[40] Small businesses also have greater opportunity to report as business expenses what are actually personal expenses, such as home office expenses or automobile expenses not related to business use.

Toder estimates that tax underreporting for nonfarm proprietor income and partnerships, S corporations, and estates and trusts amounts to $80 billion per year.[41] This is not to say that large corporations do not underreport income. But Toder estimates that large corporations underreport on average 13.9 percent of taxes, while small business underreport 28.7 percent.[42] In other words, small businesses are more likely to cheat on their taxes at the expense of their fellow citizens.

Combining all four factors, small businesses are subsidized through the tax code to the tune of almost $180 billion per year. This works out to an annual subsidy of $6,431 for each of the 27.9 million small businesses in America. This is in part why in 2013, federal income tax paid as a share of total net income was 18.2 percent for corporations with more than $250 million in sales but just 4.6 percent for firms with less than $5 million in sales.[43] Even the SBA acknowledges this difference, finding that firms organized as sole proprietorships paid, in 2004, an effective tax rate of 13.3 percent (the amount of tax paid as a fraction of net income or profit), while C corporations paid an effective rate of 17.5 percent.[44] So much for the myth that big business, with its legions of accountants, pays lower taxes than small business!

Financing and Other Subsidies

The SBA has long provided direct loans and loan guarantees for borrowers that are unable to meet commercial lenders' underwriting criteria. In 2016, SBA 7a and 504 loans amounted to over $24 billion. Moreover, more than 86 percent of SBA lending went to firms in local-serving industries where, absent the SBA money, another business without the loan would have stepped in to provide the good or service.[45] For example, the SBA supported loans worth $118 million for residential building construction, $105 million for car dealers, $312 million for liquor stores, $742 million for gas stations, and $760 million for dentists. The last is particularly ironic, as not only are dentists not a traded sector but, as Jonathan Rothwell finds, most dentists are quite well off, with 21 percent of them in the top 1 percent of earners.[46] SBA has even lent money to banks. None of this creates net new jobs. It simply means some small businesses in a particular geographic area get more sales at the expense of others in the same area who are unlucky enough to not get the subsidy. And the SBA is not alone. A number of federal agencies have their own small business lending programs, including the Treasury and Agriculture Departments.[47]

Preferential Contracting

Most governments give also small firms preferences in government contracting, even though this costs taxpayers more. Congress set a goal of giving 23 percent of federal prime contracts to small business, while the SBA set a goal of 40 percent of subcontracts to small business, and its 8(a) Business Development Program helps small business get government contracts.

Sometimes the cost to the taxpayer is obvious, as when the Federal Communications Commission (FCC) lets small telecommunications firms obtain federal wireless spectrum licenses at a discount. With the FCC's first authorization to conduct spectrum auctions in 1993, Congress mandated that the commission promote the participation of small businesses and businesses owned by minorities or women, even though in some cases the owners were multimillionaires. The "designated entity" program has been plagued by industry gaming and exploitation of loopholes, providing a gold mine for smart speculators who either act as fronts for larger businesses shut out of the auctions or resell the spectrum to larger firms for a hefty premium.[48] Taxpayers are the losers, wealthy small business owners the winners.

To take advantage of contracting set-asides, companies often set up "front companies" to qualify. For example, the SBA operates the Historically Underutilized Business Zone (HUBZone) program to provide federal contracts to small firms in economically distressed areas. The goal is worthy, but if the real goal is helping distressed areas, why limit help to small firms? Moreover, when the congressional General Accountability Office (GAO) set up four shell companies that clearly were not qualified (one listed its operating address as a Starbucks café), the SBA approved all four.[49] Thankfully, there is an advocate fighting fraud: the Small Business League, "founded by small business owners who were increasingly frustrated by abuses and loopholes, which have allowed large corporations to receive billions of dollars in federal small business contracts." The league lobbies to make sure that small companies get "their rightful" contracts.[50] US states also engage in procurement preferences, with twenty states favoring small business in their procurement rules and thirty-four having some kind of preference that requires small business certification.[51]

Justifications for Small Business Cronyism

Defenders of small is beautiful offer three main justifications for this vast array of small business preferences: fairness, efficiency, and jobs.

Fairness

Small business advocates play on people's inclination to cheer for the underdog. That's why they claim that it's fair to tilt the playing field in their direction. Otherwise, they complain, large, profit-hungry firms would run roughshod over them. They fail to mention that to the extent larger firms gain market share it is not because of any duplicity but because large firms often have natural advantages, such as higher productivity and lower prices, that benefit the economy.

While some government preferences might be justified for disadvantaged social groups and economically distressed regions, there is simply no justification for small business preferences. Businesses compete to serve customers, and those that do so best are rewarded financially. But small business wants it both ways: it wants government protection from large firm competition but also wants to pocket hefty profits if it succeeds.

Likewise, defenders complain that small firms don't have the same resources to monitor federal contracts and fill out the paperwork, so small firms should receive special preferences. A related argument is that because some government regulations impose fixed costs on businesses, large businesses have an advantage because they can amortize these costs over a larger base. As an Australian commission describes it, "Small businesses often argue that regulations and the tax system involve 'unfair' burdens on small businesses relative to larger ones. By this they mean they lack the resources of larger businesses, but are still expected to undertake similar types and amounts of paperwork to comply with uniform regulations."[52]

At first glance, this claim of an unfair regulatory burden has some validity. The SBA reports that small firms pay 67 percent more per dollar of sales to comply with the tax code than larger firms.[53] It also reports that small firms bear a regulatory cost of $10,585 per employee, 36 percent higher than the cost of regulatory compliance for large businesses.[54] Given this inequity, surely small businesses deserve exemptions.

But many forms of small business favoritism have nothing to do with the scale efficiencies of large firms. For example, allowing small firms to pay lower tax rates has no relationship to the ability of large firms to comply more efficiently. Likewise, direct subsidies, lower government fees for government services such as obtaining patents, and subsidized financing have no relationship to firm efficiency. Nor does requiring small firms to provide the same employee benefits impose relatively higher costs on small firms. For these types of obligation there is no fairness rationale to justify preferential treatment.

What about other obligations where smaller firms can't spread fixed costs over a larger revenue base? As the SBA report notes, "In large firms, these fixed costs of compliance are spread over a large revenue, output, and employee base, which results in lower costs per unit of output as firm size increases."[55] Surely in these cases it is fair to reduce small business obligations.

But these "disadvantages" simply reflect one more kind of reduced economies of scale of small business. Small business advocates don't ask for laws imposing higher taxes on big businesses simply because large firms gain scale economies from using machinery. The accepted view among most economists is that markets should be allowed to work. As Steven Bradford writes,

Economists do not usually argue that the government should protect small businesses from the negative effects of these other economies of scale. Doing so would encourage businesses to be inefficiently small. So why should regulatory economies of scale be treated any differently from these "natural" economies of scale? If small businesses cannot efficiently comply with the cost of government regulation, as with any other cost of business, they can either grow to an efficient size or be driven out of business.[56]

Finally, the problem with this notion of regulatory cost parity efficiency is that it assumes size-based market share is static. Yes, imposing the same regulatory requirements on small business will increase regulatory costs, and could lead in some cases to the costs being higher than the benefits, at least on a static basis. But on a dynamic basis, making small and large firms comply with the same regulatory requirements would mean that larger, more efficient firms would gain market share, likely more than making up for the higher compliance costs. And there are real costs to society if small firms do not have to comply with the same rules that govern large firms.

Employment discrimination, for example, is no less harmful to those on the receiving end when the employer is small than when it is large.

Exempting small firms from regulation also makes it easier for legislators to expand regulation, even if it results in costs greater than benefits. If legislators know that the costs will be limited to large firms, they may be likely to impose more regulations than might be societally optimal. In essence, small business regulatory exemptions only serve to expand, not contract, the regulatory state.

Another argument for small business preferences advanced by some progressives and populists holds that big corporations represent the "one percent," while small businesses owners represent the middle and working classes. Therefore, small business preferences are a way to redistribute wealth. Such thinking is flawed on several fronts.

First, most of the costs from small business preferences (e.g., lower taxes, reduced regulations) are borne not by the "one percent" but by the 99 percent of consumers, workers, and taxpayers. When small businesses don't pay their fair share of taxes, individuals will have to pay more taxes or receive fewer government services.

Second, small business owners as a group are wealthier than employees. As Erik Hurst and Benjamin Pugsley write, "More wealthy individuals are small business owners than poor individuals. The subsidy on small business ownership just transfers resources to the wealthy from the poor."[57] Alan Viard and Amy Roden note that "the bulk of small business income goes to high-income households; in 2006, households in the top two income tax brackets received 72 percent of all income from noncorporate firms and S corporations."[58] As one book on business size has said, "This means that to the extent that government policy favors the interests of small business owners, the direction of income redistribution will be from the bottom to the top since small business owners enjoy incomes and assets greater than those of the average American."[59] Small business subsidies are a disguised subsidy to a portion of the American rich. And let's not forget that small businesses also pay lower wages, meaning the average worker would be better off if firms were larger.

Efficiency

The second justification for small business preferences is that they allegedly boost economic efficiency. But as William Brock and David Evans write, "To justify small-business assistance programs on efficiency grounds it is necessary to identify market breakdowns that lead to too few small firms or too few small-firm jobs."[60]

Try as they might, defenders of size discrimination cannot identify these breakdowns. This doesn't stop them from trying. An SBA report notes, "If federal regulations place a differentially large cost on small business, this potentially causes inefficiencies in the structure of American enterprises, and the relocation of production facilities to less regulated countries, and adversely affects the international competitiveness of domestically produced American products and services."[61] What are these supposed inefficiencies? The SBA never says. But presumably they are not the inefficiency of propping up less efficient small firms when otherwise more efficient large firms would gain market share.

What about the supposed competiveness issue? Competitiveness is important, but if policy makers are worried about competitiveness they should be aware that favoring small firms makes competitiveness worse, not better. As noted in chapter 3, large firms are more likely to be in traded-sector industries where higher taxes or regulatory burdens would have a more detrimental impact on firms' ability to compete in international markets. Most small businesses are in local-serving industries that compete only with other small firms in the same city or even neighborhood. Small business preferences are largely irrelevant to their collective survival (although perhaps not to their owners' income). What is relevant is the strength of consumer demand. If policy makers want to help Main Street, the best way to do so is to help large firms, including those in traded sectors, as that will most effectively grow the economic pie.

The hit to growth caused by small business favoritism occurs in two ways. First, a large body of evidence shows that size-based industrial policy hurts growth by enabling less efficient small firms to gain market share. As Pugsley and Hurst show, "While policymakers and research often invoke the benefits of small business subsidies, very few discuss the costs. The results in our paper suggest the costs may be non-trivial."[62] Likewise, Scott Shane writes, "Because the average existing new firm is more productive than the average new firm, we would be better off economically if we eliminated policies that encourage people to start businesses instead of taking jobs working for others."[63]

Second, discriminatory policies provide an incentive for small firms to stay small. Why add five workers when doing so puts you over the size threshold and subjects you to a host of new regulations and restricts your access to government handouts? As the Congressional Budget Office notes, "[The] disadvantage of policies favoring small firms is that such policies may inadvertently discourage certain firms from increasing in size and losing that preferential treatment."[64] A World Bank–University College London study finds that "constraints on size can be very detrimental for the economy because they restrict firm growth."[65]

Another argument is that if we end small business affirmative action we will end up with nothing but big companies. An Australian government study justifies size discrimination because "such variation in compliance costs per unit of output would confer a competitive advantage on larger firms that may reduce the viability of small firms. In turn, this could reduce competitive pressures and lead to less efficient outcomes."[66] The obvious rebuttal is, so what? If there were only big firms, workers would have better jobs. Productivity would be higher. Exports would increase.

In reality, of course, that won't happen, because there are many local, labor-intensive industries, such as barber shops, day-care centers, and dry cleaners, where there are no returns to scale and small firms are no less competitive than large firms or chains. In other sectors, if there is a risk of monopoly, which is highly unlikely, the appropriate remedy is competition policy, not wasteful small business subsidies.

Jobs

When all else fails, the fallback position of small business advocates is that ending small business affirmative action would mean fewer jobs. This is how many small business defenders justify these policies.

The SBA states, "Because small businesses are responsible for most of the job creation and technical innovations in the United States, Congress and the president have shown great interest in encouraging the growth and health of small businesses throughout the American economy."[67] The Congressional Budget Office writes, "Policies designed to prevent discrimination or reduce pollution would probably have smaller adverse effects on employment if they exempted small firms in those cases where compliance was particularly costly for small firms."[68] Likewise, the World Bank's International Finance Corporation writes that

the strategy of promoting small- and medium-scale enterprises rests on the recognition that these enterprises constitute the largest part of the private sector in developing countries, in terms of employment. ... For this reason, one of the cornerstones of the World Bank strategy for promoting small- and medium-scale enterprises is to "level the playing field;" that is, to create a business environment that gives equal opportunities to entrepreneurs of all sizes.[69]

Even business leaders fall into this trap. Lloyd Blankfein, Michael Bloomberg, Warren Buffett, and Michael Porter write, "How can we increase the speed of job creation? A critical part of the answer lies with America's small businesses."[70]

But as we showed in chapter 6, small business is not the source of most net new jobs, big firms are. However, even if they were, job creation is a function of macroeconomic policies, such as interest rates and fiscal policy, not micro policies, such as discriminatory procurement. If government treated small and large firms the same, the result would a modest shift in output and jobs to larger firms. Production doesn't vanish; it moves to larger firms, which would expand employment to produce the output needed to serve consumer demand. While they would not in the first order create as many jobs to fulfill that demand (because they are more productive), they would also charge lower prices or provide higher wages. Because that money (consumer savings and worker wages) is not buried in the backyard but is spent on new consumption, that in turn creates more jobs. In other words, employment levels are completely unrelated to firm size.

In summary, if a business is so fragile and unsuccessful that it can't comply with sensible laws, pay its fair share of taxes, and survive without special treatment from government, then maybe it should die.

A Policy Agenda for Size Neutrality

The policy implications of this analysis are simple and clear: governments, as well as multilateral institutions like the World Bank, should embrace size neutrality and end most programs and policies designed to favor small business over large. In railing against the purported pernicious influence of big business on Washington, House Speaker Paul Ryan said, "The government does not have a stake in the fight between David and Goliath—our only concern is to make certain that it is a fair fight."[71] With that we agree. The best place to start to establish that fair fight is to end pervasive *small business cronyism.* The point is not to favor big business. It's to let market forces and consumer choice be the deciding factors in any economy's firm size structure. We discuss exactly how to implement that size neutral agenda in the next chapter.

The politics of ending small business affirmative action are not easy. Despite the benefits to workers large firms provide, most Democrats still assume that the interests of the proletariat workers and petit bourgeois small business owners are aligned against capitalist corporations. Moreover, exempting small business from regulations makes it easier for Democrats to get support for expanding the regulatory state. If small businesses knew they had to comply with new regulations they would oppose them vociferously. For Republicans, small business owners provide a key source of fundraising and are a loyal voting bloc, despite long-standing and largely fruitless Democratic efforts to woo them. And the tea party wing of the Republican Party has a decided animus toward large organizations, either government or business, which makes it tough for even the most free market Republicans to not go along with small business industrial policy. And reinforcing this for both parties are the public's favorable views of small business and relatively unfavorable views of big business.[72]

Washington's decided tilt to smallness started in the 1950s to maintain small business support. More than half a century's worth of lower productivity and less innovation was perhaps a tolerable price to pay for social harmony. But today, with the US economy facing intense global economic competition and suffering from stagnant productivity and slow wage growth, we can no longer afford to tilt the economic playing field toward small business. It is time for size neutrality.

13   Living with Giants

A key question for any advanced society is how big businesses should be. From international trade to surface transportation to intellectual property policy, all factors that affect average firm size, the question of the optimal firm size is at the heart of many of the major economic policy debates of our time.

When it comes to firm size structure and policy there are five distinct intellectual camps: global libertarianism, global neoliberalism, progressive localism, national protectionism, and national developmentalism. For America and the nations of the world, only national developmentalism provides a sustainable path forward for nations.

Holders of the global libertarian view believe there is little that ties us together as a society other than a protection of property rights and that society's job therefore is to enable individual freedom, defined as the freedom to construct any kind of business and to buy and sell anywhere in the world.

For global libertarians, national borders are an infringement on liberty. Firms should have the freedom to structure their own conduct and workers should have unlimited freedom to live and work wherever they want. For this reason, they adamantly oppose policies favoring either small or large firms. Represented by think tanks like the Cato Institute, holders of this view firmly adhere to Milton Friedman's view that the purpose of business, large or small, is to make money for its owners; all other purposes, including social responsibility, are illegitimate.

Many global libertarians believe that corporations are an aberration, only existing because transaction costs are too high and can only be managed internally by corporations, as Ronald Coase famously wrote in his 1937 essay, "The Nature of the Firm." But many of them now believe that new technologies, such as blockchain and new sharing and matching internet platforms, will enable markets to provide what corporations long had to coordinate, enabling a significant share of transactions to be coordinated by not by corporations, but by individuals and small firms in robust market empowered by new information technologies.

Even though their belief in "the market" and their antipathy toward government lead global libertarians to oppose small business preferences, seeing them as inappropriately "picking winners," they also characterize policies that benefit big business, even if in the service of increased innovation or national competitiveness, as "crony capitalism." The Republican Party, long viewed as the party of big business, has become populated by libertarians who bring their distrust of large-scale enterprise with them. Jeffrey Anderson writes in the *Weekly Standard* that "Republicans have an opportunity to enhance their reputation as the party of Main Street."[1] Former chairman of the Republican National Committee Ed Gillespie believes "we're the party of small business."[2] Is this all just election year sloganeering? Hardly. For global libertarians, their animating mission is to downsize big government, and many see an unholy alliance between big business and big government. After all, they reason, the era before big government (either before the New Deal or the Progressive era, depending on your definition) was also an era in which most businesses were small. Shrink business; therefore government shrinks, so they think.

This explains why Senator Ted Cruz (R-TX) can state, "One of the biggest lies in politics is the lie that Republicans are the party of big business. Big business does great with big government. Big business is very happy to climb in bed with big government. Republicans are and should be the party of small business and of entrepreneurs."[3] It is why Congressman Dave Brat (R-VA), a member of the House Freedom Caucus, can say, "I am not against business. I am against big business in bed with big government."[4] And it is why Republican House Speaker Paul Ryan can equate big business with a "pernicious threat to free enterprise." Big business not only generates "crony capitalism" but government nationalization of the economy. Speaker Ryan writes, "Big businesses' frenzied political dealings are not driven by party or ideology, but rather by zero-sum thinking in which their gain must come from a competitor's loss. Erecting barriers to competition is a key to maintaining advantage and market share."[5] In other words, the global libertarians understand that a globalized economy with large businesses requires an activist, developmental state, not a minimalist state, and for them, small government trumps big business, even if it means lower economic growth and reduced competitiveness.

A second camp is made up of the global neoliberals, who have been dominant among centrist Democrats and moderate Republicans. Like the global libertarians, global neoliberals tend to be agnostic about size, and they embrace unfettered global markets and division of labor. However, unlike the libertarians, they support borders, though with a high rate of immigration, both skilled and unskilled. They also support a more activist state, not to help large firms compete, an activity they often decry as inappropriate industrial policy—a term of derision for them—but rather to compensate the "losers" in the immobile national workforce who are hurt by unfettered global trade and immigration.

Unlike global libertarians, who largely see antitrust policy as limiting the freedom of entrepreneurs, including their freedom to be as big as they want and to buy whatever companies they want, global neoliberals privilege competition. For them the goal is maximizing competition in the interest of the lowest possible prices for consumers, in a competitive market embedded in an economy that is implicitly assumed to be technologically static. This is why, notwithstanding their support of large business and big banks, global neoliberals regularly sing the praises of small businesses and government policies to help them, in part to demonstrate their support of "Main Street" as a way to reduce resistance to their agenda. Emblematic is a June 2016 op-ed by Goldman Sachs CEO Lloyd Blankfein, Michael Bloomberg, Warren Buffett, and Harvard Business School professor Michael Porter that asserts: "More than six years into a sluggish recovery, we must do more to help small businesses drive a new generation of growth."[6] Championing small business is a way to signal support by neoliberals for the "losers" in the current system in order to preserve the system.

The third school is progressive localism. If global neoliberals and libertarians want a world with few or no borders, one in which firms, ideally small, compete without the help of the state, progressive localists seek an alternative economy predominantly made up of small firms, supported by big government and protected from global competition. In industries where large firms are inevitable, progressive localists would prefer to structure them as heavily regulated public utilities or to have government provide the service (e.g., municipally owned broadband providers, government funded medical R&D, and so on). For this school, local production by small firms (or even better, worker-owned co-ops or government-owned enterprises) is the desired model, and there is no need for large corporations with extended production chains. Many seek a return to an idealized prior world of national and even regional autarky in which most products and services are produced by small organizations in close geographic proximity to where they are consumed. Inspired by the motto "Think global, act local," they want to act, produce, and consume at the local level. Progressive localists are willing to sacrifice consumers' interest in the lowest possible prices and largest possible incomes, for their small producer vision, in part because they reject consumerism as a vice and a blight on the global environment.

Their outright animus toward large firms drives much of the policy advocacy of progressive localists—not only antitrust policy, which directly affects firm size, but also other policies that at first glance have little to do directly with the size of firms. This is illustrated by the indiscriminate opposition of many progressive localists to trade liberalization, even when accompanied by tough measures against foreign mercantilism. Progressives rightly understand that since the beginning of the Industrial Revolution, trade has enabled large-scale economies, which in turn enable bigness. It is no different now as global integration facilitates the growth of large corporations that can achieve global reach and scale and that can more easily generate the large-scale innovations that are difficult to achieve without access to global markets. Rather than accept the benefits from the growth of transnational corporations while seeking to align their interests with the national interest, progressive localists tend to favor national firms over transnational firms and local firms over national firms as a matter of principle.

We see the same "keep business small" logic of progressive localism playing out in a host of other issues. For example, one factor that has enabled large firms has been the growth of interstate and intracity transportation networks. When firms can easily get goods to market anywhere in the nation, they get bigger. When consumers can easily get to more stores, stores get bigger. This goes a long way toward explaining the refusal of today's gentry liberals to support highway and road expansion in favor of transit, even though personal electric cars could be even more environmentally sustainable than riding in diesel buses.[7] In their ideal world, we would be living in compact cities, walking to the locally owned mom-and-pop store to shop, and buying our organic, non-GMO food in a local farmer's market. This longing for a small business economy also explains the progressive's views toward intellectual property (IP), including patents and copyright. While IP enables firms of all sizes and in fact is used more by small firms than by large ones, many progressives see strong IP rights as something enabling big corporations alone.[8] And in fact, by enabling innovators to earn revenues from innovation, IP does enable firms of all sizes to get larger. Not only can they take more risks to invest in innovation, they can also earn revenues from it and win large market shares if the innovation is successful.

To the extent that progressive localists accept international trade, they want it conducted in a system of global governance that ensures a "level playing field" of global labor and environmental standards, all backed up by stronger global governance institutions, including global labor unions. Only then, they argue, can corporations be limited in global labor and regulatory arbitrage. Notwithstanding their largely conservative leanings, small business owners are seen as part of a global coalition of the oppressed, fighting alongside the working class against the hegemony of large soulless corporations.

One reason the progressive localist camp has grown among the left is that as big corporations moved from being multistate companies after World War II to multinational ones in the last two decades, more and more on the left have lost faith that corporate and national interests can be aligned. Rather than try to align the interests of the new global oligopolies with the national interest, as the national developmentalist school discussed below would have us do, progressive localists have simply abandoned large firms for small, which they rightly see as tied to the US economy. The problem, of course, is that an economy of small firms would consign American workers to significantly lower living standards.

The fourth school of thought about the proper role of big business today is national protectionism. Until the election of Donald Trump, this group was largely ignored. But Trump tapped into a major vein of unease with globalization and multinational corporations. National protectionists are less concerned about the size of firms than about their loyalty. National protectionists support firms of any size as long as they are strongly identi-fied with the United States, but they are skeptical of global multinationals that don't owe loyalty to the nation. President Trump has not hesitated to attack Fortune 100 companies such as Ford, Nike, and United Technologies for offshoring jobs.[9] Trump and his supporters would also likely criticize a small business that offshored jobs. In this sense, they are size agnostic. As President Trump has said, "But the small business, we are going to simplify, reduce, eliminate regulations—we're doing that for big business, too, by the way. There can't be any discrimination, right?"[10]

In contrast to the libertarians, the national protectionists reject open borders in both immigration and trade policy and see the ability and willingness to limit foreign entry as the defining characteristics of national sovereignty. And unlike both the libertarians and the neoliberals, they see globalization as rigged, not only because many other nations embrace a vast array of unfair mercantilist practices (something libertarians are indifferent to and neoliberals argue has no real negative effect on the US economy) but also because they see the simple act of competing with low-wage nations as inherently unfair and detrimental to American workers. When it comes to firm size, the nationalists are agnostic, but to the extent that their policies limit the ability of US corporations to gain global market share or have global supply chains, the net result could very well be a shift to middle-sized, non-publicly traded companies, of the kind President Trump ran for most of his career.

The fifth school, and the one to which we subscribe, can be termed national developmentalism.[11] Unlike the global libertarians and neoliberals, who fundamentally reject the notion that nations compete for economic advantage and that large firms are required to win that competition, national developmentalists see national economies in direct competition for high-value-added jobs and view the big firms that can marshal the scale needed to compete as critical national resources. Unlike the progressive localists and the national protectionists, who want to erect barriers to global integration, national developmentalists see deeper global economic integration as beneficial in many ways but only if the US federal government works to obtain the maximum benefits for workers and regions. For this reason, the national developmentalist school extends a cautious welcome to efficient global oligopolies. Developmentalists seek to maximize foreign export markets for high-value-added US exports. But they recognize that this challenge cannot be won unless there is an active developmental state that partners with companies (often big ones, but also small innovative ones) to help them innovate, be more productive, export and generally compete globally.

The first four schools have little to say about technological innovation and the productivity increases that it makes possible. Libertarians and neoliberals assume that innovation is inevitable and that government plays little role; progressives are skeptical of innovation and productivity because of their effects on worker displacement; economic nationalists tend to ignore innovation altogether. But for the school of national developmentalism, technology-driven productivity growth should be the primary objective of economic policy. From Schumpeter to Galbraith to Baumol, leading students of innovation have agreed that technological innovation is most likely when firms are big enough to reap economies of scale (sorry, producer republicans!) and are also big enough to have some control over the prices they charge; this permits them to reinvest excess profits in new rounds of competition with rivals on the basis of innovation, not price (sorry, market fundamentalists!).

Both the progressive localists and the national developmentalists, unlike the global libertarians and global neoliberals, are sometimes willing to sacrifice consumers' interest in the lowest possible prices for public purposes. For political and social reasons, progressive localists in the producer republican tradition want to protect small, inefficient producers from being driven out of business by larger, more efficient enterprises—preserving a smaller republican social order at the cost of higher prices for consumers, if necessary. The national developmental school is willing to tolerate somewhat higher consumer prices as well, but for a different reason: to give large, dynamic, oligopolistic firms the resources they need to stay ahead in their competition with their rivals, which is based on ceaseless innovation rather than relentless cost cutting. The markets rigged by progressive localists, if they succeed, may permanently raise prices for consumers. But competition to innovate among high-tech oligopolistic firms with ephemeral innovation rents usually drive down the costs of the goods and services they provide or improves quality and the development of new products or services, in part thanks to the R&D that their temporary excess profits make possible. Let us be clear: we support big firms for the practical reason that their scale and behavior can promote innovation productivity growth, in the right circumstances. We do not defend all firms that are big or all things that big firms may do. Where there are constant or diminishing returns to scale, concentration may not be beneficial and could be harmful. We would not support, for example, an attempt by a nursing home chain—to name a presently low-tech, labor-intensive industry in which there are constant or diminishing returns to scale—to buy up all the nursing homes in the United States.

Nor would we look kindly on a dynamic, efficient large innovation-based company that, instead of reinvesting its profits in the next generation of advanced machinery or R&D, squandered them in excess compensation for its executives or financial engineering like stock buy-backs that artificially boost the company's stock. That is just bad—that is, unproductive—behavior. There are many ways in which big firms can go wrong and only a few in which they can go right—but when they do go right, all of society can benefit from increased productivity, innovation, and competitiveness.

Moreover, in the perspective of the developmentalist school, the productivity that policy makers should want to maximize is the relative productivity of their own national economy, not the absolute productivity of the world economy. Nation-states are clubs run for the benefit of their members, not global charities. For the United States, if all high-value-added production were transferred by multinational corporations to other countries, leaving the United States with only low-value-added traded activities such as tourism and waste paper, in absolute terms it is possible the world as a whole might be more productive and US consumers in some scenarios could be better off. But policy makers and economists should view a country's residents not only as consumers but also as workers. This is something else which those of us of the national developmentalist school share with progressive localists and national protectionists, but not with global libertarians and neoliberals.

Most important of all, for considerations of national security in a world of rival powers, national economic policy makers must always be concerned with the distribution of relative productive capability and wealth among nations, even if academic economists prefer to ignore these strategic factors and think solely about absolute global gains from economic growth. To defend our nation-state perspective would require a book-length discussion of moral and political philosophy. Here we will simply state our premise:

the primary but not sole objective of economic policy should be maximizing national innovation and productivity growth. If this can be done in a way that boosts global productivity growth at the same time—and often it can—all the better. But the goal is higher productivity for the United States, not the United Nations.

With this in mind, we discuss first the kind of steps big corporations, particularly transnational firms, need to take to at least partially restore their tarnished reputations, before turning to the questions of how economic policy can be restructured to be size neutral and how advanced societies can learn to live with business giants without being trampled in the process.

Can We Ever Really Like Big Business?

Praising the small and attacking the big makes for good politics and nice feelings, but it's bad economics and bad policy. So restoring the reputation of big business and even getting it to the point where a majority of voters once again see big firms as a whole as a force for economic progress is a key task of our time.

This is important because, notwithstanding the beliefs of most economists and the desires of most CEOs, economics is really political economy. Like it or not, at some point, politics intrudes into economics. As the 2016 US presidential election clearly demonstrated, large numbers of voters no longer subscribe to global neoliberalism, not because they didn't study economics in college, but because it no longer works for them. Unfortunately, unless we come up with a new bargain between the democratic nation-state and big business, the political fault lines of our time will be between the progressive localists (e.g., Senator Bernie Sanders) and the national protectionists (e.g., Donald Trump). If big business is not willing to commit to fulfilling national goals, voters may favor either an economy based on small businesses or a nationalist economy that, while indifferent to firm size, puts stringent limits on the globally integrated corporation. In both cases—small businesses and nationalist-oriented larger businesses—voters see them as having the same goals they have, despite all the limitations of small business and national-only businesses.

In the 1930s, in the midst of the Great Depression and rising anger at the corporate class, which FDR termed "economic royalists," the New Deal saved capitalism from the capitalists. Today we are in need of a similar new bargain that tries to reduce the sharp contrasts between the goals of big business and the goals of host nations.

What would this new grand bargain between the multinational corporation and the democratic nation-state be based on? Global libertarianism can't be the choice as it is something only a modest number of devotees of Ayn Rand and Friedrich Hayek could embrace. As the elections in Europe and America have demonstrated, most voters reject a notion of open borders and stateless corporations and a government that leaves individuals to fend completely for themselves.

Likewise, progressive localism is a fantasy because any effort to transform the US economy into a small business paradise would be rejected by most voters for the simple reason that prices would rise and wages fall. And global labor and environmental standards at US levels will never be embraced by developing nations.

Advocates of centrist global neoliberalism continue to hold out hope that if they just make their case more clearly and loudly and increase their payouts for the "losers," voters will finally break free of their false consciousness and embrace unfettered free trade and high levels of immigration. But voters on both sides of the Atlantic are not rejecting neoliberalism because they failed Economics 101. They are rejecting it because it has failed to deliver on its promises and resulted in too much manufacturing job loss, not enough economic growth, and too much inequality. For most citizens in modern democracies, the interests of the nation have to come first. Most citizens want to avoid creating losers, not compensate them. Donald Trump tapped into this very real feeling when he said that America never wins any more.

However, despite the appeal of national protectionism in the 2016 US election, this approach can't be the answer for the simple reason that too many industries are already regional or global in structure. Trying to recreate highly autarkic national economies around the world would lead to reduced productivity, as firms in industries with increasing returns would be unable to reach the global scale they need. As of this writing, there are 193 member states of the United Nations. There cannot be 193 duplicative national aerospace or automobile or computer enterprises. Moreover, a wave of national protectionism would also quickly devolve into a politics of recrimination and hostility among countries.

What, then, should be the answer that enables big business to thrive while at the same enabling the US economy and the US worker to thrive? From the perspective of national developmentalism, the federal government, collaborating with state governments, needs to craft a new bargain with big transnational firms. Under this bargain, the federal government would help big corporations compete with the state-backed national champions of other countries by means of such programs as the Export-Import Bank, the right tax incentives for domestic investment, support for infrastructure and workforce development, and cooperative public-private R&D programs. The national government would also, within limits, allow productive firms to be big. And the government would actively defend big corporations' economic interests against those of other nations that seek to appropriate their property (physical or otherwise), force them to localize production, or unfairly subsidize and protect US corporations' foreign competitors.

In return, firms that enjoy large shares of the US market and employ significant numbers of Americans, whether they are chartered in the United States or elsewhere, would need to reciprocate, by demonstrating more deference to the well-being of the United States. That doesn't mean never moving jobs offshore; it does mean thinking twice before doing it and working first to boost productivity and innovation to try to keep work at home. It means doing more to help the workers and the communities big corporations are in and doing more to invest in America, as well as actively supporting politically a developmental state policy agenda.

To regain public acceptance, if not admiration, big business leaders, including the executives of foreign firms that do substantial business in the United States, need to do several other things as part of this bargain. First, they need to lead a repositioning of corporate governance, starting with an outright rejection of the notion that the only purpose of business is to satisfy shareholders. Nearly half a century ago Milton Friedman and other free market absolutists led the charge that asserted that the sole purpose of business was to make a profit and that any effort spent on corporate social responsibility was a violation of shareholder interest. This understanding of the nature and purpose of the firm became embedded not only in the global libertarian school but in the neoliberal school as well.

From the perspective of individual CEOs, corporate social responsibility (CSR) might be a "waste" and not part of their mission, especially if it doesn't pay off with a better reputation among their customers. But from the perspective of defending big business and corporate capitalism writ large, CSR is not a waste, it is essential. But free market advocates and the CEOs who embrace them forget that for better or for worse, there is no escaping that we live in a political economy, not just a market economy, and if voters do not have at least a modicum of good will toward big corporations, they will not support the policies needed to sustain them.

All too often corporate executives subscribe to the fiction that the firms they lead are global entities without an address, that they are not citizens of the United States but of the world. They can't have it both ways. If they want to be citizens of the world, they can't expect to enjoy the rights that citizens of the United States hold and the assistance of the US government.

Fixing this dilemma will not be easy. The first step will require corporate leaders to publicly identify it as a problem and propose solutions to fixing it. US corporations used to understand this before the rise of the shareholder value movement and the decline of the role and prominence of "corporate statesmen." They understood that it was a collective action problem that would only be addressed if all firms pitched in and free riders were shunned and shamed. Bruce Barton, a marketing executive who advocated for big companies, spoke at the National Association of Manufacturers convention in 1935, stating, "If any manufacturer says 'I do not care what the common mass of people think about my business, whether it be popular or unpopular with them, that man is a liability to all industry. No major industry has any moral right to allow itself to be unexplained, misunderstood or publicly distrusted, for by its unpopularity it poisons the pond in which we must all fish."[12]

It is probably too much to expect Wall Street to call for reform, insofar as many in the finance industry benefit the most from quarterly capitalism and unrestrained globalization. But big firms in the nonfinancial sector need to stand up and say enough is enough. More corporate leaders need to echo Jack Welch, the former CEO of General Electric, who said that it was "a dumb idea" for executives to focus so heavily on quarterly earnings and share prices.[13] More broadly this would require big-firm CEOs to play a new role: to act as many CEOs, such as GM's Charlie Wilson, GE's Reginald Jones, HP's John Young, Loral Space and Communication's Bernard Schwartz, and DuPont's Irving Shapiro, did in the past, as corporate statesmen defending not just their firm or their industry but the American system.

There are other steps big business can take. One is to do a better job of policing its own. It's a challenge that for every 50 or 100 big corporations that generally try to do the right thing there is one scofflaw, run by a CEO who cares only about his own bonus and golden parachute. That CEO and company besmirch the reputation of all large firms. Big business leaders need to make it clear that when leaders of other big firms act unethically, even if legally, they will be publicly ostracized by the corporate community.

Big business also needs to stop being reluctant to toot its own horn. Unless the leaders of big firms defend the benefits that scale provides, small business defenders will continue to successfully play the victim card. As Jonathan Bean writes, "If America is becoming a 'nation of victims,' is it a good thing, even when the so-called victims are as popular as small business? Perhaps it reflects a historical trend that a population once admired for self-reliance is now just another victimized group entitled to the solicitous care of the federal government."[14] It's time for corporate leaders to unabashedly defend bigness and not feel that they must always justify any action they take or support as valid because it also helps small firms. Explaining how big corporations support small business through purchasing and other activities can backfire by making people believe that they can have a thriving economy without big business. It is time for big corporations to stop being apologetic and clearly tell their story about how they, through their size, generate enormous benefits for the society and economy: good jobs, innovation, productivity, exports, and the like.

Finally, as both major US political parties have become more politically polarized, each for different reasons has developed an antipathy toward large business and support for small. In the 1950s and 1960s, one reason Republicans were willing to support small business policies, including the creation of the Small Business Administration (SBA), "was to deflect criticism that Republicans were the party of big business."[15] Today, many libertarian Republicans see big business as in bed with big government. Populists on the left have made common cause with these right-wing libertarians in their disdain for large business, co-opting the language of the right to paint their antipathy toward large business in the guise of support of markets. For example, the liberal crusader Lawrence Lessig wrote an article titled "The Left and Right Share a Common Enemy: Capitalists Who Corrupt Capitalism."[16]

Increasingly, any policy that even inadvertently helps big business, even if it is clearly in the public interest, is attacked on those grounds alone. For if big business is the enemy, then under no circumstances can it be helped, even if doing so would help America. We have, tragically, come to a time when what is good for GM can never be good for the nation under any circumstances.

A National Developmentalist Agenda

At the end of the day, big businesses can do only so much on their own to restore their reputation. They need government to create the conditions in which they can best contribute to national economic success. In other words, they need the support of government to help recreate Charlie Wilson's view: to better align corporate interest with national interest. But the libertarian, neoliberal, and localist camps provide no answers, delineate no path forward. The first two camps deny an active role for government, while the localists simply reject big business. And national protectionists offer only the dead end of "small government protectionism" where government abandons its role to help producers innovate or become productive, while at the same time limiting their ability to reach needed global scale.

Only national developmentalism holds the answer. Big business needs to vigorously advocate for a developmental state that helps them better align their interests with the national interests. This means that big business needs to encourage the federal government to think like a state. From Wyoming to California, from Rhode Island to Texas, all fifty states, whether red state or blue, have embraced the developmental state model.

As proponents of the developmental state, state economic development officials understand that a key driver of their state's economic health is the health of their traded sectors—the companies that do business nationally and globally. Yet in Washington, neoliberal policy makers and economists do not think this way. For them, the US economy is so large that it doesn't matter whether an establishment closes because of foreign competition or if a US firm moves production offshore. In their worldview, while individual workers might be hurt, the US economy would actually benefit as this would be a sign that the global free market was working as it should.

State "developmental economists" also understand that the goal is not just traded-sector job growth but the growth of high-wage industries and boosting productivity. It's relatively easy for a state to have lots of jobs in low-wage manufacturing or traded services such as call centers. It's quite another thing to grow jobs in higher-wage, higher-value-added manufacturing and service sector industries and firms. That's why virtually every state's economic development program, whether the governor is Republican or Democrat, "picks winners" in the sense of targeting high-value-added sectors in which the state has a potential competitive advantage. To be clear, states don't target particular firms as winners, as much as particular sectors (e.g., life sciences), broad technologies (e.g., biotechnology), or infrastructure (e.g., broadband).

This kind of "picking winners" is anathema to the libertarians and neoliberals, who believe that what a country makes does not matter. For them, targeting key sectors is "industrial policy," a concept to be derided. The chairman of the Council of Economic Advisers under President George H. W. Bush, Michael Boskin, spoke for many when he reportedly quipped, "Potato chips, computer chips, what's the difference? $100 of one or $100 of the other is still $100."[17]

So what would a federal developmental state agenda looks like? First, the federal government would consider such issues as trade, tax, talent, technology, and regulatory policy from the perspective of advancing competitiveness, innovation, and productivity. Such an agenda would include corporate tax reform that cut corporations' statutory and effective rates but also focused on ensuring that firms in traded-sector industries (e.g., manufacturing, software, traded services) paid less than firms in nontraded sectors (e.g., retail). The government would also increase tax incentives for firms to invest in the building blocks of growth in America. The bargain should be that the federal government would cut a business's taxes if that business invested in R&D, new machinery and equipment, and workforce training.

A part of this bargain should be that government expects business to work to try to keep high-value-added production at home, or bring it back, and in exchange government would work on much tougher enforcement against foreign mercantilist policies that pressure big companies to move production offshore or support their own domestic companies to capture market share. Currently too many US multinationals are defenseless against the mercantilist policies and threats by other nations that say either move production or technology here or lose access to our market. Expecting companies to say no to that on their own is naïve at best.

Another part of the deal would significantly expand federal support for R&D but target that increase not to abstract basic science but at directed research focused on solving big societal challenges, such as health care, clean energy, productivity, and industrial competitiveness and direct much of this to government-industry research partnerships. The deal would also call on businesses to increase their commitment to training American workers, with the federal government agreeing to support industry-led regional skills alliances and apprenticeship programs in which industry took the lead in organizing and funding cooperative training initiatives, with the government providing at least half the funding. It would involve expanding a range of enterprise support programs related to exporting (e.g., the Ex-Im Bank for export financing); technology (the Manufacturing USA program to help support cost-shared precompetitive R&D and the NIST Manufacturing Extension Partnerships to help small manufacturers modernize), and infrastructure (including expanding and modernizing US surface and aviation transportation systems and supporting rural broadband investment).

Getting Competition Policy Right

One component of a national developmentalist agenda is getting competition policy right. Neo-Brandeisians see big as bad and want to use competition policy to achieve their goals. But it would be a serious mistake to use competition policy to make firms smaller. As we noted in chapter 4, if the United States had the same distribution as in Europe, per capita income would be $2,060 lower as smaller firms are less productive than large ones.

To make progress in competition policy, we need to distinguish among two kinds of theories of market structure. The first kind treats firm behavior and market structure as differentiated only by size: some firms are small and some are big. The second kind of theory of market structure treats large firms and small ones as, in many cases, different in kind, as Chandler (core and periphery), Galbraith (planning system and market system), and Baumol ("innovative oligopolies" and small firms) all have done. The latter framing, large firms and small ones as different in kind, seems more accurate in the real world.

This suggests that we should recognize that firms of different sizes play different and complementary roles and that a reflexive drive for more small firms, and even more competition, misses the mark. We should let the words of Corwin D. Edwards guide us. Edwards, chairman of the policy board during World War II at the Antitrust Division of the Justice Department, had a pragmatic view that we would do well to emulate today. It's worth reproducing a statement in full from his book *Big Business and the Policy of Competition*:

The standards for a selective appraisal are easy to state, though hard to apply. Big companies should not be too few and too big. They should not have the power to exclude promising new concerns. They should not be able to destroy the independence of small companies. They should remain independent of each other and in competition with each other. Bigness that creates danger should be prevented when it contributes nothing to efficiency of operation and when its only contribution to the efficiency of the large enterprise consists of shifting risks and costs from that enterprise to weaker concerns. Big companies should, however, be big enough to operate large technological processes, to adopt economical methods of shipment, to undertake substantial programs of research and development, to integrate vertically where efficiency is increased thereby, and, in general, to perform such useful functions as require large organizations. Where the attainment of this degree of bigness endangers competition, danger that is not imminent should be accepted, though with vigilance; but clear and present danger or actual damage to competition should not be passively accepted.[18]

In other words, we need to recognize that different industries will have different size structures, that bigness can lead to considerable economic benefits, but that we also need to vigilant against abuses. This leads to six key principles.

First, antitrust provisions should be more neutral toward size and competition. The very term "antitrust" implies that trusts and other combinations are inherently bad. The more neutral European term "competition policy" is a better fit. But even that presumes that if some competition is good, more is better, which clearly is not the case. As Columbia law professor Michael Heller points out in his book *The Gridlock Economy*, there can be too much competition:

To cure underuse in an anticommons, the correct social policy should be protrust, to coin a term. Protrust should be a legitimate English word like antitrust. ... Protrust policy and antitrust enforcement together should constitute national "competition law," to use the European Union's umbrella category for this regulatory arena.[19]

Second, antitrust should have a distinct focus on improving productivity. Doing so would mean placing more weight on the impacts of actions in the marketplace on productivity and relatively less weight on short-term price effects, even if they "distort" market allocation or harm incumbent firms. As Harvard's Michael Porter argues, "Since the role of competition is to increase a nation's standard of living and long-term consumer welfare via rising productivity growth, the new standard for antitrust should be productivity growth, rather than price/cost margins or profitability."[20] This is because, as Xavier Vives points out, under certain conditions, heightened competition (at least for a market of fixed size) can actually diminish a firm's incentive to make productivity-enhancing investments and innovation because the firm is starved of the revenues it needs to make investments in productivity-enhancing technology.[21] Thus a productivity-focused view of competition policy would recognize the importance of larger firms in driving productivity, in part through the ability of large firms to marshal resources and gain scale. This is particularly important in industries with low marginal costs and high fixed costs. In these industries, a greater market share means lower overall production costs.

Third, it's important to recognize that concentration may not be problematic. For more than half a century, courts have not declared monopolies illegal per se. As Adkinson, Grimm, and Bryan write, courts "have recognized that monopoly may be obtained by superior skill and unmatched effort." They have understood that "the successful competitor, having been urged to compete, must not be turned upon when he wins."[22] In *Verizon v. Trinko*, the Supreme Court writes:

The mere possession of monopoly power, and the concomitant charging of monopoly prices, is not only not unlawful; it is an important element of the free-market system. The opportunity to charge monopoly prices—at least for a short period—is what attracts "business acumen" in the first place; it induces risk taking that produces innovation and economic growth. To safeguard the incentive to innovate, the possession of monopoly power will not be found unlawful unless it is accompanied by an element of anticompetitive conduct.[23]

Thus, rather than a focus on size and market power, the focus should be more on the abuse of market power. Market power is not the same as concentration, as there are some markets that are relatively concentrated (e.g., wireless and wireline broadband) but in which competitive forces are fairly strong, and there are some markets that are atomized but experience weak competitive forces because of collusion (e.g., optometry and sales of contact lens).[24]

In this regard, merger review should always thoroughly investigate mergers to determine the nature of market power gain. The key is to distinguish between market power that supports innovation (or other benefits, such as productivity and network externalities) and market power that enables simple abuse (higher prices with little gain in productivity or innovation). Market power can often enable the former. As Possas and Fagundes argue, "The basic lesson drawn from the neo-Schumpeterian view is that the potential direction of market power use (or abuse) should not be prejudged as necessarily harmful to competition and welfare, and consequently repressed, from a dynamic standpoint."[25] According to innovation scholar Richard Nelson, too little market power can in some cases weaken competition because competitors would be less able to innovate and engage in dynamic competition.[26] Moreover, a study by the Bureau of Labor Statistics found that mergers in concentrated industries had a higher positive effect on total factor productivity growth than mergers in less concentrated industries and that overall, "Mergers increased TFP [total factor productivity] growth by a substantial amount."[27]

More specifically, policy makers should not revise the Department of Justice's merger guidelines as the neo-Brandeisians want. The current merger guidelines are not focused narrowly on market structure but rather on the likely impact of the merger on price and output. Neo-Brandeisians want to change that and go back to a world of Brown Shoe and Vons Supermarket, where mergers were rejected for creating firms with only modest market share.[28] The reason not to do this is that market share is an arbitrary factor; it is sector specific. Again, Corwin Edwards got it right when he wrote:

The degree of bigness which is appropriate to the technology of a given industry changes from time to time as productive methods change. It may be affected by the development of assembly lines, by the substitution of electric energy for belt drives, by automation, and by a host of other influences. A limit upon size that would be appropriate to the automobile industry would be meaninglessly large for women's garments. A limit appropriate to the manufacture of biscuits and crackers would be hopelessly small for automobile manufacture. A limit suitable to the aluminum industry in 1930 might be unsuitable in 1955.[29]

Likewise, we should retain the "rule-of-reason" analysis of mergers rather than, as the neo-Brandeisians want, a per se standard, and again, for the same reason.

Fourth, any rational approach to competition policy should not automatically see interfirm collaboration as suspect. Too many believe Adam Smith when he wrote, "People of the same trade seldom meet together, even for merriment and diversion, but the conversation ends in a conspiracy against the public, or in some contrivance to raise prices."[30] Maybe this was true in an economy in which the most complicated thing people made was a wooden ship. But in a complex, technology-driven economy that requires a degree of coordination it is simply wrong.

To work effectively, the present economy requires not only competition but also cooperation (what Brandenburger and Nalebuff termed "coopetition") among firms to drive growth and innovation.[31] Indeed, many industries are characterized by complex cooperative ecosystems where firms that compete intensely against one another also collaborate on a host of issues and the collaboration results in increased productivity and innovation.[32] As Hakan Hakansson and Ivan Snehota write, interfirm "relationships make it possible to access and exploit the resources of other parties and to link the parties' activities together."[33] And as Michael Mandel writes, often one or two large firms play a key role in organizing the ecosystem for collaboration: "these ecosystems require management by a core company or companies with the resources and scale to provide leadership and technological direction. This task typically cannot be handled by a small company or startup."[34]

As Carl Shapiro has noted:

Collaboration among industry participants may be especially important in dynamic industries. ... Antitrust doctrine, with its emphasis on limiting coordination among competitors, can have difficulty distinguishing pro-competitive collaboration from collusion, especially in situations where two parties may have complex relationships that involve competition in some areas and collaboration in others. These complexities are the norm for large firms in the information technology sector of the economy.[35]

Even if this collaboration takes the form of collusion it is not necessarily always bad. As a study by Daniel Asmat, of the US Department of Justice's antitrust group, finds, collusion among semiconductor makers increased prices of chips at the end of their life cycle by up to 25 percent but decreased prices of next generation chips by up to 70 percent by letting firms produce more of the new product and gaining from economies of scale and learning curves.[36]

Fifth, competition authorities should give adequate weight in merger analysis to how the mergers affect company efficiencies and innovation. Even if a particular merger might lead to an increase in market power and a concomitant reduction in allocative efficiency and/or hurt other companies in the marketplace, such a merger might expand economic welfare if it leads to even greater efficiencies from consolidation, particularly in industries with declining marginal costs, where added scale or network effects (e.g., through de facto standardization and coordination) can drive significant cost savings. Hence, one challenge is that although potential allocative efficiency losses from a merger are relatively easy to measure, the long-term benefits from innovation and productivity are harder to visualize and measure. It is important to differentiate between market power that is anticompetitive and anticonsumer and market power that is pro-innovation. Antitrust authorities should therefore acknowledge that the task of differentiation is a necessary if difficult one to engage, and should not sweepingly condemn all market power. But even market power should not be the predominant focus; rather, the focus should be on behavior to get or maintain that market power. If companies use anticompetitive means to get or maintain market power, that should be the main focus.

Sixth, government should be humble about its ability to predict the future of any industry. Absent government protection, no business is likely to enjoy a prolonged period of dominance. As we saw with Microsoft in the 2000s and may potentially see with Google in the next decade, a modern "monopoly's" dominance in any one industry belies the competitive threat it faces from adjacent competitors and the constant onslaught of new entrants. As Shapiro and Varian note, "The information economy is populated by temporary, or fragile, monopolies. Hardware and software firms vie for dominance, knowing that today's leading technology or architecture will, more likely than not, be toppled in short order by an upstart with superior technology."[37] As Schumpeter noted, this is a different kind of competition than that envisioned in the conventional doctrine:

It is hardly necessary to point out that competition of the kind we now have in mind acts not only when in being but also when it is merely an ever present threat. It disciplines before it attacks. The businessman feels himself to be in a competitive situation even if he is alone in his field or if, although not alone, he holds a position such that investigating government experts fail to see any competition between him and any other firms in the same or neighboring field and in consequence conclude that his talk, under examination, about his competitive sorrows is all make believe.[38]

Governments should worry about the long term later. As John Maynard Keynes said, "In the long run we're all dead." The right answer usually is to let consumers reap the windfall of social and economic gains that new platforms are creating today. Most of these modern monopolies won't be dominant long enough for the downside to materialize.

The Right Small Business Policy

In addition to the right competition policy, the national developmentalist school would advocate for size neutrality, replacing small business favoritism in taxation, regulation, and other policy areas with size-neutral policies that treat all firms the same.

Doing this would mean redesigning the tax code so it treated firms of different sizes alike. To do so, governments should first eliminate differential corporate tax brackets whereby the first amount of income is taxed less than later amounts. Second, they should remove size limits on tax incentives, such as in Section 179 of the US tax code, which allows business to immediately deduct qualifying investments, but only up to $500,000. Third, they should reduce the corporate income tax rate since corporations pay taxes at both the corporate and the individual level, and if necessary should raise rates on individuals, including so-called pass-through businesses. Eliminating most special tax favors based on firm size can, according to the International Monetary Fund "potentially sizeable."[39]

Size neutrality means repealing virtually all the special preferences in government procurement designed to favor small firms. Government agencies at all levels should be able to procure goods and services from whatever firm, large or small, provides the best value. To be sure, procurement processes should be streamlined and easy for all firms to access, but they should not artificially favor small businesses at the cost to taxpayers.

Size neutrality means ending most subsidies targeted at small business. All businesses, regardless of size, should pay the same fee for equivalent services from governments, such as patent applications or spectrum fees. Governments should also eliminate small business loan programs. If a small firm is qualified it should have no trouble getting a loan in the private marketplace, even if because of lack of economies of scale (smaller loans generate less revenue per dollar of cost for banks) they may have to pay slightly higher interest rates than large firms. There is simply no need for subsidized access to capital based only on firm size. Besides, as noted in chapter 12, most government-backed small business lending simply helps some small businesses gain market share from other small businesses.

Size neutrality means eliminating most or all regulatory exemptions designed to exempt small firms from complying with regulations. If governments impose regulations, such as mandatory health care coverage or required notice to workers being laid off, they should require all firms to comply. In particular, it should be unacceptable for any firm, regardless of size, to be legally allowed under federal law to discriminate against workers on the basis of age, race, religion, sexual orientation, and gender.

To the extent governments care about regulatory burdens, the focus should be on streamlining regulations and increasing their flexibility. As an Australian government report notes, unlike reduced obligations for small business, "flexible delivery does not weaken the standard or objective of a particular regulation or tax. In these circumstances, helping smaller firms find their way through the administrative maze can reduce regulatory costs—without offsetting impacts on the regulatory benefits."[40] Toward that end, governments should work with the private sector to establish software-based tools to help all businesses easily understand the local, state, and federal regulations they need to comply with government regulations and be able to communicate in an automated way with government regarding compliance. Just as we have private sector tax preparation software for individuals to use to file their taxes, such as TurboTax, we need a tool like "TurboRegulation" to help businesses comply with government requirements.

Governments should also undertake to reduce informality by making it easier for all businesses to comply with regulations and requiring all to do so. As the US Agency for International Development found, "There is a highly statistically significant correlation between a country's overall performance on the [World Bank] Doing Business indicators and the size of its informal economy; a worse environment for doing business correlates with a larger informal economy."[41] Nations should also strengthen enforcement against individuals operating unlicensed businesses. This means requiring all "firms" to pay taxes and comply with the same rules and regulations facing the formal economy. To be clear, this does not mean that individuals who participate in the sharing economy by renting out a room in their home occasionally or selling a few items on eBay should be treated the same as a big hotel or retailer. De minimis exemptions do make sense—but not for people who engage in business full time.

Finally, in most nations, governments should increase the minimum wage, whose low levels, at least in the United States, enable more small firms to hire low paid workers, compared to large firms. Modestly increasing the minimum wage would have two salutary effects. First, at the margin it would lead to more employment at larger firms that pay more since the playing field would be more level. And second, it would help boost productivity as the evidence is clear that the higher minimum wage helps induce companies to invest in automation.[42]

There are two common responses to moving to size-neutral policies. The first is that this will mean fewer small businesses and jobs. Our response is that we hope it will mean fewer small businesses, because larger firms are better for economies. With respect to jobs, as we have shown, the consumer demand that small firms would meet will also be met by larger firms, creating jobs in the process. We don't need inefficient small companies to create jobs.

The second response is that size-neutral policies would hurt emerging new firms, some of which might grow to be big. But embracing size neutrality is not the same as embracing age neutrality. To the extent there is a rationale for policy differentiation based on firm characteristics, it should be based on age. Getting new firms off the ground can be difficult, as reflected by the fact that so many of them fail in the first five years. For this reason, policy should be more accommodating for new firms. But to the extent it is possible, the focus should be not on new firms per se but on new firms that can and want to scale up to become larger firms.

In other words, it made sense for the government to help Apple Computer get off the ground. It makes little sense for the government to help Justin and Ashley open up a pizza parlor that will never get any larger than a few employees. Policy should support the creation and growth of innovative "opportunity-seeking" startups.[43] Jorge Guzman and Scott Stern found that in the United States, there is no relationship between regional GDP growth and number of new firms, but there is a strong relationship between GDP and the number of high-growth entrepreneurial startups.[44]

Toward that end, governments should repurpose small business agencies to promote new business formation. The US Congress should transform the Small Business Administration (SBA) into the New Business Administration (NBA). The mission of the SBA's Office of Advocacy should be altered so that it focuses on eliminating or improving those regulations that act as barriers to high-growth startup companies. Among other things, this would mean eliminating the SBA loan programs, or at least targeting the loans to high-growth startups, but retaining the SBA Small Business Investment Company program, which supports equity investments in early-stage companies. It also means retaining but reforming the Small Business Innovation Research Program, a program that sets aside a small share of federal R&D expenditures for small business. Business should be limited to receiving just one or two SBIR awards, all within the first few years of the company's existence.

Governments should also focus regulatory flexibility on new firms. In the United States, Congress should reform the Regulatory Flexibility Act to allow for the review of the impact of regulations on new businesses younger than two years old and consider exempting businesses younger than two years from most regulations as they develop and implement their business plans. In addition, governments should make it easier start new companies. Governments should emulate what Portugal and Chile have done, to allow new firms to register their business on the Internet in less than an hour.

This does not mean that governments should end all support for small business, but any support should be justified on the basis of meeting national goals of productivity, innovation, or competitiveness. In the United States a case in point is the National Institute of Standards and Technology's (NIST) Manufacturing Extension Partnership program, which helps small manufacturers (many of which are suppliers to large corporations) become more productive.

Finally, this is not just an agenda for national governments. Regional governments (state and provincial) and local governments should abolish small business preferences, as well as their own anti–large business policies, such as regulations limiting big box retail stores. Local economic growth depends in large part on participation in national and global supply chains by local branches of big firms or their suppliers.

Living with Giants

The fear of giants is common enough that it even has its own scientific-sounding name: megalophobia. In myth and legend, from the biblical tale of David and Goliath to the folktale of Jack and the Beanstalk, giants are monsters who want to kill you, and may want to eat you, as well.

One of the rare exceptions in literature is the story "The Pygmies," in Nathaniel Hawthorne's retelling of Greco-Roman mythology, *The Tanglewood Tales* (1853). In Hawthorne's telling, the giant Antaeus, the son of Mother Earth, was a friend of the Pygmies—not the African people of that name but a mythical race of humans who "grew to the height of six or eight inches":

It was a happy circumstance that Antaeus was the Pygmy people's friend, for there was more strength in his little finger than in ten million of such bodies as this. ... But, being a son of Mother Earth, as they likewise were, the Giant gave them his brotherly kindness, and loved them with as big a love as it was possible to feel for creatures so very small. And, on their parts, the Pygmies loved Antaeus with as much affection as their tiny hearts could hold. He was always ready to do them any good offices that lay in his power; as for example, when they wanted a breeze to turn their windmills, the Giant would set all the sails a-going with the mere natural respiration of his lungs.[45]

Hawthorne's Pygmies would have agreed with Isabella in Shakespeare's *Measure for Measure*: "It is excellent / To have a giant's strength, but it is tyrannous / To use it like a giant."

We agree. Our argument in this book has been that the benefits provided by large, privately owned enterprises, ranging from contributions to technological innovation to the creation of well-paying jobs and increases in national and global productivity growth, will continue to make big business essential for prosperous societies. Each successive industrial revolution, from the age of steam to today's information age, has enlarged the scale of dynamic and efficient firms in industries ranging from agriculture to manufacturing to services. New technologies may make some supply chains shorter or bring them closer to the customer, but an end to increasing returns to scale in manufacturing, food production, energy, retail, and many information-based services and the rise of a high-tech-enabled small-producer world belongs to the realm of science fiction and fantasy.

At every stage in the evolution of the modern economy from the 1800s to the 2000s, some have sought to defend older economic orders characterized by more small firms and greater decentralization of power and profit. In response to public pressure, misguided analysis, and ideology, most countries protect and subsidize small businesses. But this success for the small-is-beautiful school is small consolation for more than a century of failure. The Sherman Antitrust Act and the Federal Trade Commission have never prevented the commanding heights of US manufacturing, energy, agribusiness, retail, and communications from being dominated by oligopolies of large firms. Efforts to block the spread of chain stores and supermarkets and back-to-the-land movements in each generation that have sought to revive small-scale production and artisan manufacturing have never appealed to more than a small minority. The blacksmith's shop long ago gave way to the factory. Small-town general store owners have joined other social types in extinction, such as cavalry officers and medieval knights. Like their counterparts in other modern nations, Americans love to sing the praises of mom-and-pop enterprises—while driving their Toyota cars to Walmart to buy an iPhone made by a global supply chain. And this process that reshaped advanced economies is in the process of reshaping many low-income nations, such as India. Just as in the historical American experience, small business elites in those local communities are seeking to halt the change, in the service of their own well-being, at the expense if necessary of consumers and workers in these developing nations.

None of this means that big business does not present a democratic society with serious challenges. How can corporations be prevented from evading taxes or regulations or having undue influence in politics? What, if anything, do companies owe their workers and the public as a whole? Are corporations chartered merely to promote the short-term economic interest of their shareholders, or are they social institutions created to promote public purposes, including long-term, sustainable economic growth?

These are good questions, to which the antimonopoly tradition gives bad answers: break up big firms and multiply small firms. Twentieth-century Americans created the world's leading economy and the world's first mass middle class largely by ignoring these demands. Preserving America's global status in the twenty-first century while renewing the American middle class requires us to dismiss the anachronistic answers of the nostalgic small-is-beautiful school in order to focus on plausible responses to the challenges and opportunities posed by big business.

Notes

Chapter 1

1. Quoted in Charles Brown, James Hamilton, and James Medoff, *Employers Large and Small* (Cambridge, MA: Harvard University Press, 1990), 88.

2. Quoted in ibid., 8.

3. "George Bush Sr. on Jobs," OnTheIssues.org, October 11, 1992, http://www.ontheissues.org/Celeb/George_Bush_Sr__Jobs.htm.

4. Quoted in Veronique de Rugy, "Are Small Businesses the Engine of Growth?," AEI Working Paper 123 (Washington, DC: American Enterprise Institute, December 8, 2005), https://www.aei.org/wp-content/uploads/2011/10/20051208_WP123.pdf.

5. Scott A. Shane, *The Illusions of Entrepreneurship: The Costly Myths That Entrepreneurs, Investors, and Policy Makers Live By* (New Haven, CT: Yale University Press, 2008), 146, citing White House, "President Bush Addresses Small Business Week Conference," news release, Office of the Press Secretary, April 13, 2006, https://georgewbush-whitehouse.archives.gov/news/releases/2006/10/20061011-7.html.

6. US Small Business Administration (SBA), "President Obama Proclaims National Small Business Week," news release, SBA, May 13, 2011, https://www.sba.gov/content/president-obama-proclaims-national-small-business-week.

7. Donald J. Trump, "The American dream is back. We're going to create an environment for small business like we haven't had in many, many decades!," Twitter post, @realDonaldTrump, January 30, 2017, https://twitter.com/realdonaldtrump/status/826175120238604288?lang=en.

8. Tamara Keith, "Small Businesses Get Political Hype: What's the Reality?," NPR, April 18, 2012.

9. Frank Luntz, as interviewed by Tamara Keith, ibid.

10. Republican Party, *Republican Platform: Restoring the American Dream,* https://gop.com/platform/restoring-the-american-dream.

11. Democratic Party, *Our Platform: The 2016 Democratic Platform*, https://www
.democrats.org/party-platform.

12. Brown, Hamilton, and Medoff, *Employers Large and Small*, 66, citing Sanford
L. Jacobs, "The Multibillion Dollar Wedding," *Wall Street Journal*, May 15, 1990,
41d.

13. Quoted in James Massola, "Malcolm Turnbull Unveils Reshuffled Front Bench,"
Bendigo Advertiser, July 18, 2016.

14. Quoted in Fred Lucas, "Political Money Could Dilute Edwards' Populist
Message, Analysts Say," CNSNews.com, July 7, 2008.

15. Daniela Drake, "Big Pharma Is America's New Mafia," *Daily Beast*, February 21,
2015.

16. Angelo Young, "Big Box Goes Bollywood: Wal-Mart Is Betting $1 Billion It Can
Beat Amazon.com in India," *Salon*, October 12, 2016.

17. Peter Rowe, "Venture Offers Craft Breweries an Alternative to 'Selling Out to Big
Beer,'" *Los Angeles Times*, May 4, 2016.

18. Quotes in John Eggerton, "Congress Asked to Axe FCC Broadband Privacy
Framework," *B&C Media*, January 26, 2017, http://www.broadcastingcable.com/
news/washington/congress-asked-axe-fcc-broadband-privacy-framework/162823.

19. Robert B. Reich, "Big Tech Has Become Way Too Powerful," *New York Times*,
September 18, 2105, https://www.nytimes.com/2015/09/20/opinion/is-big-tech-too
-powerful-ask-google.html.

20. Michael Pollan, "Big Food Strikes Back: Why Did the Obamas Fail to Take on
Corporate Agriculture?," *New York Times*, October 5, 2016.

21. Marta Zaraska, "This Is Why You Crave Beef: Inside Secrets of Big Meat's
Billion-Dollar Ad and Lobbying Campaigns," *Salon*, April 3, 2016, http://www.salon
.com/2016/04/03/this_is_why_you_crave_beef_inside_secrets_of_big_meats_billion
_dollar_ad_and_lobbying_campaigns.

22. Tess Owen, "The Big Chicken Industry Really Treats Its Workers Like Shit," *Vice*,
October 27, 2015.

23. Daniel Greenfield, "Dirty Big Green Criminalizes Climate Science," *Frontpage*,
April 18, 2016; Thomas Linzey, "Firing Big Green: Are National Environmental
Groups Really Serving the People?," *In These Times*, April 3, 2015; and Jason Mark,
"Naomi Klein: Big Green Is in Denial," *Salon*, September 5, 2013.

24. Pascal-Emmanuel Gobry, "Big Science Is Broken," *The Week*, April 18, 2016. The
article refers to William A. Wilson, "Scientific Regress," *First Things*, May 2016.

25. Benjamin E. Zeller, "How Big Government Enables Big Religion," *Dick and Sharon's LA Progressive*, September 12, 2011, https://www.laprogressive.com/big -government-big-religion.

26. Jonah Goldberg, "Big Bedfellows," *National Review*, March 27, 2009, http:// www.nationalreview.com/article/227168/big-bedfellows-jonah-goldberg.

27. Quoted in Keith, "Small Businesses Get Political Hype."

28. David W. Moore, "Majority of Americans Want to Start Own Business," Gallup. com, April 12, 2005, http://www.gallup.com/poll/15832/majority-americans-want -start-own-business.aspx.

29. Brown, Hamilton, and Medoff, *Employers Large and Small*, 72.

30. John Kenneth Galbraith, *The New Industrial State* (New York: Signet Books, 1968), 13–14.

31. Ibid., 311.

32. Ibid.

33. Charles P. Taft, "The Familiar Men of 1980," in Editors of *Fortune* magazine, *The Fabulous Future: America in 1980* (New York: E. P. Dutton, 1956), 176.

34. Marina Whitman, *New World, New Rules: The Changing Role of the American Corporation* (Boston: Harvard Business Review Press, 1999).

35. Michael Useem, *Investor Capitalism: How Money Managers Are Changing the Face of Corporate America* (New York: Basic Books, 1996), 64.

36. Jonathan J. Bean, *Beyond the Broker State: Federal Policies toward Small Businesses 1936–1961* (Chapel Hill: University of North Carolina Press, 1996), 119; and Roland Marchand, *Creating the Corporate Soul: The Rise of Public Relations and Corporate Imagery in American Big Business* (Berkeley: University of California Press, 1998), 358.

37. Peter F. Drucker, "'Development of Theory of Democratic Administration': Replies and Comments," *The American Political Science Review* XLVI, no. 2 (June 1952).

38. Seymour M. Lipset and William Schneider, *The Confidence Gap: Business, Labor, and Government in the Public Mind* (Baltimore: Johns Hopkins University Press, 1987), 72.

39. Ibid.

40. J. D. Harrison, "On Small Business: Who Actually Creates Jobs: Start-ups, Small Businesses or Big Corporations?," *Washington Post*, April 25, 2013, https://www .washingtonpost.com/business/on-small-business/who-actually-creates-jobs-start -ups-small-businesses-or-big-corporations/2013/04/24/d373ef08-ac2b-11e2-a8b9 -2a63d75b5459_story.html.

41. "Section 3: Public Attitudes toward Government and Business," *U.S. Politics & Policy,* Pew Research Center, October 15, 2008, http://www.people-press.org/2008/10/15/section-3-public-attitudes-toward-government-and-business.

42. Frank Newport, "Americans Trust Small-Business Owners Most on Job Creation," Gallup.com, November 3, 2011, http://www.gallup.com/poll/150545/americans-trust-small-business-owners-job-creation.aspx.

43. Hannah Fingerhut, "Millennials' Views of News Media, Religious Organizations Grow More Negative," *FactTank,* Pew Research Center, January 4, 2016, http://www.pewresearch.org/fact-tank/2016/01/04/millennials-views-of-news-media-religious-organizations-grow-more-negative.

44. "Confidence in Institutions," Gallup poll, June 1–5, 2016, http://www.gallup.com/poll/192581/americans-confidence-institutions-stays-low.aspx.

45. Scott A. Hodge, "The U.S. Has More Individually Owned Businesses Than Corporations" (Washington, DC: Tax Foundation, January 13, 2014).

46. Kirsten Grind, *The Lost Bank: The Story of Washington Mutual—The Biggest Bank Failure in American History* (New York: Simon & Schuster, 2012).

47. Richard J. Pierce, "Small Is Not Beautiful: The Case against Special Regulatory Treatment of Small Firms," *Administrative Law Review* 3 (Summer 1998): 537–578.

48. Samuel Palmisano, "The Globally Integrated Enterprise," *Foreign Affairs,* May/June 2006, https://www.foreignaffairs.com/articles/2006-05-01/globally-integrated-enterprise.

49. Cited in Marchand, *Creating the Corporate Soul,* 244.

50. Cited in ibid., 359.

51. Mark Mizruchi, *The Fracturing of the Corporate Elite* (Cambridge, MA: Harvard University Press, 2012), 16.

52. Steve Odland, "Where Have All the Corporate Statesmen Gone?," Committee for Economic Development, August 27, 2013, www.ced.org/blog/entry/where-have-all-the-corporate-statesman-gone.

53. Jonathan J. Bean, *Big Government and Affirmative Action: The Scandalous History of the Small Business Administration* (Lexington: University Press of Kentucky, 2001), 7.

54. Paul Ryan, "Down with Big Business," *Forbes,* October 12, 2009.

55. "Small Business Should Be Priority Number One," *American Interest,* April 21, 2016, https://www.the-american-interest.com/2016/04/21/small-business-should-be-priority-number-one.

56. Senator Elizabeth Warren, "Reigniting Competition in the American Economy," June 29, 2016, https://www.warren.senate.gov/?p=press_release&id=1169.

57. E. F. Schumacher, *Small Is Beautiful: A Study of Economics As If People Mattered* (London: Blond and Briggs, 1973).

58. Samuel C. Florman, "Small Is Dubious," *Harper's Bazaar*, August 1977, 12.

Chapter 2

1. "U.S. Population, 1790–2000: Always Growing," *United States History*, http://www.u-s-history.com/pages/h980.html.

2. Richard Sylla and Robert E. Wright, "Early Corporate America: The Largest Industries and Companies before 1860," *Finance Professionals' Post*, September 27, 2012, http://post.nyssa.org/nyssa-news/2012/09/early-corporate-america-the-largest-industries-and-companies-before-1860.html.

3. Michael Ratcliffe, "A Century of Delineating a Changing Landscape: The Census Bureau's Urban and Rural Classification, 1910 to 2010" (Washington, DC: US Census Bureau, n.d.), https://www2.census.gov/geo/pdfs/reference/ua/Century_of_Defining_Urban.pdf.

4. *Fortune* Editors, "Here are the Top 10 Most Successful American Companies," *Fortune*, June 6, 2016, http://fortune.com/2016/06/06/fortune-500-top-10-companies.

5. Derek Thompson, "How America Spends Money: 100 Years in the Life of the Family Budget," *Atlantic*, April 5, 2012, https://www.theatlantic.com/business/archive/2012/04/how-america-spends-money-100-years-in-the-life-of-the-family-budget/255475.

6. Thomas K. McCraw, *American Business since 1920: How It Worked*, 2nd ed. (Hoboken, NJ: Wiley-Blackwell, 2009), 1.

7. Alfred D. Chandler, *Scale and Scope: The Dynamics of Industrial Capitalism* (Cambridge, MA: Belknap Press, 1994).

8. Zoltan J. Acs and David B. Audretsch, *Innovation and Small Firms* (Cambridge, MA: MIT Press, 1991), 106.

9. Ibid.

10. Ibid.

11. Edith Penrose, *The Theory of the Growth of the Firm* (Oxford: Oxford University Press, 1995 [1959]).

12. John Kenneth Galbraith, *The New Industrial State* (Princeton: Princeton University Press, 2007 [first published in 1967]).

13. Joseph A. Schumpeter, *Capitalism, Socialism, and Democracy*, 3rd ed. (New York: Harper & Brothers, 1950 [1942]), 83.

14. Jeremy Atack, Michael Haines, and Robert A. Margo, "Railroads and the Rise of the Factory: Evidence for the United States, 1850–1870," in *Economic Evolution and Revolution in Historical Time*, ed. Paul W. Rhode, Joshua L. Rosenbloom, and David F. Weiman (Palo Alto, CA: Stanford University Press, 2011), 162–179.

15. Jean Strouse, *Morgan: American Financier* (New York: HarperCollins, 1999), 30, cited in Michael Lind, *Land of Promise: An Economic History of the United States* (New York: HarperCollins, 2012), 214.

16. George Bittlingmayer, "Decreasing Average Cost and Competition: A New Look at the Addyston Pipe Case," *Journal of Law and Economics* 25, no. 2 (October 1982): 201–229; and George Bittlingmayer, "Price-Fixing and the Addyston Pipe Case," *Research in Law and Economics* 5 (1983): 57–130. See also Dominick T. Armentaro, *Antitrust: The Case for Repeal*, rev. 2nd ed. (Auburn, AL: Ludwig von Mises Institute, 1999).

17. Naomi R. Lamoreaux, *The Great Merger Movement in American Business, 1895–1904* (Cambridge: Cambridge University Press, 1985).

18. Ibid., 1–4; Walter Adams and James W. Brock, *The Bigness Complex: Industry, Labor, and Government in the American Economy* (Palo Alto, CA: Stanford University Press, 2004), 25–27; and Lind, *Land of Promise*, 215.

19. John Bates Clark, *The Control of Trusts* (New York: Macmillan, 1901), 17, cited in Adams and Brock, *The Bigness Complex*.

20. Alfred D. Chandler, *The Visible Hand: The Managerial Revolution in American Business* (Cambridge, MA: Harvard University Press, 1977), 158.

21. Lind, *Land of Promise*, 220–221.

22. Thomas K. McCraw, "Rethinking the Trust Question," in *Regulation in Perspective: Historical Essays*, ed. Thomas K. McCraw (Cambridge, MA: Harvard University Press, 1981), 16, 206–207, note 16.

23. Atack, Haines, and Margo, "Railroads and the Rise of the Factory."

24. Jeremy Atack, Robert A. Margo, and Paul W. Rhode, "The Division of Labor and Economies of Scale in Late Nineteenth Century American Manufacturing: New Evidence," in *Enterprising America: Businesses, Banks, and Credit Markets in Historical Perspective*, ed. William J. Collins and Robert A. Margo (Chicago: University of Chicago Press, 2015), 215–244, http://www.nber.org/chapters/c13133.

25. Ibid., 215–244.

26. Alfred D. Chandler, Jr., and Takashi Hikino, "The Large Industrial Enterprise and the Dynamics of Modern Economic Growth," in *Big Business and the Wealth of Nations*, ed. Alfred D. Chandler, Jr., Franco Amatori, and Takashi Hikino (Cambridge: Cambridge University Press, 1997), 32, table 2.1.

27. Willard F. Mueller and Larry G. Hamm, "Trends in Industrial Market Concentration, 1947 to 1970," *Review of Economics and Statistics* 54, no. 4 (November 1974): 519, citing John Kenneth Galbraith, *The New Industrial State*, in *Galbraith: The Affluent Society and Other Writings, 1952–1967* (New York: Library of America, 2010), 698.

28. Marcus Biermann, "Trade and the Size Distribution of Firms: Evidence from the German Empire," CEP Discussion Paper 1450, London School of Economics, Centre for Economic Performance, October 2016, 1.

29. Chandler and Hikino, "The Large Industrial Enterprise and the Dynamics of Modern Economic Growth," 32, table 2.1.

30. Frederic L. Pryor, "An International Comparison of Concentration Ratios," *Review of Economics and Statistics* 54, no. 2 (May 1972), 130ff., citing Galbraith, *The New Industrial State*, 698.

31. Cited in McCraw, "Rethinking the Trust Question."

32. Ibid., 22, 33.

33. However, it is important to realize, as Philip Scranton has pointed out, that not all industries followed this mass production model. Many sectors, such as tools, jewelry, and printing, focused on specialized craft and batch production, in part because the production process did not enable mass production. Philip Scranton, *Endless Novelty* (Princeton, NJ: Princeton University Press, 1997).

34. Alfred D. Chandler, Jr., *Scale and Scope: The Dynamics of Industrial Capitalism* (Cambridge: The Belknap Press, 1994), 21–23.

35. McCraw, "Rethinking the Trust Question," 21.

36. Ibid, 12.

37. Glenn R. Carroll and Michael T. Hannan, *The Demography of Corporations and Industries* (Princeton, NJ: Princeton University Press, 2000), 49.

38. Ibid.

39. Lind, *Land of Promise*, 366.

40. McCraw, *American Business since 1920*, 107.

41. Lind, *Land of Promise*, 366.

42. John Byrne, "The Virtual Corporation," Bloomberg, February 8, 1993, https://www.bloomberg.com/news/articles/1993-02-07/the-virtual-corporation.

43. John Case, "The Wonderland Economy," *Inc. Magazine*, May 5, 1995, https://www.inc.com/magazine/19950515/2686.html.

44. David Hummels, "Have International Transport Costs Declined?" (mimeo, University of Chicago, Graduate School of Business, 1999).

45. Ibid., 6.

46. Harry Magdoff and Paul M. Sweezy, "Notes on the Multinational Corporation, Part Two," *Monthly Review* 21, no. 6 (November 1969): 4.

47. Stephen Hymer, "The Multinational Corporation and the Law of Uneven Development," in *International Firms and Modern Imperialism*, ed. H. Radice (Harmondsworth: Penguin, 1975), cited in Peter Nolan, "China and the Global Business Revolution," *Cambridge Journal of Economics* 26, no. 1 (2002): 119.

48. Joseph Bowring, *Competition in a Dual Economy* (Princeton, NJ: Princeton University Press, 1986), 191.

49. Peter Nolan, *Capitalism and Freedom: The Contradictory Character of Globalisation* (New York: Anthem Press, 2008).

50. Lind, *Land of Promise*.

51. Nolan, *Capitalism and Freedom*, 316, note 89.

52. Lind, *Land of Promise*, 427.

53. Nolan, *Capitalism and Freedom*, 104–105.

54. Andreas Maurer and Christophe Degain, "Globalization and Trade Flows: What You See Is Not What You Get!," Staff Working Paper ERSD-2010–12 (Geneva: World Trade Organization, Economic Research and Statistics Division, June 22, 2010), 11.

55. Christopher Minasians, "Where Are Apple Products Made?," *Macworld*, February 17, 2017, http://www.macworld.co.uk/feature/apple/where-are-apple-products-made-how-much-does-iphone-cost-make-india-3633832.

56. US Small Business Administration (SBA), Office of Advocacy, Employer Firms, Establishments, Employment, and Annual Payroll Small Firm Size Classes, 1992–2011 (database) (Washington, DC: SBA, Office of Advocacy, Research and Statistics), accessed April 14, 2017.

57. US Census Bureau, "Enterprise Statistics" (Table 1. Selected Enterprise Statistics by Sector in the US 2012), https://www.census.gov/econ/esp/2012/esp2012.html; and US Census Bureau, "1992 Enterprise Statistics: Company Summary," December 1997, http://www2.census.gov/econ/esp/1992/es92.pdf.

58. John Mullins and Mike McCall, "Analytical Highlights of CES Firm Size Employment Data" (Washington, DC: US Bureau of Labor Statistics, October 2012), 2137, https://www.bls.gov/osmr/pdf/st120070.pdf.

59. US Bureau of Labor Statistics, Current Population Survey (Labor Force Statistics Table A-9. Selected employment indicators; last modified August 8, 2015), https://www.bls.gov/webapps/legacy/cpsatab9.htm.

60. Ibid.

Chapter 3

1. US Small Business Administration (SBA), Firm Size Data (Table 2. Number of Firms, Establishments, Receipts, Employment, and Payroll by Firm Size (in Receipts) and Industry), https://www.sba.gov/advocacy/firm-size-data (accessed March 10, 2017).

2. US SBA, Firm Size Data (Detailed Industry Data, https://www.sba.gov/advocacy/firm-size-data (accessed March 10, 2017).

3. Ibid.

4. Samuel E. Henly and Juan M. Sánchez, "The U.S. Establishment-Size Distribution: Secular Changes and Sectoral Decomposition," *Economic Quarterly* 95, no. 4 (Fall 2009): 442, https://www.richmondfed.org/~/media/richmondfedorg/publications/research/economic_quarterly/2009/fall/pdf/sanchez.pdf.

5. Franco Amatori, Matteo Bugamelli, and Andrea Colli, "Italian Firms in History: Size, Technology and Entrepreneurship," paper presented at the conference "Italy and the World Economy, 1861–2011," Rome, October 12–15, 2011, https://papers.ssrn.com/sol3/papers.cfm?abstract_id=2236737.

6. Zoltan J. Acs, David B. Audretsch, and Bo Carlsson, "Flexible Technology and Firm Size," *Small Business Economics* 3, no. 4 (December, 1991): 307–319, https://link.springer.com/article/10.1007/BF01840612.

7. US Census Bureau, Business Dynamic Statistics (Firm Characteristics Data Tables: Sector), https://www.census.gov/ces/dataproducts/bds/data_firm.html.

8. US Census Bureau, Statistics of US Businesses (annual data tables 1997 and 2012).

9. Timothy H. Hannan and Gerald A. Hanweck, "Recent Trends in the Number and Size of Bank Branches: An Examination of Likely Determinants 2008-02," Finance and Economics Discussion Series (Washington, DC: Federal Reserve Board, Divisions of Research & Statistics and Monetary Affairs, 2008), https://www.federalreserve.gov/pubs/feds/2008/200802/200802pap.pdf.

10. Barry C. Lynn and Lina Khan, "The Slow-Motion Collapse of American Entrepreneurship," *Washington Monthly*, July/August 2012, http://washingtonmonthly.com/magazine/julyaugust-2012/the-slow-motion-collapse-of-american-entrepreneurship.

11. Cornelia J. Strawser, ed., *Business Statistics of the United States 2013: Patterns of Economic Change*, 18th ed. (Lanham, MD: Bernan Press, 2013), Table 10.3, 358.

12. Ian Hathaway and Robert E. Litan, "Declining Business Dynamism in the United States: A Look at States and Metros," Economic Studies at Brookings (Washington,

DC: Brookings Institution, May 2014), https://www.brookings.edu/wp-content/uploads/2016/06/declining_business_dynamism_hathaway_litan.pdf.

13. Jason Wiens and Chris Jackson, "The Importance of Young Firms for Economic Growth" (Kansas City, MO: Kauffman Foundation, September 13, 2015), http://www.kauffman.org/what-we-do/resources/entrepreneurship-policy-digest/the-importance-of-young-firms-for-economic-growth.

14. John Lettieri and Steve Glickman, "American Entrepreneurship in Decline," *Daily Beast*, July 25, 2016, http://www.thedailybeast.com/articles/2016/07/25/american-entrepreneurship-in-decline.html.

15. Hathaway and Litan, "Declining Business Dynamism in the United States," 3.

16. *America Without Entrepreneurs: The Consequences of Dwindling Startup Activity. Hearing Before the Committee on Small Business and Entrepreneurship* US Senate (June 29, 2016) (testimony of John W. Lettieri, Cofounder and Senior Director for Policy and Strategy, Economic Innovation Group), https://www.sbc.senate.gov/public/?a=Files.Serve&File_id=0D8D1A51-EE1D-4F83-B740-515E46E861DC.

17. Lynn and Khan, "The Slow-Motion Collapse of American Entrepreneurship."

18. Jim Clifton, "American Entrepreneurship: Dead or Alive?," *Business Journal*, January 13, 2015, Gallup.org, http://www.gallup.com/businessjournal/180431/american-entrepreneurship-dead-alive.aspx.

19. John Dearie, quoted in Leigh Buchanan, "American Entrepreneurship Is Actually Vanishing," *Inc.*, May 2015, http://www.inc.com/magazine/201505/leigh-buchanan/the-vanishing-startups-in-decline.html.

20. Hathaway and Litan, "Declining Business Dynamism in the United States."

21. Ian Hathaway and Robert E. Litan, "What's Driving the Decline in the Firm Formation Rate? A Partial Explanation," Economic Studies at Brookings (Washington, DC: Brookings Institution, November 2014), https://www.brookings.edu/wp-content/uploads/2016/06/driving_decline_firm_formation_rate_hathaway_litan.pdf.

22. "The Decline in Business Formation: Implications for Entrepreneurship and the Economy," testimony of Jonathan Ortmans before the US House Committee on Small Business, Subcommittee on Contracting and Workforce (Kansas City, MO: Kauffman Foundation, September 11, 2014), http://www.kauffman.org/~/media/kauffman_org/research%20reports%20and%20covers/2014/09/jonathan_ortmans_testimony_september_2014.pdf.

23. Muge Adalet McGowan and Dan Andrews, "Skill Mismatch and Public Policy in OECD Countries," OECD Working Paper ECO/WKP(2015)28 (Paris: OECD, Economics Department, April 28, 2015), https://www.oecd.org/eco/growth/Skill-mismatch-and-public-policy-in-OECD-countries.pdf.

24. Anthony B. Kim, "Economic Freedom: America's Entrepreneurial Pulse at Risk," *Daily Signal*, April 1, 2014, http://dailysignal.com//2014/04/01/economic-freedom-americas-entrepreneurial-pulse-risk.

25. Mike Konczal and Marshall Stienbaum, "Declining Entrepreneurship, Labor Mobility, and Business Dynamism: A Demand-Side Approach" (New York: Roosevelt Institute, July 21, 2016), http://rooseveltinstitute.org/declining-entrepreneurship-labor-mobility-and-business-dynamism.

26. The NFIB study is referenced in Paul Bettencourt, "Small Business Burdened by Ever-Growing Pile of Regulations," *Forbes*, September 29, 2016, https://www.forbes.com/sites/williamdunkelberg/2016/09/29/small-business-burdened-by-ever-growing-pile-of-regulations/#6a27c1f21f3c.

27. Ryan Decker, John Haltiwanger, Ron Jarmin, and Javier Miranda, "The Role of Entrepreneurship in U.S. Job Creation and Economic Dynamism," *Journal of Economic Perspectives* 28, no. 3 (Summer 2014): 19.

28. *The Kauffman Index: State Rankings* (Kansas City, MO: Kauffman Foundation, 2015) http://www.kauffman.org/kauffman-index/rankings?report=startup-activity&indicator=se-rate&type=larger.

29. Lynn and Khan, "The Slow-Motion Collapse of American Entrepreneurship."

30. Quoted in Buchanan, "American Entrepreneurship Is Actually Vanishing."

31. "Infographic: Millennial Entrepreneurs and the State of Entrepreneurship" (Kansas City, MO: Kauffman Foundation, February 11, 2015), http://www.kauffman.org/multimedia/infographics/2015/infographic-millennial-entrepreneurs-and-the-state-of-entrepreneurship.

32. Quoted in Derek Thompson, "The Myth of the Millennial Entrepreneur," *Atlantic*, July 6, 2016, https://www.theatlantic.com/business/archive/2016/07/the-myth-of-the-millennial-entrepreneur/490058.

33. Dane Stangler and Jordan Bell-Masterson, "Can Millennials Reverse America's Declining Rates of Entrepreneurship?" *Washington Monthly*, August 17, 2014, http://washingtonmonthly.com/2014/08/17/can-millennials-reverse-americas-declining-rates-of-entrepreneurship.

34. Hathaway and Litan, "What's Driving the Decline in the Firm Formation Rate?"

35. Lynn and Khan, "The Slow-Motion Collapse of American Entrepreneurship."

36. Derek Thompson, "America's Monopoly Problem: How Big Business Jammed the Wheels of Innovation," *Atlantic*, October 2016, https://www.theatlantic.com/magazine/archive/2016/10/americas-monopoly-problem/497549.

37. Stacy Mitchell, "Monopoly Power and the Decline of Small Business: The Case for Restoring America's Once Robust Antitrust Policies" (Washington, DC: Institute

for Local Self-Reliance, August 10, 2016), https://ilsr.org/monopoly-power-and-the -decline-of-small-business.

38. Mark E. Schweitzer and Scott Shane, "The Ins and Outs of Self-Employment: An Estimate of Business Cycle and Trend Effects," Working Paper 16–21 (Federal Reserve Bank of Cleveland, 2016), https://www.clevelandfed.org/newsroom-and-events/ publications/working-papers/2016-working-papers/wp-1621-ins-and-outs-of-self -employment.aspx.

39. US Census Bureau, Business Dynamics Statistics (Longitudinal Business Database, Firm Characteristics Data Tables, Firm Age by Firm Size, 1977 to 2014), https:// www.census.gov/ces/dataproducts/bds/data_firm.html (accessed March 17, 2017).

40. Robert D. Atkinson, "Enough Is Enough: Confronting Chinese Innovation Mercantilism" (Washington, DC: Information Technology and Innovation Foundation, February 28, 2012), https://itif.org/publications/2012/02/28/enough-enough -confronting-chinese-innovation-mercantilism.

41. Robert D. Atkinson, Luke A. Stewart, Scott M. Andes, and Stephen J. Ezell, "Worse Than the Great Depression: What Experts Are Missing about American Manufacturing Decline" (Washington, DC: Information Technology and Innovation Foundation, March 2012), http://www2.itif.org/2012-american-manufacturing -decline.pdf.

42. US Census Bureau, Longitudinal Business Database 1977–2014, http://www2 .census.gov/ces/bds/estab/age_size_sector.

43. Robert D. Atkinson, "Understanding and Maximizing America's Evolutionary Economy" (Washington, DC: Information Technology and Innovation Foundation, October 2014).

44. David B. Audretsch, "Technology, Life Cycles and Industry Dynamics," paper presented at the ZEW Summer Workshop on Empirical Labour and Industrial Economics, Mannheim, June 7–10, 1999, 13, http://ftp.zew.de/pub/zew-docs/sws/ audretsch.pdf.

45. US SBA, Firm Size Data (Detailed Industry Data), https://www.sba.gov/advocacy/ firm-size-data.

46. "2013 Market Measure: The Industry's Annual Report," *Hardware Retailing*, December 2013, http://www.hardwareretailing.com/wp-content/uploads/2013/11/ Market-Measure-2013.pdf.

47. Matthew E. Spencer, "Dow 30 Profile: The Home Depot," *Value Line*, May 17, 2013, http://www.valueline.com/Stocks/Highlights/2012_Highlights/Dow_30 _Profile__The_Home_Depot.aspx#.WMw8Sfnys2w.

48. "2013 Market Measure."

49. US Census Bureau, *County Business Patterns: 2012*.

50. Thompson, "America's Monopoly Problem."

51. Antoinette Schoar, "The Divide between Subsistence and Transformational Entrepreneurship," in *Innovation Policy and the Economy*, ed. Josh Lerner and Scott Stern (Chicago: University of Chicago Press, February 2010), 57–81, http://www .nber.org/chapters/c11765.

52. Ibid., 63.

53. Catherine Fazio, Jorge Guzman, Fiona Murray, and Scott Stern, "A New View of the Skew: A Quantitative Assessment of the Quality of Entrepreneurship," MIT Innovation Initiative, February 2016, https://innovation.mit.edu/assets/A-New -View_Final-Report_5.4.16.pdf.

54. J. A. Schumpeter, "Economic Theory and Entrepreneurial History," in *Explorations in Enterprise*, ed. H. G. Aitken (Cambridge, MA: Harvard University Press, 1965).

55. Osman Eroglu and Murat Picak, "Entrepreneurship, National Culture and Turkey," *International Journal of Business and Social Science* 2, no. 16 (September 2011).

56. Decker et al., "The Role of Entrepreneurship in U.S. Job Creation and Economic Dynamism."

57. Marc Andreessen (pmarca), "'There's too much entrepreneurship: Disruption running wild!' 'There's too little entrepreneurship: Economy stalling out!,'" Twitter post, January 2, 2015, 9:11 p.m.

58. Jorge Guzman and Scott Stern, "The State of American Entrepreneurship: New Estimates of the Quantity and Quality of Entrepreneurship for 15 U.S. States, 1988-2014," NBER Working Paper 22095 (Cambridge, MA: National Bureau of Economic Research, March 2016), http://www.nber.org/papers/w22095.

59. Ibid.

60. Ibid.

61. Fazio et al., "A New View of the Skew," 3.

62. Arnobio Morelix, Robert W. Fairlie, Joshua Russell, and E. J. Reedy, "2015 The Kauffman Index: Startup Activity State Trends" (Kansas City, MO: Kauffman Foundation, 2015), http://www.kauffman.org/~/media/kauffman_org/research%20 reports%20and%20covers/2015/05/kauffman_index_startup_activity_state _trends_2015.pdf.

63. Fazio et al., "A New View of the Skew," 3.

64. Acs and Audretsch, *Innovation and Small Firms*, 127.

65. Joseph A. Schumpeter, *Capitalism, Socialism, and Democracy*, 3rd ed. (New York: Harper & Brothers, 1950 [1942]), 67.

66. Ibid., 68.

67. Ibid., 83.

68. John Haltiwanger, Ian Hathaway, and Javier Miranda, "Declining Business Dynamism in the U.S. High-Technology Sector" (Kansas City, MO: Kauffman Foundation, February 2014), http://www.kauffman.org/~/media/kauffman_org/research%20reports%20and%20covers/2014/02/declining_business_dynamism_in_us_high_tech_sector.pdf.

69. Ibid.

70. Quoted in Acs and Audretsch, *Innovation and Small Firms*, 5.

71. Audretsch, "Technology, Life Cycles and Industry Dynamics," 21.

72. Carroll and Hannan, *The Demography of Corporations and Industries*, 24.

73. Francisco Louçã and Sandro Mendonça, "Steady Change: The 200 Largest U.S. Manufacturing Firms throughout the 20th Century," *Industrial and Corporate Change* 11, no. 4 (2002): 817–845, 825.

74. Ibid., 827.

75. For example, for the US retail sector, see Mark Doms, Ron S. Jarmin, and Shawn Klimek, "Information Technology Investment and Firm Performance in U.S. Retail Trade," *Economics of Innovation and New Technology* 13, no. 7 (2004): 595–613.

Chapter 4

1. Todd L. Idson and Walter Y. Oi, "Workers Are More Productive in Large Firms," *American Economic Review* 89, no. 2 (May 1999): 104–108.

2. Joachim Wagner, "Firm Size and Job Quality: A Survey of the Evidence from Germany," *Small Business Economics* 9, no. 5 (October 1997): 411–425.

3. Erik Hurst and Benjamin Wild Pugsley, "What Do Small Businesses Do?," NBER Working Paper 17041 (Cambridge, MA: National Bureau of Economic Research, May 2011), 2, http://www.nber.org/papers/w17041.pdf.

4. World Bank, "The Big Business of Small Enterprises: Evaluation of the World Bank Group Experience with Targeted Support to Small and Medium-Size Enterprises, 2006–12," March 2014, p. 35.

5. Senator Elizabeth Warren, "Reigniting Competition in the American Economy," Keynote Remarks, New America's Open Markets Program Event, Washington, D.C., June 29, 2016.

6. The average full-time hourly associate wage at Walmart is $13.38 an hour (source: Walmart Corporation). The Bureau of Labor Statistics reports that the median wage for retail salespersons is $11.01 an hour and for cashiers is $9.70 per hour (http://www.bls.gov/ooh/sales/retail-sales-workers.htm. http://www.huffingtonpost.com/entry/walmart-10-raise_us_56a01acde4b0404eb8f03b26).

7. Brianna Cardiff-Hicks, Francine Lafontaine, and Kathryn Shaw, "Do Large Modern Retailers Pay Premium Wages?," NBER Working Paper 20313 (Cambridge, MA: National Bureau of Economic Research, July 2014), http://www.nber.org/papers/w20313.

8. Claudia Goldin, "Monitoring Costs and Occupational Segregation by Sex: A Historical Analysis," *Journal of Labor Economics* 4, no. 1 (January 1986): 1–27, cited in Charles Brown, James T. Hamilton, and James Medoff, *Employers Large and Small* (Cambridge, MA: Harvard University Press, 1990), 5.

9. Charles Brown and James Medoff, "The Employer Size-Wage Effect," *Journal of Political Economy* 97, no. 5 (October 1989): 1027–1059.

10. US Bureau of Labor Statistics (BLS), Economic News Release (Table 8. Private Industry, by Establishment Employment Size, https://www.bls.gov/news.release/eccc.t08.htm (accessed March 2017).

11. Li Yu, "Three Essays on Technology Adoption, Firm Size, Wages and Human Capital" (PhD diss., Iowa State University, 2008), http://lib.dr.iastate.edu/rtd/15716.

12. Cardiff-Hicks, Lafontaine, and Shaw, "Do Large Modern Retailers Pay Premium Wages?"

13. Stéphanie Lluis, "Endogenous Choice of Firm Size and the Structure of Wages: A Comparison of Canada and the United States," Industrial Relations Center Working Paper (Minneapolis: University of Minnesota, June 2003), ftp://ftp.repec.org/opt/ReDIF/RePEc/hrr/papers/0203.pdf, 12.

14. Wagner, "Firm Size and Job Quality," 412.

15. Lluis, "Endogenous Choice of Firm Size and the Structure of Wages," 5.

16. Gregory Acs and Austin Nichols, "Low-Income Workers and Their Employers: Characteristics and Challenges," The Urban Institute, 2007, https://www.urban.org/sites/default/files/publication/46656/411532-Low-Income-Workers-and-Their-Employers.PDF.

17. Rana Hasan and Karl Robert L. Jandoc, "The Distribution of Firm Size in India: What Can Survey Data Tell Us?," ADB Economics Working Paper 213 (Manila: Asian Development Bank, August 2010), https://www.adb.org/sites/default/files/publication/28418/economics-wp213.pdf.

18. S. Thorsten Beck, A. Demirgüç-Kunt, and Ross Levine, "Small and Medium Enterprises, Growth, and Poverty: Cross-Country Evidence," World Bank Policy Research Working Paper 3178 (Washington, DC: World Bank, December 2003), 8, http://elibrary.worldbank.org/doi/abs/10.1596/1813-9450-3178.

19. Paul Reynolds and Sammis B. White, *The Entrepreneurial Process: Economic Growth, Men, Women, and Minorities* (Westport, CT: Praeger, 1997).

20. US BLS, Economic News Release (Table 8. Private Industry).

21. Walmart 401(k) Plan H, https://www.brightscope.com/401k-rating/331263/Wal-Mart-Stores-Inc/335998/Walmart-401K-PlanH (accessed April 1, 2017).

22. US BLS, *National Compensation Survey: Employee Benefits in Private Industry in the United States, March 2006*, cited in Kelly Edmiston, "The Role of Small and Large Businesses in Economic Development," *Economic Review*, Second Quarter (Kansas City Federal Reserve Bank, 2007), 73–97.

23. US Small Business Administration (SBA), "What Is the Level of Availability and Coverage of Health Insurance in Small Firms?," June 2012, https://www.sba.gov/sites/default/files/Health-Insurance.pdf.

24. Scott A. Shane, *Illusions of Entrepreneurship: The Costly Myths That Entrepreneurs, Investors, and Policy Makers Live By* (New Haven, CT: Yale University Press, 2008), 156; and David Bernstein, "Fringe Benefits and Small Businesses: Evidence from the Federal Reserve Board Small Business Survey," *Applied Economics* 34, no. 16 (2002): 2063–2067.

25. Brian Baker, "The Monthly Labor Review at 100—Part IV: Employee Benefits, Industries and Occupations, and Worker Safety and Health Since 1980," *Monthly Labor Review*, July 2016, http://www.bls.gov/opub/mlr/2016/article/the-monthly-labor-review-at-100-part-iv.htm.

26. Edmiston, "The Role of Small and Large Businesses in Economic Development."

27. Jon R. Gabel, Heidi Whitmore, Jeremy Pickreign, Christine C. Ferguson, Anjali Jain, K. C. Shova, and Hilary Scherer, "Obesity and the Workplace: Current Programs and Attitudes among Employers and Employees," *Health Affairs* 28, no. 1 (January/February 2009): 46–56.

28. US BLS, "Job Openings and Labor Turnover Survey, February 2016," news release, USDL 16-0697, US Department of Labor, April 5, 2016, https://www.bls.gov/news.release/archives/jolts_04052016.pdf.

29. Edward M. Miller, "The Extent of Economies of Scale: The Effects of Firm Size on Labor Productivity and Wage Rates," *Southern Economic Journal* 44, no. 3 (January 1978): 470–487.

30. Ibid.

31. Danny Leung, Césaire Meh, and Yaz Terajima, "Firm Size and Productivity," Bank of Canada Working Paper 2008–45 (Ottawa: Bank of Canada, November 2008), 11, http://www.bankofcanada.ca/wp-content/uploads/2010/02/wp08-45.pdf.

32. Bennett Harrison, *Lean and Mean: The Changing Landscape of Corporate Power in the Age of Flexibility* (New York: Basic Books, 1994), 62, citing Timothy Dunne, "Technology Usage in U.S. Manufacturing Industries: New Evidence from the Survey of Manufacturing Technology," Center for Economic Studies, US Census Bureau, 1991, https://www2.census.gov/ces/wp/1991/CES-WP-91-07.pdf.

33. Timothy H. Hannan and John M. McDowell, "The Determinants of Technology Adoption: The Case of the Banking Firm," *RAND Journal of Economics* 15, no. 3 (Autumn 1984): 328–335.

34. Leung, Meh, and Terajima, "Firm Size and Productivity," 11.

35. Sara Jane McCaffrey and Nancy B. Kurland, "Does 'Local' Mean Ethical? The U.S. 'Buy Local' Movement and CSR in SMEs," *Organization & Environment* 28, no. 3 (2015): 286–306, 292.

36. Ibid.

37. Ibid.

38. Ibid.

39. David B. Audretsch, "Small Firms and Efficiency," in *Are Small Firms Important? Their Role and Impact*, ed. Zoltan J. Acs (New York: Kluwer Academic, 1999), 22.

40. National Science Foundation, *Business Research and Development and Innovation: 2012* (Table 5. Worldwide R&D Paid for by the Company and Performed by the Company and Others, by Industry and Company Size: 2012), https://nsf.gov/statistics/2016/nsf16301/#chp2 (accessed March 5, 2017).

41. Ibid.

42. Tatiana Maria Correia Monteira, "Relationship between Firm Size and Export Performance: Overtaking Inconsistencies" (master's thesis, Universidade do Porto, 2013), http://www.fep.up.pt/docentes/fontes/FCTEGE2008/Publicacoes/D14.pdf.

43. Joachim Wagner, "Exports, Firm Size, and Firm Dynamics," *Small Business Economics* 7, no. 1 (February 1995): 29–39.

44. Patrick Delehanty, "Small Businesses Key Players in International Trade," *Issue Brief (SBA)* 11, December 1, 2015, https://www.sba.gov/sites/default/files/advocacy/Issue-Brief-11-Small-Biz-Key-Players-International-Trade.pdf; US Census Bureau, Statistics of US Businesses (2014 SUSB Annual Data Tables by Establishment Industry), https://www.census.gov/data/tables/2014/econ/susb/2014-susb-annual.html (accessed March 27, 2017).

45. US SBA, Office of Advocacy, "Frequently Asked Questions," September 2012, https://www.sba.gov/sites/default/files/FAQ_Sept_2012.pdf.

46. Randy A. Becker, "Air Pollution Abatement Costs under the Clean Air Act: Evidence from the PACE Survey," *Journal of Environmental Economics and Management* 50, no. 1 (July 2005): 144–169, 165.

47. Stefanie A. Haller and Liam Murphy, "Corporate Expenditure on Environmental Protection," *Environmental and Resource Economics* 51, no. 2 (February 2012): 277–296.

48. Becker, "Air Pollution Abatement Costs," 164.

49. Keith Fuglie, Paul Helsey, John King, and David Schimmelpfennig, "Rising Concentration in Agricultural Input Industries Influences New Farm Technologies," *Amber Waves*, December 3, 2012, https://www.ers.usda.gov/amber-waves/2012/december/rising-concentration-in-agricultural-input-industries-influences-new-technologies/.

50. Quoted in Fiona Tilly, "The Gap between the Environmental Attitudes and the Environmental Behavior of Small Firms," *Business Strategy and the Environment* 8, no. 4 (July/August 1999): 238–248, 241.

51. US Census Bureau, "Annual Survey of Entrepreneurs 2015 (accessed August 23, 2017), https://www.census.gov/programs-surveys/ase/data/tables.All.html.

52. "Most Small Businesses Unprepared for Cyber Criminals," Nationwide press release, November 10, 2015, https://www.nationwide.com/about-us/111015-cyber-security.jsp.

53. National Small Business Association, "2013 Small Business Technology Survey," http://www.nsba.biz/wp-content/uploads/2013/09/Technology-Survey-2013.pdf.

54. Joel Slemrod, "The Economics of Corporate Tax Selfishness," NBER Working Paper 10858 (Cambridge, MA: National Bureau of Economic Research, 2004), 14, http://www.nber.org/papers/w10858.

55. Ibid., 6.

56. Farahnaz Orojali Zadeh and Alireza Eskandari, "Firm Size as Company's Characteristic and Level of Risk Disclosure: Review on Theories and Literatures," *International Journal of Business and Social Science* 3, no. 17 (September 2012): 9–17.

57. Giampaolo Arachi and Allesandro Santoro, "Tax Enforcement for SMEs: Lessons from the Italian Experience," *eJournal of Tax Research* 5, no. 2 (2007): 225–243.

58. Ibid., 234.

59. Susan Cleary Morse, Stewart Karlinsky, and Joseph Bankman, "Cash Businesses and Tax Evasion," *Stanford Law and Policy Review* 20, no. 1 (2009): 37–68.

60. Jane G. Gravelle, "Federal Tax Treatment of Small Business: How Favorable? How Justified?," in *Proceedings of 100th Annual Conference, National Tax Association* (Washington, DC, 2007), 152–158, 158, https://www.ntanet.org/wp-content/uploads/proceedings/2007/017-gravelle-federal-tax-treatment-2007-nta-proceedings.pdf.

61. Morse, Karlinsky, and Bankman, "Cash Businesses and Tax Evasion," 67.

62. Ibid., 64.

63. Ibid., 49.

64. Bernd Frick, "The Effect of Employment Protection Legislation on Dismissals in Germany," *Vierteljahrshefte zur Wirtschaftsforschung* 63, nos. 1–2 (1994): 85–89.

65. Rudolf Winter-Ebmer, "Does Layoff Risk Explain the Firm-Size Wage Differential?," *Applied Economics Letters* 2, no. 7 (1995): 211–214.

66. Garnett Picot, "Workers on the Move: Permanent Layoffs," *Perspectives on Labour and Income* 4, no. 3 (Autumn 1992), http://www.statcan.gc.ca/pub/75-001-x/1992003/47-eng.pdf.

67. Decker et al., "Role of Entrepreneurship."

68. William A. Brock and David S. Evans, "Small Business Economics," *Small Business Economics* 1, no. 1 (1989): 7–20.

69. Patricia M. Anderson and Bruce D. Meyer, "The Extent and Consequences of Job Turnover," *Brookings Paper: Microeconomics* (1994): 177–248.

70. US BLS, "Job Openings and Labor Turnover Survey (Experimental JOLTS Estimates by Establishment Size Class," last modified February 21, 2017), https://www.bls.gov/jlt/sizeclassmethodology.htm.

71. US BLS, Economics News Release (Table 8. Private Industry).

72. Ibid.

73. The reduction in the number of small coal-mining companies accounted for about four fewer deaths per year because small firms had less safe working conditions. George R. Neumann and Jon P. Nelson, "Safety Regulation and Firm Size: Effects of the Coal Mine Health and Safety Act of 1969," *Journal of Law & Economics* 25, no. 2 (October 1982): 183–199.

74. D. McVittie, H. Banikin, and W. Brocklebank, "The Effects of Firm Size on Injury Frequency in Construction," *Safety Science* 27, no. 1 (October 1997): 19–23.

75. David E. Cantor, Thomas M. Corsi, Curtis M. Grimm, and Prabhjot Singh, "Technology, Firm Size, and Safety: Theory and Empirical Evidence from the U.S. Motor-carrier Industry," *Transportation Journal* 55, no. 2 (Spring 2016): 149–167.

76. US BLS, (Table Q1. Incidence Rates of Total Recordable Cases of Nonfatal Occupational Injuries and Illnesses, by Quartile Distribution and Employment Size, 2012), https://www.bls.gov/iif/oshwc/osh/os/ostb3585.pdf (accessed January 20, 2017).

77. Lluis, "Endogenous Choice of Firm Size and the Structure of Wages," 12.

78. Unpublished data from the Pennsylvania Keystone Research Center, Harrisburg.

79. Frick, "The Effect of Employment Protection Legislation."

80. Brown, Hamilton, and Medoff, *Employers Large and Small*, 54.

81. *OECD Science, Technology and Industry Scoreboard 2015: Innovation for Growth and Society* (Paris: OECD, 2015), 41 (Chart 1.29. Investment in Firm-Specific On-the-Job Training, by Firm Size, 2011-12), http://dx.doi.org/10.1787/sti_scoreboard-2015-en.

82. Barbara F. Reskin, Debra B. McBrier, and Julie A. Kmec, "The Determinants and Consequences of Workplace Sex and Race Composition," *Annual Review of Sociology* 25 (1999): 335–361.

83. "Affirmative Action Plans," *FindLaw*, http://smallbusiness.findlaw.com/employment-law-and-human-resources/are-employers-required-to-have-affirmative-action-plans.html.

84. "Title VII of the Civil Rights Act of 1964," Equal Employment Opportunity Commission, https://www.eeoc.gov/laws/statutes/titlevii.cfm.

85. Jonathan D. Glater and Martha M. Hamilton, "Affirmative Action's Corporate Converts," *Washington Post*, March 19, 1995, https://www.washingtonpost.com/archive/business/1995/03/19/affirmative-actions-corporate-converts/99c3261c-3d42-47db-a8a5-86b2310b0ae0/?utm_term=.30f06739d8e3.

86. Harry J. Holzer, "Why Do Small Establishments Hire Fewer Blacks Than Large Ones?," IRP Discussion Paper 1119–97 (Lansing: Michigan State University, Department of Economics, Institute for Research on Poverty, 1997), http://www.irp.wisc.edu/publications/dps/pdfs/dp11997.pdf.

87. Brian Headd, "The Characteristics of Small-Business Employees," *Monthly Labor Review* (April 2000): 13–18, http://www.bls.gov/opub/mlr/2000/04/art3full.pdf.

88. US Census Bureau, American Fact Finder (Series: SB1200CSA12, 2012 Survey of Business Owners) (database), https://factfinder.census.gov/faces/nav/jsf/pages/index.xhtml (accessed March 27, 2017)

89. Robert W. Fairlie and Alicia M. Robb, "Gender Differences in Business Performance: Evidence from the Characteristics of Business Owners Survey," *Small Business Economics* 33 (2009): 375–395.

90. Louis H. Amato and Christie H. Amato, "The Effects of Firm Size and Industry on Corporate Giving," *Journal of Business Ethics* 72, no. 3 (May 2007): 229–241.

91. Jan Lepoutre and Aimé Heene, "Investigating the Impact of Firm Size on Small Business Social Responsibility: A Critical Review," *Journal of Business Ethics* 67, no. 3 (September 2006): 257–273.

92. Ibid.

93. Ibid.

94. Crystal L. Owen and Robert Scherer, "Social Responsibility and Market Share," *Review of Business* 15, no. 1 (Summer/Fall 1993).

95. "Common Dreams," *Common Dreams*, http://www.commondreams.org.

96. Stephen Brammer and Andrew Millington, "Firm Size, Organizational Visibility and Corporate Philanthropy: An Empirical Analysis," *Business Ethics: A European Review* 15, no. 1 (January 2006): 6–18.

97. Kevin Cochrane, "Shopping 'Local' Doesn't Make Sense," *The Weekly Standard*, August 31, 2017, http://www.weeklystandard.com/shopping-local-doesnt-make-sense/article/2009481.

98. Foundation Center, "Foundation Stats: Aggregate Fiscal Data for Top 50 FC 1000 Foundations Awarding Grants, 2012," http://data.foundationcenter.org/#/fc1000/subject:all/all/top:foundations/list/2012.

99. Thomas Piketty, *Capital in the Twenty-First Century* (Cambridge, MA: Belknap Press of Harvard University Press, 2013), 315.

100. Jason Furman and Peter Orszag, "A Firm-Level Perspective on the Role of Rents in the Rise in Inequality," paper presented at "A Just Society," Centennial Event in Honor of Joseph Stiglitz, Columbia University, New York, October 16, 2015, https://obamawhitehouse.archives.gov/sites/default/files/page/files/20151016_firm_level_perspective_on_role_of_rents_in_inequality.pdf.

101. Holger M. Mueller, Paige P. Ouimet, and Elena Simintzi, "Wage Inequality and Firm Growth," NBER Working Paper 20876 (Cambridge, MA: National Bureau of Economic Research, January 2015), http://www.nber.org/papers/w20876.

102. Ibid., 4.

103. Ibid.

104. Jae Song, David J. Price, Fatih Guvenen, Nicholas Bloom, and Till von Wachter, "Firming Up Inequality," NBER Working Paper 21199 (Cambridge, MA: National Bureau of Economic Research, May 2015), http://www.nber.org/papers/w21199, 29.

105. Unpublished estimates from the US BLS, National Compensation Survey: Employer Costs for Employee Compensation, provided to the authors on June 4, 2016.

106. Song et al., "Firming Up Inequality."

107. Ibid., p. 29.

108. Robert W. Van Giezen, "Occupational Pay by Establishment Size," *Compensation and Working Conditions,* Spring 1998, 28–36, https://www.bls.gov/opub/mlr/cwc/occupational-pay-by-establishment-size.pdf.

109. Holger M. Mueller, Paige P. Ouimet, and Elena Simintzi, "Within-Firm Pay Inequality," January 2016, https://papers.ssrn.com/sol3/papers.cfm?abstract_id =2716315.

110. Ibid., 6.

111. Gerald F. Davis and J. Adam Cobb, "Corporations and Economic Inequality around the World: The Paradox of Hierarchy," *Research in Organizational Behavior* 30 (2010): 35–53.

112. Gerald Davis, *The Vanishing American Corporation* (Oakland, CA: Berrett-Koehler, 2016), 136.

113. Shane, *Illusions of Entrepreneurship*, 106, citing Michael S. Gutter and Tabassum Saleem, "Financial Vulnerability of Small Business Owners," *Financial Services Review* 14, no. 2 (Summer 2005): 133–47.

114. Ibid., 107.

115. Erik G. Hurst and Benjamin W. Pugsley, "Wealth, Tastes, and Entrepreneurial Choice," Staff Report 747 (Federal Reserve Bank of New York, October 2015), https://papers.ssrn.com/sol3/papers.cfm?abstract_id=2677571.

116. "Sources of Flow-Through Business Income by Expanded Cash Income Percentile; Current Law, 2016" (Washington, DC: Urban Institute and Brookings Institution, Tax Policy Center, August 23, 2016) (Table T16-0184), http://www.taxpolicycenter.org/model-estimates/distribution-business-income-august-2016/t16-0184-sources-flow-through-business.

117. Jonathan Rothwell, "Why Elites Want More Competition for Everyone Except Themselves," *Evonomics*, April 2, 2016, http://evonomics.com/why-elites-want-more -competition-for-everyone-except-themselves.

118. Ibid.

119. Jonathan Rothwell, email exchange with Robert Atkinson, based on his analysis using the 2013 American Community Survey (via IPUMS-USA), May 2016.

120. Steven N. Kaplan and Joshua Rauh, "Wall Street and Main Street: What Contributes to the Rise in the Highest Incomes?," *Review of Financial Studies* 23, no. 3 (2010): 1004–1050.

121. Ibid.

Chapter 5

1. Alice Dechêne, Christoph Stahl, Jochim Hansen, and Michaela Wänke, "The Truth about the Truth: A Meta-Analytic Review of the Truth Effect," *Personality and Social Psychology Review* 14, no. 2 (2009): 238–257, https://www.researchgate.net/publication/40730710_The_Truth_About_the_Truth_A_Meta-Analytic_Review_of_the_Truth_Effect.

2. White House, Office of Management and Budget, "Supporting Small Businesses and Creating Jobs," ObamaWhiteHouseArchives.gov, n.d., https://obamawhitehouse.archives.gov/omb/factsheet/supporting-small-businesses-and-creating-jobs.

3. Bennett Harrison, *Lean and Mean: The Changing Landscape of Corporate Power in the Age of Flexibility* (New York: Basic Books, 1994), 42.

4. Catherine Armington, "Entry and Exit of Firms: An International Comparison," paper presented at the UK conference on Job Formation and Economic Growth, London, March, 1986.

5. Steven J. Davis, John Haltiwanger, and Scott Schuh, "Small Business and Job Creation: Dissecting the Myth and Reassessing the Facts," NBER Working Paper 4492 (Cambridge, MA: National Bureau of Economic Research, October 1993), http://www.nber.org/papers/w4492.

6. John C. Haltiwanger, Ron S. Jarmin, and Javier Miranda, "Who Creates Jobs? Small vs. Large vs. Young," NBER Working Paper W16300 (Cambridge, MA: National Bureau of Economic Research, 2010), 30.

7. "The Middle Market Power Index: Catalyzing U.S. Economic Growth," American Express and Dunn & Bradstreet, April 2015, http://about.americanexpress.com/news/docs/2015x/MMPI-FINAL-14April15.pdf.

8. Haltiwanger, Jarmin, and Miranda, "Who Creates Jobs?," 30.

9. Tim Kane, "The Importance of Startups in Job Creation and Job Destruction" (Kansas City, MO: Kauffman Foundation, July 2010), http://www.kauffman.org/~/media/kauffman_org/research%20reports%20and%20covers/2010/07/firm_formation_importance_of_startups.pdf.

10. Ryan Decker, John Haltiwanger, Ron Jarmin, and Javier Miranda, "The Role of Entrepreneurship in U.S. Job Creation and Economic Dynamism," *Journal of Economic Perspectives* 28, no. 3 (Summer 2014).

11. Jonathan S. Leonard, "On the Size Distribution of Employment and Establishments," NBER Working Paper 1951 (Cambridge, MA: National Bureau of Economic Research, June 1986), http://www.nber.org/papers/w1951.pdf.

12. John Haltiwanger, Ron S Jarmin, Robert Kulick, and Javier Miranda, "High Growth Young Firms: Contribution to Job, Output, and Productivity Growth," US Census Bureau, Center for Economic Studies Working Papers, vol. 16, no. 49, November 2016, 30.

13. US Small Business Administration (SBA), Office of Advocacy, "Frequently Asked Questions" (Washington, DC: SBA, September 2012), https://www.sba.gov/sites/default/files/FAQ_Sept_2012.pdf.

14. Zoltan J. Acs, *Are Small Firms Important? Their Role and Impact* (Boston: Kluwer Academic, 1999), 32.

15. David Neumark, Brandon Wall, and Junfu Zhang, "Do Small Businesses Create More Jobs? New Evidence for the United States from the National Establishment Time Series," IZA Discussion Paper 3888 (Bonn: Forschungsinstitut zur Zukunft der Arbeit, Institute for the Study of Labor, December 2008), ftp://repec.iza.org/pub/SSRN/pdf/dp3888.pdf.

16. Scott A. Shane, *The Illusions of Entrepreneurship: The Costly Myths That Entrepreneurs, Investors, and Policy Makers Live By* (New Haven, CT: Yale University Press, 2010).

17. Stephen J. Davis, John C. Haltiwanger, and Scott Schuh, *Job Creation and Destruction* (Cambridge, MA: MIT Press, 1996).

18. Kevin L. Kliesen and Julia S. Maués, "Are Small Businesses the Biggest Producers of Jobs?," *Regional Economist*, Federal Reserve Bank of St. Louis, April 2011, 8.

19. Decker et al., "The Role of Entrepreneurship in U.S. Job Creation and Economic Dynamism."

20. Charles Brown, James T. Hamilton, and James Medoff, *Employers Large and Small* (Cambridge, MA: Harvard University Press, 1990), 5.

21. John Mullins and Mike McCall, "Analytical Highlights of CES Firm Size Employment Data," Joint Statistical Meeting 2012, October 2012, https://www.bls.gov/osmr/pdf/st120070.pdf.

22. US Census Bureau, National Quarterly Workforce Indicators (Data, Firm-Size Disaggregation, 2015 Q3 release), http://lehd.ces.census.gov/data/qwi/us/R2015Q3/DVD-sa_fs (accessed January 2016).

23. Benjamin Wild Pugsley and Erik Hurst, "What Do Small Businesses Do?," paper presented at the Brookings Conference on Economic Activity, Washington, DC, Fall 2011, https://www.brookings.edu/bpea-articles/what-do-small-businesses-do.

24. Giuseppe Moscarini and Fabien Postel-Vinay, "The Contribution of Large and Small Employers to Job Creation in Times of High and Low Unemployment," *American Economic Review* 102, no. 6 (2012): 2509–2539, http://dx.doi.org/10.1257/ aer.102.6.2509.

25. Ibid.

26. Catherine Armington and Zoltan J. Acs, "The Determinants of Regional Variation in New Firm Formation," *Regional Studies* 36, no. 1 (2002): 33–45 .

27. Moscarini and Postel-Vinay, "The Contribution of Large and Small Employers to Job Creation."

28. Ibid., 2522.

29. Shane, *The Illusions of Entrepreneurship*, 25.

30. Ibid., 7.

31. Harrison, *Lean and Mean*, 19.

32. SBA, Office of Advocacy, "Frequently Asked Questions."

33. Ibid.

34. US Census Bureau, Business Dynamics Statistics (Longitudinal Business Database, Firm Characteristics Data Tables, Firm Age by Firm Size, 1977 to 2014, https://www.census.gov/ces/dataproducts/bds/data_firm.html (accessed March 17, 2017).

35. Pugsley and Hurst, "What Do Small Businesses Do?"

36. Shane, *The Illusions of Entrepreneurship*, 43.

37. Ibid., 66.

38. Pugsley and Hurst, "What Do Small Businesses Do?" 73.

39. Shane, *The Illusions of Entrepreneurship*, 154.

40. Ibid.

41. Dane Stangler, "High-Growth Firms and the Future of the American Economy" (Kansas City, MO: Kauffman Foundation, March 2010), 12, http://www.kauffman .org/what-we-do/research/firm-formation-and-growth-series/highgrowth-firms-and -the-future-of-the-american-economy.

42. Spencer Tracy, "Accelerating Job Creation in America: The Promise of High-Impact Companies" (Washington, DC: SBA, July 2011), 19.

43. Ibid.

44. Ibid., 41.

45. Ibid., 28.

46. Pugsley and Hurst, "What Do Small Businesses Do?"

47. Harrison, *Lean and Mean*, 13.

48. Data provided by the Boeing Company, March 23, 2017.

49. Eurostat, "Statistics on Small- and Medium-Sized Enterprises: Dependent and Independent SMEs and Large Enterprises," Eurostat Statistics Explained, September 2015, http://ec.europa.eu/eurostat/statistics-explained/index.php/Statistics _on_small_and_medium-sized_enterprises (accessed June 3, 2017).

50. John Dearie and Courtney Geduldig, *Where the Jobs Are: Entrepreneurship and the Soul of the American Economy* (Hoboken, NJ: John Wiley & Sons, 2013), 16.

Chapter 6

1. Quoted in Walter Isaacson, "Stewart Brand Responds," *Medium*, December 27, 2013, https://medium.com/@walterisaacson/stewart-brand-responds-f857b2e8da26.

2. Quoted in Malcolm Gladwell, "Creation Myth: Xerox PARC, Apple, and the Truth about Innovation," *New Yorker*, May 16, 2011, http://www.newyorker.com/ magazine/2011/05/16/creation-myth.

3. Vannevar Bush, "As We May Think," *Atlantic Monthly*, July 1945.

4. Dylan Tweney, "Dec. 9, 1968: The Mother of All Demos," *Wired*, December 9, 2010.

5. "The Xerox PARC Visit," in *Making the Macintosh: Technology and Culture in Silicon Valley*, Stanford University, web.stanford.edu.

6. Chris Nuttall, "Silicon Valley's Founding Fathers," *Financial Times*, October 30, 2007.

7. Benjamin Pimentel, "High Tech's Lowly Birthplace," *SFGATE*, November 27, 2005.

8. Gary P. Pisano and Willy C. Shih, "Restoring American Competitiveness," *Harvard Business Review*, July/August 2009, https://hbr.org/2009/07/restoring -american-competitiveness.

9. Joseph A. Schumpeter, *The Theory of Economic Development* (Cambridge, MA: Harvard University Press, 1934 [1911]), 91.

10. Joseph A. Schumpeter, *Capitalism, Socialism, and Democracy*, 3rd ed. (New York: Harper & Brothers, 1950 [1942]).

11. Ibid., 132.

12. Ibid., 100–101.

13. John Kenneth Galbraith, *American Capitalism: The Concept of Countervailing Power* (New York: Houghton Mifflin, 1952), 91.

14. William J. Baumol, *The Free-Market Innovation Machine* (Princeton, NJ: Princeton University Press, 2002), 287.

15. Joseph Bowring, *Competition in a Dual Economy* (Princeton, NJ: Princeton University Press, 1986), 11.

16. J. R. Hicks, *Value and Capital* (Oxford: Oxford University Press, 1946), 83–84, cited in John Bellamy Foster, Robert W. McChesney, and R. Jamil Jonna, "Monopoly and Competition in Twenty-First Century Capitalism," *Monthly Review* 62, no. 11 (April 2011), https://monthlyreview.org/2011/04/01/monopoly-and-competition-in-twenty-first-century-capitalism.

17. John Kenneth Galbraith, *The New Industrial State*, 4th ed. (Princeton, NJ: Princeton University Press, 2007), 746.

18. Galbraith, *American Capitalism*, 85.

19. Kenneth J. Arrow, "Economic Welfare and the Allocation of Resources for Invention," in *Essays in the Theory of Risk-Bearing*, ed. Kenneth J. Arrow (Amsterdam: North-Holland, 1971), 144–160.

20. White House, Council of Economic Advisers, "Benefits of Competition and Indicators of Market Power," Council of Economic Advisors Issue Brief, ObamaWhiteHouseArchives.gov, May 2016, 3, https://obamawhitehouse.archives.gov/sites/default/files/page/files/20160502_competition_issue_brief_updated_cea.pdf.

21. Ester Fano, "Technical Progress as a Destabilizing Factor and As an Agent of Recovery in the United States between the Two World Wars," *History and Technology* 3 (1987): 262–263, http://www.tandfonline.com/doi/abs/10.1080/07341518708581671?journalCode=ghat20.

22. Zvi Griliches, "Recent Patent Trends and Puzzles," Brookings Papers on Economic Activity (Washington, DC: Brookings Institution, 1989), 291–330, cited in Baumol, *The Free-Market Innovation Machine*, 34.

23. "Research and Development in Industry, 1974" (Washington, DC: National Science Foundation, September 1976), cited in Galbraith, *The New Industrial State*, 38–39.

24. Henry Kressel and Thomas V. Lento, *Entrepreneurship in the Global Economy: Engine for Economic Growth* (Cambridge: Cambridge University Press, 2012), 44.

25. Michael Mandel, "Scale and Innovation in Today's Economy" (Washington, DC: Progressive Policy Institute, December 2011), 3.

26. Eric Hobsbawm, *Industry and Empire: From 1750 to the Present* Day (Harmondsworth: Penguin, 1969), 40.

27. David Autor, David Dorn, Gordon H. Hanson, Gary Pisan, and Pian Shu, "Foreign Competition and Domestic Innovation: Evidence from US Patents" (working paper, Department of Economics, Massachusetts Institute of Technology, November 2016), http://economics.mit.edu/files/11708.

28. Fred Block, "Swimming against the Current: The Rise of a Hidden Developmental State in the United States," *Politics & Society* 36, no. 2 (2008): 169–206, See also Walter Powell, "The Capitalist Firm in the 21st Century: Emerging Patterns in Western Enterprise," in *The Twenty-First Century Firm: Changing Economic Organization in International Perspective*, ed. Paul DiMaggio (Princeton, NJ: Princeton University Press, 2001), 35–68; and Raymond E. Miles, Grant Miles, and Charles C. Snow, *Collaborative Entrepreneurship: How Communities of Networked Firms Use Continuous Innovation to Create Economic Wealth* (Palo Alto, CA: Stanford University Press, 2005), 36, note 56.

29. Ashish Arora, Sharon Belenzon, and Andrea Patacconi, "Killing the Golden Goose? The Changing Nature of Corporate Research, 1980–2007" (faculty paper, Fuqua School of Business, Duke University, and Norwich Business School, University of East Anglia, January 9, 2015), https://faculty.fuqua.duke.edu/~sb135/bio/Science%201%2091%2015.pdf.

30. Ibid.

31. Cited in Chris Matthews, "The Death of American Research and Development," *Fortune*, December 21, 2015, http://fortune.com/2015/12/21/death-american-research-and-development.

32. Bill George, "Dow-DuPont Raises Even More Concerns America Is Abandoning Corporate Research," *Fortune*, December 12, 2015, http://fortune.com/2015/12/12/dow-dupont-corporate-research-america.

33. Moshe Y. Vardi, "The Rise and Fall of Industrial Research Labs," *Communications of the ACM* 58, no. 1 (January 2015): 5, http://delivery.acm.org/10.1145/2690000/2687353/p5-vardi.pdf.

34. "Microsoft's Expenditure on Research and Development from 2002 to 2016 (in Million US Dollars), Statista.com, n.d., https://www.statista.com/statistics/267806/expenditure-on-research-and-development-by-the-microsoft-corporation.

35. Peter Nolan, Jin Zhang, and Chunhang Liu, *The Global Business Revolution and the Cascade Effect: Systems Integration in the Global Aerospace, Beverage and Retail Industries* (New York: Palgrave Macmillan, 2007), 146.

36. Scott A. Shane, *The Illusions of Entrepreneurship: The Costly Myths That Entrepreneurs, Investors, and Policy Makers Live By* (New Haven, CT: Yale University Press, 2008), 30.

37. Sam Hogg, "Why Small Companies Have the Innovation Advantage," *Entrepreneur*, November 15, 2011, https://www.entrepreneur.com/article/220558.

38. Anthony Breitzman and Diana Hicks, "An Analysis of Small Business Patents by Industry and Firm Size," cited in *The Small Business Economy, 2009: A Report to the President* (Washington, DC: US GPO, 2009), 29, https://www.sba.gov/sites/default/files/files/sb_econ2009.pdf.

39. Jose M. Plehn-Dujowich, "Product Innovations by Young and Small Firms," (Washington, DC: SBA, Office of Advocacy, May 2013), 5, https://www.sba.gov/sites/default/files/files/rs408tot.pdf.

40. Jose M. Plehn-Dujowich, "The Effect of Firm Size and Age on R&D Productivity" (faculty paper, Department of Economics, SUNY at Buffalo, n.d., 435), https://editorialexpress.com/cgi-bin/conference/download.cgi?db_name=IIOC2008&paper_id=510.

41. US SBA, Office of Advocacy, "Frequently Asked Questions" (Washington, DC: SBA, September 2012), https://www.sba.gov/sites/default/files/FAQ_Sept_2012.pdf.

42. Justin Hicks, "Knowledge Spillovers and International R&D Networks" (Washington, DC: Information Technology and Innovation Foundation, May 7, 2012), http://www2.itif.org/2012-knowledge-spillover-hicks.pdf.

43. Shane, *The Illusions of Entrepreneurship*, 65.

44. Ibid.

45. Erik Hurst and William Pugsley, "What Do Small Businesses Do?," paper presented at the Brookings Conference on Economic Activity, Washington, DC, Fall 2011, 21, https://www.brookings.edu/bpea-articles/what-do-small-businesses-do.

46. Ibid.

47. Anthony Breitzman and Diana Hicks, "An Analysis of Small Business Patents by Industry and Firm Size," in Rowan University, *Faculty Scholarship for the College of Science & Mathematics* (Glassboro, NJ, November 2008), iii.

48. Nolan, Zhang, and Liu, *The Global Business Revolution and the Cascade Effect*, 146, table 6.1.

49. National Science Foundation, "Business Research and Development and Innovation: 2012," NSF 16-301 (Arlington, VA: NSF, October 29, 2015), table 5, https://nsf.gov/statistics/2016/nsf16301/#chp2.

50. Ibid., table 51.

51. Michael Mandel, "Scale and Innovation in Today's Economy" (Washington, DC: Progressive Policy Institute, December 2001), 3, http://progressivepolicy.org/wp-content/uploads/2011/12/12.2011-Mandel_Scale-and-Innovation-in-Todays-Economy.pdf.

52. Adams Nager, David Hart, Stephen Ezell, and Robert D. Atkinson, "The Demographics of Innovation in the United States" (Washington, DC: Information Technology and Innovation Foundation, February 2016), http://www2.itif.org/2016-demographics-of-innovation.pdf?_ga=1.150326719.884756560.1448881039.

53. Luc L. G. Soete, "Firm Size and Inventive Activity: The Evidence Reconsidered," *European Economic Review* 12, no. 4 (October 1979): 319–340, https://ideas.repec.org/a/eee/eecrev/v12y1979i4p319-340.html.

54. Wesley M. Cohen and Steven Klepper, "A Reprise of Size and R & D," *Economic Journal* 106, no. 437 (July 1996): 948, http://www.jstor.org/stable/2235365.

55. Ibid.

56. Ibid.

57. Anne Marie Knott and Carl Vieregger, "Reconciling the Firm Size and Innovation Puzzle," Center for Economic Studies Paper 16-20 (Washington, DC: US Census Bureau, March 2016), https://www2.census.gov/ces/wp/2016/CES-WP-16-20.pdf.

58. Zeina Alsharkas, "Firm Size, Competition, Financing and Innovation," *International Journal of Management and Economics (Zeszyty Naukowe KGŚ)* 44 (December 2014): 58, http://kolegia.sgh.waw.pl/pl/KGS/publikacje/Documents/IJME44_ZN%2044%20(1).pdf.

59. "SMEs in Japan: A New Growth Driver?," Economist Intelligence Unit, December 2010, https://www.eiuperspectives.economist.com/sites/default/files/EIU_Microsoft_JapanSMEs_FINAL-WEB.pdf.

60. Patrizio Pagano and Fabiano Schivardi, "Firm Size Distribution and Growth," *Scandinavian Journal of Economics* 105, no. 2 (2003): 272, http://onlinelibrary.wiley.com/doi/10.1111/1467-9442.t01-1-00008/abstract.

61. Alsharkas, "Firm Size, Competition, Financing and Innovation," 58.

62. Shane, *The Illusions of Entrepreneurship*, 23.

63. Ibid.

64. Keith Pavitt, Michael Robson, and Joe Townsend, "The Size Distribution of Innovating Firms in the UK: 1945–1983," *Journal of Industrial Economics* 35, no. 3 (1987): 297–316, http://econpapers.repec.org/article/blajindec/v_3a35_3ay_3a1987_3ai_3a3_3ap_3a297-316.htm.

65. Giovanni Dosi, Alfonso Gambardella, Marco Grazzi, and Luigi Orsenigo, "The New Techno-Economic Paradigm and Its Impact on Industrial Structure," in *Techno-Economic Paradigms: Essays in Honor of Carlota Perez*, ed. Wolfgang Dreschsler, Rainer Kattel, and Erik S. Reinert (London: Anthem Press, 2011), 84.

66. Acs and Audretsch, *Innovation and Small Firms*, 50.

67. Ibid., 55.

68. Paroma Sanyal and Linda R. Cohen, "Powering Progress: Restructuring, Competition, and R&D in the U.S. Electric Utility Industry," *Energy Journal* 30, no. 2 (2009): 41–79, https://www.jstor.org/stable/41323233?seq=1#page_scan_tab_contents.

69. John M. Vernon and Peter Gusen, "Technical Change and Firm Size: The Pharmaceutical Industry," *Review of Economics and Statistics* 56, no. 3 (August 1974): 294–302, http://www.jstor.org/stable/1923966.

70. Robert P. Rogers, "Staff Report on the Development and Structure of the U.S. Electric Lamp Industry" (Washington, DC: Federal Trade Commission, Bureau of Economics, February 1980), https://www.ftc.gov/sites/default/files/documents/reports/bureau-economics-staff-report-development-and-structure-u.s.electric-lamp-industry/198002electriclampindustry.pdf.

71. Keith Fuglie, Paul Heisey, John Kind, and David Schimmelpfennig, "Rising Concentration in Agricultural Input Industries Influences New Farm Technologies" (Washington, DC: US Department of Agriculture, December 3, 2012), http://www.ers.usda.gov/amber-waves/2012/december/rising-concentration-in-agricultural-input-industries-influences-new-technologies.

72. Antonio J. Revilla and Zulima Fernández, "The Relation between Firm Size and R&D Productivity in Different Technological Regimes," *Technovation* 32, no. 11 (November 2012): 609–623, https://www.researchgate.net/publication/257002756_The_Relation_between_Firm_Size_and_RD_Productivity_in_Different_Technological_Regimes.

73. Ibid.

74. Quoted in Acs and Audretsch, *Innovation and Small Firms*, 50.

75. Barry C. Lynn, "Antitrust: A Missing Key to Prosperity, Opportunity, and Democracy" (New York: Demos, New Economic Paradigms, and Rockefeller Foundation, n.d.), http://www.demos.org/sites/default/files/publications/Lynn.pdf.

76. Seth Goldman, personal conversation with Robert Atkinson, November 4, 2016.

77. Hurst and Pugsley, "What Do Small Businesses Do?" 73.

78. Ibid., 75.

79. Ibid., 96.

Chapter 7

1. "Self-Employment Rate," OECD data, 2016, https://Data.Oecd.Org/Emp/Self
-Employment-Rate.Htm (accessed March 19, 2017).

2. Central Intelligence Agency, *CIA World Factbook* (2016), https://www.cia.gov/
library/publications/the-world-factbook.

3. Ben Ryan, "Nearly Three in 10 Workers Worldwide Are Self-Employed," Gallup.
com, August 22, 2014, http://www.gallup.com/poll/175292/nearly-three-workers
-worldwide-self-employed.aspx.

4. World Bank, "International Tourism, Receipts (% of Total Exports)" (database
and graph), http://data.worldbank.org/indicator/ST.INT.RCPT.XP.ZS.

5. Gerald F. Davis and J. Adam Cobb, "Corporations and Economic Inequality
around the World: The Paradox of Hierarchy," Administrative Science Quarterly 62,
no. 2: 304–340, http://journals.sagepub.com/doi/10.1177/0001839216673823#articl
eCitationDownloadContainer.

6. Klaus Schwab, ed., *The Global Competitiveness Report: 2015–2016* (Geneva: World
Economic Forum, 2015), http://www3.weforum.org/docs/gcr/2015-2016/Global
_Competitiveness_Report_2015-2016.pdf.

7. Emilio Congregado, Antonio A. Golpe, and André Stel, "The Role of Scale Economies in Determining Firm Size in Modern Economies," *Annals of Regional Science* 52,
no. 2 (March 2014): 431–455, https://www.researchgate.net/publication/260762630
_The_role_of_scale_economies_in_determining_firm_size_in_modern_economies.

8. Serguey Braguinsky, Lee G. Branstetter, and Andre Regateiro, "The Incredible
Shrinking Portuguese Firm," NBER Working Paper 17265 (Cambridge, MA: National
Bureau of Economic Research, July 2011), http://www.nber.org/papers/w17265
.pdf.

9. Ibid., 46.

10. Shanji Zin, "Firm Size and Economic Growth in China" (faculty paper, Department of Economics, Seoul National University, June 2015), https://editorialexpress
.com/cgi-bin/conference/download.cgi?db_name=WCCE2015&paper_id=418.

11. Robert D. Atkinson, "The Real Korean Innovation Challenge: Services and Small
Businesses," Korea Economic Institute of America, March 4, 2016, https://itif.org/
publications/2016/03/04/real-korean-innovation-challenge-services-and-small
-businesses.

12. "SMEs: Employment, Innovation and Growth," Washington Workshop, OECD,
1996, https://www.oecd.org/cfe/smes/2090756.pdf.

13. Benedict Dellot, "The Second Age of Small: Understanding the Economic Impact of Micro Businesses" (London: RSA Action and Research Centre, June 2015), https://www.thersa.org/globalassets/pdfs/reports/rsa_second_age_of_small.pdf.

14. Ibid.

15. International Monetary Fund, "Finland: Selected Issues," IMF Staff Country Report 15/312 (Washington, DC: IMF, 2015), http://www.imf.org/en/Publications/CR/Issues/2016/12/31/Finland-Selected-Issues-43397.

16. Bart van Ark and Erik Monnikhof, "Size Distribution of Output and Employment: A Data Set for Manufacturing Industries in Five OECD Countries, 1960s-1990," OECD Economics Department Working Paper 166, January 1, 1996, http://www.oecd-ilibrary.org/economics/size-distribution-of-output-and-employment_207105163036?crawler=true.

17. Danny Leung, Cesaire Meh, and Yaz Terajima, "Firm Size and Productivity," Bank of Canada Staff Working Paper 2008-45 (Ottawa: Bank of Canada, February 2010), 3, http://www.bankofcanada.ca/wp-content/uploads/2010/02/wp08-45.pdf.

18. Ibid.

19. Fukao Kyojirietirieti, "Explaining Japan's Unproductive Two Decades," RIETI Policy Discussion Paper Series 13-P-021 (Tokyo: Research Institute of Economy, Trade and Industry, October 22, 2013), http://www.rieti.go.jp/jp/publications/pdp/13p021.pdf.

20. S. Thorsten Beck, A. Demirgüç-Kunt, and Ross Levine, "Small and Medium Enterprises, Growth, and Poverty: Cross-Country Evidence," World Bank Policy Research Working Paper 3178 (Washington, DC: World Bank, December 2003), http://elibrary.worldbank.org/doi/abs/10.1596/1813-9450-3178.

21. John Page and Måns Söderbom, "Is Small Beautiful? Small Enterprise, Aid and Employment in Africa," *African Development Review* 27, Suppl. 1 (2015): 44–55, http://soderbom.net/smallbeautiful_feb2015.pdf.

22. Rana Hasan and Karl Robert L. Jandoc, "The Distribution of Firm Size in India: What Can Survey Data Tell Us?," ADB Economics Working Paper 213 (Manila: Asian Development Bank, August 2010), https://www.adb.org/sites/default/files/publication/28418/economics-wp213.pdf.

23. Johannes Van Biesebroeck, "Firm Size Matters: Growth and Productivity Growth in African Manufacturing," *Economic Development and Cultural Change* 53 (2005): 546–583, http://www.journals.uchicago.edu/doi/abs/10.1086/426407.

24. Donald R. Snodgrass and Taylor Biggs, *Industrialization and Small Firm: Patterns and Policies* (San Francisco: International Center for Economic Growth, 1996).

25. US Small Business Administration, "The Small Business Economy" (compilation of databases, covering multiple years, on small business and the economy), https://www.sba.gov/advocacy/small-business-economy.

26. Snodgrass and Biggs, *Industrialization and Small Firm.*

27. Scott Shane, *The Illusions of Entrepreneurship: The Costly Myths That Entrepreneurs, Investors, and Policy Makers Live By* (New Haven, CT: Yale University Press, 2008), 151.

28. Ibid., 152.

29. Ibid., 18.

30. Leung, Meh, and Terajima, "Firm Size and Productivity."

31. Ibid., 3.

32. This is based on the 18 percent productivity gap between the two nations and the fact that the firm size component of the gap is 19 percent.

33. Krishna B. Kumar, Raghuram G. Rajan, and Luigi Zingales, "What Determines Firm Size?," NBER Working Paper 7208 (Cambridge, MA: National Bureau of Economic Research, July 1999), http://www.nber.org/papers/w7208.

34. Australia, Austria, Belgium, Bulgaria, Czech Republic, Denmark, Finland, Germany, Greece, Hungary, Israel, Italy, Japan, Latvia, Lithuania, Luxembourg, Mexico, New Zealand, Poland, Portugal, Romania, Slovak Republic, Slovenia, Spain, Sweden, Turkey, Switzerland, United Kingdom, and the United States.

35. Robert E. Lucas, Jr., "On the Size Distribution of Business Firms," *Bell Journal of Economics* 9, no. 2 (1978): 508–523, https://www.jstor.org/stable/3003596?seq=1#page_scan_tab_contents.

36. Markus Poschke, "The Firm Size Distribution across Countries and Skill-Biased Change in Entrepreneurial Technology" (Economics Department, McGill University, November 2011), http://www.ub.edu/ubeconomics/wp-content/uploads/2013/05/mposchke_skillbias1.pdf.

37. Jan Eeckhout and Boyan Jovanovic, "Occupational Choice and Development," NBER Working Paper 13686 (Cambridge, MA: National Bureau of Economic Research, March 2012), http://trove.nla.gov.au/work/25837889?q&sort=holdings+desc&_=1494451397913&versionId=178164501.

38. Farrukh Iqbal Shujiro Urata, "Small Firm Dynamism in East Asia: An Introductory Overview," *Small Business Economics* 18, no. 1 (February 2002): 1–12.

39. Rafael Laporta, Florencio Lopez-De-Silanes, Andrei Shleifer, and Robert W. Vishny, "Trust in Large Organizations," *American Economic Review Papers and Proceedings* 87, no. 2 (May 1997), 333–338.

40. Nicholas Bloom, Raffaella Sadun, and John Van Reenen, "The Organization of Firms across Countries" (working paper), *Quarterly Journal of Economics* 127, no. 4(2012): 1663–1705, https://academic.oup.com/qje/article-abstract/127/4/1663/ 1842108/The-Organization-of-Firms-Across-Countries?redirectedFrom=PDF.

41. Kumar, Rajan, and Zingales, "What Determines Firm Size?"

42. Ibid., 22.

43. Luc Laeven and Christopher Woodruff, "The Quality of the Legal System, Firm Ownership, and Firm Size" (Washington, DC: World Bank Group, March 2004), http://elibrary.worldbank.org/doi/abs/10.1596/1813-9450-3246.

44. Kumar, Rajan, and Zingales, "What Determines Firm Size?," 22.

45. European Commission, "Putting Small Businesses First: Europe Is Good for SMEs, SMEs Are Good for Europe" (European Commission, 2008), http://ec.europa .eu/docsroom/documents/2278/attachments/1/translations/en/renditions/pdf.

46. Adalberto Cardoso and Telma Lage, *As normas e os factos* (Rio de Janeiro: Editora FGV, 2007).

47. Gabriel Sánchez, "Understanding Productivity Levels, Growth and Dispersion in Argentina: The Case of Supermarkets" (faculty paper, IERAL, Buenos Aires, draft of February 13, 2008), www.merit.unu.edu/meide/papers/2009/1236010806_GS .pdf.

48. Stephen Ezell, "Stephen Ezell on Innovation Matters," *Bridges* 41 (October 2014) (Washington, DC: Office of Science and Technology Austria), http://ostaustria.org/ bridges-magazine/item/8284-stephenezell-on-innovation-matters.

49. Bill Lewis, Heinz-Peter Elstrodt, David Edelstein, et al., "Productivity: The Key to an Accelerated Development Path for Brazil" (Washington, DC: McKinsey Global Institute, March 1998), http://www.mckinsey.com/global-themes/americas/ productivity-is-the-key-to-development-path-for-brazil.

50. Chang-Tai Hsieh and Benjamin A. Olken, "The Missing 'Missing Middle,'" NBER Working Paper 19966 (Cambridge, MA: National Bureau of Economic Research, March 2014), 100, http://www.nber.org/papers/w19966.

51. Bikky Khosla, "SME Policy: What China Is Doing and We're Not," *SME Times*, January 27, 2015, http://www.smetimes.in/smetimes/editorial/2015/Jan/27/sme -policy-what-china-doing-and-we-are-not29921.html.

52. R. S. Jones and M. Kim, "Fostering a Creative Economy to Drive Korean Growth," OECD Economics Department Working Paper 1152 (Paris: OECD, 2014), 9, http://dx.doi.org/10.1787/5jz0wh8xkrf6-en.

53. Ibid., 24.

54. European Commission, *Handbook on Community State Aid Rules for SMEs* (European Commission, February 25, 2009), http://ec.europa.eu/competition/state_aid/studies_reports/sme_handbook.pdf.

55. Ibid.

56. Scott Shane, "Why Encouraging More People to Become Entrepreneurs Is Bad Public Policy," *Small Business Economics* 33, no. 2 (August 2009): 141–149, https://link.springer.com/article/10.1007/s11187-009-9215-5.

57. Soumitra Dutta, ed., *The Global Innovation Index 2012: Stronger Innovation Linkages for Global Growth* (Fontainebleu: INSEAD and WIPO, 2012), https://www.globalinnovationindex.org/userfiles/file/gii-2012-report.pdf.

58. Kim So-Hyn, "8 Firms Get Poor Shared Growth Marks," *Korea Herald*, May 28 2013, http://m.koreaherald.com/view.php?ud=20130527000961&ntn=1.

59. Robert Atkinson, "The Real Korean Innovation Challenge: Services and Small Businesses," *Korea's Economy* 30 (2015): 47–54, http://keia.org/sites/default/files/publications/kei_koreaseconomy_atkinson_0.pdf.

60. Ibid.

61. Luis Garicano, Claire LeLarge, and John Van Reenen, "Firm Size Distortions and the Productivity Distribution: Evidence from France," NBER Working Paper 18841 (Cambridge, MA: National Bureau of Economic Research, February 2013), http://www.nber.org/papers/w18841.

62. Ibid., 25.

63. Serguey Braguinsky, Lee Branstetter, and Andre Regateiro, "The Incredible Shrinking Portuguese Firm," NBER Working Paper 17265 (Cambridge, MA: National Bureau of Economic Research, July 2011), http://www.nber.org/papers/w17265.

64. Rana Hasan and Karl Robert L. Jandoc, "Labor Regulations and the Firm Size Distribution in India Manufacturing," paper presented at the conference "India: Reforms, Economic Transformation and the Socially Disadvantaged," Columbia University, New York, September 2012, http://indianeconomy.columbia.edu/sites/default/files/paper_4-hasan.pdf.

65. Fabiano Schivardi A. and Roberto Torrini, "Identifying the Effects of Firing Restrictions through Size-Contingent Differences in Regulation," *Labour Economics* 15, no. 3, (June 2008): 482–511, http://www.sciencedirect.com/science/article/pii/S0927537107000206.

66. Kazuki Onji, "The Response of Firms to Eligibility Thresholds: Evidence from the Japanese Value-Added Tax," *Journal of Public Economics* 93 (2009): 766–775, http://www.sciencedirect.com/science/article/pii/S0047272708001953.

67. Nezih Guner, Gustavo Ventura, and Xu Y, "Macroeconomic Implications of Size-Dependent Policies," *Review of Economic Dynamics* 11 (2008): 721–744, http://fmwww.bc.edu/repec/sed2005/up.14973.1107121049.pdf.

68. Montek S. Ahluwalia, "Economic Reforms in India since 1991: Has Gradualism Worked?," *Journal of Economic Perspectives* 16, no. 3 (Summer 2002): 67–88.

69. Gurcharan Das, *India Grows at Night: A Liberal Case for a Strong State* (New Delhi: Penguin, 2012), 35.

70. Hasan and Jandoc, "The Distribution of Firm Size in India.Error!Hyperlinkrefere ncenotvalid.

71. Ibid.

72. Robert C. Young, "Enterprise Scale, Economic Policy and Development: Evidence on Policy Biases, Firm Size, Efficiency, and Growth," Occasional Paper 52 (International Center for Economic Growth, 1994), 15, http://213.154.74.164/invenio/record/15889/files/iceg52.pdf.

73. Chang-Tai Hsieh and Peter J. Klenow, "Misallocation and Manufacturing TFP in China and India," *Quarterly Journal of Economics* 124, no. 4 (2009): 1403–1448, http://klenow.com/MMTFP.pdf.

74. Shahid Yusuf and Danny Leipziger, eds., *How Economies Grow* (Washington, DC: Growth Dialogue, 2014), http://dannyleipziger.com/documents/How%20Economies%20Grow.pdf.

75. Cardoso and Lage, *As normas e os factos.*

76. Stoyan Tenev, Amanda Carlier, Omar Chaudry, and Quynh-Trang Nguyen, "Informality and the Playing Field in Vietnam's Business Sector" (Washington, DC: IFC, World Bank, and MPDF, 2003), https://www.ifc.org/wps/wcm/connect/9aae680 047adb52f9311f7752622ff02/VN-informality-playing-field-VN.pdf?MOD=AJPERES.

77. "The Informal Workforce and Public Policy" (interview with Luis Videgaray Caso), *Revista Este País* 267 (July 2013), http://www.wiego.org/sites/default/files/publications/files/Videgaray-Informal-Workforce-Public-Policy.pdf.

78. James Manyika, Jonathan Woetzel, Richard Dobbs, Jaana Remes, Eric Labaye, and Andrew Jordan, "Can Long-Term Global Growth Be Saved?" (Washington, DC: McKinsey Global Institute, January 2015), http://www.mckinsey.com/global -themes/employment-and-growth/can-long-term-global-growth-be-saved.

79. "Policies & Programmes," Women in Informal Employment: Globalizing and Organizing website, http://wiego.org/informal-economy/policies-programmes.

80. "EU Accountability Report 2012 on Financing for Development: Review of Progress of the EU and Its Member States," European Commission Staff Working

Paper (European Commission, July 9, 2012), 40, http://ec.europa.eu/europeaid/sites/devco/files/swp-accountability-report-199-main-report_en.pdf.

81. United Nations, "Sustainable Development Knowledge Platform," http://www.un.org/sustainabledevelopment/development-agenda.

82. World Bank, "The Big Business of Small Enterprises: Evaluation of the World Bank Group Experience with Targeted Support to Small and Medium-Size Businesses, 2006–2012" (Washington, DC: World Bank, 2014), xi

83. James Militzer, "Most Influential Post Nominee: 10 Takeaways from the World Bank Forum on Microcredit's (Lack of) Social Impact," NB Financial Innovation, December 25, 2015, http://nextbillion.net/10-takeaways-from-the-world-bank-forum-on-microcredits-lack-of-social-impact.

Chapter 8

1. The anecdote, from the notes of Dr. James McHenry, a delegate to the Constitutional Convention from Maryland, was first published in the *American Historical Review*, volume 11 (1906), p. 618.

2. Barry C. Lynn and Phillip Longman, "Populism with a Brain: Ten Old/New Ideas to Give Power Back to the People," *Washington Monthly*, June/July/August, 2016.

3. Quoted in Melvin I. Urofsky, *Louis D. Brandeis: A Life* (New York: Schocken Books, 2009), 309.

4. Ibid.

5. Ibid.

6. Friedrich August Hayek, *The Road to Serfdom* (New York: George Routledge & Sons, 1944), 204.

7. Urofsky, *Louis D. Brandeis*, 346.

8. See Quentin Skinner, "A Third Concept of Liberty," *Proceedings of the British Academy* 117, no. 237 (2002): 262; Quentin Skinner, *Liberty before Liberalism* (Cambridge: Cambridge University Press, 1998); and Philip Pettit, *Republicanism: A Theory of Freedom and Government* (Oxford: Oxford University Press, 1999).

9. Aristotle, *The Politics and the Constitution of Athens*, 3.7.

10. Quoted in Alex Gourevitch, *From Slavery to the Cooperative Commonwealth: Labor and Republican Liberty in the Nineteenth Century* (Cambridge: Cambridge University Press, 2015), 103.

11. J. G. A. Pocock, ed., *The Political Works of James Harrington: Part One* (Cambridge: Cambridge University Press, 1977), 170.

12. Charles Francis Adams, ed., *The Works of John Adams*, 10 vols. (Boston: Little, Brown, 1854), 9:376.

13. Abraham Lincoln, "Address before the Wisconsin State Agricultural Society, Milwaukee, Wisconsin," September 30, 1859, in Roy P. Basler, ed., *The Collected Works of Abraham Lincoln*, 9 vols. (New Brunswick, NJ: Rutgers University Press, 1953), 3:478–479.

14. Ibid.

15. Alexis de Tocqueville, *Democracy in America*, trans. and ed. Harvey C. Mansfield and Delba Winthrop (Chicago: University of Chicago Press, 2000), 532, xxvii.

16. Thomas Jefferson, letter to General Thaddeus Kosciusko, in *The Works of Thomas Jefferson*, 12 vols. (New York: Cosimo Classics, 2009), 11:260.

17. "Lewis Mumford Quotes," Goodreads.com, https://www.goodreads.com/author/quotes/51834.Lewis_Mumford?page=2.

18. "Whole Earth Systems," *Whole Earth Catalog*, http://www.wholeearth.com/issue/1010/article/196/the.purpose.of.the.whole.earth.catalog.

19. Alvin Toffler, *The Third Wave* (New York: Morrow, 1980).

20. Matea Gold and Anu Narayanswamy, "The New Gilded Age: Close to Half of All Super-PAC Money Comes from 50 Donors," *Washington Post*, April 10, 2016, https://www.washingtonpost.com/politics/the-new-gilded-age-close-to-half-of-all-super-pac-money-comes-from-50-donors/2016/04/15/63dc363c-01b4-11e6-9d36-33d198ea26c5_story.html?utm_term=.9d4ba5dc549a.

21. Open Secrets, Center for Responsive Politics, https://www.opensecrets.org.

22. Martin Gilens and Benjamin I. Page, "Testing Theories of American Politics: Elites, Interest Groups, and Average Citizens," *Perspectives on Politics* 12, no. 3 (September 2014): 564–581.

23. "Lobbying: Top Spenders," Maplight.org, http://maplight.org/us-congress/lobbying.

24. Open Secrets, Center for Responsive Politics, "Top Pacs," https://www.opensecrets.org/pacs/toppacs.php.

25. Charles Brown, James T. Hamilton, and James Medoff, *Employers Large and Small* (Cambridge, MA: Harvard University Press, 1990), 4, cited in Carol Matlack, "Mobilizing a Multitude," *National Journal*, October 17, 2596.

26. "Government Regulation and Regulatory Reform," National Federation of Independent Businesses, http://www.nfib.com/advocacy/government-and-regulatory-reform.

27. "Issues and Committees," Business Roundtable, http://businessroundtable.org/issues.

28. Frank R. Baumgartner, Jeffrey M. Berry, Marie Hojnacki, David C. Kimball, and Beth L. Leech, *Lobbying and Policy Change: Who Wins, Who Loses, and Why* (Chicago: University of Chicago Press, 2009).

29. Ibid.

30. Joe Kennedy, "Tax Reform Not Unfair to Small Business," *Triangle Business Journal*, November 11, 2016, http://www.bizjournals.com/triangle/news/2016/11/11/guest-opiniontax-reform-not-unfair-to-small.html.

Chapter 9

1. Richard Hofstadter, *The Paranoid Style in American Politics* (New York: Vintage, 2008 [1965]), 205.

2. Thurman W. Arnold, *The Bottlenecks of Business* (New York: Reynal & Hitchcock, 1940).

3. Charles W. Calomiris and Stephen H. Haber, *Fragile by Design: The Political Origins of Banking Crises and Scarce Credit* (Princeton, NJ: Princeton University Press, 2014).

4. Roland Marchand, *Creating the Corporate Soul: The Rise of Public Relations and Corporate Imagery in American Big Business* (Berkeley: University of California Press, 1998), 4.

5. *Congressional Record*, 51st Cong., 1st Sess., House, 20 June (1890) 4100, quoted in Thomas J. DiLorenzo, "The Origins of Antitrust: An Interest-Group Perspective," *International Review of Law and Economics* (1985), 5, 80–81.

6. Quoted in Glenn Porter, *The Rise of Big Business, 1860–1920*, 3rd ed. (Wheeling, IL: Harlan Davidson, 2006 [1973]), 98.

7. Millard E. Tydings, US Senator, 1938, quoted in Jonathan J. Bean, *Beyond the Broker State: Federal Policies toward Small Businesses 1936–1961* (Chapel Hill: University of North Carolina Press, 1996), 1.

8. Dissent of Justice William O. Douglas in *Standard Oil of California and Standard Stations, Inc. v. United States* (June 13, 1949).

9. "The Omaha Platform: Launching the Populist Party," *History Matters*, historymatters.gmu.edu.

10. Lippmann quoted in Nicholas Lemann, "Notorious Big: Why the Specter of Size Has Always Haunted American Politics," *New Yorker*, March 28, 2106.

11. Ibid.

12. John Bates Clark, "The Limits of Competition," in John Bates Clark and Franklin H. Giddings, *The Modern Distributive Process* (New York: D. Appleton, 1889), 74, quoted in William L. Letwin, "Congress and the Sherman Antitrust Law: 1887–1890," *University of Chicago Law Review* 23, no. 2 (Winter 1956): 238.

13. Richard T. Ely, "The Nature and Significance of Corporations," *Harper's Magazine* 75 (June/November 1887), quoted in Letwin, "Congress and the Sherman Antitrust Law: 1887–1890," 238.

14. *Socialist Campaign Book of 1900* (Chicago, 1900), 31, cited in Jack Blicksilver, *Defenders and Defense of Big Business in the United States, 1880–1900* (New York: Garland, 1985), 66.

15. Eugene Debs, "A Study of Competition," *Appeal to Reason* (socialist newspaper), May 28, 1910, at 2, cited in Daniel A. Crane, "All I Really Need to Know about Antitrust I Learned in 1912," *Iowa Law Review* 100, no. 5 (2015): 2030.

16. *The Nationalist*, quoted in Lilliam Symes and Travers Clement, *Rebel America: The Story of Social Revolt in the United States* (New York: Harper & Brothers, 1934), 186–187, cited in Blicksilver, *Defenders and Defense of Big Business in the United States, 1880–1900*, 73.

17. Quoted in David Noble, *Progress without People: New Technology, Unemployment, and the Message of Resistance* (Toronto: Between the Lines, 1995).

18. Thorstein Veblen, *The Engineers and the Price System* (New York: B. W. Huebsch, 1921).

19. Stuart Chase, *Technocracy: An Interpretation* (New York: John Day, 1933).

20. "President Gompers' Report," in American Federation of Labor, *Proceedings* (1889), cited in Blicksilver, *Defenders and Defense of Big Business in the United States, 1880–1900*, 355.

21. Samuel Gompers, "Labor and Its Attitude toward Trusts," *American Federationist*, 1907, 1–7.

22. Herbert Croly, *The Promise of American Life* (New York: Macmillan, 1914), 115.

23. Ibid., 357–359.

24. Theodore Roosevelt, "Fifth Annual Message" (December 5, 1905), *The American Presidency*, http://www.presidency.ucsb.edu/ws/?pid=29546.

25. Quoted Daniel A. Crane, "All I Really Need to Know about Antitrust I Learned in 1912," *Iowa Law Review* 100, no. 5 (2015): 2029.

26. Martin J. Sklar, *The Corporate Reconstruction of American Capitalism* (Cambridge: Cambridge University Press, 1988), 346.

27. Crane, "All I Really Need to Know about Antitrust," 2029.

28. Letter from President Theodore Roosevelt to Arthur B. Farquhar (Aug. 11, 1911), in *Theodore Roosevelt: Letters and Speeches*, ed. Louis Auchincloss (New York: Library of America, 2004), 652, cited in Crane, "All I Really Need to Know about Antitrust," 2029–2030.

29. Theodore Roosevelt, "Editorial: The Trusts, the People, and the Square Deal," Nov. 18, 1911, reprinted in *The Making of Competition Policy: Legal and Economic Sources*, ed. Daniel A. Crane and Herbert Hovenkamp (New York: Oxford University Press, 2013), 110–111, cited in Crane, "All I Really Need to Know about Antitrust," 2029.

30. "The Progressive Party Platform of 1912: November 5, 1912," in *Political Party Platforms: Parties Receiving Electoral Votes: 1840–2012*, The American Presidency Project, http://www.presidency.ucsb.edu/ws/index.php?pid=29617.

31. Ibid.

32. Ibid.

33. Melvin I. Urofsky, *Louis D. Brandeis: A Life* (New York: Schocken, 2012).

34. Thomas K. McCraw, *Prophets of Regulation: Charles Francis Adams, Louis D. Brandeis, James M. Landis, Alfred E. Kahn* (New York: Belknap Press, 1984), 108.

35. *Hearing Before the Committee on Interstate Commerce,* US Senate, 62d Cong. (statement of Louis D. Brandeis, Esq., Attorney at Law, of Boston, Mass., Thursday, December 14, 1911) (Washington, DC: GPO, 1912), 1, 1174.

36. Quoted in Sklar, *The Corporate Reconstruction of American Capitalism,* 416–418.

37. Quoted in Urofsky, *Louis D. Brandeis*, 346.

38. Crane, "All I Really Need to Know about Antitrust," 2028.

39. Tony A. Freyer, *Antitrust and Global Capitalism, 1930–2004* (New York: Cambridge University Press, 2006).

40. David M. Hart, "Antitrust and Technological Innovation in the US: Ideas, Institutions, Decisions, and Impacts, 1890–2000," *Research Policy* 30, no. 6 (2001): 923–936.

41. Ibid., 926.

42. William H. Page, "Ideological Conflict and the Origins of Antitrust Policy," *Tulane Law Review* 66, no. 1 (1991).

43. *United States v. Aluminum Co. of Am. (Alcoa)*, 148 F.2d 416, 430 (2d Cir. 1945).

44. Franklin Delano Roosevelt, Commonwealth Club Address, San Francisco, September 23, 1932, in *The New Deal: Franklin D. Roosevelt Speeches* (Pepperdine

University, School of Public Policy), https://publicpolicy.pepperdine.edu/academics/research/faculty-research/new-deal/roosevelt-speeches/fr092332.htm

45. Quoted in Jordan A. Schwarz, *Liberal: Adolf A. Berle and the Vision of an American Era* (New York: Free Press, 1987), 106.

46. Quoted in Lawrence M. Friedman, "Law and Small Business," in *Small Business in American Life*, ed. Stuart W. Bruchey (New York: Columbia University Press, 1980), 309.

47. Morton Keller, "The Pluralist State: American Economic Regulation in Comparative Perspective, 1900–1930," in *Regulation in Perspective: Historical Essays*, ed. Thomas K. McCraw (Cambridge, MA: Harvard University Press, 1981), 93.

48. Stanley C. Hollander, "The Effects of Industrialization," in Bruchey, ed., *Small Business in American Life*, 212–236.

49. Quoted in Marc Levinson, *The Great A&P and the Struggle for Small Business in America* (New York: Hill & Wang, 2011), 146.

50. Quoted in ibid., 152.

51. Ibid., 155, 161.

52. Ibid., 171–172.

53. Ibid., 183.

54. Hollander, "The Effects of Industrialization, 230.

55. Thomas D. Clark, *Pills, Petticoats, and Plows: The Southern Country Store* (Indianapolis: Bobbs-Merrill, 1944), vii–viii, quoted in Roger L. Sansom and Richard Sutch, *One Kind of Freedom: The Economic Consequences of Emancipation*, 2nd ed. (Cambridge: Cambridge University Press, 2001), 126.

56. Sansom and Sutch, *One Kind of Freedom*, 187.

57. Quoted in Charles H. Otken, *The Ills of the South* (New York: G. P. Putnam's Sons, 1894), 57, emphasis in the original, quoting the *New York Ledger* (1889), quoted in Sansom and Sutch, *One Kind of Freedom*, 149.

58. Sansom and Sutch, *One Kind of Freedom*, 169–70.

59. Raghuram G. Rajan and Rodney Ramcharan, "Land and Credit: A Study of the Political Economy of Banking in the United States in the Early 20th Century," NBER Working Paper 15083 (Cambridge, MA: National Bureau of Economic Research, June 2009).

60. Raghuram G. Rajan and Rodney Ramcharan, "Constituencies and Legislation: The Fight over the McFadden Act of 1927," Finance and Economics Discussion

Series (Washington, DC: Federal Reserve Board, Divisions of Research & Statistics and Monetary Affairs 2012).

61. Thomas K. McCraw, "Rethinking the Trust Question," in *Regulation in Perspective: Historical Essays*, ed. Thomas K. McCraw (Cambridge, MA: Harvard University Press, 1981), 54.

Chapter 10

1. Thurman W. Arnold, *The Bottlenecks of Business* (New York: Reynal & Hitchcock, 1940), 125.

2. David Hart, "Antitrust and Technological Innovation in the U.S.," *Issues in Science and Technology* 15, no. 2 (Winter 1999).

3. Quoted in Alan Brinkley, *The End of Reform: New Deal Liberalism in Recession and War* (New York: Alfred A. Knopf, 1996), 60, and cited in Ganesh Sitaraman, *The Crisis of the Middle-Class Constitution* (New York: Alfred A. Knopf, 2017), 198.

4. Thurman W. Arnold, letter to Fred Friendly, August 9, 1961, quoted in Eugene Gressley, ed., *Voltaire and the Cowboy: The Correspondence of Thurman Arnold* (Boulder: University Press of Colorado, 1977), 439, and quoted in Spencer Weber Waller, "The Antitrust Legacy of Thurman Arnold," *St. John's Law Review* 78 (2004): 611–612.

5. Thurman Arnold, *The Folklore of Capitalism* (New Haven, CT: Yale University Press, 1937), 217, quoted in Waller, "The Antitrust Legacy of Thurman Arnold," 575.

6. Quoted in Brinkley, *The End of Reform*, 114.

7. "The Lessons of 1937," *Economist*, June 18, 2009.

8. Robert H. Jackson, *That Man: An Insider's Portrait of Franklin D. Roosevelt*, ed. John Q. Barrett (New York: Oxford University Press, 2003), 124, quoted in Waller, "The Antitrust Legacy of Thurman Arnold," 570.

9. Jefferson B. Fordham, "Review of *The Bottlenecks of Business* by Thurman W. Arnold, *Louisiana Law Review* 3, no. 4 (May 1941): 842.

10. Franklin D. Roosevelt, "Message to Congress on Curbing Monopolies, April 29, 1938," *The American Presidency Project*, University of California at Santa Barbara, http://www.presidency.ucsb.edu/ws/?pid=15637.See also William Kolasky, "Robert H. Jackson: How a 'Country Lawyer' Converted Franklin Roosevelt into a Trustbuster," *Antitrust* 27, no. 2 (Spring 2013).

11. Friedrich August Hayek, *The Road to Serfdom* (London: Routledge, 2004 [1944]), 47–49.

12. Senator Elizabeth Warren, "Senator Elizabeth Warren Delivers Remarks on Reigniting Competition in the American Economy," news release, June 29, 2016, https://www.warren.senate.gov/?p=press_release&id=1169.

13. Elaine S. Tan, "Champernowne Model Estimates of Aggregate Concentration in the United States, 1931–2000," research paper, October 15, 2008 (last revised October 20, 2008), https://ssrn.com/abstract=1285070.

14. *Report of the White House Task Force on Antitrust Policy* (Washington, DC: US Government Printing Office, July 5, 1968), reprinted in *Congressional Record*, May 27, 1969, p. 13890 (although submitted in 1968, the report did not become public until 1969).

15. Carl Kaysen and Donald F. Turner, *Antitrust Policy: An Economic and Legal Analysis* (Cambridge, MA: Harvard University Press, 1959).

16. George J. Stigler, "The Case against Big Business," *Fortune*, May 1952.

17. *Brown Shoe Co., Inc. v. United States*, 370 US 294 (1962).

18. Adolf A. Berle, *The American Economic Republic* (New York: Harcourt, Brace & World, 1963), 153.

19. John Steele Gordon, "The Antitrust Monster," *American Heritage* 4, no. 3 (May/June 1998), http://www.americanheritage.com/content/antitrust-monster.

20. Barry C. Lynn and Phillip Longman, "Who Broke America's Jobs Machine?," *Washington Monthly*, March/April 2012, http://washingtonmonthly.com/magazine/marchapril-2010/who-broke-americas-jobs-machine-3.

21. Ibid.

22. Barry C. Lynn, "Estates of Mind," *Washington Monthly*, July/August 2013, http://washingtonmonthly.com/magazine/julyaugust-2013/estates-of-mind.

23. Rob Glidden, "RCA under Fire," *Time*, March 3, 1958, 79.

24. Ibid.

25. Ibid.

26. Abegglen quoted in Robert Sobel, *RCA* (New York: Stein and Day, 1986), 212.

27. Richard N. Langlois, "Organizing the Electronic Century" (working paper, Department of Economics, University of Connecticut, March 2007), 21, http://digitalcommons.uconn.edu/cgi/viewcontent.cgi?article=1099&context=econ_wpapers.

28. Kenneth L. Simons, "Engine of Dominance: Competence-Enhancing Process Innovation," paper presented at the Industry Studies Conference, Minneapolis, May 24–26, 2016.

29. Margaret B. W. Graham, *RCA and the VideoDisc* (New York: Cambridge University Press, 1986), 81.

30. Gordon, "The Antitrust Monster."

31. Marcus A. Hollabaugh and Robert Wright, 85th Cong. 2d Sess. (1958). *Compulsory Licensing under Antitrust Judgments*, staff report of the Subcommittee on Patents, Trademarks and Copyrights, Senate Committee on the Judiciary (Washington, DC, 1960), 2–5.

32. Gordon, "The Antitrust Monster."

33. Gary Jacobson and John Hillkirk, *Xerox: American Samurai* (New York: Macmillan, 1986), 72.

34. Ibid., 72.

35. Mark Blaxill and Ralph Eckardt, "The Innovation Imperative: Building America's Invisible Edge for the 21st Century," PatentHawk.com, Winter 2009 blog, 5, http://www.patenthawk.com/blog_docs/The%20Innovation%20Imperative.pdf.

36. Ibid.

37. William J. Kolasky, "Conglomerate Mergers and Range Effects: It's a Long Way from Chicago to Brussels," address before the George Mason University Symposium, Washington, DC, November 9, 20001, https://www.justice.gov/atr/speech/conglomerate-mergers-and-range-effects-its-long-way-chicago-brussels.

38. Walter Kiechel, *Lords of Strategy*, eBook ed. (Cambridge, MA: Harvard Business School, 2010).

39. "FTC Requires NXP Semiconductors N.V. to Divest RF Power Amplifier Assets as a Condition of Acquiring Freescale Semiconductor Ltd.," news release, Federal Trade Commission, November 25, 2015, https://www.ftc.gov/news-events/press-releases/2015/11/ftc-requires-nxp-semiconductors-nv-divest-rf-power-amplifier.

40. Robert H. Bork, *The Antitrust Paradox: A Policy at War with Itself* (New York: Basic Books, 1993).

41. Robert D. Atkinson and David Audretsch, "Economic Doctrines and Policy Differences: Has the Washington Policy Debate Been Asking the Wrong Questions?" (Washington, DC: Information Technology and Innovation Foundation, September 2008), https://itif.org/publications/2008/09/12/economic-doctrines-and-policy-differences-has-washington-policy-debate-been.

42. Joseph A. Schumpeter, *Capitalism, Socialism, and Democracy*, 3rd ed. (New York: Harper & Brothers, 1950 [1942]), 84.

43. John Kenneth Galbraith, "American Capitalism: The Concept of Countervailing Power," in *Galbraith: The Affluent Society and Other Writings, 1952–1967* (New York: Library of America, 2010), 78–81.

44. Ibid., 82.

45. Ibid., 49–54.

46. Schumpeter, *Capitalism, Socialism, and Democracy.*

47. Philip Cullis, "The Limits of Progressivism: Louis Brandeis, Democracy and the Corporation," *Journal of American Studies* 30, no. 3, pt. 3 (December 1996): 381–404.

48. William J. Baumol, *The Free-Market Innovation Machine* (Princeton, NJ: Princeton University Press, 2002), 182.

49. Adolf A. Berle, *The American Economic Republic* (New York: Harcourt, Brace & World, 1963), 4.

50. Michael E. Porter, "Competition and Antitrust: Toward a Productivity-Based Approach to Evaluating Mergers and Joint Ventures," *Antitrust Bulletin* 46 (2001): 919–958.

51. Lina Khan, "New Tools to Promote Competition," *Democracy Journal* 42 (Fall 2016).

52. Thompson, "America's Monopoly Problem."

53. Ibid.

54. Khan, "New Tools to Promote Competition."

55. Lina Khan and Sandeep Vaheesan, "Market Power and Inequality: The Antitrust Counterrevolution and Its Discontents," *Harvard Law and Policy Review* 11, no. 1 (February 2017), http://harvardlpr.com/wp-content/uploads/2017/02/HLP110.pdf.

56. Barry C. Lynn and Phillip Longman, "Populism with a Brain," *Washington Monthly*, June/July/August 2016, http://washingtonmonthly.com/magazine/junejulyaug-2016/populism-with-a-brain.

57. Nell Abernathy, Mike Konczal, and Kathryn Milani, "Untamed: How to Check Corporate, Financial, and Monopoly Power" (New York: Roosevelt Institute, June 2016), http://rooseveltinstitute.org/untamed-how-check-corporate-financial-and-monopoly-power.

58. Marc Jarsulic, Ethan Gurwitz, Kate Bahn, and Andy Green, "Reviving Antitrust: Why Our Economy Needs a Progressive Competition Policy" (Washington, DC: Center for American Progress, June 2016), https://www.americanprogress.org/issues/economy/reports/2016/06/29/140613/reviving-antitrust.

59. Robert Reich, "Why We Must End Upward Presdistribution to the Rich," blog post, RobertReich.org, September 25, 2015, http://robertreich.org/post/129996780230.

60. Khan, "New Tools to Promote Competition."

61. US Bureau of Labor Statistics, Series ID (CMU2010000000111D, CMU2010000000112D, CMU2010000000121D, CMU2010000000122D, CUUR0000SA0), https://data.bls.gov/cgi-bin/srgate (accessed May 9, 2017).

62. Jason Furman and Peter Orszag, "A Firm-Level Perspective on the Role of Rents in the Rise in Inequality," paper presented at "A Just Society," Centennial Event in Honor of Joseph Stiglitz, Columbia University, New York, October 16, 2015.

63. Khan, "New Tools to Promote Competition."

64. Barry C. Lynn, "Antitrust: A Missing Key to Prosperity, Opportunity, and Democracy," Demos.org, n.d., 13, http://www.demos.org/sites/default/files/publications/Lynn.pdf.

65. K. Sabeel Rahman, "Curbing the New Corporate Power," *Boston Review*, May 4, 2015, http://bostonreview.net/forum/k-sabeel-rahman-curbing-new-corporate-power.

66. Louis Brandeis, quoted in "Progressive Reform and the Trusts," *Digital History*, University of Houston, http://www.digitalhistory.uh.edu/disp_textbook.cfm?smtID=11&psid=3823.

67. Lynn, "Antitrust,"11.

68. Abernathy, Konczal, and Milani, "Untamed," 18.

69. Tim Wu, "Small Is Beautiful," *New Yorker*, January 24, 2015, http://www.newyorker.com/business/currency/small-bountiful-small-business-craft-beer.

70. Thompson, "America's Monopoly Problem."

71. US Department of Commerce, Bureau of Labor Statistics, National Data (Table 6.1. National Income; Table 6.16. Corporate Profits by Industry).

72. This assumes a 6 percent share of profits of GDP from 2011 to 2016 instead of the 8.2 percent actual rate.

73. Craig Pirrong, "Antitrust to Attack Inequality? Fuggedaboutit: It's Not Where the Money Is," StreetwiseProfessor.com, January 5, 2006, http://streetwiseprofessor.com/?p=10020.

74. Jonathan Lewellen and Katharina Lewellen, "Investment and Cash Flow: New Evidence," *Journal of Financial and Quantitative Analysis* 51, no. 4 (August 2016): 1135–1164.

Chapter 11

1. Senator Elizabeth Warren, "Senator Elizabeth Warren Delivers Remarks on Reigniting Competition in the American Economy," news release, June 29, 2016, https://www.warren.senate.gov/?p=press_release&id=1169.

2. Barry C. Lynn and Phillip Longman, "Who Broke America's Jobs Machine?," *Washington Monthly*, March/April, 2010, http://washingtonmonthly.com/magazine/marchapril-2010/who-broke-americas-jobs-machine-3.

3. Nell Abernathy, Mike Konczal, and Kathryn Milani, "Untamed: How to Check Corporate, Financial, and Monopoly Power" (New York: Roosevelt Institute, June 6, 2016), http://rooseveltinstitute.org/untamed-how-check-corporate-financial-and-monopoly-power/.

4. Jason Furman, "Productivity Is Slowing and Inequality Is Growing. Here's What's Causing It: Productivity, Inequality, and Economic Rents," *Evonomics*, July 9, 2016, http://evonomics.com/productivity-is-slowing-inequality-is-growing-heres-whats-causing-it.

5. Elaine S. Tan, "Champernowne Model Estimates of Aggregate Concentration in the United States, 1931–2000," working paper, October 20, 2008 (last revision), https://papers.ssrn.com/sol3/papers.cfm?abstract_id=1285070.

6. John Bellamy Foster, Robert W. McChesney, and R. Jamil Jonna "Monopoly and Competition in Twenty-First Century Capitalism," *Monthly Review* 62, no. 11, April 2011, https://monthlyreview.org/2011/04/01/monopoly-and-competition-in-twenty-first-century-capitalism.

7. Ibid.

8. IRS, SOI Tax Stats, Table 5—Returns of Active Corporations, 1994 and 2013 (database, last modified May 25, 2016), https://www.irs.gov/uac/soi-tax-stats-table-5-returns-of-active-corporations.

9. Federal Trade Commission, Annual Competition Reports: Annual Reports to Congress Pursuant to the Hart-Scott-Rodino Antitrust Improvements Act of 1976, https://www.ftc.gov/policy/reports/policy-reports/annual-competition-reports.

10. White House, "Benefits of Competition and Indicators of Market Power," Council of Economic Advisers Issue Brief, updated May 2016, https://obamawhitehouse.archives.gov/sites/default/files/page/files/20160502_competition_issue_brief_updated_cea.pdf.

11. Asher Schechter, "Economists: "Totality of Evidence" Underscores Concentration Problem in the US," Pro-Market, March 31, 2017, https://promarket.org/economists-totality-evidence-underscores-concentration-problem-u-s.

12. The US government uses the North American Industrial Classification system to classify industries. Six digits is the most finely detailed industry sector. For example, flour milling is classified as 311211.

13. US Census Bureau, *Economic Census 2002 and 2012* (Concentration by Largest Firms by Industry), http://factfinder.census.gov/faces/nav/jsf/pages/index.xhtml (accessed July 6, 2016).

14. Ryan Decker, John Haltiwanger, Ron Jarmin, and Javier Miranda, "The Role of Entrepreneurship in U.S. Job Creation and Economic Dynamism," *Journal of Economic Perspectives* 28, no. 3, (Summer 2014): 3–24.

15. These are raw averages, not adjusted for sales (data from US Census Bureau, "Manufacturing: Subject Series: Concentration Ratios: Share of Value Added Accounted for by the 4, 8, 20, and 50 Largest Companies for Industries: 2002, 2007, 2012").

16. John Baldwin, "The Dynamics of the Competitive Process" (mimeo, Queen's University, 1991).

17. Robert H. McGuckin and Sang V. Nguyen, "On Productivity and Plant Ownership Change: New Evidence from the Longitudinal Research Database," *RAND Journal of Economics* 26, no. 2 (Summer 1995): 257–276.

18. David M. Szymanski, Sundar G. Bharadwaj, and P. Rajan Varadarajan, "An Analysis of the Market Share-Profitability Relationship," *Journal of Marketing* 57, no. 3 (July 1993): 1–18.

19. Ibid., 13.

20. Michael D. Giandrea, "Industry Competition and Total Factor Productivity Growth," BLS Working Paper 399 (Washington, DC: US Bureau of Labor Statistics, September 2006), 2.

21. Jan De Loecker and Jan Eeckhout, "The Rise of Market Power and the Macroeconomic Implications," NBER Working Paper No. 23687 (Cambridge, MA: National Bureau of Economic Research, August 2017), http://www.nber.org/papers/w23687.

22. Ibid.

23. General Electric Co. financials, https://www.gurufocus.com/financials/GE.

24. IRS, SOI Tax Stats, Statistics of Business (Table 5. Selected Balance Sheet, Income Statement, and Tax Items, by Sector, by Size of Business Receipts), https://www.irs.gov/uac/soi-tax-stats-table-5-returns-of-active-corporations.

25. Ibid., Table 5 for Tax Year 2013.

26. Abernathy, Konczal, and Milani, "Untamed." See also White House, "Benefits of Competition and Indicators of Market Power," Council of Economic Advisers Issue

Brief, April 2016, https://obamawhitehouse.archives.gov/sites/default/files/page/files/20160414_cea_competition_issue_brief.pdf.

27. OECD, *The Future of Productivity* (Paris: OECD Publishing, July 2015), http://www.oecd.org/eco/growth/OECD-2015-The-future-of-productivity-book.pdf.

28. Ibid, 12.

29. James Manyika, Susan Lund, Jacques Bughin, Jonathan Woetzel, Kalin Stamenov, and Dhruv Dhingra, "Digital Globalization: The New Era of Global Flows" (Washington, DC: McKinsey Global Institute, February 2016), http://www.mckinsey.com/business-functions/mckinsey-digital/our-insights/digital-globalization-the-new-era-of-global-flows.

30. White House, "Benefits of Competition and Indicators of Market Power," Council of Economic Advisers Issue Brief, updated May 2016, https://obamawhitehouse.archives.gov/sites/default/files/page/files/20160502_competition_issue_brief_updated_cea.pdf.

31. Olivia LaVecchia and Stacy Mitchell, "North Dakota's Pharmacy Ownership Law," Institute for Local Self-Reliance, October 2014, http://ilsr.org/wp-content/uploads/2014/10/ND_Pharmacy_Ownership_Report.pdf.

32. Peng Cheng Zhu and Peter E. Hilsenrath, "Mergers and Acquisitions in U.S. Retail Pharmacy," *Journal of Health Care Finance*, October/November 2014, http://healthfinancejournal.com/index.php/johcf/article/view/20.

33. US Bureau of Labor Statistics, Annual Index of Labor Productivity (2007 = 100) for NAICS 446110, Pharmacies and Drug Stores.

34. Barry C. Lynn and Phillip Longman, "Who Broke America's Jobs Machine?," *Washington Monthly*, March/April, 2010, http://washingtonmonthly.com/magazine/marchapril-2010/who-broke-americas-jobs-machine-3.

35. Robert Reich, "Why We Must End Upward Predistribution to the Rich," *Huffington Post*, September 27, 2015, http://www.huffingtonpost.com/robert-reich/why-we-must-end-upward-pr_b_8204796.html.

36. See figure 2.36 in OECD, *OECD Digital Economy Outlook 2015* (Paris: OECD Publishing, 2015), http://ec.europa.eu/eurostat/documents/42577/3222224/Digital+economy+outlook+2015/dbdec3c6-ca38-432c-82f2-1e330d9d6a24.

37. Richard Bennett, Luke A. Stewart, and Robert D. Atkinson, "The Whole Picture: Where America's Broadband Networks Really Stand" (Washington, DC: Information Technology and Innovation Foundation, February 2013), https://itif.org/publications/2013/02/12/whole-picture-where-america%E2%80%99s-broadband-networks-really-stand.

38. Andrea DiVirgilio, "10 Countries with The Highest Cost of Food," *The Richest*, November 6, 2013, http://www.therichest.com/expensive-lifestyle/food/countries -with-the-most-expensive-cost-of-food.

39. "Aviation Price Index," *Kiwi*, https://kiwi.com/stories/aviation-price-index/usd.

40. "World Retail Banking Report," CapGemini, ING, and the European Financial Management & Marketing Association (EFMA), 2007, https://www.capgemini .com/resource-file-access/resource/pdf/World_Retail_Banking_Report_2007.pdf. See also Oxera, "The Price of Banking: An International Comparison—Report Prepared for British Bankers' Association," November 2006, http://www.oxera.com/getmedia/ dfa0bbfd-ce3e-4509-b434-c456464edbbb/The-price-of-banking%E2%80%94an -international-comparison.pdf.aspx?ext=.pdf.

41. Barry Lynn, *Cornered: The New Monopoly Capitalism and the Economics of Destruction* (New York: John Wiley & Sons, 2011).

42. "The Superstar Company: A Giant Problem: The Rise of the Corporate Colossus Threatens Both Competition and the Legitimacy of Business," *Economist*, September 17, 2016, http://www.economist.com/news/leaders/21707210-rise -corporate-colossus-threatens-both-competition-and-legitimacy-business.

43. Raghuram G. Rajan, Krishna B. Kumar, and Luigi Zingales, "What Determines Firm Size?" NBER Working Paper 7208 (Cambridge, MA: National Bureau of Economic Research, 1999), http://www.nber.org/papers/w7208.pdf.

44. Matt Stoller, tweet, August 20, 2017, https://twitter.com/matthewstoller/ status/899305284920856577.

45. The Boston Consulting Group, *Perspectives on Experience* (Boston: Boston Consulting Group, 1970), 12.

46. Ibid., 49.

47. White House, "Benefits of Competition and Indicators of Market Power," 2, https://obamawhitehouse.archives.gov/sites/default/files/page/files/20160502 _competition_issue_brief_updated_cea.pdf.

48. Robert P. Rogers, "Staff Report on the Development and Structure of the U.S. Electric Lamp Industry" (Washington, DC: Federal Trade Commission, February 1980), 138.

49. Ibid., 141.

50. Vojislav Maksimovic and Gordon Phillips, "The Market for Corporate Assets: Who Engages in Mergers and Asset Sales and Are There Efficiency Gains?," *Journal of Finance* 66, no. 6 (December 2001.

51. Barry C. Lynn, "Antitrust: A Missing Key to Prosperity, Opportunity, and Democracy," Demos, October 2013, http://www.demos.org/sites/default/files/ publications/Lynn.pdf.

52. US Census Bureau, Concentration Ratios by Industry, Finance 2002, 2012 (Series ID: EC1252SSSZ6 & EC0252SSSZ6) (database), http://factfinder.census.gov/faces/nav/jsf/pages/index.xhtml.

53. Roisin McCord, Edward Simpson Prescott, and Tim Sablik, "Explaining the Decline in the Number of Banks since the Great Recession," Economic Brief 15-03 (Federal Reserve Bank of Richmond, March 2015), https://www.richmondfed.org/-/media/richmondfedorg/publications/research/economic_brief/2015/pdf/eb_15-03.pdf.

54. Ibid.

55. "How Does the U.S. Banking System Compare with Foreign Banking Systems?" (Federal Reserve Bank of San Francisco, April 2002), http://www.frbsf.org/education/publications/doctor-econ/2002/april/us-banking-system-foreign.

56. David C. Wheelock and Paul W. Wilson, "The Evolution of Scale Economies in U.S. Banking," Working Paper 2015-021C, revised (Federal Reserve Bank of St. Louis, Research Division, February 2017), https://research.stlouisfed.org/wp/2015/2015-021.pdf.

57. Ibid., 21.

58. David C. Wheelock and Paul W. Wilson, "Do Large Banks Have Lower Costs? New Estimates of Returns to Scale for U.S. Banks," *Journal of Money, Credit and Banking*, January 27, 2012, http://onlinelibrary.wiley.com/doi/10.1111/j.1538-4616.2011.00472.x/abstract.

59. Sandra E. Black and Philip E. Strahan, "Business Formation and the Deregulation of the Banking Industry," in *Public Policy and the Economics of Entrepreneurship*, ed. Douglas Holtz-Eakin and Harvey S. Rosen (Cambridge, MA: MIT Press, 2004), 73.

60. Kwangwoo Park and George Pennacchi, "Harming Depositors and Helping Borrowers: The Disparate Impact of Bank Consolidation," *Review of Financial Studies* 22, no. 1 (2009): 1–40, 34.

61. Emek Basker, Shawn Klimek, and Pham Hoang Van, "Supersize It: The Growth of Retail Chains and the Rise of the 'Big-Box' Store," *Journal of Economics & Management Strategy* 21, no. 3 (2012): 541–582, 576.

62. Dominic Gates, "Boeing Celebrates 787 Delivery as Program's Costs Top $32 Billion," *Seattle Times*, September 24, 2011, http://seattletimes.com/html/businesstechnology/2016310102_boeing25.html.

63. Antonio Vezzani and Sandro Montresor, "The Production Function of Top R&D Investors: Accounting for Size and Sector Heterogeneity with Quantile Estimations," IPTS Working Papers on Corporate R&D and Innovation 02/2013 (Seville: European Commission, Joint Research Center, 2013).

64. For a review of this debate, see Carl Shapiro, "Competition and Innovation: Did Arrow Hit the Bull's Eye?," http://faculty.haas.berkeley.edu/shapiro/arrow.pdf.

65. William J. Baumol, *The Free-Market Innovation Machine* (Princeton, NJ: Princeton University Press, 2002), 176.

66. Ibid., 162.

67. Bronwyn H. Hall, "Investment and Research and Development at the Firm Level: Does the Source of Financing Matter?," NBER Working Paper 4096 (Cambridge, MA: National Bureau of Economic Research, 1992); and Lorne Switzer, "The Determinants of Industrial R&D: A Funds Flow Simultaneous Equation Approach," *Review* of *Economics and Statistics* 66, no. 1 (1984): 163–168, cited in George Symeonidis, "Innovation, Firm Size and Market Structure: Schumpeterian Hypotheses and Some New Themes," OECD Economic Department Working Paper 161 (Paris: OECD, 1996).

68. Antonio Vezzani and Sandro Montresor, "The Production Function of Top R&D Investors: Accounting for Size and Sector Heterogeneity with Quantile Estimations," *Research Policy* 44, no. 2 (2015), http://www.sciencedirect.com/science/article/pii/ S0048733314001462.

69. US Congress, Office of Technology Assessment (OTA), Pharmaceutical R&D: Costs, Costs, Risks and Rewards OTA-H-522 (Washington, DC: US Government Printing Office, February 1993), 2, http://ota.fas.org/reports/9336.pdf.

70. F. M. Scherer, "Pricing, Profits, and Technological Progress in Pharmaceutical Industry," *Journal of Economic Perspectives* 7, no. 3 (1993): 97–115.

71. Organisation for Economic Co-operation and Development (OECD), Pharmaceutical Pricing Policies in a Global Market (Paris: OECD, September 2008), 190, http://www.oecd.org/els/pharmaceutical-pricingpolicies-in-a-global-market.htm.

72. Joseph Farrell and Michael L. Katz, "Competition or Predation? Schumpeterian Rivalry in Network Markets," *Journal of Industrial Economics* 53, no. 2 (2005): 203–231.

73. Joseph A. Schumpeter, *Capitalism, Socialism and Democracy* (New York: Harper & Brothers, 1950), 84.

74. Derek Thompson, "The 100-Year March of Technology in 1 Graph," *Atlantic*, April 7, 2012, http://www.theatlantic.com/technology/archive/2012/04/the-100 -year-march-of-technology-in-1-graph/255573.

75. Baumol, *The Free-Market Innovation Machine*.

76. Abernathy, Konczal, and Milani, "Untamed," 18.

77. US Census Bureau, "2012 Statistics of U.S. Businesses," https://www.census.gov/ data/datasets/2012/econ/susb/2012-susb.html.

78. Barry Lynn and Philip Longman, "Populism with a Brain," *Washington Monthly*, June/July/August, 2016, http://washingtonmonthly.com/magazine/junejulyaug -2016/populism-with-a-brain.

79. "Annual U.S. Domestic Average Itinerary Fare in Current and Constant Dollars" (Washington, DC: U.S. Department of Transportation, Bureau of Transportation Statistics), http://www.rita.dot.gov/bts/airfares/programs/economics_and_finance/ air_travel_price_index/html/AnnualFares.html. To be fair, this does not include the fact that more airlines now charge for items and services, such as for pillows or to check bags, than did before. But even including these adjustments would still likely see total costs increasing less than the rate of inflation.

80. US Bureau of Labor Statistics, Figure 5. Multifactor Productivity in Air Transportation and Private Nonfarm Business (data derived from US Bureau of Labor Statistics, US Bureau of Economic Analysis, and US Bureau of Transportation Statistics), https://www.bls.gov/opub/mlr/2017/images/data/russell-fig5.stm.

81. Lynn and Longman, "Populism with a Brain."

82. US Department of Transportation, Bureau of Transportation Statistics, "Table 11. Air Travel Price Index: Top 85 Markets Ranked by Percentage Change from 1995," http://www.rita.dot.gov/bts/programs/economics_and_finance/air_travel _price_index/html/table_11.html.

83. John Duke, Diane Litz, and Lisa Usher, "Multifactor Productivity in Railroad Transportation," *Monthly Labor Review*, August, 1992, https://www.bls.gov/mfp/ mprduk92.pdf.

84. Craig Pirrong, "Antitrust to Attack Inequality? Fuggedaboutit: It's Not Where the Money Is," StreetwiseProfessor.com, January 5, 2006, http://streetwiseprofessor .com/?p=10020.

85. White House, "Benefits of Competition and Indicators of Market Power," May 2, 2016, https://obamawhitehouse.archives.gov/sites/default/files/page/files/20160502 _competition_issue_brief_updated_cea.pdf.

86. "The Superstar Company: A Giant Problem," *Economist*, September 17, 2016, http://www.economist.com/news/leaders/21707210-rise-corporate-colossus -threatens-both-competition-and-legitimacy-business.

87. Foster, McChesney, and Jonna, "Monopoly and Competition in Twenty-First Century Capitalism."

88. Ibid.

89. Lynn and Longman, "Who Broke America's Jobs Machine?"

90. Robert D. Atkinson, *Enough Is Enough: Confronting Chinese Mercantilism* (Washington, DC: Information Technology and Innovation Foundation, 2012),

https://itif.org/publications/2012/02/28/enough-enough-confronting-chinese
-innovation-mercantilism.

91. "China's Semiconductor Grab," *Asia Today*, August 24, 2014, http://www
.asiatoday.com/pressrelease/chinas-semiconductor-grab.

92. "China's Tsinghua Unigroup Plans $23B bid for Micron Technology," *CNBC*,
July 13, 2015, https://www.cnbc.com/2015/07/13/chinas-tsinghua-unigroup-makes
-23b-bid-for-micron-technology.html.

93. "New Masters of the Universe: How State Enterprise Is Spreading," *Economist*,
January 21, 2012, http://www.economist.com/node/21542925.

94. US Department of State, "U.S. Relations with China" (fact sheet, Bureau of East
Asian and Pacific Affairs, January 21, 2015), http://www.state.gov/r/pa/ei/bgn/
18902.htm.

95. Yasheng Huang, "Business and Government Relations in China," presentation,
MIT Sloan School of Management, Cambridge, MA, August 2015, 57; see also OECD,
Statistics, FDI Statistics According to Benchmark Definition 4th Edition (BMD4), FDI
Main Aggregates: Summary: FDI Financial Flows—USD Million," accessed August 20,
2017), http://stats.oecd.org/#.

96. Huang, "Business and Government Relations in China."

97. K. Sabeel Rahman, "Curbing the New Corporate Power," *Boston Review*, http://
bostonreview.net/forum/k-sabeel-rahman-curbing-new-corporate-power.

98. Ibid.

99. Ibid.

100. K. Sabeel Rahman, "Curbing the New Corporate Power," *Boston Review*, May
5, 2015, http://bostonreview.net/forum/curbing-new-corporate-power/dean-baker
-dean-baker-response-curbing-new-corporate-power.

101. White House, "Benefits of Competition and Indicators of Market Power,"
May 2, 2016, https://obamawhitehouse.archives.gov/sites/default/files/page/files/
20160502_competition_issue_brief_updated_cea.pdf, 2.

102. Robert D. Atkinson, "Break Up the Contact Lens Cartel to Give Consumers
More Choice," *The Hill*, October 8, 2016, http://thehill.com/blogs/pundits-blog/
healthcare/301641-break-up-the-contact-lens-cartel-to-give-consumers-more
-choice.

103. Yevgeniy Feyman and Jonathan Hartley, "The Perils of Hospital Consolidation," *National Affairs*, Summer 2016, https://www.nationalaffairs.com/publications/
detail/the-perils-of-hospital-consolidation.

Chapter 12

1. Quoted in Wyatt Wells, *Antitrust and the Formation of the Postwar World*, (New York: Columbia University Press, 2002), 29.

2. Charles Brown, James T. Hamilton, and James Medoff, *Employers Large and Small* (Cambridge, MA: Harvard University Press, 1990), 66, cited in John E. Jackson, "The Climate for Entrepreneurial and Small Business" (mimeograph, University of Michigan, Department of Political Science, 1986).

3. Small Business Majority, "Policy Agenda," SmallBusinessMajority.org, https://www.smallbusinessmajority.org/economic-agenda.

4. Robert Reich, "The Revolt of Small Business Republicans," blog post, RobertReich.org, May 8, 2015, http://robertreich.org/post/119297219035.

5. Alan D. Viard and Amy Roden, "Big Business: The Other Engine of Economic Growth" (Washington, DC: American Enterprise Institute, June 2009).

6. Jane G. Gravelle, "Federal Tax Treatment of Small Business: How Favorable? How Justified?," in *Papers and Proceedings of the 100th Annual Conference on Taxation* (Washington, DC: National Tax Association, 2007), 152–158, http://www.ntanet.org/images/stories/pdf/proceedings/07/017.pdf.

7. Richard J. Pierce, Jr., "Small Is Not Beautiful: The Case against Special Regulatory Treatment of Small Firms," *Administrative Law Review* 50, no. 3 (Summer 1998): 537–578.

8. *United States v. Aluminum Co. of America*, 148 F.2d 416 (1945), 429.

9. Senator William Proxmire, *Can Small Business Survive?* (Chicago: Henry Regnery, 1964), v.

10. Ernst Morris, *Utopia 1976* (New York: Rinehart, 1955), 84.

11. Willam H. Whyte, *The Organization Man* (New York: Simon & Schuster, 1956).

12. Proxmire, *Can Small Business Survive?*, 9.

13. Ibid., 160.

14. John Kenneth Galbraith, *The Liberal Hour* (New York: Houghton Mifflin, 1964), 110.

15. Quoted in Melvin I. Urofsky, *Louis D. Brandeis* (New York: Schocken Books, 2009), 92.

16. Brown, Hamilton, and Medoff, *Employers Large and Small*, 6.

17. Jonathan J. Bean, *Big Government and Affirmative Action: The Scandalous History of the Small Business Administration* (Lexington: University Press of Kentucky, 2001), 3.

18. Ibid., 2.

19. Brown, Hamilton, and Medoff, *Employers Large and Small*, 83.

20. Andrew Reamer, "Federal Efforts in Support of Entrepreneurship: A Reference Guide (Working Draft)" (George Washington Institute of Public Policy, George Washington University, April 13, 2017).

21. Bean, *Big Government and Affirmative Action*, 2.

22. Bennett Harrison, *Lean and Mean: The Changing Landscape of Corporate Power in the Age of Flexibility* (New York: Basic Books, 1994), 16.

23. Jonathan J. Bean, *Beyond the Broker State: Federal Policies toward Small Businesses 1936–1961* (Chapel Hill: University of North Carolina Press, 1996), 176.

24. Randy A. Becker, "Air Pollution Abatement Costs under the Clean Air Act: Evidence from the PACE Survey" (Washington, DC: Center for Economic Studies, US Census Bureau, 2001), 163.

25. "Small Businesses May Be Exempt From Some Regulations," Lawyers.com, http://business-law.lawyers.com/business-planning/small-businesses-may-be-exempt-from-some-regulations.html.

26. Richard Carlson, "The Small Firm Exemption and the Single Employer Doctrine in Employment Discrimination Law," *St. John's Law Review* 80, no. 4 (2012): 1197.

27. Ibid., 1198.

28. Richard Carlson, "The Small Firm Exemption and the Single Employer Doctrine in Employment Discrimination Law," *St. John's Law Review* 80, no. 4 (2012), article 2, http://scholarship.law.stjohns.edu/lawreview/vol80/iss4/2.

29. Gerald Davis, *The Vanishing American Corporation* (Oakland, CA: Berrett-Koehler, 2016), 8.

30. Pierce, "Small Is Not Beautiful," 548.

31. Becker, "Air Pollution Abatement Costs under the Clean Air Act," 150.

32. Brown, Hamilton, and Medoff, *Employers Large and Small*, 84.

33. Thomas D. Hopkins, *Profiles of Regulatory Costs. Report to the U.S. Small Business Administration*, US Department of Commerce, National Technical Information Service #PB96 128038, November 1995, http://www.sba.gov/advo.

34. John Dearie and Courtney Geduldig, *Where the Jobs Are: Entrepreneurship and the Soul of the American Economy* (Hoboken, NJ: John Wiley & Sons, 2013), 122.

35. Eric Toder, "Does the Federal Income Tax Favor Small Business?" (Washington, DC: Urban Institute and Urban-Brookings Tax Policy Center, 2007).

36. Ibid., 11.

37. Gravelle, "Federal Tax Treatment of Small Business," 152.

38. Ibid.

39. Ibid.

40. Toder, "Does The Federal Income Tax Favor Small Business?," 14.

41. Ibid.

42. Ibid., 15.

43. IRS, SOI Tax Stats, Table 5. Returns of Active Corporations: Selected Balance Sheet, Income Statement, and Tax Items, by Sector, by Size of Business Receipts, Tax Year 2013, IRS.gov, https://www.irs.gov/uac/soi-tax-stats-table-5-returns-of -active-corporations.

44. US Small Business Administration (SBA), Office of Advocacy, "Frequently Asked Questions," September 2012, https://www.sba.gov/sites/default/files/FAQ _Sept_2012.pdf.

45. Defined as industries other than agriculture, mining, manufacturing and infor- mation (US SBA, "SBA 7(a) & 504 Loan Data Reports," https://www.sba.gov/about -sba/sba-performance/open-government/foia/frequently-requested-records/sba-7a -504-loan-data-reports).

46. Jonathan Rothwell, "Why Elites Want More Competition for Everyone except Themselves," Evonomics, April 2, 2016, http://evonomics.com/why-elites-want-more -competition-for-everyone-except-themselves.

47. Reamer, "Federal Efforts in Support of Entrepreneurship."

48. Congressional Budget Office (CBO), "Small Bidders in License Auctions for Wireless Personal Communications Services," October 2005, https://www.cbo.gov/ sites/default/files/109th-congress-2005-2006/reports/10-24-fcc.pdf.

49. Government Accountability Office, "HUBZONE PROGRAM: SBA's Control Weaknesses Exposed the Government to Fraud and Abuse," July 17, 2008, http:// www.gao.gov/products/GAO-08-964T.

50. American Small Business League, "Our History," http://www.asbl.com/ ourhistory.html.

51. National Association of State Procurement Officers, 2016 Survey, http://www .naspo.org/2016Survey.

52. Ian Bickerdyke and Ralph Lattimore, "Reducing the Regulatory Burden: Does Firm Size Matter?" (Canberra: Commonwealth of Australia, Industry Commission, December 1997), 54.

53. Nicole V. Crain and W. Mark Crain, "The Impact of Regulatory Costs on Small Firms" (Washington, DC: SBA, 2010), https://www.sba.gov/sites/default/files/The%20Impact%20of%20Regulatory%20Costs%20on%20Small%20Firms%20(Full).pdf.

54. Ibid.

55. Ibid., 8.

56. Steven Bradford, "Does Size Matter? An Economic Analysis of Small Business Exemptions from Regulation," *Journal of Small and Emerging Business Law* 8 (2004): 1–37, 30.

57. Erik G. Hurst and Benjamin W. Pugsley, "Wealth, Tastes, and Entrepreneurial Choice," Staff Report 747 (Federal Reserve Bank of New York, October 2015), https://www.newyorkfed.org/medialibrary/media/research/staff_reports/sr747.pdf.

58. Allan D. Viard and Amy Roden, "Trade and Tax Issues Relating to Small Business Job Creation" (Washington, DC: American Enterprise Institute, March 9, 2010), http://www.aei.org/publication/trade-and-tax-issues-relating-to-small-business-job-creation/print.

59. Brown, Hamilton, and Medoff, *Employers Large and Small*, 89.

60. William A. Brock and David S. Evans, "Small Business Economics," *Small Business Economics* 1, no. 1 (1989): 7–20, 11.

61. Crain and Crain, "The Impact of Regulatory Costs on Small Firms," 6.

62. Benjamin Wild Pugsley and Erik Hurst, "What Do Small Businesses Do?," paper presented at the Brookings Conference on Economic Activity, Washington, DC, Fall 2011, https://www.brookings.edu/bpea-articles/what-do-small-businesses-do.

63. Shane, *The Illusions of Entrepreneurship*, 163.

64. CBO, "Small Firms, Employment, and Federal Policy," March 2012, http://www.cbo.gov/sites/default/files/cbofiles/attachments/SmallFirms_0.pdf.

65. Rita Almeida and Pedro Carneiro, "Enforcement of Labor Regulation and Firm Size" (World Bank and University College London, May 8, 2008), http://www.ucl.ac.uk/~uctppca/brasil_mar12_08.pdf.

66. Lattimore and Bickerdyke, "Reducing the Regulatory Burden: Does Firm Size Matter?"

67. Barry L. McVay, "Getting Started in Federal Contracting, Chapter 11," (Federal Government Contracts Center, 2009), http://www.fedgovcontracts.com/chap11 .pdf,

68. CBO, "Small Firms, Employment, and Federal Policy."

69. Mirjam Schiffer and Beatrice Weder, "Firm Size and the Business Environment: Worldwide Survey Results,: Discussion Paper 43 (Washington, DC: International Finance Corporation, 2001), IV.

70. Lloyd Blankfein, Michael Bloomberg, Warren Buffett, and Michael Porter, "To Grow the Economy, Grow Small Businesses: Bloomberg & Buffett," *USA Today*, June 7, 2016, http://www.usatoday.com/story/opinion/2016/06/07/grow-economy-grow -small-businesses-bloomberg-buffett-column/85526778.

71. Paul Ryan, "Down with Big Business," *Forbes*, December 11, 2009. http://www .forbes.com/2009/12/11/business-government-politics-reform-opinions -contributors-paul-ryan.html.

72. Polling Report, "Major Institutions," http://www.pollingreport.com/institut .htm.

Chapter 13

1. Jeffrey H. Anderson, "Republicans Fight for Small, Democrats for Big, Business," *Weekly Standard*, December 14, 2012, http://www.weeklystandard.com/republicans -fight-for-small-democrats-for-big-business/article/691098.

2. PBS, "Interview with Ed Gillespie," *Frontline*, April 12, 2005, http://www.pbs.org/ wgbh/pages/frontline/shows/architect/interviews/gillespie.html.

3. Quoted in Jackie Calmes, "For 'Party of Business,' Allegiances Are Shifting," *New York Times*, January 15, 2013, http://www.nytimes.com/2013/01/16/us/politics/ a-shift-for-gop-as-party-of-business.html.

4. David Weigel, "David Brat: Half Elizabeth Warren, Half Ludwig von Mises," *Slate*, June 11, 2014, http://www.slate.com/blogs/weigel/2014/06/11/david_brat _half_elizabeth_warren_half_ludwig_von_mises.html.

5. Paul Ryan, "Down with Big Business," *Forbes*, October 12, 2009.

6. Lloyd Blankfein, Michael Bloomberg, Warren Buffett, and Michael Porter, "To grow the economy, grow small businesses: Bloomberg and Buffett," *USA Today*, June 7, 2016, https://www.usatoday.com/story/opinion/2016/06/07/grow-economy -grow-small-businesses-bloomberg-buffett-column/85526778.

7. Robert D. Atkinson, "How Transportation Became the Latest Victim of America's Culture Wars," *Washington Post*, November 5, 2015, https://itif.org/publications/

2015/11/06/how-transportation-became-latest-victim-america%E2%80%99s-culture -wars.

8. Paul H. Jensen and Elizabeth Webster, "Firm Size and the Use of Intellectual Property Rights," *Economic Record*, March 8, 2006, http://onlinelibrary.wiley.com/ doi/10.1111/j.1475-4932.2006.00292.x/full.

9. Tim Fernholz, "The Alliance between Big Business and the Republican Party Is in Shambles," *Quartz*, May 31, 2016, https://qz.com/682125/the-alliance-between-us -businesses-and-the-republican-party-is-in-shambles.

10. Quoted in Jean Card, "Big Business Donald: Don't Let the President Get Away with Using Small Businesses as Props," *U.S. News and World Report*, February 2, 2017, https://www.usnews.com/opinion/thomas-jefferson-street/articles/2017-02-02/ donald-trump-uses-small-business-as-a-big-business-prop.

11. The term "developmental state" was coined first to describe postwar East Asian capitalism. See Meredith Woo-Cumings, *The Developmental State* (Ithaca, NY: Cornell University Press, 1999); and Chalmers Johnson, *Japan: Who Governs? The Rise of the Developmental State* (New York: W. W. Norton, 2001). The practice as well as the theory of developmental capitalism is much broader and older. See Richard Nelson, *An Evolutionary Theory of Economic Change* (Cambridge, MA: Harvard University Press, 1982); Erik Reinert, *How Rich Countries Got Rich … and Why Poor Countries Continue to Stay Poor* (New York: Carroll and Graf, 2007); Ralph E. Gomory and William J. Baumol, *Global Trade and Conflicting National Interests* (Cambridge, MA: MIT Press, 2001); William J. Baumol, *The Free-Market Innovation Machine: Analyzing the Growth Miracle of Capitalism* (Princeton, NJ: Princeton University Press, 2002); Carlota Perez, *Technological Revolutions and Financial Capital: The Dynamics of Bubbles and Golden Ages* (Cheltenham: Edward Elgar, 2002); Robert D. Atkinson, *The Past and Future of America's Economy: Long Waves of Innovation That Power Cycles of Growth* (Cheltenham: Edward Elgar, 2005); Robert D. Atkinson and Stephen J. Ezell, *Innovation Economics: The Race for Global Advantage* (New Haven, CT: Yale University Press, 2012); and Michael Lind, *Land of Promise: An Economic History of the United States* (New York: HarperCollins, 2012).

12. Quoted in Roland Marchand, *Creating the Corporate Soul: The Rise of Public Relations and Corporate Imagery in American Big Business* (Berkeley: University of California Press, 1998), 203.

13. Quoted in Francesco Guerrera, "Welch Condemns Share Price Focus," *Financial Times*, March 12, 2009, https://www.ft.com/content/294ff1f2-0f27-11de-ba10 -0000779fd2ac.

14. Jonathan J. Bean, "Review: *Small Business Policy and the American Creed* by Sandra M. Anglund," *The Business History Review* 74, no. 3 (Autumn, 2000): 538–540, https://www.jstor.org/stable/3116459?seq=1#page_scan_tab_contents.

15. Jonathan J. Bean, *Big Government and Affirmative Action: The Scandalous History of the Small Business Administration* (Lexington: University Press of Kentucky, 2001), 7.

16. Lawrence Lessig, "The Left and Right Share a Common Enemy: Capitalists Who Corrupt Capitalism," *Evonomics*, January 16, 2016, http://evonomics.com/how-capitalists-corrupt-capitalism.

17. George R. Hoguet, "Arguments for Industrial Policy," OMFIF, https://www.omfif.org/analysis/the-bulletin/2016/may/arguments-for-industrial-policy.

18. Corwin D. Edwards, *Big Business and the Policy of Competition* (Cleveland: Press of Western Reserve University, 1956), 107–108.

19. Michael Heller, *The Gridlock Economy: How Too Much Ownership Wrecks Markets, Stops Innovation, and Costs Lives* (New York: Basic Books, 2008), 185.

20. Michael E. Porter, "Competition and Antitrust: A Productivity-Based Approach" (faculty paper, Harvard Business School, May 30, 2002), http://www.isc.hbs.edu/Documents/pdf/053002antitrust.pdf.

21. Xavier Vives, "Games of Strategic Complementarities: An Application to Bayesian Games," *Spanish Economic Review* 9 (December 2007): 237–247.

22. William F. Adkinson, Jr., Karen L. Grimm, and Christopher N. Bryan, "Enforcement of Section 2 of the Sherman Act: Theory and Practice," FTC Working Paper (Washington, DC: Federal Trade Commission, November 3, 2008), https://www.ftc.gov/system/files/documents/public_events/section-2-sherman-act-hearings-single-firm-conduct-related-competition/section2overview.pdf.

23. "*Verizon Communications, Inc. v. Law Offices of Curtis V. Trinco, LLP.*" Oyez, November 1, 2017, www.oyez.org/cases/2003/02-682.

24. Robert Atkinson, "Break Up the Contact Lens Cartel to Give Consumers More Choice" *The Hill*, October 18, 2016, http://thehill.com/blogs/pundits-blog/healthcare/301641-break-up-the-contact-lens-cartel-to-give-consumers-more-choice.

25. Mario L. Possas and Jorge Fagundes, "Competition, Strategic Behaviour and Antitrust Policy: An Evolutionary Approach," *Revista Brasileira de Economia* 52, no. 1 (1998): 111–144.

26. Richard R. Nelson, *Technology, Institutions, and Economic Growth* (Cambridge, MA: Harvard University Press, 2005).

27. Michael D. Giandrea, "Industry Competition and Total Factor Productivity Growth," US Department of Labor, Bureau of Labor Statistics, Working Paper 399 (Washington, DC, September 2006), https://www.bls.gov/ore/pdf/ec060110.pdf.

28. Nell Abernathy, Mike Konczal, and Kathryn Milani, "Untamed How to Check Corporate, Financial, and Monopoly Power" (New York: Roosevelt Institute, June

2016), http://rooseveltinstitute.org/untamed-how-check-corporate-financial-and -monopoly-power.

29. Edwards, *Big Business and the Policy of Competition*, 108–109.

30. Adam Smith, *Wealth of Nations*, ed. C. J. Bullock (New York: P. F. Collier & Son, 1909–14), www.bartleby.com/10.

31. Adam M. Brandenburger and Barry J. Nalebuff, *Co-opetition: A Revolution Mindset That Combines Competition and Cooperation: The Game Theory Strategy That's Changing the Game of Business* (New York: Doubleday, 1998).

32. Quoted in James F. Moore, "Business Ecosystems and the View from the Firm," *Antitrust Bulletin* 51, no. 1 (Spring 2006): 31.

33. Hakan Hakansson and Ivan Snehota, "No Business Is an Island: The Network Concept of Business Strategy," *Scandinavian Journal of Management* 22 (2006): 261.

34. Michael Mandel, "Scale and Innovation in Today's Economy" (Washington, DC: Progressive Policy Institute, December 2011), 2.

35. Carl Shapiro, "Antitrust, Innovation, and Intellectual Property" (faculty paper, University of California, Berkeley, November 8, 2005), http://faculty.haas.berkeley .edu/shapiro/amcinnovation.pdf.

36. Danial Asmat, "Collusion Along the Learning Curve: Theory and Evidence from the Semiconductor Industry" (Washington, DC: US Department of Justice, Antitrust Division, June 20, 2016), https://www.justice.gov/atr/collusion-along -learning-curve-theory-and-evidence-semiconductor-industry.

37. Carl Shapiro and Hal R. Varian, *Information Rules: A Strategic Guide to the Network Economy* (Boston: Harvard Business School Press, 1999).

38. Joseph A. Schumpeter, *Capitalism, Socialism and Democracy* (New York: Harper & Brothers, 1950).

39. Dora Benedek, Nina Budina, Pragyan Deb, Borja Gracia, Sergejs Saksonovs, and Anna Shabunina, "The Right Kind of Help? Tax Incentives for Staying Small," (Washington, DC: International Monetary Fund, June 2017), http://www.imf.org/ en/Publications/WP/Issues/2017/06/13/The-Right-Kind-of-Help-Tax-Incentives-for -Staying-Small-44958.

40. Ian Bickerdyke and Ralph Lattimore, "Reducing the Regulatory Burden: Does Firm Size Matter?" (Canberra: Commonwealth of Australia, Industry Commission, December 1997), v.

41. US Agency for International Development, "Removing Barriers to Formaliza- tion: The Case for Reform and Emerging Best Practice" (Washington, DC: USAID, March 2005), http://www.businessenvironment.org/dyn/be/docs/73/Session2 .1WelchDoc.pdf.

42. Noah Smith, "Higher Minimum Wages Will Give High Tech a Boost," *Bloomberg View*, August 22, 2017, https://www.bloomberg.com/view/articles/2017-08-22/higher-minimum-wages-will-give-high-tech-a-boost.

43. Robert D. Atkinson, "Understanding and Maximizing America's Evolutionary Economy" (Washington, DC: Information Technology and Innovation Foundation, 2014), https://itif.org/publications/2014/10/02/understanding-and-maximizing-americas-evolutionary-economy.

44. Jorge Guzman and Scott Stern, "The State of American Entrepreneurship: New Estimates of the Quantity and Quality of Entrepreneurship for 15 US States, 1988–2014" (working paper, MIT and NBER, Cambridge, MA, March 2016), http://jorgeg.scripts.mit.edu/homepage/wp-content/uploads/2016/03/Guzman-Stern-State-of-American-Entrepreneurship-FINAL.pdf.

45. Nathaniel Hawthorne, "The Pygmies," in *The Tanglewood Tales* (New York: H. M. Caldwell, 1853).

Index